AMPLIFIED ENCYCLO.
ONE HIT W ᴏɴᴅᴇʀꜱ ᴏꜰ
THE 50'S, 60'S, 70'S AND 80'S

COMPILED BY IAN HALL

ISBN-13: 978-1987757057

ISBN-10: 198775705X

Table of Contents

THE ULTIMATE BOOK OF MUSIC TRIVIA: ONE HIT WONDERS

INTRODUCTION...

Love them or hate them, One Hit Wonders fascinate every music lover, and I include you in that august group, just because you're reading this. Whether in the huge market of the U.S.A. or in some remote backwater, the story of how one band or artist makes it big, sometimes huge, then fades completely from the public eye, is the stuff of music trivia legend.

These stars shine like the brightest supernova suns, on occasion selling millions of records, then sink back to the obscurity of dark matter. Some artists bask in the limelight for a single chart week, some spurts of fame last a month or two.

But some bring a fresh air to the music world; their songs are often unique, iconic, and thus bring back so many vivid memories to so many music lovers. They conjure places and dates which our subconscious has forgotten; some of these songs are the backdrop of our lives whether we like it or not.

I find they fall into three distinct categories...

THE TRUE OHW; THE FLASH IN THE PAN...

Like the gunpowder from the actual saying, some of the celebrities in this book are plucked from such depths of obscurity in mere days and lifted into the bright light of the sun. In some cases their meteoric rise finds them unprepared for such instant exposure; blinded by the limelight, for a myriad of reasons they slink back into the dark woods they were dragged from.

They are the true One Hit Wonders, the stuff of legend, the ones which have passed from the media which raised them, the ones of which we wonder; "Where are they now?"

Example;

CYNDI GRECCO - MAKING OUR DREAMS COME TRUE

Cyndi Grecco is the quintessential one hit wonder. Her only hit was used as the theme song for the smash TV show, Laverne & Shirley. It reached #25 in the U.S. Billboard Hot 100, spending 16 weeks on the chart, and reached #16 in Canada. She never charted again.

THE CHANCE OHW; THE HARD-WORKING MUSICIANS...

These are the artists who have chosen to work in the profession, slaving for years on sub-burger-flipper wages in order to keep their 'career' going. I include here the artists who play in bars, pubs, small clubs, who dream of success, and then find it… the big hit… only to have it snatched from them, perhaps even before they can fully appreciate the feel of its glory.

Some of these musicians become stars in their own fields, working in genres like Country Music, Soul, R&B, Death Rock, Comedy, etc, but only when they find their 'crossover' hit to the mainstream charts do the main body of music lovers find them.

This book is full of such 'greats', hard working men and women who make a living giving you entertainment, and just once have had their fifteen minutes of mainstream fame.

I find that depending on the level of hit, these musicians usually again fall into two categories; those who milk the hit for all its worth, and those who chase the next bright star, never quite making the mark.

Example;

TEN YEARS AFTER – I'D LOVE TO CHANGE THE WORLD

Written by band leader, Alvin Lee, it was the first single from the British Rockers album, A Space in Time. It is the band's only Top 40 hit, reaching #40 in the Billboard Hot 100. Although the band sold millions of albums, they never charted a single again.

THE FREAK OHW; STARS IN THEIR OWN LAND…

Then there are the stars in their own land; they've had a string of hit singles or reasonable music careers in their own country, but never broken out of its porous borders. Suddenly with a huge hit on their hands, they think the doors to worldwide fame have finally opened… only to have them slammed shut in their faces. In their own country, they've had their biggest hit… in the country into which they've thrust themselves temporarily; they're banished to the ignominy and the completely mistaken identity of the One-Hit-Wonder bin.

Example;

THIN LIZZY - THE BOYS ARE BACK IN TOWN

This is one of a few one hit wonders that shocked me.

Despite millions of plays on US rock radio stations, despite 33 single releases and 58 albums, this song was their only USA chart hit. From the album, Jailbreak, it reached #1 in Ireland, #8 in the UK and Canada, and a #12 hit in the Billboard Top 100.

Billboard ranked it as the #97 song from 1976.

Although many of their singles are now played in every USA Rock radio station, they only charted once.

THE FREAKS IN THIS FREAK SHOW... I'M ONLY HUMAN...

Speaking as the collector of these pieces of detritus, I'm only human, I have my moments of clarity, and my headstrong bursts of idiocy. I mention this because, despite my efforts to be impartial, I know I'm going to indulge my own favorites, and there's little that I (or you that matter) can do about it.

So...

I'm going to apologize now; there's going to be a little bit of me in this list.

Oh, and sometimes I'll not just find a way to include songs just because I like them, sometimes I'll list songs just to show the idiosyncrasies of the pop market.

For instance, here's one of music's wonderful weirdities...

Led Zeppelin, one of the greatest musical groups that the UK has ever produced... are a one hit wonder in the UK.

Yes, you can thank me now for digging this one up, and quote me to your friends at the pub. Led Zeppelin released singles in the USA and other countries, but NOT the UK, where they were content with album sales. However, in 1997 they did release a commemorative single; Whole Lotta Love. It got to #21 in the UK Charts, amazingly their only single UK chart entry. I'm afraid for all you Led Zep fans out there, by any criteria you may devise, that makes Led Zeppelin a One Hit Wonder in the UK.

And so to the nitty gritty stuff...

THE CRITERIA BEHIND THE ORDER...

WHAT MAKES A ONE HIT WONDER...

There's a few things we should set straight before we begin our book in earnest.

The criteria which defines one hit wonder-ness is quite easy...

1. The artist must have had one hit in the top 40 of the following countries; USA, UK, Ireland, Canada, Australia, New Zealand, or South Africa.

2. The artist must not have had a different hit single in the top 40 in the country in which they are a one hit wonder. (For instance, a band may have had one big hit in more than one country, but if his other hits were limited to one country, he's a one hit wonder everywhere else.)

Example in point... British band, Right Said Fred, had a worldwide hit with I'm Too Sexy, topping the charts in over 6 countries, including the USA Billboard Hot 100. Their follow up single Simply Dippy, failed to chart in the USA, but was a sizable hit elsewhere. Therefore, Right said Fred are a one hit wonder in the USA; they get into the book.

Another example... The Spin Doctors had a worldwide hit with Two Princes, but their follow-up single Little Miss Can't be Wrong also charted in a few countries; they don't get into the book, I'm afraid. Even I'm not a big enough zealot to dig into the minor world charts and find a top 40 somewhere that their second single bombed.

Now I'm using USA and the UK as my major music charts of note here, with Canada, Australia, New Zealand, Ireland and South Africa as my one hit wonder second-strings.

I know Germany will have its own one hit wonders, Finland too, and Kazakhstan, Thailand and 167 other countries.

But I write in English, so I'm hitting the English-speaking world as my theatre, and perhaps we'll get other language editions later, if this one sells at all.

GETTING THE YEAR CORRECT...

Now this was a major problem, because hits don't always occur in the year the single was released. Obviously some singles released in the end of a year can be a hit the year after. Similarly some hits take time to travel around the world.

Some like Roger Whittaker's, The Last Farewell, took four years to chart properly. Yes, I said FOUR YEARS!

The answer?

Well, I don't have one, I've tried to list the one hit wonder entry in the year it had its major impact. Did I get it right all the time? Probably/definitely not. So if you're looking for your favorite one hit wonder, check the years before and after too. You might get lucky. Or check the song index at the end of the book.

MUSIC RECORDING SALES CERTIFICATION...

Basically what I'm talking about here is silver, gold and platinum awards for sales of recorded units.

And, to be precise, this involved just 78's in the old days, then as the medium changed, singles and albums, and today it also involves digital download sales.

One extremely important fact to remember is that originally these awards were numerically the same for every country, (a single in 1970 selling one million copies in one country got awarded a 'gold' record for that country) but today, these parameters have changed. Every country now has their own silver, gold and platinum threshold. Just because a record is awarded 'gold' in France and the USA, does not mean that the record sold the same number of copies in those countries.

Both singles and albums have their own award system, but since we are talking about one hit wonders, I will restrict the details to singles only.

The History.

In the dim and distant past, the first 'award' discs were handed out by the labels themselves. The first silver award was given by Regal Zonophone Records to the UK's George Formby in 1937, for sales of 100,000 copies of, 'The Window Cleaner'.

The first gold disc award was given by RCA Victor records to Glenn Miller in February 1942, for exceeding 1 million sales of the single, 'Chattanooga Choo Choo'.

As Billboard revamped the chart system in 1958, introducing the Hot 100, the Recording Industry Association of America (RIAA) took over the award process, and the same year awarded their first 'gold' award to Perry Como's hit single, 'Catch a falling Star'. The soundtrack for 'Oklahoma' was the first 'gold' album awarded, just months later.

In 1976, the RIAA revamped the whole certification process, and other countries followed suit. It's here that the number of sales to qualify for 'gold' level began to vary from country to country. This new system made sense; small countries wanted to award their own stars too, but some smaller countries didn't have the record sales to reach the heady million copy mark. Mostly the countries followed America's lead, having gold, platinum, then (in more modern times) diamond awards.

In the USA, 'gold' was 500,000 units, and 'platinum' was 1,000,000 units. Diamond was for ten times the platinum level; 10,000,000 sales.

In Canada, the goals were vastly reduced; 'gold' was 5,000 sales (one hundredth of the USA levels), and 'platinum' was 10,000. Their diamond award was given for sales of 100,000, again ten times the level of platinum sales.

Elsewhere, the countries were less uniform.

In France, 'gold' meant 75,000 sales, and 'platinum' was 150,000 sales. Diamond was awarded for 250,000, just two and a half times the platinum level.

In the UK, they went with a different system entirely; a 'silver' award meant sales of 200,000, and 'gold' was awarded for sales of 400,000. Their top tier was a platinum award, but just for 600,000 sales, one and a half times the middle level.

Clear? Yeah, like so many of the world's 'standards', in the murky waters of the international music business, nothing is ever easy.

TRIVIA; WEIRD OHW FACTS...

During the research into the book, I came across some weird facts that although they fall under the category of trivia, they are not really all that related to the actual one hit wonder entry itself.

So I included these as '**Weird OHW Facts**', and hope you like them.

Now, I make no apology for the frequency that these facts are presented... some of the 'facts' came easily, obscure singers with lots of fun facts. Other bands were so blindly boring, I could find nothing interesting to say about them.

The best one?

Undoubtedly... here's the question you 70's musical nuts will ask your friends in the bar...

QUESTION; What do one hit wonders, MINNIE RIPERTON (LOVIN' YOU), and VAN McCOY (THE HUSTLE) have in common.

(Yeah, we know they're both African American, and they're musically inclined)

ANSWER; It's in four parts...

1. They both had one hit wonders.
2. They both had those one hit wonders in the same year, 1975.
3. They both died (just six days apart) in July 1979 in totally unrelated fashion. (Riperton died of breast cancer, McCoy died from a heart attack.)
4. They were both in their thirties (Riperton was 31, McCoy was 39)

Weird, right?

That's what trivia is all about!

GETTING THE LIST IN ORDER...

We've done this in date order, split into separate years, not to confuse anyone, more to make it at least searchable in some way or another...
The initial quandary...
Do we list them alphabetically? No. Some folks don't give much of a crap for anything old; they just want to see the twenty years or so of their youth.
Do we list by artist name, alphabetically? No, for much of the same reason; true some one-hit wonders last in the airwaves forever, but the majority are time stamped. How many of us have heard a song on the radio from our youth, and can remember exactly where we were, what we were wearing, what we were doing, and who we were with?
We considered doing a list by artist name, or by song title... Nope, it just wasn't going to work.
So we did it by date...
But from what date...?

THE BIRTH OF ROCK AND ROLL...

We decided to start where the charting of rock and roll began. 1955.
Before 1955, the American charts were split into three, each giving a different aspect of single 'sales'. The three charts were, 'Best Sellers in Stores', 'Most Played by Jockeys', and 'Most Played in Jukeboxes'. Charts in this time would have been incredibly difficult to find any kind of actionable data. There were sometimes three number ones, there were state lists, city lists, regional charts, and there were local parochial lists.
In 1955, Billboard pushed through a groundbreaking phenomenon and produced the first ever USA Top 100. This list was sampled on a large scale from thousands of outlets, and did take into consideration radio and juke box play.
Now this new service morphed for a couple of years, but by the end of 1958, the various charts had been amalgamated into one brand new service, the Billboard Hot 100.
Yeah, you'll have your own date, you'll have your own birthplace of your music, but we had to start somewhere.

THE ORGANIZATION OF THE LIST...

To our best ability, we placed the hits in the year of their best sales (I know, different music hit different countries at different times, but we did have to put them somewhere). Once we'd broken them into a particular year, we listed them in alphabetical order for ease of reference.

Basically the one-hit-wonders are in the year they were hits, and in alphabetical order within that year.

(Please note, that in band names, the word, 'the' has been ignored for alphabetical purposes; The Beatles are listed under 'B'. But other titles, beginning with an 'A', have been kept; A Flock of Seagulls, for instance, is listed under 'A'.)

We've also listed them in pure alphabetical order, for instance Charlie Pride is listed under C, not listed as Pride, Charlie, which I always have found confusing.

Then, just when you thought we'd done enough organizing... we made a list of song titles, and stuck it in the back as an additional index. That way if you can just remember the name of the song, you've got a better chance of finding it.

Clear?

As mud? Who cares?

A LITTLE BILLBOARD CHART HISTORY...

CHARTS IN THE USA...

In the USA, prior to 1955, Billboard did not have a national unified chart which encompassed all facets of single 'sales'.

First established in 1936, when most record sales were for 10 inch shellac discs spinning at 78rpm, 'Best Sellers in Stores' was technically the very first Billboard chart. It recorded and ranked the best-selling singles in the large retail stores, and gave a chart as the Top 20, then Top 50 positions.

'Most Played by Jockeys' was Billboard's chart of radio station airplay, but again with the expanding radio boom, these figures depended on the disc jockeys themselves reporting in, and thus included a variety of human factors; accuracy, honesty, and regular reporting. This national chart usually had 20 positions, but never could be said to be completely accurate.

'Most Played in Jukeboxes' was a weekly list of the top 20 juke box rankings, so depended again on a variety of factors; some juke boxes featured local singers, some kept popular, outdated songs. Run by the club owner, it was open to personal opinion and again relied on integrity in reporting.

On the week ending November 12, 1955, Billboard published The Top 100 for the very first time, effectively replacing and revamping all the three existing chart systems. The Top 100 was the first modern chart, and combined all aspects of a single's performance (sales, airplay and jukebox activity). The whole Top 100 list was based on a points system that generally gave sales (purchases) more weight on the chart than radio airplay or jukebox plays. They boasted the new Top 100 was faster, more accurate, and un-cheatable. For three years the other charts, The Best Sellers In Stores, Most Played by Jockeys and Most Played in Jukeboxes charts were published alongside the new Top 100 chart.

With the rapid increase in broadcasting radio stations, on June 17, 1957, Billboard discontinued the 'Most Played in Jukeboxes' chart.

The week ending July 28, 1958, was the end of the old era; the 'Most Played By Jockeys' and Top 100 charts, featured their very last chart.

One week later, the Billboard Hot 100 was released. The 'Best Sellers in Stores' chart struggled for a couple of months, then it too succumbed to the new modern juggernaut. The new Hot 100 chart was scientifically tested, scientifically reported, and featured new releases far faster than any other method.

It was now the job of the record producers and distributors to keep up with this new coast-to-coast chart service.

CHARTS IN THE UK...

Oh boy, where do I start?

Basically for the first decade or so, it was run by Music newspapers.

In the UK, the first chart was run by the music newspaper, The New Musical Express, in 1952. They phoned a selection of 20 record stores and compiled a Top 12. This became a hit, and was copied by the Record Mirror in 1955. Their rival music newspaper, Melody Maker, began theirs in 1956.

Then, if it had been clear, it gets misty.

The newspaper Record Mirror starts printing/copying NME's charts.

Then the newspaper Record Retailer begins to produce an album chart and a top 50 singles chart, and Record Mirror starts publishing their data.

Somewhere in the mish-mash, the figures used in the UK charts begin to be Record Retailer figures.

Incredibly this system carried on until 1969, when the Record Retailer and the BBC commissioned the brand new British Market Research Bureau (BMRB) to compile music charts.

And they're still arguing yet...

THE AMERICAN RECORD INDUSTRY...

In the fledgling years of the mid-fifties, there was no industry so cut-throat and yet disorganized as the American Record Industry. Big record companies trod mercilessly over each other to find the next big name. Searching for the same product, small recording studios sprung up on every corner, and many big names began their career as a one-time pressing or a small limited edition run. As their song hit the local 'chart', the songs sometimes gained traction on a regional basis. Contracts at this level were extremely fragile, with the small labels selling out the song's contract to larger labels who could cope with the wider and bigger distribution problems.

On an international basis, this became even more pronounced. In the early days, launching a new single into uncharted territory was a risky business, and often ended with the record company losing money.

Selling the rights for a record which may or may not actually chart in the foreign country was easier to do than a gamble on an overseas record success.

In reality, a local record company could copy the song and release it before the original got any headway and before the poor artist could negotiate a foreign release deal, the song had been copied by the record label's own star, making them a far greater percentage on the deal.

Take, for instance, Endless Sleep, written and by rockabilly novice Jody Reynolds. His #5, one million seller hit was not released in the UK or Germany. In the UK, the song was taken to #4 in the UK Charts by Marty Wilde (father of 'We're The Kids In America' fame, Kim Wilde). In Germany the hit was recorded by a German star, but did not chart.

It was a strange time, but fascinating.

SONGWRITER'S RIGHTS...

Basically there was no such thing. The songwriter published the sheet music, and got a royalty for each copy sold. If the song was recorded, the writer got a royalty per record sold or per radio play.

On hearing a 'great record', all a person had to do was buy the sheet music and make a recording. In smaller countries this process of hi-jacking a hit was less prevalent as the chart itself was small. In a huge country like America, with its regional charts, and the length of time a record took to become popular, this practice became the norm.

The song, Let Me Go, Lover!, is a prime example. It was written by Jenny Lou Carson and Al Hill in 1954, and originally called, Let Me Go, Devil, a song about alcoholism. The song with new lyrics specially written for the TV program, Studio One, an anthology drama series was featured on the show as Let Me Go, Lover! It aired on November 15, 1954, the song sung by Joan Weber. Remember that date. It's November 15th, just 45 days until the end of the year.

The aim of the show, Studio One, was to demonstrate how pop songs go from recording to the public. The music stores were pre-stocked with Weber's single, ready for the public to go wild. The day after the show, they did. Because of the sales-ready stock, the record sold 100,000 copies in the first week. Joan Weber's version quickly got to US #1.

However, just THREE DAYS after the show had been aired, on November 18, 1954, the song had been already recorded by Teresa Brewer and The Lancers, and immediately put into pressing by Coral Records; there were records in the stores just a week later, her version reached #6 in the US, and #9 in the UK.

No more than a week after that, Peggy Lee also released the song. Her version was less successful, but it still charted.

The rush wasn't over. And remember, it was only two weeks after the show had been aired.

Still in 1954, Canadian Country singer Hank Snow, changed the lyrics again. Let Me Go, Woman got to #1 in the Canadian Country Chart.

In December 1954, Dean Martin recorded a version for his new four track EP, for release in the UK and Australia only. It reached #3 in the UK, and #1 in Australia.

Finally, in March 1955, Ruby Murray's version reached #5 in the UK.

And, let's face it, that's only the versions we know about!

Songs could be 'hi-jacked' by unscrupulous or powerful record labels so quickly, it was sometimes impossible for members of the public to know which version was the original. Good songs were assigned or recorded by other artists for the larger regional or national audience. Sometimes up to ten different versions of the same song would vie for sales in the same chart, and this practice still existed into the early seventies; the example of the Hillside Singers and the New Seekers 'teaching the world to sing' in 1972 is a prime example.

Yes, it was a crazy time in the record industry.

And this is the time to tell of the most despicable 'thefts' in the early music industry.

Before the Sex Pistols album of the same name, came a few thousand claims to the title... but in the world of one hit wonders, this story takes every kind of biscuit.

We begin our story in the dim and distant days of 1960... Here's his entry in our great book of tragedies.

GARRY MILLS - LOOK FOR A STAR

This might be the most blatant trans-Atlantic 'cover' version snatch ever performed. Let's see if we can shed light on the devious, nefarious, and most barefaced musical plot in the history of pop music... (okay, I may be getting a bit passionate here, but hear me out)

Written by British songwriter, Tony Hatch (under the pseudonym, Mark Anthony) it was featured in the 1960 horror movie, Circus of Horrors, sung by British pop singer, Garry Mills. On Top Rank Records, it got to #7 in the UK Charts, which he followed by two other hits...

However, Garry Mills' single got released in the USA, and the floodgates opened. Garry Mill's song eventually reaches #26 in the Billboard Hot 100, his only US Chart hit, making him a one hit wonder in the USA and a bit of cash and fame. Wonderful. (You can probably tell he's not the bad guy here)

Weirdest OHW Fact Ever... This story is worthy of a movie plot.

Deane Hawley records the song, and her version gets to #29 in the Billboard Chart. (This gal is also not the bad person in this plot)

Billy Vaughn, band leader with many hits under his belt, makes an instrumental of the song... it reaches #19 in the Billboard Chart. (Amazingly, he's also not the bad guy here, in fact, so far no-one has done anything really bad)

Enter Nashville's **James E. 'Buzz' Cason**... (the bad guy)... he was a founding member of Nashville's first rock band, The Casuals, and with Richard Williams and Hugh Jarrett of The Jordanaires, he had recorded songs as 'The Statues for Liberty'.

Suddenly (I'm thinking with no malice or forethought... my tone dripping heavily with spicy sarcasm), James E. 'Buzz' Cason decides to change his name to **Garry Miles** (MILES) and go off and have a solo career, oh, and he decides to record for his first solo single, Look For a Star, a new song bubbling under the US Chart by a Brit called **Garry Mills** (MILLS).

Now is it me, or is that some cauldron-bubbling heap of coincidence?

However, history shows that the two versions of the songs are in the chart at the same time. They rise in the chart together. They are played by the same radio stations at the same time. Thousands of record buyers look up at the chart on music store walls wondering which version they've heard on the radio, and which one they should buy?

The two songs peak at their respective highest points just ONE WEEK APART.

As Brit, Garry Mills reaches #26 in the Billboard Top 100, James E. 'Buzz' Cason/Garry Miles reaches #16 in the Billboard Hot 100, decides against the solo career, and immediately reverts back to his old name. Yup, he's a one hit wonder too.

Now, Buzz Cason goes on to have a great middling music career, but I sure think he went one step too far in the search for personal stardom. What do you think?

THE SPECIALIST BILLBOARD CHARTS IN THE USA...

In a music industry where success in your genre can be a lucrative career, and where a listener can be focused on just his or her particular genre, I fully understand the necessity for specialist charts.

The Hip-hop/Black chart speaks for itself, it's not a race separation, it's more a style or a rythym matter. The Rock chart is exactly the same, (Rock is where my head is, I get it), Latin, Country, Christian, Jazz and Dance charts supply information and remove all other genres to let you, the specialist customer, see a better picture. Most of these genres speak for themselves, but let's take a look at two and see how they've evolved over the years.

'BLACK' SINGERS AND MUSICIANS...

From the early days of the modern music industry (I'm thinking 1940's here) there has been a separate chart to house the records of 'black' or African American music. While the chart is not totally segregated, (some 'white', or 'non' black music is included), but usually it is music of R&B, hip-hop or blues in nature.

The chart has undergone many name-changes during the years, and I have tried to use the names in this book, the chart was even discontinued between 1963 and 1965, but however no matter how hard I've tried, I know I've got some wrongly labelled, and for that I apologize.

In the early 1940's the black chart was called, 'The Harlem Hit Parade', but that was changed in 1945 to The Race Chart. (Yeah, political correctness was not predominant in those days). Until October 1958, there were two or three charts depicting sales, blues and R&B, but these were amalgamated together to for the official Billboard R&B Sides.

During the years, the Billboard 'black' music chart has been called... Hot Rhythm & Blues Singles, Best Selling Soul Singles, Hot Soul Singles, Hot Black Singles, Hot R&B Singles, Hot R&B Singles & Tracks, Hot R&B/Hip-Hop Singles & Tracks, and eventually, Hot R&B/Hip-Hop Songs.

Since 1958 the black chart (like the mainstream Billboard Hot 100) has always been based on a mixture of different figures. Initially it was based on a measure of radio airplay, sales data, and juke-box play. Nowadays it uses radio airplay, sales data and streaming activity.

Initially with a chart of 100 positions, it was shortened in 2012 to a Top 50.

For the sake of clarity, I must add that the R&B Chart was discontinued from November 1963 to January 1965. They stopped it because so many Motown recordings were charting in the R&B and the Hot 100, making the charts very similar. The British Invasion changed the figures in 1964, and the chart was reinstated, now as 'Hot Rhythm & Blues Singles'. Oh how fickle we are...
Anyway...
From its ancient days of jazz, blues and doo-wop, it moved through phases of rhythm & blues (R&B), rock and roll, soul, disco, funk, and today it is predominantly R&B and hip hop.

I hope that clears the air rather than Muddy's Waters (my wee black R&B joke).

ADULT CONTEMPORARY CHART? WHAT DOES THAT TERM EVEN MEAN?

Contemporary... "living or occurring at the same time".
Even hearing the dictionary definition, I'm not even certain what that means about music charts. However...
(I'm sure by now you're getting the idea that I' not 'into' the purpose of this chart)
The Adult Contemporary chart does not chart by record sales, rather it lists the most popular songs played on 'adult contemporary' radio stations in the United States that are members of the Adult Contemporary radio panel.
However, like every facet of the US music business, it hasn't always been know as such.
It began as the Easy Listening Chart, (1961–1962), switches to Middle-Road Singles, (1962 – 1964), then to become as clear as mud to its purpose, its name was changed for a single year to Pop-Standard Singles (1964–1965). By now I'm starting to shake my head, see red, and throw the whole idea away, all at once. However, it gets worse... not happy with 'Pop-Standard Singles', it switches back to calling itself the Easy Listening Chart, (1965–1979). In 1979, however, comes the term, contemporary, and the idea behind the chart becomes clear (can you hear the sarcarm dripping from my words?), and the chart is named Hot Adult Contemporary Tracks (1979–1982) and Adult Contemporary (1983–present).
Yeah, Billboard, your executives have far too much time on their hands.

THE TOP 20 ONE HIT WONDERS... EVER!

First, I'm going to introduce the biggest selling top 20 one-hit-wonders... the TOP 20 of all time. Not all one hit wonders were oddballs, this list of 20 songs contains 19 of the top 75 best-selling singles ever recorded; quite a bragging right.

Now, I'm not guaranteeing this list is absolutely positively swear-on-a-bible accurate, but after all the digging I did, this is the list I've accrued from the data I sifted through. See how many you recognize.

NUMBER 1... 1970.

MUNGO JERRY – IN THE SUMMERTIME
Reached #1 in Australia, Austria, Belgium, Canada, Denmark, France, Germany, Ireland, Italy, Netherlands, New Zealand, Norway, South Africa, Sweden, Switzerland, and UK.
Sold more than 30 million copies.
The 4th biggest selling single of all time.
The consummate one hit wonder, the debut single by British rock band Mungo Jerry reached #1 in 26 charts all around the world. It became one of the best-selling singles of all-time.

However, not all plaudits were at the same level; Billboard ranked the record as the USA's #53 song of 1970.

Weird OHW Fact... The song's lyrics "have a drink, have a drive, go out and see what you can find" led to the song's use in a UK campaign 'Drinking and Driving Wrecks Lives'.

Weird OHW Fact... The band's name comes from the TS Elliot poem, Mungojerrie and Rumpleteazer, from Old Possum's Book of Practical Cats.

Weird OHW Fact... When they got suddenly booked onto Top of the Pops, the band leader, Ray Dorset, had to ask his boss for time off work.

NUMBER 2... 1958.

DOMENICO MODUGNO - NEL BLU DIPINTO DI BLU (VOLARE)
Reached #1 in USA.
Sold over 22 million copies.
The 6th biggest selling single of all time.
Written by Franco Migliacci and Domenico Modugno, it won the Sanremo Music Festival, and became a worldwide success. It topped the Billboard Charts for 5 weeks, with combined versions selling 22 million copies worldwide. It also won 2 Grammy Awards.

Weird OHW fact... This song, the 6th biggest selling single EVER, only came in 3rd as the Italian entry in the 1958 Eurovision Song Contest.
Weird OHW Fact... The title means 'In the Blue That is Painted Blue'.

NUMBER 3... 1984.
USA FOR AFRICA - WE ARE THE WORLD
Reached #1 in USA, UK, Australia, Ireland, Canada, New Zealand, and more than 20 other countries.
Sold over 20 million copies.
The 9th biggest selling single of all time.
Written by Michael Jackson and Lionel Richie after an original idea by Harry Belafonte, the USA's charity record for Africa was released just seven weeks after UK Band Aid's super-hit, Do They Know It's Christmas? The US single topped the charts in too many countries to count, and charted everywhere, raising millions for Ethiopia.
It also starred 'everybody'.
However, despite the huge world sales, Billboard rated the song as only #20 of 1985.
Weird OHW Fact... To show unity with the British effort, Phil Collins played drums, and Bob Geldof sang on the chorus.
Weird OHW Fact... Again, Like Band Aid's 'aftershocks', We Are The World 25 For Haiti raised millions for the island after the earthquake of 2010.

NUMBER 4... 1989.
KAOMA – LAMBADA
Reached #1 in Austria, Belgium, Finland, France, Germany, Italy, Netherlands Norway, Spain, Sweden, and Switzerland.
Sold over 15 million copies.
The 12th biggest selling single of all time.
French pop group Kaoma, with guest vocals by Brazilian, Loalwa Braz, hit it big right out of the blocks. Their first single from their debut album blew their world apart. It reached #1 in eleven countries and #4 in the UK, and Ireland, #5 in Australia, #10 in New Zealand, #12 in Japan, and a lowly #46 in the Billboard Hot 100.
Weird OHW Fact... Kaoma's version was unauthorized by the original writers, Bolivian pop group Los Kjarkas, and they successfully sued for damages in 1990.

NUMBER 5... 1963.
KYU SAKAMOTO - SUKIYAKI
Reached #1 in USA.

Sold more than 13 million copies.
The 17th biggest selling single of all time.
Written by Rokusuke Ei and Hachidai Nakamura, the song was recorded by 22 year old Japanese Actor and singer, Kyu Sakamoto. His worldwide hit, sung in Japanese, Ue o Muite Arukō, ('I look up when I walk') was known as 'Sukiyaki' to most of the world, and sold more than 13 million copies. It reached #1 in the USA Billboard Hot 100, and #6 in the UK Charts.
Weird OHW Fact... It was the first Japanese song to enter either the US or the UK chart.
Weird OHW Fact... Sakamoto died in the crash of Japan Airlines Flight 123 in 1985, aged just 43.

NUMBER 6... 1981.

TRIO - DA DA DA
Reached #1 in Austria, New Zealand, South Africa, and Switzerland.
Sold over 13 million copies.
The 18th biggest selling single of all time.
German band Trio consisted of Stephan Remmler, Gert 'Kralle' Krawinkel, and Peter Behrens. This annoying song from their debut album was a complete hit in over 30 countries. It can't be counted as a #1 hit, but more as a Top 10, because it made the top 10 in most countries in the world. It ended up being the 18th biggest single ever sold, selling over 13 million copies.
It has been dubbed, copied, translated, lampooned and parodied. The writers don't care; they made millions.

NUMBER 7... 1996.

ANDREA BOCELLI AND SARAH BRIGHTMAN - TIME TO SAY GOODBYE
Reached #1 in Belgium, France, Austria, Germany, Ireland and Switzerland.
Sold more than 12 million copies.
The 21st biggest selling single of all time.
Originally written by Francesco Sartori and Lucio Quarantotto, and originally sung by just Bocelli, the song was already a hit. A new version, partly in English, paired English Soprano, Sarah Brightman and Italian tenor Andrea Bocelli which became a worldwide smash hit. It stayed at #1 in Belgium for 12 weeks, in Germany for 14 weeks, in France and Switzerland for 6 weeks. It reached #2 in the UK, #8 in the Netherlands, and #31 in Sweden.

NUMBER 8... 1984.
BAND AID - DO THEY KNOW IT'S CHRISTMAS?
Reached #1 in the UK, Australia, Austria, Belgium, Denmark, Germany, Ireland, Italy, Netherlands, New Zealand, Norway, Sweden, Switzerland, and many more.
Sold more than 12 million copies.
The 23rd biggest selling single of all time.
Almost worth a chapter on its own, this charity ensemble changed history. Written by Bob Geldof (Boomtown Rats) and Midge Ure (Ultravox), and sung/recorded in a single day by a plethora of British stars, it shot straight to #1 for Christmas, staying there for 5 weeks. With the record producers working for free, it sold a million copies in the first week, eventually over 12 million were sold, raising £8 million for Ethiopia.
It reached #13 in the Billboard Hot 100.
Weird OHW Fact... Band Aid II in 1989 also had a UK #1 with the song (see 1989 entry) with a new cast of singers and performers.
Weird OHW Fact... In 2004, Band Aid 20 did a 30 year anniversary version, (most of the singers were very young when it was first released). This also got to #1 in the UK, Denmark, Italy, Norway and New Zealand.

NUMBER 9... 1974.
CARL DOUGLAS - KUNG FU FIGHTING
Reached #1 in UK, Australia, Austria, Belgium, Canada, France, Germany, Ireland, Netherlands, Norway, South Africa, USA.
Sold over 11 million copies.
The 25th biggest selling single of all time.
An epic one hit wonder, this single topped the charts all over the world, but it wasn't overnight; the disco hit charted slowly, gaining momentum as it hit the clubs. He never charted again.
Weird OHW Fact... Amazingly, Carl Douglas is NOT a one hit wonder in the UK. His follow-up, Do the Kung Fu, reached #35 in the UK Charts and #48 in the Billboard Hot 100.

NUMBER 10... 1975.
ROGER WHITTAKER - THE LAST FAREWELL
Reached #1 in USA and in 11 other countries.
Sold over 11 million copies.
The 28th biggest selling single of all time.
This chart hit is one of the slowest climbers ever. Released back in 1971, it was heard four years later and played in a radio station in Atlanta,

Georgia. The listeners liked it, requested it again, and it soon began selling. It reached #19 in the Billboard Hot 100, and #1 in the contemporary chart.

The success in America rocketed sales all over the world; #2 in UK, and #1 in eleven countries.

NUMBER 11... 1995.

LOS DEL RÍO – MACARENA

Reached #1 in over 13 countries, including USA, Australia, and Israel.

Sold over 10 million copies.

The 33rd biggest selling single of all time.

Written by Rafael Ruiz Perdigones and Antonio Romero Monge, Los del Rio began their work on the song as a rumba in 1992. By the time of the Bayside Boys remix three years later, they had perfected the sound, and it had gone global. Hitting #1 in 13 countries including USA, it was top three in every major chart except Canada (#16). Its 14 week stay at the top of the Billboard Chart was record breaking, and only the Spice Girls kept it from the top place in the UK.

Billboard ranked it as the #1 song of 1996.

Weird OHW Fact... Los del Rio means 'Those from the River'.

NUMBER 12... 1998.

PANJABI MC - MUNDIAN TO BACH KE

Reached #1 in Belgium and Italy.

Sold over 10 million copies.

The 36th biggest selling single of all time.

Written by Glen Larson, Stu Philips, Panjabi MC, and Labh Janjua, the song in Punjabi reached massive sales when linked with Jay Z. It reached #1 in Belgium and Italy, #2 in Austria and Germany. Topping out at #5 in the UK, it even reached #33 in the Billboard Hot 100. It was Top ten in every major music chart.

Weird OHW Fact... Mundian To Bach Ke, means 'Beware of the Boys.

NUMBER 13... 1955.

THE PENGUINS - EARTH ANGEL (WILL YOU BE MINE)

Reached #1 in USA.

Sold more than 10 million copies.

The 38th biggest selling single of all time.

Written by Curtis Williams, Jesse Belvin, and Gaynel Hodge, it was recorded by American doo-wop group from Los Angeles. Earth Angel got to every facet of #1 in America, the Juke Box Chart, Best Sellers in Stores and Most Played, and even reached #4 in the UK Chart. It eventually sold more than 10 million copies, although the writing credits were disputed for years.

NUMBER 14... 1985.
PAUL HARDCASTLE – 19
Reached #1 in Austria, Belgium, Germany, Ireland, Italy Netherlands Norway, New Zealand, Sweden Switzerland, and UK.
Sold over 8 million copies.
The 49th biggest selling single of all time.
Written by Paul Hardcastle, William Coutourie, and Jonas McCord, '19' was recorded on Hardcastle's third album. Helped by versions in French, Spanish, German and Japanese, it was a number one all over the world; topping 13 charts.
In the USA, despite the Viet Nam subject matter, and despite reaching #2 in Canada, the song topped out at just #15 in the Billboard Charts.
Weird OHW Fact... Due to other hits, Paul Hardcastle is NOT a one hit wonder in UK, Ireland, New Zealand, Netherlands and Germany.
Weird OHW Fact... Manchester United used the track to celebrate their 19th Premier League title; the song dipped back into the UK Top 40.

NUMBER 15... 1970.
SHOCKING BLUE – VENUS
Reached #1 in Australia, Belgium, Canada, Denmark, France, Italy, Spain, Switzerland, and USA.
#2 in Austria, Germany, Japan.
Sold 8 million copies worldwide.
The 57th biggest selling single of all time.
Written by Dutch band member Robbie van Leeuwen, he took the song to #1 in nine countries, reaching #2 in Austria, Germany and Japan, #3 in Netherlands, #8 in the UK and Finland and #10 in Ireland.
Weird OHW Fact... As a cover in 1986, Bananarama returned the song to #1 in seven countries.

NUMBER 16... 2002.
LAS KETCHUP - THE KETCHUP SONG (ASEREJÉ)
Reached #1 in EVERY music chart except USA.
Sold over 7 million copies.
The 65th biggest selling single of all time.
Written by Manuel Ruiz, and sung by Muñoz sisters Lucía, Lola, Pilar, and Rocío, it took three record companies to cope with the song's success. First signed to a parochial Altra Moda, then Columbia, then

Sony. It hit #1 in virtually every country in the world, with the exception of the USA (#54 in the Billboard Hot 100).

Weird OHW Fact... There is a controversy about the lyrics containing references to Satanism and demons.

NUMBER 17... 1967.

SCOTT MCKENZIE - SAN FRANCISCO (BE SURE TO WEAR FLOWERS IN YOUR HAIR)

Reached #1 in the UK.

Sold more than 7 million copies.

The 66th biggest selling single of all time.

Written by John Phillips (Mamas & the Papas) who played guitars and sitar on the track, the song was recorded by Scott McKenzie for his album, The Voice of Scott McKenzie. It was an instant hit, reaching #4 in the Billboard Hot 100, and getting to #1 in the UK.

Weird OHW Fact... The Bee Gees, Massachusetts, is an answer to McKenzie's song, about an easterner who goes to San Francisco, and is homesick for Massachusetts.

NUMBER 18... 1972.

ROYAL SCOTS DRAGOON GUARDS - AMAZING GRACE

Reached #1 in UK, Ireland, Australia, New Zealand, Canada and South Africa.

Sold over 7 million copies.

The 70th biggest selling single of all time.

Bringing the sound of the mass pipes and drums to the world, the regimental band toured extensively, playing in competitions, concerts and parades. Their recording of Amazing Grace reached #1 in charts all over the world, and #11 in the Billboard Chart.

NUMBER 19... 1969.

THE ARCHIES - SUGAR, SUGAR

Reached #1 in Austria, Belgium, Canada, Germany, Ireland, Norway, Spain, UK and USA.

Sold over 6 million copies.

The 77th biggest selling single of all time.

Written by Jeff Barry and Andy Kim, the song was performed by studio musicians for the TV cartoon series, The Archie Show. It reached #1 in the Billboard Hot 100 (for 4 weeks), in the UK (for 8 weeks) and in 8 other countries. It also reached #2 in Denmark, Switzerland, and #3 in Netherlands.

Weird OHW Fact... In 1970, Wilson Pickett covered the song, and it became a hit all over again.

NUMBER 20... 1973.
TERRY JACKS - SEASONS IN THE SUN
Reached #1 in Australia, Austria, Belgium, Canada, Denmark, France, Germany, Ireland, Norway, South Africa, Switzerland, New Zealand, UK and USA.

Sold more than 5 million copies.

The 109th biggest selling single of all time.

Originally written by Belgian Jacques Brel, new English lyrics were added by Rod McKuen. The result was a worldwide hit for Canadian Terry Jacks. A Christmas chart-topper in over 20 countries, it would probably be easier to list the countries it didn't top the chart in.

Billboard ranked it as the #2 song of 1973.

Weird OHW Fact... The Beach Boys started to record the song, but abandoned the project.

THE TWO KINGS OF ONE HIT WONDERS...

1. KING SONGWRITER, AMERICA'S JOHN D. LOUDERMILK...

One Hit Wonders is the name of this book, and John D. Loudermilk wrote a staggering... NINE of them!

John D. Loudermilk Jr. was born in Durham, North Carolina, and learned guitar as a young boy. His first true composition was his own poem, put to music, A Rose and Baby Ruth. Country star George Hamilton heard it, and recorded it in 1956. Eddie Cochran had his first ever hit with a Loudermilk composition in 1957; Sittin' on the balcony reached #18 in the US Chart, and #23 in Canada.
Loudermilk's career was set.
With contracts with Columbia and RCA records, he recorded 9 albums, and 5 Country Hits.
However, as a songwriter he would become famous. His songs have been recorded in every genre, and every decade since the 1950's.
Everyone has recorded his songs; The Everly Brothers, Eddie Cochran, Johnny Cash, Connie Francis, Paul Revere and The Raiders, Roy Orbison, Glen Campbell, Marianne Faithfull, Jefferson Airplane, Nora Jones, and David Lee Roth, to name just a few.
But more importantly (for this book), he is here as the Songwriting King of One Hit Wonders...

It began in 1957, in his first recording contract, he chose the stage name; Johnny Dee.

1957... JOHNNY DEE - SITTIN' IN THE BALCONY
Written and recorded by John D. Loudermilk (Johnny Dee), on Colonial Records, it reached #38 in the Billboard Top 100, and #20 in the UK. It would be his only hit as Johnny Dee; the 1962 single, Road Hog, was the best of his follow-ups, reaching #65.
Weird OHW Fact... The 'D' in his name did not stand for anything; his father had the same middle initial.

He teamed with the legendary Marijohn Wilkin, of, Long Black Veil, and, One day at a Time, fame.

1959... STONEWALL JACKSON – WATERLOO

Written by John D. Loudermilk and Marijohn Wilkin, it was recorded by country singer Stonewall Jackson. The single topped the Country Music Chart and spent five weeks at #1. It also reached #4 in the Billboard Hot 100, staying sixteen weeks in the mainstream chart.

1960... JOHNNY FERGUSON - ANGELA JONES
Written by John D. Loudermilk, the song was recorded by Johnny Ferguson on MGM Records, reaching #27 in the Billboard Hot 100.
Weird OHW Fact... Loudermilk was first to record the song, but it did not chart.

And in the UK...

1960... MICHAEL COX - ANGELA JONES
Written by John D. Loudermilk, the song was the only hit on Joe Meek's ill-fated Triumph label. The song reached #7 in the UK Charts, but it stalled from low record production in the factory, and would have climbed higher. Cox's follow-up, Along Came Caroline, was released on HMV Records, but it just got to #41. So close, yet so far.

As a solo artist under his real name, he charted only once...

1961... JOHN D. LOUDERMILK - LANGUAGE OF LOVE
Written by John D. Loudermilk, Language of Love, reached #32 in the Billboard Hot 100 in 1960, and Top 20 in the UK.
Loudermilk would never hit the Top 40 as a solo artist again.

1962... KRIS JENSEN - TORTURE
Written by John D. Loudermilk Jr., it was recorded by Kris Jensen, from New Haven, Connecticut, on Hickory Records. The song reached #20 in the Billboard Hot 100, but despite recording many more songs, it would be Jensen's only hit.
Weird OHW Fact... Loudermilk originally wrote the song for The Everly Brothers, but only after witnessing Jensen's success did the Everly brothers record the song.

1964... THE NASHVILLE TEENS - TOBACCO ROAD
Written and first recorded by John D. Loudermilk in 1960, this pop band from Surrey, England, recorded the song on Decca Records after being spotted by Mickey Most touring with Chuck Berry. With Most's production, it was an instant hit, reaching #6 in the UK Chart. It crossed the Atlantic well, getting to #14 in the Billboard Hot 100. They followed

it up with another Loudermilk song, Google Eye, which reached #10 in the UK, but failed to chart in the USA, stalling at #117.

Weird OHW Fact... The Nashville Teens were producer Mickey Most's third acquisition, following The Animals, Herman's Hermits.

1967... THE CASINOS – THEN YOU CAN TELL ME GOODBYE

Written by John D. Loudermilk, and first released as a country song in 1962 by Don Cherry, it was the doo-wop version by Cincinnati's the Casinos that many people remember. It reached #6 in the Billboard Hot 100 and #28 in the UK. Their subsequent singles did not chart.

1968... DON FARDON - INDIAN RESERVATION

Sold over 1 million copies.

Don Fardon (born Donald Arthur Maughn), from Coventry, started his musical life as a singer for The Sorrows. Once he had gone solo, he recorded Indian Reservation (Written by John D. Loudermilk) and took the song to #3 in the UK Chart, #20 in the Billboard Hot 100, and #4 in Australia. His best follow-up, Follow Your Drum, reached #16 in Australia, but did not chart in the UK or USA.

Yup... John D. Loudermilk; the supreme King of one hit writing...

2. KING SINGER, BRITAIN'S TONY BURROWS...

The man's name is Tony Burrows.
His claim to fame?
Well, he was the lead singer in several one-hit wonder bands, including
The Flower Pot Men, Edison Lighthouse, White Plains, The Pipkins, The
Brotherhood of Man and The First Class.
Basically he holds the record for one hit wonders with ALL the above
bands. Yup, he's had a hand in SIX of them.
The story starts in the early years of the 1960's...

Anthony Burrows was born in Exeter, Devon, South England, in 1942,
the middle of World War 2. In the early 1960s, he sang with The
Kestrels, a vocal group which included the future songwriting team
Roger Greenaway and Roger Cook.
Roger Greenaway and Roger Cook have written and co-written a host
of hit songs; 'You've Got Your Troubles, (Fortunes UK #2), I'd Like to
Teach the World to Sing (in Perfect Harmony)' (New Seekers UK #1)
and, Long Cool Woman in a Black Dress, (The Hollies US #2).
Unknown to Tony, working hard with Roger, Roger and The Kestrels,
there was a duo working elsewhere who would influence his life
forever...
John Carter and Ken Lewis were essentially songwriters. They wrote
Mike Sarne's 1962 single, Will I What? (UK #18) and wrote Herman's
Hermits 1965 hit, 'Can't You Hear My Heartbeat', (US #2) and John
Carter provided lead vocals for The New Vaudeville Band's 1966 hit,
'Winchester Cathedral', (US #1, UK #4). They also featured Jimmy Page
in their band for a short time.
The Ivy League was assembled essentially to showcase carter and
Lewis's songs, and the initial line up included Jimmy Page (later of Led
Zeppelin) and Viv Prince (later of the Pretty Things). However, the band
soon settled down to a Birmingham trio, and comprised John Carter,
Ken Lewis (previously with Carter-Lewis and the Southerners) and
Perry Ford. The Ivy League provided The Who with the backing vocals
on, I Can't Explain, and were making moves in the music world. Their
second single, 'Funny How Love Can Be, reached #8 in the UK Charts,
and a year later, 'Tossing and Turning', got to #3.
The Flower Pot Men. When Carter and Lewis left the band to start
Sunny Records, Tony Burrows and Neil Landon were hired to fill their
places. After a disappointing single, The Willow Tree, (UK #50) in 1966,
the band was expanded and its name was changed to The Flower Pot
Men, (after characters in a popular childrens TV show, and an obvious

association with 'Flower Power', and the word 'Pot', linked with Cannabis). Two founding members of Deep Purple, Jon Lord and Nick Simper, were also part of this early band.

RELEASED AUGUST 1967.
THE FLOWER POT MEN - LET'S GO TO SAN FRANCISCO
Written by John Carter and Ken Lewis, this was the only charting single by British band, The Flower Pot men, which included Jon Lord of Deep Purple. Tony Burrows sang vocals, and the California Sound single reached #4 in the UK, and Top ten in many European countries, including #9 in Norway.
Weird OHW Fact... The song is so close to the Beach Boys sound, it has been mistaken for them.
Weird OHW Fact... In the USA, DJ's had to refer to them as the 'Flower Men', to drop the association with cannabis.

The Flower Pot Men's follow-up had a similar sound, but didn't chart except in Holland (#4). By 1968, they needed new ideas, and even a name change (Piccolo Man, was released under the band name 'Friends') did not alter the downward spiral. Roger Greenaway and Roger Cook came onboard to help, and when more bandmembers left in 1969, they changed the name again to White Plains and began to record.
The Brotherhood of Man. Around the same time of the decline of The Flower Pot Men, in an era of flux and uncertainty, Burrows was brought into another ensemble put together by Roger Greenaway; The Brotherhood of Man. They recorded in the winter of '69, releasing their hit single, United We Stand, in January 1970.

RELEASED JANUARY 1970.
THE BROTHERHOOD OF MAN - UNITED WE STAND
Written by Tony Hiller and Peter Simmons, it was the band's first and only international hit, peaking at #13 in the Billboard Hot 100, #9 in Canada, #8 in Australia, and #10 in the U.K.
The song has become an anthem in times of disunity, used as a football chant and by various political themes.
Billboard ranked the record as the #64 song of 1970.
Weird OHW Fact... The song was used as the closing credits of the TV show The Brady Bunch Hour.

Unbeleivably, Burrows juggled these three projects well, even doing quick clothes changes in the Top of the Pops studio, floating from one band's performance to another.

RELEASED JANUARY 1970.
WHITE PLAINS - MY BABY LOVES LOVIN'
Written by Roger Cook and Roger Greenaway, and released on Decca records, the British pop group White Plains had their one and only hit. It reached #4 in Canada, #9 in UK, and #13 in the USA. The band did have other hits in the UK; When You Are A King, (UK #13) and, Lovin' You Baby (Canada #35), but never again in the USA.

The White Plains. January would be a busy time for Tony Burrows. Continuing his leadership of White Plains, he joined Edison Lighthouse for the recording of their hit single, Love Grows (Where My Rosemary Goes), then he promptly left the band. The single was a hit, but none of their subsequent material charted.
Tony Burrows didn't mind, he was being considered for the next Roger Greenaway project.

RELEASED JANUARY 1970.
EDISON LIGHTHOUSE - LOVE GROWS (WHERE MY ROSEMARY GOES)
Reached #1 in UK, New Zealand.
The single hit #1 in the UK Singles Chart for a total of five weeks, #2 in Australia, #3 in Canada and South Africa, and #5 in the Billboard Hot 100. Their follow-ups, It's Up to You, Petula, reached the UK Top 50, but nothing else charted.
Billboard ranked the record as the #40 song of 1970.

The Pipkins. After the furore of having three concurrent hits in the charts, Burrows was free to join Roger Greenaway's newest project; The Pipkins. In all, twelve songs were recorded, but only one was a hit. From Albert Hammond and Mike Hazlewood's musical work, Oliver in the Underworld, Gimme Dat Ding was a novelty song, combining Burrows and Greenaway's voices.

RELEASED 1970
THE PIPKINS - GIMME DAT DING
Written and composed by Albert Hammond and Mike Hazlewood on EMI Columbia, the gimmick single reached #6 in UK, #9 in USA, and #7 in Canada.
The original version of the song, performed by Freddie Garrity, was released on the album, Oliver in the Overworld.

Weird OHW Fact... Gimme Dat Ding was used (as Gimme Dat Ring) by Coca-Cola to advertise their new Ring Pull Cans in the early 1970's.

Having had five one hit wonders, Burrows wasn't done. As White Plains began to run out of success, he met John Carter, who was putting a band together. With songs written with his wife, Carter provided the material, Burrows belted it out. Their first single was an international hit.

RELEASED MAY 1974.
THE FIRST CLASS - BEACH BABY
Reached #1 in Canada.
Written by London husband and wife team John Carter and Gillian Shakespeare, and sugng by one hit wonder king, Tony Burrows, the song reached #1 in Canada, #4 in the Billboard Hot 100, #13 in their native UK, and #11 in Australia.
Weird OHW Fact... Neither Burrows nor Carter wanted to tour, so they sent a 'dummy' band on tour with the song; the new musicians who mimed on pop shows never sang a note. The First Class recorded two albums, but did not score another hit.
Billboard ranked it as the #94 song for 1974.

Burrows claims that he was the first and only artist to appear on Top of the Pops fronting three bands in one show. This is yet to be confirmed, but one thing is true; he did perform fronting two bands on a single show on four occasions. He also claims to have been 'banned' by the BBC.

Weird OHW Fact... Although he reached the Top 40 as the lead singer of 6 different groups, he only managed one chart single as a solo artist. In 1970, in the US, he dipped inside the Billboard Hot 100 with 'Melanie Makes Me Smile, which only peaked at #87.

And if you think that Britain was alone in having a one-hit-wonder king, you'd be wrong... they're not quite in the same league as Britain's Tony Burrows, but this bunch from Los Angeles had a chameleon-like idea of the music business. It all began quite innocuously...

In Los Angeles, in 1955, a group of African Americans formed a group called The Jay Hawks.

1956... THE JAY HAWKS – STRANDED IN THE JUNGLE

The group was an African-American soul vocal ensemble from Los Angeles, California. In 1956, they released a single called 'Stranded in the Jungle', written by Ernestine Smith and the band's first tenor, James Johnson. We think the complete line-up was; Don Bradley, Carl Fisher, Dave Govan, James Johnson and Ricky Owens. The song reached #18 in the Billboard Hot 100, but subsequent attempts as The Jay Hawks were unsuccessful.

So they changed their record label to Chess Records, and their name to... The Vibrations, but in typical style couldn't resist recording one song as... The Marathons.

1961...THE MARATHONS – PEANUT BUTTER

Written by Hidle Brown Barnum, Martin Cooper, Fred Smith and Cliff Goldsmith, it was recorded on Arvee Records. The line-up at this stage was Jimmy Johnson (Lead), Carl Fisher (Ténor), Dave Govan (Baritone), and Carver Bunkum (Bass). It reached #20 in the Billboard Hot 100 in 1961. Supposedly, the Olympics were on tour so their manager secretly signed the Vibrations to record this song as 'The Marathons'. Unfortunately for the band, Chess Records discovered the fraud and stopped Arvee records from releasing further copies. It was also released on Argo records.

Weird OHW Fact... This connection is rather tenuous; the peanut bar, Snickers, was called 'Marathon' in the UK for many years.☐

But the band couldn't help themselves. Concurrent with the release of, Peanut Butter, they released another single as The Vibrations.

1961... THE VIBRATIONS – THE WATUSI

Written by Hall, Temple and the band member, Jimmy Johnson, the 'new dance' song was recorded on Checker records. (Not to be confused with

Watusi Time, released in 1964) the single reached #25 in the Billboard Hot 100.

However, the name, The Vibrations, seemed to stick, and their next hit came three years later...

1963... THE VIBRATIONS – MY GIRL SLOOPY
Supposedly written by Wes Farrell and Bert Berns, My Girl Sloopy was first recorded by The Vibrations in 1964, on Atlantic Records. It reached #26 in the Billboard Hot 100, and #10 in the R&B Chart.
At last the group had beat their one-hit-wonder status!
The band recorded off and on until 1976, when they finally broke up.

Before we get to the meat of the book, the one hit wonders, here's a list you might enjoy.

Now here, we're not talking about artists, but the actual songs, taking into account every single cover version, in every guise, and in every genre imaginable. Obviously, the earlier the song was a hit, gives it more time to be covered, and the more the songs were covered, the more airplay the song had. The figures, given out in 1999 by the BMI are as accurate as they can be, taking into consideration the diverse state of radio on the planet...

1. More than 8 Million plays; You've Lost That Lovin' Feelin'
Written by Barry Mann, Phil Spector, and Cynthia Weil
First recorded by; the Righteous Brothers
Covered by; Joan Baez with Phil Spector, Nancy Wilson, Cilla Black, Dionne Warwick, Roberta Flack and Donny Hathaway, Long John Baldry, Hall & Oates, The Pozo-Seco Singers, Nancy Sinatra and Lee Hazlewood, The Blossoms, Elvis Presley, Isaac Hayes, Siw Malmkvist, Barry Mann, Bill Medley, Barbara Fairchild, The Human League, Grant & Forsyth, Carroll Baker, Günther Neefs, Jackie Leven, André Hazes & Johnny Logan, Erasure, Jessie J and Tom Jones.

2. More than 7 million plays; Never My Love
Written by American brothers Donald and Richard Addrisi.
First recorded by the Association
Covered by; The Association, 5th Dimension, Hans Christian (a.k.a. Jon Anderson, Later of Yes) in 1968, Booker T. & the M.G.'s, Vikki Carr, Percy Faith, Peter Nero, Blue Suede, The Four Tops, Lou Christie, Billy Crawford, Astrud Gilberto, Etta James, Steve Lawrence, Brenda Lee, The Lennon Sisters, The Lettermen, The Sandpipers, David Hasselhoff, Pekinška Patka, Henry Mancini, Johnny Mathis, Smokey Robinson, Donny Hathaway, Tinkerbells Fairydust, Tom Scott, Sylvia, Cal Tjader, The Ventures, Kathy Troccoli, Andy Williams, Boris Gardiner, Sarah Vaughan, Vern Gosdin, Samantha Jones.

3. "Yesterday" by Lennon–McCartney
First recorded by The Beatles, Yesterday, is one of the most recorded songs in the history of popular music; its entry in Guinness World Records states that, by January 1986, 1,600 cover versions had been made.[2] After Muzak switched in the 1990s to programs based on commercial recordings, its inventory grew to include about 500

"Yesterday" covers.[38] At the 2006 Grammy Awards, McCartney performed the song live as a mash-up with Linkin Park and Jay Z's "Numb/Encore"

But enough waffle... let's get to the massive list of songs...

THE FIFTIES...
1955...

As the Billboard Top 100 consolidates and 'supposedly' supersedes all other American record charts, the year begins...
At 19, Jim Henson makes his first Kermit puppet, , the first nuclear-powered submarine, the USS Nautilus sails on its maiden voyage, death at Le Mans as a two car crash kills 83, Ruth Ellis is hanged for murder in London, the last woman to be executed in the UK, Gunsmoke debuts on the CBS, and The Vietnam War begins.

AL HIBLER – UNCHAINED MELODY
Written in 1955 by Alex North and Hy Zaret for the virtually unknown prison movie, Unchained, it was recorded by three artists in the same year. Les Baxter, Al Hibbler, and Roy Hamilton charted in the Billboard Top 10 in the United States, Hibbler reaching #2. Hibbler went on to have more success in the USA, but Unchained Melody would be his only UK hit, reaching #2.
Weird OHW Fact... Four versions were in the UK chart at the same time, a record still unbeaten. Versions by Al Hibbler, Les Baxter, Jimmy Young, and Liberace all charted in the UK Top 20.

BONNIE LOU - DADDY-O
From Illinois, country singer Bonnie Lou signed with her first record company in 1953, King Records in Cincinnati, Ohio. She hit the Country Charts, then moved on to sing rockabilly numbers and soon hit the chart with Daddy-O, reaching #14 in the new Billboard Chart. She found it difficult to follow-up the success, and soon dropped out of the music scene.

CATERINA VALENTE - THE BREEZE AND I (ANDALUCIA)
With classical roots, the original song was written by Ernesto Lecuona and Emilio de Torre, with English lyrics by Al Stillman. Jimmy Dorsey's 1940 recording is considered the best, but it was covered by Italian singer Caterina Valente in 1955. It reached #5 in the UK Charts, then moved to the US, charting at #13 in the Billboard Top 100.

CHUCK MILLER - THE HOUSE OF BLUE LIGHTS
Born in Wellington, Kansas, he was a club singer before he was 25. The song was written in 1946 by Don Raye and Freddie Slack, and was Miller's only chart hit, reaching #9 in the Billboard Top 100 Chart. His

only successful follow-up, The Auctioneer, only reached # 59 the next year.

DEJOHN SISTERS - (MY BABY DON'T LOVE ME) NO MORE
Written by Leo J. De John, Julie De John and Dux De John. Recorded by the DeJohn Sisters on Epic Records, the song reached #6 in the Billboard Top 100. They had no other hit.

Weird OHW Fact... The McGuire Sisters version on Coral Records peaked at #23, and #20 in the UK, but the DJ's began to play the B-side, Sincerely, which got to #1 and sold a million copies.

THE DREAM WEAVERS - IT'S ALMOST TOMORROW
Written in 1953 by then high-schoolers Gene Adkinson and Wade Buff, known as The Dream Weavers (see other listings), they recorded the song for Decca, and it was an immediate hit. It reached #7 in the US Billboard Top 100, staying in the chart for 21 weeks, and #1 in the UK for 2 weeks in 1956, lingering in that chart for 18 weeks (Where they are a one hit wonder).

Weird OHW Fact... In the USA, the Dream Weavers had another hit, A Little Love Can Go A Long Way, reaching #33 in the Billboard 100.

Weird OHW Fact... At one point there were FOUR different versions in the US Chart; David Carroll (#20), Snooky Lanson (#20), and Jo Stafford (#14).

EL DORADOS - AT MY FRONT DOOR (CRAZY LITTLE MAMA)
Formed in Chicago in 1952, and previously called Pirkle Lee and the Five Stars, doo wop group The El Dorados had many attempts at the fame game. They eventually hit it big with, At My Front Door, reaching #1 in the R&B Chart and #17 in the Billboard Top 100. Their follow-up, I'll Be Forever Loving You, made the R&B Top Ten, but did not chart mainstream.

FELICIA SANDERS - BLUE STAR
Adapted from Victor Young's Theme for the TV show, Medic, lyrics were added by Edward Heyman, and the collaboration called 'Blue Star'. As usual, in the rush to record the song, six different versions hit the chart in the last half of 1955. New Yorker Felicia Sanders's version reached #29 in the Billboard Top 100.

FERKO STRING BAND - ALABAMA JUBILEE
Written by George L. Cobb and Jack Yellen it made popular by comedians Collins & Harlan in 1915, and Red Foley in 1951. The version

by the Ferko String Band was an instrumental, and reached #14 in the Billboard Chart, and #20 in the UK Charts

JOAN WEBER - LET ME GO, LOVER!
Reached #1 in USA.
Sold over 1 million copies.
Joan Weber's story is as tragic as any Hollywood weepie. She was pregnant when given the song, and recorded it immediately. The song was featured on TV show, Studio One, and it went straight to #1 in the Billboard Chart, and #16 in the UK. Her follow-up, Lover Lover (Why Must We Part), did not chart, and because of her advancing pregnancy, she could not promote any further singles. She was checked into a mental hospital, and her royalty checks were 'returned to sender'. She died in an institution, in 1981, the same day Pope John Paul II was assassinated.
Weird OHW Fact... Because of its popularity it was immediately covered many times and charted;
Late 1954, Teresa Brewer and The Lancers, #6 US, #9 UK. Late 1954, Peggy Lee, #26 Cash Box Chart. 1955, Hank Snow #1 US Country Chart. 1955, Dean Martin, #3 UK. 1955, Ruby Murray #5 UK.

JOHNNY ACE - PLEDGING MY LOVE
Written by Ferdinand Washington and Don Robey, this is another song covered by many artists in 1955. The highest chart release was by Johnny Ace (John Marshall Alexander) from Memphis, Tennessee. After making the recording, Ace accidentally shot and killed himself. Duke records released the record posthumously and it reached #1 in the R&B Chart, #17 in the Billboard Top 100.

JULIE LONDON - CRY ME A RIVER
Written by Arthur Hamilton in 1953, it was made into an institution by actress Julie London from Santa Rosa, California. Originally intended for Ella Fitzgerald in the movie, Pete Kelly's Blues, the song was surprisingly dropped from the soundtrack. Peggy King also declined the song. Julie London's performance in the movie, The Girl Can't Help It, broke the floodgates. It reached #9 in the Billboard Top 100, and #22 in the UK.

KITTY KALLEN - LITTLE THINGS MEAN A LOT
Sold more than 2 million copies.
Reached #1 in USA and UK.

Written by Edith Lindeman and Carl Stutz, it was recorded by Philadelphia's Kitty Kallen, who took it to #1 in the US Pop Chart (a Top 12 at that time), where it stayed at the top for 9 weeks, and in the chart for a staggering 7 months. It also reached #1 in the UK, where she was a one hit wonder.

Weird OHW Fact... It was covered many times, principally by Alma Cogan who reached UK #11 in the same year, and by Dana, who reached #27 in her native Ireland.

LILLIAN BRIGGS - I WANT YOU TO BE MY BABY
Sold a million copies.
Written by Jon Hendricks for Louis Jordan, it was recorded by comedian Lillian Briggs which resulted in an immediate cover version by singer Georgia Gibbs. Both versions raced into production, with some DJ's receiving copies for broadcast the same day. Gibbs did actually chart higher, #14, but Briggs comedic version had more longevity, reaching #18 and staying in the chart to get a gold disc award.

Weird OHW Fact... In the UK two versions were released, one by Annie Ross, and one by Don Lang. neither reached the charts.

MARION MARLOWE - THE MAN IN THE RAINCOAT
Written by Warwick Webster. Marion Townsend was a singer from the age of five. She had her own radio show from age 9 to 13. She sang on stage, but her only chart success was The Man in the Raincoat, which reached #14 in the Billboard chart.

Weird OHW Fact... Think of her stage name... she was a room-mate of Marilyn Monroe in Hollywood.

NAPPY BROWN - DON'T BE ANGRY
Written by Nappy Brown, Rose Marie McCoy, and Fred Mendelsohn, it was recorded by Brown (born Napoleon Brown Goodson Culp) and would be his first hit. Don't be Angry Brown reached #2 in the Billboard R&B charts, and #25 in the Billboard Top 100. His follow-ups came close... Little By Little #57, and It Don't Hurt No More #89.

Weird OHW Fact... The Crew Cuts (A Canadian singing group who 'captured' popular songs) version got to #14.

Weird OHW Fact... UK punk band Bad Manners recorded a version in 1981.

PEGGY KING - MAKE YOURSELF COMFORTABLE

Pennsylvania native Peggy King will best be remembered as a TV actress and singer. She had many minor hits, her only chart entry being Make Yourself Comfortable, getting to #30 in the Billboard Chart.

THE PENGUINS - EARTH ANGEL (WILL YOU BE MINE)

Reached #1 in USA.
Sold more than 10 million copies.
Written by Curtis Williams, Jesse Belvin, and Gaynel Hodge, it was recorded by The Penguins, an American doo-wop group from Los Angeles. Earth Angel got to #1 in every chart in America, the Juke Box Chart, Best Sellers in Stores and Most Played. It eventually sold more than 10 million copies, although the writing credits were disputed for years.
Weird OHW Fact... The best cover version was by Canadian band, the Crew-Cuts. Their version peaked at number three on the pop charts, and hit #4 in the UK Charts, where the original did not chart.

PRISCILLA WRIGHT - MAN IN THE RAINCOAT

Written by Warwick Webster. Priscilla Wright from Ontario, Canada, came from a musical family, and at just 14 years old had a hit with Man in the Raincoat, reaching #16 in the Billboard Pop Chart. It was just one of three versions of the song in the charts at that time.

RICKY ZAHND AND THE BLUE JEANERS - (I'M GETTIN') NUTTIN' FOR CHRISTMAS

Written by Sid Tepper and Roy C. Bennett, it's yet another example of multiple chart entries. The song was so popular, there were five different recordings in the chart at the one time. The highest entry (#6) was Art Mooney and His Orchestra, with a six-year-old Barry Gordon as lead vocalist. Our one hit wonders, however, were Ricky Zahnd and the Blue Jeaners, whose version got to #21. They never charted again.

THE SINGING DOGS – OH SUSANNAH

Sold over a million copies.
Danish recording engineer Carl Weismann dubbed barking dogs into the melody of the Stephen Foster song, Oh! Susanna, and a novelty hit was born. It reached #22 in the US Billboard Pop Singles chart, and eventually was awarded a gold record. Thankfully the follow-up was not a hit.

STEVE ALLEN - AUTUMN LEAVES

Written in French in 1945 by Joseph Kosma, Johnny Mercer, and Jacques Prévert, it was originally called, *Les Feuilles Mortes* (literally, The Dead Leaves). Allen's version reached #35 in the newly formed Billboard Top 100.

Weird OHW Fact... It has been copied many times, notably by Andy Williams, and lately by Eva Cassidy, whose version still haunts me.

THE SUNNYSIDERS - HEY! MR. BANJO

Recorded by The Sunnysiders,
Written by comedian Spike Jones, and with The Sunnysiders TV appearance on the Bandstand, Hey! Mr. Banjo reached #12 in the Billboard Top 100 and encouraged Kapp Records to give the trio an LP contract. Unfortunately, they did not chart again.

Weird OHW Fact... Band member, Margie Rayburn, had another one hit wonder in 1957, with her solo recording, I'm Available.

THE THREE CHUCKLES – RUNAROUND

Written by a truck driver named Cirino Colacrai, it was recorded by Brooklyn rock & rollers The Three Chuckles. The song became a hit, reaching #20 in the Billboard Pop Chart. They quickly followed it up, but their subsequent singles did not chart well... Times Two, I Love You (#67), and And the Angels Sing (#70). The band broke up in 1958.

THE VOICES OF WALTER SCHUMANN - THE BALLAD OF DAVY CROCKETT

American composer, Walter Schumann, gathered a singing ensemble (they were not a choir!) and recorded many popular songs. One of these, The Ballad of Davy Crockett, reached #29 in the Billboard Pop Chart.

Weird OHW Fact... Schumann also wrote the theme to TV show Dragnet.

1956...

As Elvis Presley enters the United States music charts for the first time, with Heartbreak Hotel, the year begins...
Morocco and Tunisia declare independence from France, boxing legend Rocky Marciano retires undefeated, the first Eurovision Song Contest is broadcast from Lugano, Switzerland, the first Lockheed U-2 spy plane flight over the Soviet Union, and the UK and France bomb Egypt to force the reopening of the Suez Canal.

THE BLUE STARS - LULLABY OF BIRDLAND
Written by George Shearing and George David Weiss in 1952, it was recorded by The Blue Stars in 1956, who took it to #16 in the Billboard Top 100.
Weird OHW Fact... The title of the song is a reference to Charlie 'Bird' Parker and the Birdland jazz club named after him.

BOBBY SCOTT - CHAIN GANG
Sold over 1 million copies.
Not to be confused with Sam Cooke's 1960 song, this song of the same name was recorded by New York's Bobby Scott. It reached #13 in the Billboard Top 100 and was awarded gold status.
Weird OHW Fact... Bobby Scott won a Grammy for 'A taste of Honey', in 1963, and co wrote the Hollies smash hit, 'He Ain't Heavy, He's My Brother'.

BONNIE SISTERS - CRY BABY
Three nurses at Bellevue Hospital began singing together at work. They got a TV spot, a record deal, and hit it big with their first release. Cry Baby got to #16 in the Billboard Top 100, but their follow-ups 'Track That Cat', 'Wandering Heart', and 'Confess', did not chart.
Weird OHW Fact... Following their brief sojourn in the music business, they returned to nursing.

THE CADETS - STRANDED IN THE JUNGLE
Written by Ernestine Smith and The Jayhawk's first tenor, James Johnson, this doo-wop song was recorded by The Cadets (also from Los Angeles, California) as soon it was off the Jayhawks press. The Jayhawks reached #18 in the Billboard Top 100, but the Cadets did better, and probably have the best-remembered version, reaching #15 in the Billboard Top 100, and #3 in the R&B Chart in the same week.

Weird OHW Fact... The Gadabouts version got to #39 just one week later. (see Gadabouts and JayHawks entry).

CARL PERKINS - BLUE SUEDE SHOES

Written by Carl Perkins in 1955, it is recognized as the first rock-a-billy song, and has been covered many times by Elvis, Buddy Holly, and Eddie Cochrane to name a few.. Perkins' version shot to #2 in the Billboard Top 100, but it would be his only charting single. The follow up, 'Boppin' the Blues', just got to #70.

Weird OHW Fact... Johnny Cash told Perkins a story about a man with blue suede shoes, and when Perkins was playing one night, he heard a dancer complain to his girl; "Don't step on the suede!" Perkins wrote the song that night, and even spelled suede wrong... swade.

CATHY CARR - IVORY TOWER

Written by Jack Fulton and Lois Steele, three versions hit the charts in 1956. Cathy Carr's version reached #2 in the Billboard Top 100, and #2 in Australia, and was by far the most successful. Actress/singer Gale Storm reached #6, and a R&B version by Otis Williams got to #11 in the R&B chart.

Weird OHW Fact... Cathy Carr's real name was Angelina Helen Catherine Cordovano.

COUNT BASIE - APRIL IN PARIS

Written in 1932 by Vernon Duke and Yip Harburg for the Broadway musical, Walk a Little Faster, Count Basie recorded it on his first album. It reached #28 in the Billboard Top 100, but would be his only chart hit.

Weird OHW Fact... Count Basie has won nine Grammys.

DON ROBERTSON - THE HAPPY WHISTLER

Sold over 1 million copies.

Written by singer/songwriter Donald Irwin Robertson, this is the only time he hit the chart with his own composition. It reached #6 in the Billboard Top 100, and #8 in the UK Chart. Robertson is better known for his songwriting, recorded by many American greats including Elvis, Les Paul and Jim Reeves.

EDDIE COOLEY – PRISCILLA

Written by Eddie Cooley, and recorded by Eddie Cooley and the Dimples, the song reached #20 in the Billboard Top 100. Unused to vocals, it would be his only chart hit.

Weird OHW Fact... Cooley co-wrote 'Fever', which was a R&B #1 for Little Willie John in 1956.

EDDIE LAWRENCE - THE OLD PHILOSOPHER

This may be the weirdest single ever; comedian Lawrence lists random sort-of comedic phrases and one liners. Nonetheless, it reached #34 in the Billboard Top 100, and spring-boarded his comedy career. Lawrence appeared on Broadway and on film and television for many years.

ELMER BERNSTEIN - MAIN THEME FROM THE MAN WITH THE GOLDEN ARM

From the 1955 Frank Sinatra movie, Elmer Bernstein's original version reached #32 in the Billboard Top 100, while Billy May and his Orchestra had the #6 hit in the UK.

Weird OHW Fact... The McGuire Sisters had a hit with a version with lyrics by Sylvia Fine. The song reached #37 in the Billboard Top 100 and #24 in the UK Chart in 1956. In an even weirder twist, the lyrics had no correlation to the film content whatsoever.

THE FOUR VOICES - LOVELY ONE

This Tennessee vocal quartet released a string of singles for Columbia Records. This, their third single, was the only one to hit the chart. It reached #20 in the Billboard Top 100. Despite regular television appearances, they will remain one hit wonders.

THE GADABOUTS - STRANDED IN THE JUNGLE

Written by Ernestine Smith and The Jayhawk's first tenor, James Johnson, the doo-wop song was recorded by The Gadabouts. This was a song with three versions in the chart at the same time. The Jayhawks reached #18 in the Billboard Top 100, The Cadets got to #15 in the same week, and the Gadabouts reached #39 one week later. (See the Cadet's and Jay Hawks entry)

GOGI GRANT – THE WAYWARD WIND

Reached #1 in the USA.
Sold over 1 million copies.
Written by Stanley Lebowsky and Herb Newman, this country song was released by Gogi Grant, Tex Ritter, and Jimmy Young. Grant's version was the most notable, reaching #1 in the Billboard Top 100, #9 in the UK, and #9 in Australia. However, Grant is only a one hit wonder in the

UK and Australia, as she had a previous US hit in 1955 with, Suddenly There's A Valley (US #9).

Tex Ritter's version reached #28 in the US, #8 in the UK, and Jimmy Young's version reached #27 in the UK.

Weird OHW Fact... Frank Ifield would have a #1 hit in the UK with the, The Wayward Wind, in 1961 (Ireland #3, Australia #16)

Weird OHW Fact... The Wayward Wind was played by the Beatles in their live show in 1960 and 1961, but no recording was ever made.

GRACE KELLY - TRUE LOVE

Written by Cole Porter, and featured in the movie, High Society, the song was a duet by Bing Crosby and Grace Kelly. The song reached #4 in the Billboard Top 100, and #4 in the UK Charts. Although Kelly only sings on the last verse, the single gave her credit for her part; it was her only chart hit.

Weird OHW Fact... True Love is actually the name of the yacht in the movie.

Weird OHW Fact... In real life, Bing Crosby bought a 55-foot yacht, which he named, True Love.

HELMUT ZACHARIAS - WHEN THE WHITE LILACS BLOOM AGAIN

Probably taken from the 1953 German film, When the White Lilacs Bloom Again, it was recorded by Helmut Zacharias, German violinist and composer. The record got to #12 in the Billboard Top 100, but was his only US Success.

Weird OHW Fact... In November 1964, he reached #9 in the UK Singles Chart with a tune called, Tokyo Melody, used by the BBC as a theme for the Winter Olympics.

THE HIGHLIGHTS - CITY OF ANGELS

Written by Bev Dusham and Nicholas Jovan, this Chicago vocal quintet approached Bailly Records with their song, Jingle-Lo. The record company gave them City of Angles instead and it reached #19 in the Billboard Top 100. The follow-up, 'To Be With You', reached #84 the next year. By then the band were dissatisfied with being a back-up band for the lead singer, and split up.

IVORY JOE HUNTER - SINCE I MET YOU BABY

Sold over 1 million copies.

Written by pianist Ivory Joe Hunter, he recorded it himself, reaching the top of the R&B Chart for three consecutive weeks. The song got to #12 in the mainstream Billboard Top 100.

It has been covered many times, and been a hit in most decades.

JANE POWELL - TRUE LOVE
Born Suzanne Lorraine Burce, Powell is perhaps better known for her many acting roles. The Cole Porter song, True Love, was featured in the film, High Society, a duet with Bing Crosby and Grace Kelly (#4 US and #4 UK, see listing above). Powell recorded the song and released it the same year. Her version reached #15 in the Billboard Top 100.
Weird OHW Fact... It got to #2 in the UK in 1993 with Elton John and Kiki Dee.

THE JAY HAWKS - STRANDED IN THE JUNGLE
Written by Ernestine Smith and the band's first tenor, James Johnson, the doo-wop song was first recorded by the Jayhawks. This was a song with three versions in the chart at the same time. The Jay Hawks reached #18 in the Billboard Top 100. (See featured spot above, The American One-Hit-Wonder Kings...)
Weird OHW Fact... Yup, The Cadets version reached #15 at the same time. The Gadabouts version got to #39 just one week later. (see their entries above)

JERRY LEWIS - ROCK-A-BYE YOUR BABY WITH A DIXIE MELODY
Sold over 1 million copies.
Written by Jean Schwartz, Sam M. Lewis, and Joe Young, it was featured in the musical, Sinbad, sung by Al Jolson, getting to #1 in 1918. Actor and comedian Jerry Lewis's version reached #10 in the Billboard Top 100, and was awarded a gold record.

JOE 'FINGERS' CARR - PORTUGUESE WASHERWOMEN
Reached #1 in Australia.
From Louisville Kentucky, Louis Ferdinand Busch worked in the music industry in the 40's and 50's. In 1955 he changed his name to Joe 'Fingers' Carr, and had a nostalgic hit with Portuguese Washerwomen , which reached #25 in the Billboard Top 100. It also charted in Australia, topping the chart there for three weeks, the #11 song of the year there.

JOE VALINO - GARDEN OF EDEN
Written by Dennise Haas Norwood, the song was first recorded by Philadelphia's Joe Valino, (born Joseph Paolino, Jr) on RCA records, whose version went to #12 in the Billboard Top 100. It would be Valino's only chart entry (see Weird OHW Fact below). In the UK,

Frankie Vaughan had his first #1 with the song the next year, staying at the top for 4 weeks.

Weird OHW Fact... In 1957 Valino's girlfriend claimed that he had arranged for her illegal abortion. He denied it, but was convicted anyway, receiving a 17-year probation. As a result of this conviction, his music was removed from sale in shops and banned from all radio play.

KAY THOMPSON - ELOISE

Kay Thompson is the writer and creator of the 'Eloise' books for children, written in the 1950's. She made one recording, entitled, Eloise, in 1956, and it reached #39 in the Billboard Top 100.

Weird OHW Fact... Thompson mentored/tutored Andy Williams in the 50's and early 60's, bringing him into the limelight. In his memoirs, Williams admitted to having a longtime affair with Thompson, despite their 20 year age difference.

KIT CARSON - BAND OF GOLD

Written by Jack Taylor and lyrics by Bob Musel, its biggest hit was Don Cherry in 1955. One hit wonder Kit Carson (born Liza Morrow) recorded it and had a hit the next year, reaching #11 in the Billboard Top 100.

Weird OHW Fact... Petula Clark had the hit in the UK.

THE LENNON SISTERS - TONIGHT YOU BELONG TO ME

Written in 1926 by Lee David and Billy Rose, it was recorded by The Lennon Sisters and reached #16 in the Billboard Top 100. It was their only US hit. However, they are actually one hit wonders twice over.

Weird OHW Fact... In 1961, their single, Sad Movies (Make Me Cry), reached #1 in Japan, but just got to #56 in the USA.

LITTLE JOE AND THE THRILLERS - PEANUTS

Philadelphia's Joseph Cook had sung in church from an early age. His only chart recording was his self-penned falsetto song, Peanuts. It reached #22 in the Billboard Top 100. He performed in clubs for many years, and in a group with his daughters scored a minor R&B hit, Pop Pop Pop-Pie.

LOU BUSCH AND HIS ORCHESTRA - 11TH HOUR MELODY

Written by King Palmer and Carl Sigman, Louis Ferdinand Busch was a Kentucky pianist who is in this book already (5 entries above this one) as Joe 'Fingers' Carr. On Capitol Records, he recorded his only charting hit, the piano driven song called, 11th Hour Melody. It reached #35 in the Billboard Top 100.

MORRIS STOLOFF AND THE COLUMBIA PICTURES ORCHESTRA - MOONGLOW AND THEME FROM PICNIC

Moonglow was written in 1933 by Will Hudson, Irving Mills and Eddie DeLange, and Theme from Picnic written in 1955 by George Duning and Steve Allen. Morris Stoloff put them together as a medley for the William Holden movie, Picnic. Stoloff's version got to #2 in the Billboard Top 100, and #1 in minor charts. Another version, by George Cates, charted at #4.

RICHARD HAYMAN AND JAN AUGUST - (A THEME FROM) THE THREE PENNY OPERA (MORITAT)

Written by Bertolt Brecht and Elizabeth Hauptmann, the full title of the song is Die Moritat von Mackie Messer, better known as, The Ballad of Mack the Knife. This version got to #12 in the Billboard Top 100, although the more known version would come from Frank Sinatra.

RICHARD MALTBY AND HIS ORCHESTRA - (THEMES FROM) THE MAN WITH THE GOLDEN ARM

Richard Eldridge Maltby Sr. was an American conductor and bandleader. His only charting recording, however was, Themes From The Man with the Golden Arm, from the movie starring Frank Sinatra. It reached #32 in the Billboard Top 100.

Weird OHW Fact... Richard Maltby Sr. is the father of Broadway director Richard Maltby Jr.

THE ROVER BOYS - GRADUATION DAY

Written by Joe and Noel Sherman, it was recorded by Canadian vocal group, The Rover Boys, featuring Billy Albert, on ABC Paramount Records. The song reached #16 in the Billboard Top 100, but their follow-up, From A School Ring To A Wedding Ring, only got to #79. The Four Freshmen also charted at #17 with the same song in the same month.

SANFORD CLARK - THE FOOL

Written by Lee Hazlewood, it was recorded by American country-rockabilly singer and guitarist, Sandford Clark, on MCI Records. It was his debut single, and reached #7 in the Billboard Top 100, #5 in the Black Singles Chart, and #14 in the Country Chart. His follow-up single, The Cheat, was a minor hit, but did not break the mainstream chart.

SIL AUSTIN - SLOW WALK

From Dunelin, Florida, this self-taught saxophonist studied at Julliard School of music in New York. Despite making 30 albums for Mercury Records, he only scored one mainstream hit, Slow Walk, reaching #17 in the Billboard Top 100.

THE SIX TEENS - A CASUAL LOOK

From Los Angeles, California, the singing group were all, well teenagers. A Casual Look was their third attempt at fame, and reached #25 in the Billboard Top 100, and #7 in the Black Singles Chart. Moving briefly to Hawaii, they did not score another hit.

SONNY KNIGHT - CONFIDENTIAL

From Maywood, Illinois, this singer/songwriter had a few penned songs already sold to others when he decided to try his own luck at singing. Written by Dorinda Morgan, Confidential reached #17 in the Billboard Top 100, and #8 in the R&B Charts.

TEDDI KING - MR. WONDERFUL

Written by Jerry Bock, George David Weiss, and Larry Holofcener, it was the title song of the Broadway musical starring Sammy Davis Jr. Three versions fought in the charts for sales, Peggy Lee's reached #14 in the Billboard Top 100, #5 in the UK, and #10 in Australia, Sarah Vaughan reached #17, and the one hit wonder, Teddi King, got to #18 in the Billboard Top 100. Teddi's follow-ups, 'Married I Can Always Get, and 'Say It Isn't So' sneaked into the Top 100, but were not hits.

THE TEEN QUEENS - EDDIE MY LOVE

Written by Maxwell Davis (who played sax on the Teen Queens doo-wop recording), Aaron Collins, Jr., and Sam Ling, it was recorded by numerous artists in 1956. The Teen Queens reached #14 in the Billboard Top 100, and #3 in the R&B Chart. The Chordettes version also got to #14, and The Fontane Sisters charted at the same time.

THE TURBANS - WHEN YOU DANCE

Philadelphia's African American doo-wop vocal group recorded When You Dance in 1955, and sales were at first sluggish. It eventually reached #33 in the Billboard Top 100, (staying in the chart for 5 months) and #3 in the R&B Chart. They continued recording, but faced with little success, broke up in 1962.

VINCE MARTIN AND THE TARRIERS - CINDY, OH CINDY

Written by Robert Nemiroff and Burt D'Lugoff (Barron & Long), it uses the melody of 'Pay Me My Money Down'. Originally recorded by Vince Martin and the Tarriers, it was rapidly covered by Eddie Fisher. Both versions made the charts; Fisher's version got to #10 in the Billboard Top 100, and #5 in the UK. Martin's version reached #9 in the Billboard Top 100, and would be his only charting single.

Weird OHW Fact... Eddie Fisher is the father of Princess Leia, Carrie Fisher.

1957...

As Dwight D. Eisenhower is sworn in for a second term as the 34th President of the USA, the year begins...
The Wham-O Company produces the first Frisbee, movie legend Humphrey Bogart dies, Dr. Seuss' The Cat in the Hat is published, John Lennon and Paul McCartney meet as teenagers at a garden fete, the movie, The Bridge on the River Kwai, opens in the U.K. and the USSR launch Sputnik, the Sputnik 2 with a dog named Laika on board.

BILL JUSTIS - RAUNCHY
Sold over 1 million copies.
Written by William Everett 'Bill' Justis, Jr., from Birmingham, Alabama, his rock and roll instrumental was so popular that it had three different entries in the Billboard Top 100 in 1957 by three different artists; Justis on Sun Records (#2), Ernie Freeman on Imperial Records (#4)(see later entry), and Billy Vaughn on Dot Records (#10). Justis's version reached #2 in the Billboard Top 100 and also reached #11 in the UK Charts. He only 'just' makes the one hit wonder book, however, his follow-up, College Man, reached #42 in the US.

BILLY MYLES - THE JOKER (THAT'S WHAT THEY CALL ME)
Written by Billy Myles, it was the second song he ever wrote. It was a hit in Canada, and reached #25 in the Billboard Top 100, and #13 in the R&B Chart. Versions by The Hilltoppers (#22) and Oliver Hazell were also in the chart at the same time.
Weird OHW Fact... Myles went on to write many hits for Jackie Wilson and the song, 'Have You Ever Loved A Woman, a hit for Derek and the Dominos, Eric Clapton, and Van Morrison.

THE BOBBETTES - MR. LEE
From East Harlem, New York, this R&B girl group hit the chart with their debut single, reaching #6 in the Billboard Top 100, and #1 in the R&B Charts, where it stayed at the top for 4 weeks. They were the first girl group to top the R&B Chart and get top ten in the Billboard Top 100.
Weird OHW Fact... Considering the title of their hit, their best follow-up, however, only got to #52, curiously entitled 'I Shot Mr. Lee'.

BONNIE GUITAR - DARK MOON
Written by Ned Miller for Dorsey Burnette, it was recorded instead by Bonnie Buckingham (Guitar). Her crossover version got to #6 in the

Billboard Top 100, and #14 in the Country Chart. Gale Storm recorded it immediately, getting to #4, and Britain's Tony Brent had the hit in the UK, reaching #17.

Weird OHW Fact... Considering her real name (Buckingham), Bonnie Guitar went on to launch the career of the band, the Fleetwoods, (themselves UK one hit wonders in 1959). (Fleetwood Mac/Lindsay Buckingham reference there, in case you missed it)

BUDDY KNOX – PARTY DOLL

Reached #1 in the USA.

Sold over 1 million copies.

Having already had a one hit wonder with Jimmy Bowen With The Rhythm Orchids - I'm Stickin' With You, Buddy Knox went solo. His first single, Party Doll, written by the same partnership, Buddy Knox and Jimmy Bowen, reached #1 in the Billboard Top 100 and #3 in the R&B Chart, and #29 in the UK Chart, where he is a one hit wonder. Four of his subsequent US singles reached Top 40 status.

CHARLES MCDEVITT SKIFFLE GROUP - FREIGHT TRAIN

Written by Elizabeth Cotton, (Label says James-Williams) it was recorded by Scottish skiffle player, Charles James McDevitt. Originally a male voice recording, he was encouraged to incorporate a female vocal version by fellow Scot Nancy Whiskey. The record was a huge hit, reaching #5 in the UK Charts, and #40 in the Billboard Top 100. He still entertains today, although this was his only chart entry.

DAVE GARDNER - WHITE SILVER SANDS

Written by Charles 'Red' Matthews, it was recorded by at least three artists in 1957. One hit wonder comedian and drummer Dave Gardner on OJ Records reached #22 in the Billboard Top 100, Don Rondo had the bigger hit, reaching #7 in the Billboard Top 100, and #2 in Australia. The Owen Bradley Quintet also recorded a version.

THE DUBS - COULD THIS BE MAGIC

Written by band member Richard Blandon, it was recorded by the Harlem doo-wop group as their second single on Gone Records. It reached #23 in the Billboard Top 100, but the group suffered from line-up changes, and ostensibly broke up in 1962.

ERNIE FREEMAN - RAUNCHY

Written by William Everett "Bill" Justis, Jr., (see entry above) it was recorded by Ernie Freeman on Imperial Records who reached #4 in the

Billboard Top 100, and #1 in the R&B Chart. It shared the charts with 2 other versions, but Freeman's follow-up, Indian Love Call, only reached #59. He continued to record until 1963 as a solo act and with other artists.

THE HOLLYWOOD FLAMES - BUZZ BUZZ BUZZ
Written by John Gray and Bobby Day, and was performed by The Hollywood Flames on EBB Records. The lead vocals on the recording were by Earl Nelson, later of Bob & Earl. It reached #11 in the Billboard Top 100 and #5 in the R&B Chart. They never entered the Top 100 again.
Billboard ranked the song as #94 of 1958.

JODIE SANDS - WITH ALL MY HEART
Born in Philadelphia, real name Eleanor DiSipio, Jodi gets her second mention. Her first single, With All My heart was her only USA hit in 1957. Her second attempt bombed in the US but hit #14 in the UK Chart, making her a one hit wonder twice.
Her third single, Love Me Forever, bombed in both countries.

JOE BENNETT & THE SPARKLETONES - BLACK SLACKS
Written by Joe Bennett and Jimmy Denton, it was recorded on ABC Paramount Records as their debut single. The band from Spartanburg, South Carolina too the song to #17 in the Billboard Top 100, and #11 in the R&B Chart. They only just claim one hit wonder status, however, as their follow-up, Penny Loafers and Bobby Socks, got to #43.
Billboard ranked the song as #100 of 1957.
Weird OHW Fact... Although the hit was not major, the band's constant touring kept the song in the Top 100 for over 4 months.

JOY LAYNE - YOUR WILD HEART
From Chicago, Illinois, Layne was signed to mercury records at the age of fifteen. Her first single was a version of The Poni-Tails album track, 'Your Wild Heart'. It reached #20 in the Billboard Top 100. Her next singles, recorded at the same session, My Suspicious Heart, and, After School, were unsuccessful.

JOHNNIE & JOE - OVER THE MOUNTAIN; ACROSS THE SEA
Written by Rex Garvin, the song was recorded by the Bronx R&B duo Johnnie Louise Richardson and Joe Rivers on Chess Records. It reached #8 in the Billboard Top 100, and #3 in the R&B Chart. Their follow-ups,

I'll Be Spinning", got to #10 in the R&B Chart, and, My Baby's Gone, was a #15 R&B hit, but neither charted in the mainstream chart.

JOHNNY DEE - SITTIN' IN THE BALCONY
Written and recorded by John D. Loudermilk (Johnny Dee), on Colonial Records, it reached #38 in the Billboard Top 100, and #20 in the UK. It would be his only hit; the 196 single, Road Hog got to #65. Concentrating on songwriting, he wrote, Indian Reservation", a 1971 U.S. #1 hit for Paul Revere & the Raiders, Ebony Eyes, a 1961 U.K. #1 and U.S. #8 for the Everly Brothers, among many others.
Weird OHW Fact... The 'D' in his name did not stand for anything; his father had the same middle initial.

JIMMY BOWEN WITH THE RHYTHM ORCHIDS - I'M STICKIN' WITH YOU
Sold over 1 million copies.
Written by Jimmy Bowen and Buddy Knox, it was recorded by Jimmy Bowen with The Rhythm Orchids on Roulette Records. It reached #14 in the Billboard Top 100 and #9 in the R&B Chart. Bowen would not chart again.
Weird OHW Fact... Bowen's songwriting partner, Buddy Knox went on to have a good musical career, releasing hit singles into the 70's and having a UK one hit wonder in 1957 with Party Doll, UK #29.

JIMMY MCCRACKLIN WITH HIS BAND - THE WALK
Written by Jimmy McCracklin (born James David Walker Jr.) it was recorded by the African American pianist. After an appearance on Dick Clark's American Bandstand, the single reached #7 in the Billboard Top 100, and #5 in the R&B Chart. McCracklin had a 70 year musical career, releasing 30 albums, and awarded 4 gold discs, but he only charted once.

JIMMY C NEWMAN - A FALLEN STAR
From Big Mamou, Louisiana, this country legend peppered the country chart for many years, but his only crossover into the mainstream chart was the 1957 hit, A Fallen Star. It reached #2 in the US Country Chart, and #23 in the Billboard Top 100.
Weird OHW Fact... Newman was responsible for Dolly Parton's first appearance at the Grand Ole Opry in 1959, when he gave up one of his two performance slots to let Parton (just 13 years old) to perform.

Weird OHW Fact… Newman was born Jimmy Yves Newman, but is better known as Jimmy C. Newman. The initial 'C', stands for Cajun, one of his main singing styles.

THE JIVE BOMBERS - BAD BOY
Written by Lil Armstrong and Avon Long in 1936, it was recorded by The Jive Bombers on Savoy Records. The song reached #35 in the Billboard Top 100 and #7 in the R&B Chart. Despite other singles, it would be the band's only chart entry.

KEN COPELAND - PLEDGE OF LOVE
With the authorship attributed on the single sleeve to R. Redd, it was recorded by Lubbock Texas crooner and soon-to-be evangelist. The single got to #17 in the Billboard Top 100, and stayed in the top 100 for 15 weeks. It would be his only chart entry, born-again in 1962, he has been a minister ever since.
Weird OHW Fact… The songwriter, R. Redd is probably Ramona Redd, the wife of country singer, Mitchell Torok.

LOU STEIN - ALMOST PARADISE
This American jazz pianist from Philadelphia played with Glenn Miller and Ray McKinley during World War II. Later, he recorded some records as a bandleader and Almost Paradise reached #31 in the Billboard Top 100. Although his version of, Got A Match, reached the Cashbox Top 60 the following year, he never charted mainstream again.

MARGIE RAYBURN - I'M AVAILABLE
Written by Dave Burgess, it was recorded by Madera, California's Margie Rayburn on Liberty Records. It reached #9 in the Billboard Top 100, but despite releasing nearly 20 singles, she never charted again.
Weird OHW Fact… As a member of The Sunnysiders, she had a one-hit-wonder Top 40 hit in the US in 1955 with, Hey! Mr. Banjo. (See previous entry)

MARVIN RAINWATER - GONNA FIND ME A BLUEBIRD
Written by Marvin Karlton Rainwater, his recording reached #18 in the Billboard Top 100, and #3 in the Country Chart. His duet with Connie Francis, The Majesty of Love, did not chart but was the first of four gold records. Amazingly he had a UK #1 with, Whole Lotta Woman, and followed it up with a #19 hit. But in his native USA, he will be known as a one hit wonder.

Weird OHW Fact... He was 25% Cherokee, and commonly wore Native American-themed outfits on stage.

THE MELLO-TONES - ROSIE LEE
Written by the lead singer Jerry Carr, this Detroit doo-wop song on Fascination Records reached #24 in the Billboard Top 100. Although they recorded many songs, this was their only chart entry.

MICKEY & SYLVIA - LOVE IS STRANGE
Written by Bo Diddley under the name of his wife, Ethel Smith, this crossover hit was released by R&B duo, Mickey & Sylvia. It reached #1 in the R&B Chart, and #11 in the Billboard Top 100. They continued to record until 1961, but failed to chart again.
Weird OHW Fact... This is a R&B classic, covered many artists; Lonnie Donegan, Wings, and The Everly Brothers.
Weird OHW Fact... The song was featured in the movie, Dirty Dancing.

MOE KOFFMAN QUARTETTE - THE SWINGIN' SHEPHERD BLUES
Toronto Sax and Flautist, Koffman, recorded The Swinging Shepherd Blues on his first of 28 albums. It would be his only chart hit, reaching #23 in the Billboard Top 100.

RANDY STARR - AFTER SCHOOL
Born Warren Nadel, Starr only scored one hit with his own songs. After School reached #32 in the Billboard Top 100, and Starr would go on to sing with The Islanders, scoring another one hit wonder in 1959, The Enchanted Sea.
Weird OHW Fact... Starr wrote 12 songs used by Elvis Presley either in film or record.

THE RAYS - SILHOUETTES/DADDY COOL
With both songs/sides written by Bob Crewe and Frank Slay, this doo-wop single on Cameo Records reached #3 in the Billboard Top 100. Unsurprisingly, Canadian doo-wop band The Diamonds, covered both sides of the single and reached #10.
Weird OHW Fact... In 1971, in Australia, Drummond reached 31 with Daddy Cool. In 1977 in the UK, Darts version reached #6.

ROY BROWN - LET THE FOUR WINDS BLOW
Written by Fats Domino and Dave Bartholomew, it was recorded by hard working Louisiana native, Roy James Brown. A regular in the R&B Chart, (with 2 #1's) his first and only crossover came on his 14th

attempt. The song reached #29 in the Billboard Top 100, and #5 in the R&B Chart.

RUSSELL ARMS - CINCO ROBLES (FIVE OAKS)
American actor and singer from Berkley, California, is perhaps better known for his film and TV appearances, but in 1957, he did chart. Cinco Robles (Five Oaks), reached #22 in the Billboard Top 100, and stayed in the Top 100 for 15 weeks.

RUSS HAMILTON - RAINBOW
Written and performed by Russ Hamilton, the record was already a hit in the UK (#2 with We Will Make Love, Rainbow's B-side). For some obscure reason, the US DJ's began playing the more melodic B-side, and Rainbow became a strange hit. It reached #7 in the Billboard Top 100, and #10 in the R&B Chart in 1957. His follow up, Wedding Ring, reached #20 in the UK, but did not chart in the USA.

Weird OHW Fact... When Hamilton was at #2 in the UK, the record company, Oriole Records went on holiday, and due to no records being available in the shops, he missed the #1 spot.

Weird OHW Facts... The single in the USA was a bit of a novelty, because Hamilton's speech impediment meant he couldn't correctly sing his 'R's. His UK follow-up, considering the problem, was called Wedding Ring.

Weird OHW Fact... The single remains the only one to have a different side be a hit on either side of the Atlantic.

SHEPHERD SISTERS - ALONE (WHY MUST I BE ALONE)
Written by Morty and Selma Craft, and first recorded by the Shepherd Sisters on Craft's Vee-Jay Record label. It was the Shepherd's Sisters only hit, reaching #18 in the Billboard Top 100, and #14 in the UK Charts. Also in the UK, Petula Clark took her version to #8, and another version by The Southlanders, reached #17.

THE TECHNIQUES - HEY LITTLE GIRL
Written by band member Buddy Funk (born Beauford Harold Funk), and recorded by The techniques on Roulette Records, it reached #29 in the Billboard Top 100, the only hit for the group. All band members met as students at Georgia Tech University.

TERRY GILKYSON AND THE EASY RIDERS - MARIANNE
Sold over 1 million copies.

Written by the trio, Terry Gilkyson, Richard Dehr and Frank Miller, and recorded on Columbia Records, Marianne got to #4 in the Billboard Top 100, was awarded a gold disc and sold a million copies. The trio wrote and recorded until the 1960's then broke up, but had no more charting hits of their own. Their song, The Cry of the Wild Goose, was a #1 hit for Frankie Laine, and they penned songs for the Kingston Trio, Gale Storm, Harry Belafonte, Doris Day, and Burl Ives.

Weird OHW Fact... Their interpretation of the 1927 song, Tell the Captain, led directly to the Beach Boys song, Sloop John B.

Weird OHW Fact... Gilkyson left the group to work for Disney and wrote the Oscar-nominated, The Bear Necessities, for Disney's movie, The Jungle Book.

Weird OHW Fact... They wrote, Memories Are Made of This, a doo-wop favorite and #1 for Dean Martin. In 1956, the song was taken up by the Hungarians, and renamed Honvágy-dal ('The Song of Homesickness'). In Germany, it was called 'Heimweh' (Homesickness) and performed by Freddy Quinn with German lyrics by Ernst Bader and Dieter Rasch. The song sold 8 million copies worldwide, and spent 14 weeks at #1 in Germany.

THURSTON HARRIS - LITTLE BITTY PRETTY ONE
Sold more than 1 million copies.
Written by Bobby Day, (Bobby Day and the Satellites, US #57) it was recorded by Thurston Harris Aladdin Records. It reached #6 in the Billboard Top 100, and #2 in the R&B Chart. His former band, The Sharps, provided backing vocals.

TONY PERKINS - MOONLIGHT SWIM
Written by Sylvia Dee and Ben Weisman, it was recorded by a very young Tony Perkins on RCA Victor Records, possibly his first recording. Anthony Perkins will probably be best known for his portrayal as Norman Bates from Alfred Hitchcock's Psycho, but after his first six films, he did release 2 albums. Moonlight Swim reached #24 in the Billboard Top 100, and he went on to movie stardom in 1960.

Weird OHW Fact... After the release of Psycho, Tony Perkins was probably the last person on Earth that a young woman would want to have a Moonlight Swim with!

THE TUNE WEAVERS - HAPPY, HAPPY BIRTHDAY BABY
Written by band members Margo Sylvia & Gilbert Lopez, the song was recorded on Casa Grande Records. It would be their only hit, reaching #5 in the Billboard Top 100, and #4 in the R&B Chart.

Weird OHW Fact... The single's verse inspired, I'm On The Outside (Looking In), by Little Anthony and the Imperials (US #15 in 1964) and the chorus inspired, Wasted Days and Wasted Nights, by Freddy Fender (US #8 in 1975).

VICTOR YOUNG AND HIS SINGING STRINGS - (MAIN THEME) AROUND THE WORLD

Written by Harold Adamson and Victor Young, it was the theme tune from the 1956 movie Around the World in 80 Days. With Young's recording on the A-side, and Bing Crosby's vocal version on the B-side, it reached #26 in the Billboard Top 100, #5 in the UK, and also a hit in Australia.

Weird OHW Fact... The single was released after Young's death in 1956.

WILL GLAHÉ AND HIS ORCHESTRA - LIECHTENSTEINER POLKA

German accordionist Will Glahé hit it big in the US with his version of the Liechtensteiner Polka, reaching #16 in the Billboard Top 100. His follow-up, Sweet Elizabeth, charted but not in the top 40.

1958...

(Please note... The Billboard Hot 100 was first issued in November of this year, so for the sake of continuity all chart positions will be given as 'Billboard **Hot** 100'.)

As the USSR's satellite Sputnik, falls from orbit and burns up in the atmosphere, the year begins...

At just 14, Bobby Fischer wins the US Chess Championship, 7 Manchester United footballers are killed in the Munich air disaster, the first branch of Pizza Hut opens, NASA is formed and launches Pioneer 1, and figures showed that more people traveled by air than by sea.

THE AQUATONES - YOU

Discovered at a talent show at a local New York high school, the four-part harmony group Aquatones won, and got a record deal with Fargo Records. Their ballad reached #21 in the Billboard Hot 100, but their follow-ups were not so well received.

ART AND DOTTY TODD - CHANSON D'AMOUR (SONG OF LOVE)

Written by Wayne Shanklin, it was recorded by American husband and wife singing duo, who had already had success in 1953 in the UK with Broken Wings at #6. Chanson D'Amour reached #6 in the US Billboard Hot 100 and #20 in the Melody Maker Chart in the UK. It would be their only US hit.

BOBBY DAY - ROCKIN ROBIN

Written by Leon René under the pseudonym of Jimmie Thomas, this song was recorded by Robert James Byrd under the stage name of Bobby Day, who sang with the California R&B group, The Hollywood Flames. The song reached #2 in the Billboard Hot 100, and topped the R&B Chart. His follow-up, Over and Over, just reached #41... making him a 'just' a one hit wonder, and no more.

BOBBY HENDRICKS - ITCHY TWITCHY FEELING

Written by Bobby Hendricks, this singer from Columbus, Ohio once sang lead for the Drifters. His only solo hit, however, reached #5 in the Black Singles chart and #25 in the Billboard Hot 100. The follow-up, Psycho, only got to #73.

THE CHAMPS – TEQUILA

Reached #1 in USA.

Sold over 1 million copies.

Written by the band's saxophone player Danny Flores, it was the B-side for the first single of this American rock and roll band. While the A-side languished, a Cleveland DJ played the B-side, and the rest is history. The song reached #1 in the USA, and #5 in the UK. The follow-up, Too Much tequila, got to #30 in the US, but only #49 in the UK, making them a UK one hit wonder.

Weird OHW Fact... Flores was credited as Chuck Rio; at the time, he was under contract to another record label.

Weird OHW Fact... They took their name from Champion, Gene Autry's horse, (they were signed to gene Autry Records).

Weird OHW Fact... Flores only said 'Tequila' three times on the record.

THE CRESCENDOS - OH JULIE
Sold over 1 million copies.

Discovered at a talent show, this American rock and roll group from Nashville, Tennessee recorded only three songs, all on the Nasco label. The first, Oh Julie, got to #4 in the US Black Singles Chart and reached #5 in the Billboard Hot 100, the other two did not chart at all. The band split up the next year.

DALE WRIGHT WITH THE ROCK-ITS – SHE'S NEAT
Born Harlan Dale Riffe, in Middletown, Ohio, he started life as a DJ in Dayton. She's Neat was his only charting hit, reaching #38 in the Billboard Hot 100. His follow up, Don't Do It, only got to #77.

He went back to DJ'ing, hosting a chat show and becoming program Director at WCKU in Kentucky.

THE DANLEERS - ONE SUMMER NIGHT
Sold over 1 million copies.

Written by the band's manager, Danny Webb, the song was recorded on the band's very first recording session. It was released on AMP 3 Record label, then on Mercury Records for better distribution. It reached #4 on the Black Singles Chart, then #7 in the Billboard Hot 100.

Weird OHW Fact... The band's name came from the manager's name, Danny.

DOMENICO MODUGNO - NEL BLU DIPINTO DI BLU (VOLARE)
Reached #1 in USA.

Sold over 22 million copies (Combined cover versions).

Written by Franco Migliacci and Domenico Modugno, it won the Sanremo Music Festival, and became a worldwide success. It topped the

Billboard Charts for 5 weeks, selling 22 million copies worldwide. It also won 2 Grammy Awards.

Weird OHW fact... This song, the 6th biggest selling single EVER, only came in 3rd in the 1958 Eurovision Song Contest.

Weird OHW Fact... The title means 'In the Blue That is Painted Blue'.

DON LANG & HIS FRANTIC FIVE – WITCH DOCTOR

Born Gordon Langhorn in Halifax, England, this English trombone player and singer led his own band. The band recorded the theme for the TV show, Six Five Special, but it was the cover version of Davie Seville's Witch Doctor that became their only hit, reaching #10 in the UK Charts.

Weird OHW Fact... Lang played trombone on Revolution 1, on the Beatles White album.

EARL GRANT - THE END

Written by Jimmy Krondes and Sid Jacobson, it was recorded by Grant on Decca Records. It spent 19 weeks in the chart, reaching #7 in the Billboard Hot 100. A German version also charted, getting to #16 in the German Charts, It was Grant's only hit.

EDDIE PLATT – TEQUILA

Edward R. "Eddie" Platakis was born in Cleveland, Ohio, and played in his first band at age 16. He covered The Champs' (already a OHW 1958 entry) song, Tequila, and took it to #20 in the Billboard Hot 100. It would be his only hit.

ED TOWNSEND - FOR YOUR LOVE

Written and performed by Ed Townsend, this singer/songwriter from Fayetteville, Tennessee, was active from 1957-77. Thinking of interesting Nat 'King' Cole with the song, he took it to Capitol Records, who were so impressed, they signed him up to record it himself. The song reached #7 in the US R&B Chart, and #13 in the Billboard Hot 100. He did not have any more luck as a solo artist, but penned songs for many others.

Weird OHW Fact... He served with the Marine Corps in the Korean War.

THE ELEGANTS - LITTLE STAR

Reached #1 in USA.

Written by band members Vito Picone and Arthur Venosa of this Staten Island, teenage New York doo wop band, the music was an interpretation of the nursery rhyme, Twinkle Twinkle Little Star. It immediately topped the R&B Chart, then the mainstream Billboard Hot 100, reaching #25 in the UK Charts.

FRANKIE ERVIN – YOU CHEATED

From Blythe, California, Frank Miller Ervin recorded the song with a put-together backing line up, called The Shields. You Cheated reached #12 in the Billboard Hot 100, and #11 in the R&B Chart. Subsequent singles did not chart.

FRANKIE VAUGHAN - JUDY

With UK hits galore, Liverpool's Frankie Vaughan (born Frank Ableson) had tried to crack the US before and failed. His hit, Judy, reached #22 in the Billboard Hot 100, but it didn't open the USA as he'd hoped. Despite regular UK Chart appearances, he didn't chart in the US again.

Weird OHW Fact... He chose the stage name Vaughan because his Russian grandmother called him her 'number 'von' grandson'.

THE FIVE BLOBS - THE BLOB

Written by Burt Bacharach and Mack David, this bunch of session musicians were assembled by Bernie Knee to sing the theme of the Steve McQueen B-movie, The Blob. The Five Blobs were never destined to be a long-time operation, and the single reached #33 in the Billboard Hot 100. They did release follow-ups, but they never charted.

GENE ALLISON - YOU CAN MAKE IT IF YOU TRY

Written by Ted Jarrett, it was recorded by Nashville's Gene Allison (born Versie Eugene Allison). It reached #3 in the Black Singles Chart, and #36 in the Billboard Hot 100. His follow ups, charted in the Black Singles Chart, but the highest, Have Faith, only reached #73 in the Hot 100.

Weird OHW Fact... He used his royalties to open a 24-hour soul food restaurant in Nashville, called Gene's Drive-In.

HUEY "PIANO" SMITH AND THE CLOWNS - DON'T YOU JUST KNOW IT

Sold a million copies.

A piano player for Little Richard's band, Huey Pierce Smith was performing from 15 years old. His first hit, Rockin' Pneumonia and the Boogie Woogie Flu, sold a million records, but only charted at #52. His only chart success was Don't You Just Know It, reaching #9 in the Billboard Hot 100, and #4 in the R&B Chart.

THE JAMIES - SUMMERTIME, SUMMERTIME

Written by band members Serena Jameson and Sherman Feller, this Boston band released Summertime, Summertime, on Epic Records. It reached #26 in the US Billboard Hot 100, but none of their follow-ups met with any chart success. Re-released in 1962, it reached #38. It has been covered many times.

Weird OHW Fact... The name, The Jamies, came from the surname of band siblings, Tom and Serena Jameson.

JAN AND ARNIE - JENNIE LEE

American rock duo William Jan Berry and Dean Ormsby Torrence are considered pioneers of the American 'beach sound', however, in a short hiatus before becoming the famous 'Jan and Dean', Berry joined with school band mate, Arnold P. "Arnie" Ginsburg, and recorded a song as 'Jan & Arnie'. Jennie Lee reached #8 in the Billboard Hot 100, but their follow-up, Gas Money, only reached #81.

Weird OHW Fact... Berry's dad was the project manager of Howard Hughes' Spruce Goose, and flew with Hughes on its first and only flight.

JIM BACKUS AND FRIEND - DELICIOUS

James Gilmore Backus is probably best known for the voice of near blind cartoon character Mr. Magoo. However, in 1958, Backus released a novelty album, which spawned two singles. The only one to chart was Delicious, which reached #40 in the Billboard Hot 100, the flimsiest of one hit wonders.

Weird OHW Fact... The cartoon, which first appeared in 1949 has a cute trivia fact... Mr Magoo's first name is Quincy, and he had a nephew named Waldo.

JODY REYNOLDS - ENDLESS SLEEP

Written by Jody Reynolds after hearing Elvis Presley's Heartbreak Hotel. The actual record label credited the song to Reynolds and a Dolores Nance, but it is thought it was just for show. The rockabilly song reached #5 in the Billboard Hot 100, spawning a whole wave of songs of teenage tragedy.

Weird OHW Fact... The original version had the girl dying at the end. Reynolds only got a record deal when he changed the ending to her surviving.

Weird OHW Fact... In the UK, the song was recorded by Marty Wilde (father of 'We're The Kids In America' fame, Kim Wilde), and it got to #4 in the UK Charts.

Weird OHW Fact... In 1979 Jody Reynolds' version did actually chart in the UK, (#66) after a re-release.

JODIE SANDS - SOMEDAY (YOU'LL WANT ME TO WANT YOU)

Born in Philadelphia, real name Eleanor DiSipio, Jodi gets her second mention. Her first single, With All My Heart was her only USA hit in 1957. Her second attempt bombed in the US but hit #14 in the UK Chart, making her a one hit wonder twice.
Her third single, Love Me Forever, bombed in both countries.

JOHNNY OTIS SHOW - WILLIE AND THE HAND JIVE

Written by Johnny Otis, it was recorded by an ensemble called the Johnny Otis Show. The Bo Diddley beat song reached #9 in the Billboard Hot 100, topped out at #1 in the Billboard R&B chart, but did not chart in the UK, where he'd already had 2 Top 20 singles.
Weird OHW Fact... It has been covered many times, most famously Eric Clapton, Cliff Richard, George Thorogood and The Grateful Dead.

JOHN ZACHERLEY - DINNER WITH DRAC–PART 1

Born John Zacherle, he was an American television and radio personality, most often associated with horror movies and skits. His novelty rock and roll song, Dinner With Drac, reached #6 in the Billboard Hot 100 on Cameo Records.
Weird OHW Facts... Broadcaster, Dick Clark, nicknamed Zacherley... 'The Cool Ghoul'.

THE KALIN TWINS - WHEN

Reached #1 in the Netherlands and UK.
Written by Jack Reardon and Paul Evans, it was recorded by The Kalin Twins (Harold and Herbert) from Port Jervis, New York. It topped the UK Chart and the Dutch Chart for five weeks, and reached #5 in the Billboard Hot 100. Their second single, Forget Me Not, reached #12 in the US, making them UK one hit wonders.
Weird OHW Fact... The Kalin twins were the first twins to have a number one.
Weird OHW Fact... UK band Showaddywaddy took the song to #3 in the UK in 1977.

KIRBY STONE FOUR - BAUBLES, BANGLES AND BEADS

With their swing jazz style, this vocal band got many TV appearances; The Ed Sullivan Show, and The Judy Garland Show. Their version of

Baubles, Bangles and Beads on Columbia Records reached #25 in the Billboard Hot 100.

Weird OHW Fact... The band was named after their leader, Kirby Stone.

LAURIE LONDON - HE'S GOT THE WHOLE WORLD IN HIS HANDS

Reached #1 in USA.

Sold over 1 million copies.

This American spiritual, first published in 1927, became a worldwide hit by 13 year old English schoolboy Laurie London from Bethnal Green. His version charted in the UK, reaching #12 in the UK Charts, then it hit America. It reached #1 in the Billboard Hot 100, and #3 in the R&B Charts. It was the first and only gospel song to reach #1 in the Billboard Hot 100.

Weird OHW Fact... London did record until he reached 19, his music 'trended' towards a German influence, singing many German songs.

MARION RYAN – LOVE ME FOREVER

Born in Middlesborough, England, Marion was a popular songstress on the Grenada ITV quiz show, Spot That Tune. Love Me Forever was her only hit, and it reached #5 in the UK Chart.

THE MONOTONES – WHO WROTE THE BOOK OF LOVE?

Written by band members Warren Davis, George Malone and Charles Patrick, the New Jersey doo wop sextet released the song on the Mascot Record label. It reached #3 in the R&B Chart, #5 in the Billboard Hot 100, and #5 in Australia.

Weird OHW Fact... Supposedly singer Charles Patrick heard a Pepsodent toothpaste commercial which contained the line, 'wonder where the yellow went'. That gave him the idea of 'I wonder, wonder, wonder who, who wrote the book of love'.

Weird OHW Fact... Don McLean, in his classic American Pie, makes reference to the 'book of love'.

Weird OHW Fact... Led Zeppelin in the song, Rock and Roll, also make reference... 'been a long time since the book of love'.

NICK TODD - AT THE HOP

Written by Artie Singer, John Medora, and David White, Danny & the Juniors had the original hit in 1957. Nick Todd, (Cecil Altman Boone), the younger brother of pop singer Pat Boone released it as his second single, and it reached #21 in the Billboard Hot 100. His first single, Plaything, had reached #41, rendering Todd a one hit wonder.

Weird OHW Fact... Told to find a stage name, he chose Todd, as it was 'Dot' Records backwards.

THE PASTELS - BEEN SO LONG
DiFosco "Dee" T. Ervin Jr. formed the Pastels while in the Air Force in Greenland, performing for the military. After being discharged, their first single reached #4 in the R&B chart and #24 in the Billboard Hot 100. Their follow-up, You Don't Love Me Anymore, was not a hit, and they broke up soon afterwards.

THE PETS - CHA-HUA-HUA
From Los Angeles, California, session musicians Plas Johnson, Rene Hall, Richard Podolor, and Earl Palmer got together. Their only hit, on Arwin Records, was Cha Hua Hua, and it reached #34 in the Billboard Hot 100.
Weird OHW Fact... Arwin Records was owned by Marty Melcher, Doris Day's husband.

THE PONI-TAILS - BORN TOO LATE
Written by Charles Strouse and Fred Tobias, this song was recorded by girl singing group from Cleveland, Ohio. On the ABC-Paramount label, it reached #5 in the UK Singles Chart, and #7 in the Billboard Hot 100. Their follow-ups did not chart, but a later single, Early to Bed, reached #26 in the UK, making them a USA one hit wonder.
Weird OHW Fact... In 1973 the song was on the soundtrack of the David Essex movie, That'll Be the Day.

THE QUIN-TONES - DOWN THE AISLE OF LOVE
From York, Pennsylvania, doo wop group the Quin-Tones recorded four singles for Chess Records. Ding Dong did not chart, but Down the Aisle of Love reached #5 in the Black Singles chart and #18 in the Billboard Hot 100. The band dissolved soon afterwards.

RENATO CAROSONE - TORERO
A musical legend in his native Italy and Europe, this crooner hit the big time with Torero, a cha-cha originally recorded for a Spanish tour. It reached #18 in the Billboard Hot 100, and has had countless cover versions made.

THE RINKY DINKS - EARLY IN THE MORNING
Written by Bobby Darin and Woody Harris, about the era of Darin's first hit, Splish Splash, Darin, (under contract with Atco Records), took the song to Brunswick, who released the first version under the fictional

name, The Ding Dongs, then The Rinky Dinks. Once Atco discovered the ruse, future releases were under Darin's name. It reached #24 in the Billboard Hot 100.

ROBERT & JOHNNY - WE BELONG TOGETHER
Written by Robert Carr, Johnny Mitchell, and Hy Weiss it was recorded by the doo-wop duo from The Bronx. It reached #12 in the R&B Chart and #32 in the Billboard Hot 100. The follow-up, I Believe In You, only reached #93

ROBIN LUKE - SUSIE DARLIN'
Sold over 1 million copies.
Written by Robin Luke, named after his five year old sister, this Hawaii native recorded the rockabilly song and it went straight to #5 in the Billboard Hot 100, and to #25 in the UK.
Luke quit the music business in 1965, getting a degree, and becoming a college professor.

RONALD & RUBY – LOLLIPOP
Written by Julius Dixson and Beverly Ross, it was recorded by the duo Ronald & Ruby. Ronald was a 13 year old black neighbor of Dixson's, and Ruby was Beverly Ross herself. Although the more successful version was by the Chordettes, Ronald & Ruby's version reached #20 in the Billboard Hot 100.
Weird OHW Fact... The fact that the duo were of differing ages, and inter-racial, caused them to keep publicity to a minimum.
Weird OHW Fact... The song was inspired by Dixson's daughter getting a lollipop stuck in her throat.

SHEB WOOLEY - PURPLE PEOPLE EATER
Reached #1 in Australia, and USA.
Written and performed by actor and singer Shelby Fredrick 'Sheb' Wooley, who took this novelty song to the top of the US and Australian charts. The song, which described an alien creature who comes to Earth to join a rock band, which reached #1 in the Billboard Hot 100, #1 in Australia, and #12 in the UK.
Weird OHW Fact... Wooley played Ben Miller in High Noon, and Travis Cobb in the Clint Eastwood classic, The Outlaw Josey Wales.

THE SILHOUETTES - GET A JOB
Reached #1 in USA.
Sold more than 1 million copies.

Written by Philadelphia doo-wop band members Earl Beal, Raymond Edwards, Richard Lewis, and William Horton, this single took four months to reach the top of the Billboard Hot 100 and the R&B Charts. Get a Job was originally intended as the B-side to, I Am Lonely.

TEDDY BEARS - TO KNOW HIM IS TO LOVE HIM
Reached #1 in USA.
Sold over 2½ million copies.
Written by nineteen year old Phil Spector for his group, The Teddy Bears, it was taken up by ERA's Dore label. It went on to be a worldwide hit, topping the Billboard Hot 100 for 3 weeks, and reaching #2 in the UK.
Weird OHW Fact... At just nineteen, Spector showed his genius, having a hand in every facet of the record.
Weird OHW Fact... The words, To Know Him Is To Love Him, were taken from Spector's father's gravestone.

TIMMIE 'OH YEAH' ROGERS - BACK TO SCHOOL AGAIN
Born Timothy John Anerum, he ran away from home at 12, and ended up in a dance troupe, then comedian, speaking nine languages. His only hit was Back to School Again, which reached #36 in the Billboard Hot 100.

THE TOMMY DORSEY ORCHESTRA AND WARREN COVINGTON - TEA FOR TWO CHA CHA
Sold over 1 million copies.
When Tommy Dorsey died in 1956, Decca records approached Warren Covington to head the leaderless orchestra. His only hit with the band was, Tea for Two Cha Cha. This tune sold over 1 million copies, and reached #7 in the Billboard Hot 100, #3 in the UK Chart.

TONI ARDEN - PADRE
Sold over 1 million copies.
Originally titled *Padre Don José*, and written by Jacques Larue and Alain Romans, it was given English lyrics by Paul Francis Webster. New York's Toni Arden (born Antoinette Ardizzone) reached #13 in the Billboard Hot 100 with her version.
Weird OHW Fact... Marti Robbins got to #5 in 1970 with a cover.
Weird OHW Fact... Elvis once said that Arden's version was his favorite song; he recorded it on the album, The Fool, in 1973.

VALERIE CARR - WHEN THE BOYS TALK ABOUT THE GIRLS

New Yorker, Carr, signed with Roulette Records in 1958, having immediate success with this single, reaching #19 in the Billboard Hot 100, and top 40 in the UK. The B-side of the singe was, Padre, (just look at the listing directly above) and her version was considered a better one.

OH SO CLOSE... BUT NO CIGAR...

LORD ROCKINGHAM'S XI - HOOTS MON
Written by front man Harry Robinson, this novelty song is often considered a one hit wonder. However the band (who were put together for ITV pop show, Oh Boy!) had another hit!
Hoots Mon got to #1 in the UK for three weeks, but the follow-up, Wee Tom, actually reached #16. Sorry lads.
Weird OHW Fact... The 'real' Lord Rockingham challenged the name of the band, and the case was settled out of court.

1959...

As the USA (after owning Alaska for 91 years), finally announce it as the 49th state, and Hawaii is added as the 50th, the year begins...
The Marx Brothers make their last TV appearance, NASA announces the selection of the first U.S. astronauts, "The Mercury Seven", western TV series Bonanza premieres in color, the USSR's Luna 3 sends back the first photos of the far side of the Moon, Che Guevara and Fidel Castro arrive in Havana, and MGM release Ben-Hur, starring Charlton Heston.

BARRETT STRONG - MONEY (THAT'S WHAT I WANT)
Written by Tamla founder Berry Gordy and Janie Bradford, it was the first hit for the new label. Barrett Strong provided piano and vocals, and the single went to #2 in the R&B Chart, #23 in the Billboard Hot 100, and #5 in the UK Chart.

THE BELL NOTES - I'VE HAD IT
From Long Island, New York, The Bell Notes recorded, I've Had It, for just $50. It was a hit, reaching #6 in the Billboard Hot 100, and #19 in the R&B Chart. Their follow-up, Old Spanish Town, only reached #76. It was their only hit.

BILLY GRAMMER - GOTTA TRAVEL ON
Sold over 1 million copies.
Written by David Lazar, Larry Ehrlich, Paul Clayton and Tom Six, the song was recorded by country singer Billy Grammer from Benton, Illinois. The song was one of the first major country cross-overs, reaching #5 in the Hot Country Chart, #14 in the R&B Chart, and #4 in the Billboard Hot 100.
He would have many hits in the country genre in the US and Canada, but he never hit the mainstream chart again.

BO DIDDLEY - SAY MAN
Ellas Otha Bates (Bo Diddley) was born in McComb, Mississippi, and went on to become one of the icons of popular music, often cited as the founder of Rock and Roll. He's made 37 singles and 24 studio albums, and yet he's here in this book. No stranger to the R&B Charts, his only mainstream US Top 40 hit was, Say Man, reaching #20 in the Billboard Hot 100, and #3 in the R&B Chart.
Weird OHW Fact... In the UK, he had 2 hits, Pretty Thing (#34 in 1955) and Hey Good Lookin' (#39 in 1965).

CARL MANN - MONA LISA

Carl Mann, from Huntingdon, Tennessee, is a rockabilly style singer and pianist. Signed to Sun Records, he recorded a rockabilly version of Nat King Cole's standard, Mona Lisa. It got to #24 in the Black Singles Chart, and #25 in the Billboard Hot 100.

Weird OHW Fact... Both Mann and Conway Twitty released their own versions at the same time. Twitty's more standard recording fell short, just reaching #29 in the US, but it did go to #1 in Australia and #5 in the UK.

CHAN ROMERO - HIPPY HIPPY SHAKE

Written and recorded by Chan Romero (Robert Lee 'Chan' Romero from Billings, Montana), it was a hit in 1959 long before the Swinging Blue jeans version in 1964. Just 17 years old at the time, the song reached #3 in Australia. Making it a one hit wonder for the first time. (See 1964 entry).

Weird OHW Fact... Romero befriended Ritchie Valens mother immediately after the star's death, and even slept in Valens' bedroom while visiting.

CHRIS BARBER'S JAZZ BAND - PETITE FLEUR (LITTLE FLOWER)

Sold over 1 million copies.

Born in Welwyn Garden City, Hertfordshire, England, Donald Christopher Barber was a band leader and trombonist. He had chart success in the UK, but his only single in the US was, Petite Fleur (Little Flower). It reached #5 in the Billboard hot 100, and #3 in the UK Charts.

Weird OHW Fact... Barber is responsible for bringing Lonnie Donegan into the music world.

DANCER, PRANCER AND NERVOUS - THE HAPPY REINDEER

Record producer Russ Regan put himself on the other side of a microphone to record the Christmas novelty song inspired by the Chipmunks. Under the comedic stage name of Dancer, Prancer and Nervous, Regan's song reached #34 in the Billboard Hot 100, and needless to say, was a one hit wonder.

DODIE STEVENS - PINK SHOE LACES

Sold over 1 million copies.

Written by Mickie Grant, the song was given to thirteen year old Stevens by the chairman of Crystalette records after seeing her at a local talent show. It was an inspired decision; the song reached #3 in the Billboard

Hot 100, and #5 in the R&B Chart. The best follow-up, Yes, I'm Lonesome Tonight, only reached #60.

EDWARD BYRNES - KOOKIE, KOOKIE (LEND ME YOUR COMB)
Sold over 1 million copies.
Born Edward Byrne Breitenberger, he is probably best remembered as an actor in the TV series 77 Sunset Strip. In the show, Kookie persistently tends Byrnes' ducktail hairstyle, prompting the song. The recording (with Connie Stevens) reached #4 in the Billboard Hot 100.
Weird OHW Fact... At the top of his fame, Byrnes received over 15,000 fan letters a week.

ERNIE FIELDS - IN THE MOOD
Sold over 1 million copies.
From Nacogdoches, Texas, Fields led the studio band of Rendezvous Records in Los Angeles. Playing orchestra standards in an R&B style, Glenn Miller's, In the Mood, was a perfect choice. It reached #4 in the Billboard Hot 100, and #13 in the UK Chart.

EUGENE CHURCH AND THE FELLOWS - PRETTY GIRLS EVERYWHERE
Written by Eugene Church and Thomas Williams, it was recorded by the band and became their only hit. It reached #6 in the R&B Chart, and #36 in the Billboard Hot 100. The follow-up, Miami, only reached #67 in the Hot 100.

THE FALCONS - YOU'RE SO FINE
Formed in Detroit, Michigan, The Falcons had much influence in the popular soul music of the next decade. You're So Fine was their only national hit, and reached #17 in the Billboard Hot 100.
Weird OHW Fact... Wilson Pickett sang lead from 1960-63.
Weird OHW Fact... Ike and Tina Turner recorded it on their River Deep - Mountain High, album in 1966.

THE FIESTAS - SO FINE
Written by Johnny Otis (who also wrote the 1958 one hit wonder, Willie and the Hand Jive), the song was recorded by New Jersey R&B group, The Fiestas. It reached #3 in the R&B Chart, and #11 in the Billboard Hot 100. Subsequent singles did not chart.

THE FIREFLIES - YOU WERE MINE

Written by band member Paul Giacalone, this doo wop group from Long Island, New York, recorded it, and it became their only hit. It reached #21 in the Billboard Hot 100, and stayed in the chart for 16 weeks. It also reached #15 in the Canadian Chart. Their follow-up singles did not chart, the highest, I Can't Say Goodbye, reached #90.

Weird OHW Fact... The Fireflies were actually the first all-white vocal harmony group to sing at The Apollo Theater.

THE FLEETWOODS - COME SOFTLY TO ME
Reached #1 in Canada and USA.
Written by the band members, Gretchen Christopher, Barbara Ellis and Gary Troxel, it was released from the new Dolphin Records label. It reached #1 in the Billboard Top 100 and Canada, and got to #6 in the UK, where it remains a one hit wonder. They did have many more hits in the USA and Canada.

Weird OHW Fact... Originally titled, Come Softly, it was thought so risqué, and it was changed to, Come Softly to Me. The new title phrase does not appear in the song's lyrics.

FLOYD ROBINSON - MAKIN' LOVE
Written by Nashville's Floyd Eugene Robinson, he recorded the song himself, and had his only hit. Makin' Love reached #20 in the Billboard Hot 100, #27 in the Black Singles Chart, and #9 in the UK Singles Chart.

Weird OHW Fact... He also wrote The Little Space Girl, see one hit wonder Jesse Lee Turner, below. **Weird OHW Fact...** Although it reached #20, it was soon banned for its sexual content.

FRANCK POURCEL'S FRENCH FIDDLES - ONLY YOU
Sold over 3 million copies.
Born in Marseilles, France, composer and orchestra conductor Pourcel immigrated to the US in 1952. His only hit was a 1956 recording, Only You. It was a very slow chart riser, and reached #9 in the Billboard Hot 100 in the summer of 1959, staying in the chart for 16 weeks.

Weird OHW Fact... As a conductor of many famous orchestras, Pourcel has recorded 250 albums, and over 3000 songs. He has won many awards and is considered a French musical legend.

FRANKIE FORD - SEA CRUISE
Sold over 1 million copies.
Written by Huey 'Piano' Smith and His Clowns, the song was recorded by Frankie Ford (born Vincent Francis Guzzo), who made it such a hit, it is now considered the 'definitive' version. Using Smith's original

backing track, and with added ships horns and bells Ford reached #14 in the Billboard Hot 100, and #11 in the R&B Chart. Subsequent singles charted in the high #70's, but never in the Top 40.

Weird OHW Fact... The record company decided to release Ford's version, as Piano Smith was on tour.

GARY STITES - LONELY FOR YOU

Gary Stites was a fleeting chapter in the history of music. Remembered only for the one hit which was said to be more than a touch reminiscent of Conway Twitty's, It's Only Make Believe. The song reached #24 in the Billboard Hot 100, but his follow-up, Starry Eyed, only reached #77.

Weird OHW Fact... Michael Holliday took Starry Eyed to #1 in the UK later the same year.

GERRY GRANAHAN - NO CHEMISE, PLEASE

From Pittston, Pennsylvania, DJ Gerald Granahan tried through many bands to have a musical career. His only hit, however, was No Chemise, Please. It reached #23 in the Billboard Hot 100.

Weird OHW Fact... Granahan had a voice akin to Elvis Presley's, he subsequently got a job making demos of songs to be considered by Elvis.

HARRY SIMEONE CHORALE - THE LITTLE DRUMMER BOY

Written by Katherine Kennicott Davis in 1941, and originally entitled, Carol of the Drum, Simeone recorded it for an album of Christmas songs. He changed the original arrangement and re-named it, Little Drummer Boy. It reached #13 in the Billboard Hot 100, and has been a frequent chart visitor ever since.

Weird OHW Fact... The Beverley Sisters' version reached #6 in the UK Singles Chart the same year.

Weird OHW Fact... It has been covered many hundreds of times, here's just a few... David Bowie and Bing Crosby, The Jackson Five, Rush (yes, RUSH!), Jimi Hendrix, and Christopher Lee.

THE IMPALAS - SORRY (I RAN ALL THE WAY HOME)

Sold over a million copies.

Written by Artie Zwirn and Aristides Giosasi, the song was recorded by the Impalas, a multi-racial singing group from Brooklyn, New York. Suddenly signed to MGM Records, the song reached #2 in the Billboard Hot 100, #14 in the R&B Chart, and #28 in the UK. Their follow-ups, 'Bye Everybody, and Oh What A Fool, did not chart.

THE ISLANDERS - THE ENCHANTED SEA

Written by band member Randy Starr, this recording was the band's only hit. The Enchanted Sea reached #15 in the Billboard Hot 100 and led to a one album deal on Mayflower Records. Randy Starr also co-wrote Kissin' Cousins, for Elvis Presley.

Billboard rated the song as #5 of 1959.

Weird OHW Fact... Randy Starr was a one hit wonder on his own in 1957 (see previous entry) with After School.

IVO ROBIC AND THE SONG-MASTERS - MORGEN

Written by Peter Moesser, Morgen, (Morning) was recorded by Ivo Robić and The Song-Masters in Germany. It was a hit in their native land, then later in the US. Still sung in German, it reached #13 in the Billboard Hot 100, one of the highest German songs to chart. A few English versions were quickly released (now titled One More Sunrise) but none charted in the US.

In the UK, Dickie Valentine's cover reached #14 in the UK Charts, spending 7 weeks in the chart.

JERRY KELLER - HERE COMES SUMMER

Reached #1 in the UK.

Sold over a million copies.

Written by Jerry Keller, and the size of the hit recognized by his manager, the song was released on Kapp Records nationally in the US, and given to London Records for UK release. In the US it reached #14 in the Billboard Chart, and stayed in the chart for 13 weeks. Elsewhere, it reached #1 in the UK, #4 in Canada, and #8 in Norway. Keller turned to song writing, film scores and jingles.

Weird OHW Fact... It was covered by Cliff Richard And The Shadows and The Dave Clark Five.

JESSE BELVIN - GUESS WHO

Written by his wife, Jo Ann Belvin, this Texan had great promise as a song-writer. One of Jesse Lorenzo Belvin's first songs, Dream Girl, reached #2 in the R&B charts, Goodnight My Love reached #7 in the R&B chart. In 1959, his wife wrote Guess Who in an effort to change his style, and the song reached #31 in the Billboard Hot 100. With this new laid back look, he was considered a rival to Nat King Cole.

He died in a car crash less than a year later, aged 27, his driver having fallen asleep at the wheel.

JESSE LEE TURNER - THE LITTLE SPACE GIRL

Written by Floyd Robinson, he gave it to his cousin, Jesse Lee Turner from Addicks, Texas. Turner recorded songs for several labels, but this was the one that made it big. The single reached #20 in the Billboard Hot 100. His follow-ups, Thinkin', and Do I Worry, failed to chart. He is now a Christian evangelist.

THE MARK IV - I GOT A WIFE
A short-lived ensemble from Chicago, The Mark IV soon had a hit on their hands. The novelty song on Mercury Records, I Got A Wife, reached #24 in Billboard Hot 100 chart, and #14 in Canada. None of their other records charted, but (Make With) The Shake, was performed on American Bandstand and got to #22 in Canada.

MICKEY MOZART QUINTET - LITTLE DIPPER
Written by Robert Maxwell (born Max Rosen), the song was recorded under the dubious name of the Mickey Mozart Quintet. It reached #30 in the Billboard Hot 100. None of his other compositions did near as well.

MORMON TABERNACLE CHOIR - BATTLE HYMN OF THE REPUBLIC
From 1869, the Mormon Tabernacle Choir grew from humble beginnings to a full 360 person choir. They toured extensively, both in America and overseas, and were featured on radio as one of America's greatest choirs. In 1959, they recorded the Battle Hymn of the Republic, and it got to #13 in the Billboard Hot 100.
Weird OHW Fact... The choir still runs today, and have 5 gold albums to their credit.

THE MYSTICS - HUSHABYE
Written by Doc Pomus and Mort Shuman, it was recorded by the Brooklyn doo-wop group, the Mystics (Initially called The Overons). It was a thumping hit, reaching #20 in the Billboard Hot 100, and spending 16 weeks in the chart.
Weird OHW Fact... It was covered by the Beach Boys and The Kingsmen.

NINA SIMONE - I LOVES YOU, PORGY
Written by George and Ira Gershwin in 1935, the song is a duet from the opera Porgy and Bess. North Carolina's Nina Simone (born Eunice Kathleen Waymon) recorded it on her debut album, Little Girl Blue, and it reached #18 in the Billboard Chart and #2 in the R&B Chart.
Weird OHW Fact... Although this was her only US hit, Simone went on have many chart entries in the UK, reaching #2 twice and #5 twice.

Weird OHW Fact... Nina Simone recorded 48 albums in her lifetime.
Weird OHW Fact... Aspiring to be a concert pianist, and fresh from Juilliard, she was refused entry to the Curtis Institute of Music in Philadelphia, perhaps because of racial discrimination. Decades later, just two days before she died, the Curtis Institute of Music gave her an honorary degree.

THE NUTTY SQUIRRELS - UH! OH! PART 2
The Chipmunks had a hit with a song called Uh-Oh, and it reached #45, but the cartoon was delayed in release. The Nutty Squirrels (jazz musicians Don Elliott and Granville 'Sascha' Burland) did their own cartoon and got it published before the Chipmunks, imitated the falsetto voices, then recorded a similar song. Their version got to #14 in the Billboard Hot 100.
Weird OHW Fact... For a short time, both cartoons fought for ratings, but the Chipmunks won.

PHIL PHILLIPS WITH THE TWILIGHTS - SEA OF LOVE
Sold over a million copies.
Written by Philip Phillips and George Khoury, the song was first produced on Khoury's own label, then on Mercury Records. The song reached #1 in the R&B Chart, and #2 in the Billboard Hot 100. Philips never had another hit.
Weird OHW Fact... In the UK, Marty Wilde reached #3 with a hastily recorded cover, while Phillip's single did not chart.
Weird OHW Fact... Robert Plant's 'Honeydrippers' reached#3 in the Billboard Chart with their 1891 version.
Weird OHW Fact... Phillips has stated that despite the million plus sales, he only received $6800.

PRESTON EPPS - BONGO ROCK
Written by Preston Epps, he recorded the rock instrumental and had a hit on his hands. It reached #14 in the Billboard Hot 100, and #20 in Canada. His follow-up, Bongo Bongo Bongo, reached #78.
Weird OHW Fact... Epps' bongo-themed singles kept coming, all in vain... Bongo in the Congo, Bongo Rocket, Bootlace Bongo, Bongo Boogie, Flamenco Bongo, Mr. Bongo, and Bongo Shuffle.
Weird OHW Fact... The Incredible Bongo Band recorded a cover version, Bongo Rock '73, also a minor hit.

RAY PETERSON – THE WONDER OF YOU

Written by Baker Knight, it was Texan Peterson's first hit, and reached #23 in the UK, #25 in the Billboard Hot 100, and #22 in Australia. Subsequent hits were, Tell Laura I Love Her (US #7, AUS #10), and Corinna Corinna (US #9, AUS #4, UK #41). Tell Laura I Love Her did not chart in the UK at all, considered in bad taste by Decca Records, helping make Peterson a UK one hit wonder.

Weird OHW Fact... It was also a UK hit for Hull's Ronnie Hilton, reaching #22.

Weird OHW Fact... Elvis's version was one of his biggest UK hits, staying at #1 for six weeks in 1970.

Weird OHW Fact... It has been the football crowd anthem at Arsenal, Port Vale, and Ross County.

REG OWEN - MANHATTAN SPIRITUAL

Born in hackney, London, conductor Reginald Owen played saxophone from his teenage years, and wrote film scores in the late 1950's. his one surprise hit, Manhattan Spiritual, reached #10 in the Billboard Hot 100, and #20 in the UK Charts. His follow up, Obsession, only got to #43 in the UK.

THE REVELS - MIDNIGHT STROLL

From Philadelphia, Pennsylvania, doo wop quintet The Revels worked hard for their first hit. Their chiller, set for the Halloween market, reached #35 in the Billboard Hot 100, and became the band's only hit. Their follow-up, another chiller, Foo Man Choo, failed to chart.

ROCCO GRANATA AND THE INTERNATIONAL QUINTET - MARINA

Reached #1 in Belgium and Germany.

Sung by Italian accordionist and singer Rocco Granata, Marina became his first international hit and only US chart entry. After topping the German and Belgian charts in late 1959, it reached #31 in the Billboard Hot 100 in 1960, becoming his best known song by far.

THE ROCK-A-TEENS - WOO HOO

Written by George Donald McGraw, the song is a 12 bar blues riff with just one lyric, yeah, you've guessed it, Woo Hoo. Richmond, Virginia's The Rock-A-Teens, version reached #16 in the Billboard Hot 100, becoming their only hit. Their follow-up, Twangy, did not chart.

ROD BERNARD - THIS SHOULD GO ON FOREVER

Written by Louisiana's Bernard 'King Karl' Jolivette, it is a prime example of 'swamp pop'. Fellow swamp popper, Rod Bernard, heard a performance and on hearing that King Karl had no views to record the song, asked permission to do so. Bernard released the single, and of course, fueled by success, King Karl followed suit. Bernard's version reached #20 in the Billboard Hot 100, and is considered to be the definitive version.

RONNIE HAWKINS AND THE HAWKS - MARY LOU

Born in Arkansas, he moved to Canada after forming The Hawks. In 1959, they recorded their only US hit single, Mary Lou. The song reached #26 in the Billboard Hot 100. They slipped into more 'country' music and had success there, but they not chart mainstream again.

Weird OHW Fact... The move to Canada caused changes in the band, and most left. Drummer Levon Helm and the other 'Hawks' left Hawkins in 1964, to form... The Band, of Last Waltz fame.

STONEWALL JACKSON – WATERLOO

Written by prolific songwriters John D. Loudermilk and Marijohn Wilkin, it was recorded by country singer Stonewall Jackson. The single topped the chart and spent five weeks at #1 in the Country Music Chart. It also reached #4 in the Billboard Hot 100, staying sixteen weeks in the mainstream chart.

THE TEMPOS - SEE YOU IN SEPTEMBER

Written by Sid Wayne and Sherman Edwards, the song was accepted by the second New York record company they approached. The Tempos version, however, was released in July, and may have been influenced by changes in the Billboard reporting system. It reached #23 in the new Billboard Hot 100.

Weird OHW Fact... The Happenings reached #3 in 1966 with their cover version.

Weird OHW fact... The tempos' version was included in the American Graffiti soundtrack.

THOMAS WAYNE AND THE DELONS – TRAGEDY

Sold 1 million copies.

Written by Gerald H. Nelson and Fred B. Burch, it was recorded by Thomas Wayne (born Thomas Wayne Perkins) who was the brother of Johnny Cash's guitarist, Luther Perkins. The single reached #20 in the Black Singles Chart and #5 in the Billboard Top 100.

Weird OHW Fact... Wayne, who recorded many singles which became charters for different artists, never recorded an album.

TOMMY DEE - THREE STARS

Sold over 1 million copies.

Three Stars was written by DJ Tommy Dee as a tribute to Buddy Holly, Ritchie Valens, and The Big Bopper, who died in a plane crash earlier in 1959. The song reached #11 in the Billboard Hot 100, and was awarded a gold disc.

Weird OHW Fact... Eddie Cochrane recorded a cover version, then died in a car crash a year later; Cochrane is heard sobbing on the second verse.

TOMMY FACENDA - HIGH SCHOOL U.S.A.

From Portsmouth, Virginia, Facenda joined Gene Vincent's Blue Caps in 1957, but left a year later to follow a solo career. The novelty song, High School U.S.A., was recorded 28 different times with different schools mentioned. The combined sales reached #28 in the Billboard Hot 100, and #30 in the Black Singles Chart. His follow-up, Bubba Ditty, did not chart.

TONY BELLUS - ROBBIN THE CRADLE

Written by Chicago native Tony Bellus (born Anthony J. Bellusci), the ballad rose to #25 in the Billboard Hot 100, and stayed in the chart for a then record-breaking 26 weeks. He never reached the chart again, his time in the army interrupting his career.

TRAVIS AND BOB - TELL HIM NO

Written by Travis, the duo Travis Pritchett and Bob Weaver from Jackson, Alabama, recorded Tell Him No on Sandy Records in nearby Mobile, Alabama. It reached #8 in the Billboard Hot 100 and #21 in the R&B Chart. It was their only chart success.

Weird OHW Fact... A year later, they sued Sandy Records for royalties of the single.

THE WAILERS – TALL COOL ONE

Written by band members Richard Dangel, Kent Morrill and John Greek this 5 piece band from Tacoma in Washington state, had one single which threatened to boost them out of their local stomping grounds. The instrumental Tall Cool One reached #24 in the R&B Chart and #36 in the Billboard Hot 100. Their follow up, Mau-Mau got to #68, and Wailin' failed to chart.

Weird OHW Fact... The song's name was suggested by Morrill's mother.

THE VIRTUES - GUITAR BOOGIE SHUFFLE

Guitar Boogie was written by Arthur Smith in 1945, it was recorded by Philadelphia band, Frank Virtue and the Virtues, who added 'Shuffle' to the title. The single reached #5 in the Billboard Hot 100 and #27 in the R&B Chart.

Weird OHW Fact... In the same year in the UK, Bert Weedon reached #10 in the UK Charts with his cover version.

WINK MARTINDALE - DECK OF CARDS

First a hit in 1948, and traceable back to 1762, game show host Martindale's version is the highest charting cover. It reached #7 in the Billboard Hot 100, and #11 in the Country Chart, and may have reached #1 in some charts worldwide. The song tells of a soldier found with a deck of cards. He then tells how the cards are his bible, and is supposedly not charged.

Weird OHW Fact... In the UK, the song got to #13 by Max Bygraves in 1973.

THE SIXTIES...
1960...

As U.S. Senator John F. Kennedy announces his candidacy for the Democratic presidential nomination, the year and the decade begin...
Lucille Ball files for divorce from Desi Arnaz, Ben-Hur wins eleven Oscars, Gary Powers' Lockheed U-2 spy plane is shot down over Russia, Muhammad Ali (Cassius Clay) wins the gold medal at the Olympic Games in Rome, and Britain's 'farthing' coin becomes obsolete.

AL BROWN'S TUNETOPPERS FEATURING COOKIE BROWN – THE MADISON
Written by Al Brown, this dance record was released on Amy Records, and got to #23 in the Billboard Hot 100. Another version, led by the Ray Bryant Combo, also charted, reaching #30 (see entry below).

BILLY BLAND - LET THE LITTLE GIRL DANCE
Written by Spencer and Glover, it was recorded by Billy Bland (from Wilmington, North Carolina) on Old Town Records. It reached #7 in the Billboard Hot 100, and #11 in the R&B Chart. Bland had two other minor hits the same year, Harmony got to #91, and, You Were Born to Be Loved, reaching #94.
Weird OHW Fact... In the 1980s, he opened a soul food restaurant in Harlem, New York.

BOBBY MARCHAN - THERE'S SOMETHING ON YOUR MIND
The song is attributed to B. J. McNeely, but he did admit to buying it from John Harris who got most of the song from a gospel tune. It was recorded by Ohio's Bobby Marchan (born Oscar James Gibson) on Fire Records. It reached #31 in the Billboard Hot 100, and topped the R&B Chart. His subsequent singles did not chart.

BOB LUMAN - LET'S THINK ABOUT LIVING
Written by Boudleaux Bryant, the song is a spoof of popular teenage tragedy song genre of the time. Recorded by Luhman on Warner Brothers Records, on the album of the same name, it reached #7 in the Billboard Hot 100, #3 in Australia and #3 in Norway. Luhman peppered the Country Chart until his early death in 1978. He was just 41 years old.

Weird OHW Fact... The first line states... "In every other song that I've heard lately, some fellow gets shot...".

BUSTER BROWN - FANNIE MAE

Written and recorded by Georgia blues and R&B singer, Buster Brown, the song reached #38 in the Billboard Hot 100 and #1 in the US Billboard R&B chart. His follow-up, Is You Is or Is You Ain't My Baby, reached # 81 and Sugar Babe, got to #99.

Weird OHW Fact... Brown was 50 years old when he had his only hit.

Weird OHW Fact... The song was featured on the American Graffiti soundtrack.

BUZZ CLIFFORD – BABY SITTIN' BOOGIE

Sold more than 1 million copies.

Written by Johnny Parker, it was recorded by Buzz Clifford (born Reese Francis Clifford) on Columbia Records on his 1961 album, Baby Sittin' with Buzz Clifford. It reached #6 in the Billboard Hot 100, #27 on the R&B chart, and #28 on the U.S. country chart. Overseas it got to #17 in the UK Charts, and #4 in Norway. Clifford was thrust into the limelight of such as Perry Como on American Bandstand, but his follow-up, Three Little Fishes, flopped at #102.

Billboard ranked the song as #67 of 1961.

CHARLIE RYAN AND THE TIMBERLANE RIDERS - HOT ROD LINCOLN

Written by Charlie Ryan, and first released in 1955, to little success. Re-released in late 1959, it reached #33 in the Billboard Hot 100, and #14 in the Country Chart. After a stint in the Korean War, Ryan toured with country giants, Jim Reeves and Johnny Horton, but never charted again.

Weird OHW Fact... Commander Cody and His Lost Planet Airmen's version reached #9 in the Billboard Hot 100, #28 Adult Contemporary, and #7 in Canada.

DANTE & THE EVERGREENS - ALLEY OOP

Written by Dallas Frazier, it was released by a host of artists in 1960 (see Hollywood Argyles entry below). The Prehistorics, The Dyno-Sores (#59) and Dante & the Evergreens competed with the Hollywood Argyles #1). Dante reached a creditable #15 in the Billboard Hot 100. Their follow-up single, Time Machine, hit #73 in the Billboard Hot 100.

DEANE HAWLEY - LOOK FOR A STAR

See 1960 entry below, (Garry Mills – Look for a Star)

THE DEMENSIONS - OVER THE RAINBOW
This doo wop group from The Bronx, New York, recorded the Judy Garland song (Written by Harold Arlen and Yip Harburg) on Mohawk Records. It reached #16 in the Billboard Hot 100, but the best of their follow-ups was, My Foolish Heart, (#95 in 1963).

DORSEY BURNETTE - (THERE WAS A) TALL OAK TREE
Originally in a trio with his younger brother Johnny (who had a few hits in the USA and UK), Singer/songwriter Dorsey Burnette's fame extended to one song. Originally offered to Ricky nelson, Burnette recorded it himself. It reached #23 in the Billboard Hot 100. The follow-up, Hey Little One' just got to #48... so close, yet so far.

ETTA JONES - DON'T GO TO STRANGERS
Sold over a million copies.
Hard working South Carolina singer, Etta Jones, had one shot at fame, and it was a good one. Despite just reaching #36 in the Billboard Hot 100, it got to #5 in the R&B Chart, received wide critical acclaim, and was awarded gold record status. The album was also nominated for a Grammy.
Weird OHW Fact... The afore-mentioned 'hard-working' tab is proper for this artist; she released over 40 albums in a 50 year career.

THE FENDERMEN - MULE SKINNER BLUES
Written by Jimmie Rodgers and George Vaughan in 1930, it was recorded by Madison, Wisconsin-based duo on Soma Records. Their version, played on fender guitars (hence their name) reached #5 in the Billboard Hot 100, #16 in the Country Chart, #2 in Canada, and #32 in the UK Charts. Their only other hit, Don't You Just Know It, only got to #110.
Weird OHW Fact... Despite their short career, their version of Ghost Riders In The Sky, is well worth a listen to with twanging fenders and heavy sax.
Weird OHW Fact... Their guitars, one telecaster, and one Stratocaster, were both plugged into the one amplifier.

GARRY MILLS - LOOK FOR A STAR
This might be the most blatant trans-Atlantic 'cover' version snatch ever performed. Let's see if we can shed light on the devious, nefarious, and most barefaced musical plot in the history of pop music... (okay, I may be getting a bit passionate here, but hear me out)

Written by British songwriter, Tony Hatch (under the pseudonym, Mark Anthony) it was featured in the 1960 horror movie, Circus of Horrors, sung by British pop singer, Garry Mills. On Top Rank Records, it got to #7 in the UK Charts, which he followed by two other hits...

However, Garry Mills' single got released in the USA, and the floodgates opened. Garry Mill's song eventually reaches #26 in the Billboard Hot 100, his only US Chart hit, making him a one hit wonder in the USA and a bit of cash and fame. Wonderful. (You can probably tell he's not the bad guy here)

Weirdest OHW Fact Dump Ever... This story is worthy of a movie plot.

Deane Hawley records the song, and her version gets to #29 in the Billboard Chart. (This gal is also not the bad person in this plot)

Billy Vaughn, band leader with many hits under his belt, makes an instrumental of the song... it reaches #19 in the Billboard Chart. (Amazingly, he's also not the bad guy here, in fact, so far no-one has done anything really bad)

Enter Nashville's **James E. 'Buzz' Cason**... (the bad guy)... he was a founding member of Nashville's first rock band, The Casuals, and with Richard Williams and Hugh Jarrett of The Jordanaires, he had recorded songs as 'The Statues for Liberty'.

Suddenly (I'm thinking with no malice or forethought... my tone dripping heavily with spicy sarcasm), James E. 'Buzz' Cason decides to change his name to **Garry Miles** (MILES) and go off and have a solo career, oh, and he decides to record for his first solo single, Look For a Star, a new song bubbling under the US Chart by a Brit called **Garry Mills** (MILLS).

Now is it me, or is that some cauldron-bubbling heap of coincidence?

However, history shows that the two versions of the songs are in the chart at the same time. They rise in the chart together. They are played by the same radio stations at the same time. Thousands of record buyers look up at the chart on music store walls and wonder which version they've heard, and which one they should buy?

The two songs peak at their respective highest points just ONE WEEK APART.

As Brit, Garry Mills reaches #26 in the Billboard Top 100, James E. 'Buzz' Cason/Garry Miles reaches #16 in the Billboard Hot 100, decides against the solo career, and immediately reverts back to his old name. Yup, he's a one hit wonder too.

Now, Buzz Cason goes on to have a great middling music career, but I sure think he went one step too far in the search for personal stardom. What do you think?

GARRY MILES - LOOK FOR A STAR

Yup, this entry is just a little out of alphabetical order.

James E. 'Buzz' Cason, AKA Garry Miles reached #16 in the Billboard Top 100.

(see above entry for details)

HANK LOCKLIN - PLEASE HELP ME, I'M FALLING

Written by Don Robertson and Hal Blair, this country classic was first recorded by Hank Locklin on RCA Victor records. The song reached #1 in the Country Chart, where it topped the chart for 14 weeks (his second Country #1). It then crossed over to the Billboard Hot 100 reaching #8, #9 in the UK Chart, and #4 in Norway.

Weird OHW Fact... Later the same year, Skeeter Davis had answered the record with, (I Can't Help You) I'm Falling Too, which reached #39 in the Billboard Hot 100, #2 in the Country Chart. It was her first US hit of many.

HAROLD DORMAN - MOUNTAIN OF LOVE

Written by Harold Kenneth Dorman on Rita Records, the song spent 19 weeks in the Billboard Hot 100, reaching #21, #7 in the R&B Chart, and #25 in the Canadian Chart. It would be his only hit.

Weird OHW Fact... In the UK, Kenny Lynch had the hit, reaching #33 in the UK Chart.

Weird OHW Fact... With Mountain of Love, in 1981, Charlie Pride topped the US and Canadian Country Charts.

THE HOLLYWOOD ARGYLES - ALLEY OOP

Written by Dallas Frazier, the song was based on a newspaper strip cartoon. The novelty song was recorded by the studio-formed band, The Hollywood Argyles, and it got to #1 in the Billboard Hot 100, #3 in the R&B chart, and #24 in the UK.

Weird OHW Fact... Gary Paxton, who sang vocals, was the leader of Bobby "Boris" Pickett's Crypt-**Weird OHW Fact...** The song was covered by The Bonzo Dog Doo-Dah Band, and George Thorogood & the Destroyers.

HUGO & LUIGI - JUST COME HOME

More used to producing music, these moguls took to vinyl just once. With the artist labelled on the RCA Victor record as 'Hugo & Luigi, Their Orchestra and Chorus', the song reached #35 in the Billboard Hot 100.

Weird OHW Fact... They began working in the 1950's, producing such greats as Perry Como, Elvis Presley, and Sam Cooke... they closed in 1970's managing the Stylistics.

THE IVY THREE - YOGI
Written by Lou Stallman and Sid Jacobson (founders of Shell Records) and band member Charles Koppelman the song was recorded by the pop band from Garden City, Long Island, New York. It was a hit, reaching #8 in the Billboard Hot 100, and #22 in the R&B Chart. The band broke up the next year.

JEANNE BLACK - HE'LL HAVE TO STAY
Sold over 1 million copies.
Written by Audrey Allison, Charles Grean, and Joe Allison as an answer to Jim Reeve's song, He'll Have To Go. Recorded by Jeanne Black on Capitol Records, on her only album, A Little Bit Lonely, it reached #4 in the Billboard Hot 100, #6 in the Country Chart, #11 in the R&B chart, and only #41 in the UK. Her follow-up, Lisa, just got to #43.
Billboard ranked the song as #52 of 1960.

JESSIE HILL - OOH POO PAH DOO–PART II
Written by Jessie Hill, this Louisiana R&B and blues singer's song would be covered by over 100 artists. His original version, polished on stage, reached #5 in the R&B Chart, and #28 in the Billboard Hot 100. He wrote songs for Ike and Tina Turner, Sonny and Cher, and Willie Nelson.

JIMMY CHARLES - A MILLION TO ONE
Written by Phil Medley and first recorded on Promo Records by Jimmy Charles and the Revelletts. The single reached #5 in the Billboard Hot 100, and #8 in the R&B Chart. His follow-up single, The Age for Love, just missed out at #47.

JOE JONES - YOU TALK TOO MUCH
Written by Fats Domino's brother-in-law, Reginald Hall, it was recorded by New Orleans singer, Joseph Charles "Joe" Jones, who had played with B. B. King. The song reached a lofty #3 in the Billboard Hot 100, but it would be his only hit. His follow-ups did not chart.
Weird OHW Fact... Fats Domino turned down the song.

JOHN D. LOUDERMILK - LANGUAGE OF LOVE
Written by John D. Loudermilk, the singer/songwriter is more known for his songwriting rather than his recordings, many of which have been

hits (See section on One Hit Wonder Kings, at the beginning of this book). His single, Language of Love, reached #32 in the Billboard Hot 100 in 1960, and Top 20 in the UK. He would never hit the Top 40 as a solo artist again.

Weird OHW Fact... A previous 'solo' single in 1957, Sittin' in the Balcony, did hit the Billboard Hot 100 at #38. BUT... he released it under the name, Johnny Dee, on Colonial Records.

JOHNNY BOND - HOT ROD LINCOLN

Originally a one hit wonder by Charlie Ryan (see Charlie Ryan's entry above, 1960) recounting a car race, Johnny Bond's (born Cyrus Whitfield Bond) version on Republic Records changes the plot slightly, (from a V-12 to a V-8) and reached #26 in the Billboard Hot 100.

Weird OHW Fact... Johnny Bond had 11 hits in the Country Chart, and appeared in more than 40 movies.

Weird OHW Fact... Bond released a sequel to Hot Rod Lincoln, called, X-15, set in 1997, changing the car-race plot to that of an airplane race. It did not chart.

JOHNNY FERGUSON - ANGELA JONES

Written by John D. Loudermilk, the song was recorded by Johnny Ferguson on MGM Records, reaching #27 in the Billboard Hot 100. The song was a hit in the Uk by Michael Cox (see entry below).

Weird OHW Fact... Loudermilk was first to record the song, but it did not chart.

LARRY HALL - SANDY

Written by Terry Feif, it was recorded by Hall (born Lawrence Kendall Hall), from Hamlett, Ohio, on Strand Records. Hall had a short recording career, releasing just six singles. His only charting hit, Sandy, reached #15 in the Billboard Hot 100 chart.

LARRY VERNE - MR. CUSTER

Reached #1 in the USA.

Sold over 1 million copies.

Written by Al De Lory, Fred Darian, and Joseph Van Winkle, the song tells the story of a soldier's letter to general Custer, telling him that the soldier did not want to fight. It reached #1 in the Billboard Hot 100 for one week. Verne's follow-up, Mr. Livingston, just reached #75.

Weird OHW Fact... Charlie Drake had the hit in the UK, taking it to #12 in the UK Charts.

THE LITTLE DIPPERS - FOREVER

Written by Buddy Killen, it was recorded by The Little Dippers (AKA the Anita Kerr Singers) on University Records. It reached #9 in the Billboard Hot 100, spending 14 weeks in the chart, and also getting to #13 in the Canadian Chart.

LOLITA - SAILOR (YOUR HOME IS THE SEA)

Reached #1 in Norway and Sweden.

Sold over 2 million copies.

Written in German by Werner Scharfenberger and Fini Busch, the song became an international hit, covered by a myriad of artists. Austrian singer Lolita (Edith Einzinger) recorded the original version, a #2 hit in Germany, #14 in Australia, #7 in the Netherlands and #8 in New Zealand. In the US on Kapp Records, and with a short over-dubbed English narration, it reached #5 in the Billboard Hot 100.

Weird OHW Fact... Lolita's version stayed at #1 in Norway for 9 weeks and at #1 in Sweden for 11 weeks.

Weird OHW Fact... Petula Clark got to #1in the UK Chart, #1 in the New Zealand Chart and had the hit in France and (#12) Belgium, Anne Shelton (#10) charted in the UK, Caterina Valente (#10) in Belgium, Towa Carson (#5) in Sweden, Jan Høiland (#2) in Norway, and Virginia Lee (#8) in South Africa.

Weird OHW Fact... It was the first German language top 5 hit in the USA, not surpassed until another one hit wonder, Nena's 99 Luftballons.

LYN CORNELL – NEVER ON SUNDAY

Cornell was a member of the girl bands, The Vernons Girls, The Carefrees (One hit wonders in 1964, see entry) and The Pearls, and had at least one hit with all groups. She recorded, Never On Sunday, as a solo artist on Decca Records, and it reached #30 in the UK Charts. Her Christmas follow-up, The Angel and the Stranger, did not reach the charts.

MARK DINNING - TEEN ANGEL

Written by husband and wife Jean Dinning and Red Surrey, it was recorded by Jean's brother, Mark Dinning. It would be the song that started off the teen-death song craze of the early 1960s. The song was a slow charter, with US radio stations considering the theme macabre, but it soon rose to #1 in the Billboard Hot 100. It also got to #37 in the UK Charts despite being banned.

Weird OHW Fact... Dinning's nephew played bass for the band, Toad the Wet Sprocket.

MAURICE WILLIAMS AND THE ZODIACS - STAY
Reached #1 in USA.
Sold more than 8 million copies.
Written by Williams in 1953 when he just was 15 years old, it was eventually recorded by his band seven years later. It reached #1 in the Billboard Hot 100, where it stayed for just one week.
Weird OHW Fact... The song holds the record for the shortest recording ever to reach #1... it is just 1 minute 36 seconds.
Weird OHW Fact... It was featured in the soundtrack of Dirty Dancing.

MICHAEL COX - ANGELA JONES
Written by John D. Loudermilk, the song was recorded by Johnny Ferguson in the US (See entry above). The record was the only hit on Joe Meek's ill-fated Triumph label. The song reached #7 in the UK Charts, but it stalled from low record production in the factory, and would have climbed higher. Cox's follow-up, Along Came Caroline', was released on HMV Records, but it just got to #41. So close, yet so far.

MONTY KELLY - SUMMER SET
Written by English clarinetist Acker Bilk (a US one hit wonder in 1962) and pianist Dave Collette, the title is a pun on Bilk's home county of Somerset. Monty Kelly and his orchestra released the single in the USA and it reached #30 in the Billboard Hot 100.
Weird OHW Fact... Bilk's version reached #5 in the UK Chart, kicking off his career.

THE PARADONS - DIAMONDS AND PEARLS
From Bakersfield, California, The Paradons were a short-lived pop group on Milestone Records. Their only hit was their debut single, which reached #27 in the R&B Chart, and #18 in the Billboard Hot 100 in 1960. Appearing on American Bandstand and at the Apollo Theatre, the band broke up a year later. Their follow-ups never charted.

RAY BRYANT TRIO - THE MADISON TIME–PART 1
Written by Al Brown (see entry above) this was the second version of The Madison to be released in 1960. Born Raphael Homer Bryant, he played piano from the age of six. He played with Charlie Parker, Miles Davis, and Aretha Franklin. His only 'solo' hit was The Madison Time, on Columbia Records, which reached #30 in the Billboard Hot 100.

RAY SMITH - ROCKIN' LITTLE ANGEL

Sold over 1 million copies.

Rockabilly Ray Smith recorded the song on Judd Records, taking some influence from the old 1844 American classic, Buffalo Gals. The song only reached #22 in the Billboard hot 100, but must have had some longevity as it was awarded a gold disc.

RICHIE VALENCE – TELL LAURA I LOVE HER

Reached #1 in the UK.

Sold over 1 million copies.

Written by Jeff Barry and Ben Raleigh, and a #7 hit in the US by Ray Petersen, the original lyrics tell that the hero dies in a rodeo accident. The lyrics were changed to a stock car race, and the teenage death song was complete. It reached #1 in the UK Charts and was Welshman Valence's only UK hit. Follow up singles, Jimmy's Girl, and Moving Away, reached #1 in both Scandinavia and Australia.

Weird OHW Fact... Decca Records in the UK smashed 20,000 copies of Ray Peterson's 1959 version, choosing not to release as they considered the lyrics to be in bad taste.

Weird OHW Fact... The BBC refused to play 'American death songs' and the single reached the UK audience by plays on Radio Luxembourg.

ROD LAUREN - IF I HAD A GIRL

Born Rod Lawrence Strunk is probably better known for his acting work on Alfred Hitchcock Presents and Gomer Pyle, U.S.M.C.. His only dabble into the music world was his one hit wonder, If I Had A Girl, which reached #31 in the Billboard Hot 100.

Weird OHW Fact... His wife, Bianca, was found stabbed to death in the Philippines in 2001. He fled the country, fearing extradition; others were eventually charged with her murder.

Weird OHW Fact... He committed suicide in 2007 in Tracy, California.

RON HOLDEN - LOVE YOU SO

A pop and rhythm and blues singer from Seattle, Washington, he was discovered by Larry Nelson. Holden recorded, Love You So, which reached #11 in the R&B Chart and #7 in the Billboard Hot 100. His highest charting follow-up, Can You Talk?, only reached #49 in the R&B Chart.

ROSIE AND THE ORIGINALS – ANGEL BABY

Written by Rosie Hamlin, it was eventually taken up by Highland records, recorded by her own band. The song reached #5 in the R&B Chart, and #5 in the Billboard Hot 100, where it stayed for 15 weeks. A year later it reached #6 in Canada.

Weird OHW Fact... Because she had omitted to add her name as the writer, Rosie got little to no royalties... years of legal wrangling followed.

Weird OHW Fact... In 1973, John Lennon recorded a version of the song. It was included on the 1986 compilation album Menlove Ave.

THE SAFARIS - IMAGE OF A GIRL

From Los Angeles, California, The Safaris were a short-lived pop group. Formed in 1959, they released their only hit single a year later on ELDO Records. Image of a Girl reached #6 in the Billboard Hot 100. The band broke up in 1962.

Weird OHW Fact... It was released by Mark Wynter in the UK, reaching #11 in the UK Charts.

SPENCER ROSS - TRACY'S THEME

Written by Robert Mersey under the pseudonym, 'Spencer Ross' to avoid contract problems, it would be featured in a new NBC TV production of The Philadelphia Story. With record stores primed for its release, the instrumental reached #13 in the Billboard Hot 100.

Billboard ranked it as the #81 song of 1960.

THE TEMPTATIONS - BARBARA

Not The Temptations of Motown fame, but a vocal group from New York. Their only claim to fame was the hit, Barbara, on Goldisc Records. It reached #38 in Cash Box Chart, and #29 in the Billboard Hot 100.

Weird OHW Fact... The group were managed by Arthur 'Artie' Ripp, the founder of Kama Sutra Records, and the first to sign Billy Joel.

TOBIN MATTHEWS AND CO. - RUBY DUBY DU

A guitarist from Calumet City, Illinois, Tobin recorded the slow guitar tune, Ruby Duby Du, on Chief Records. Further released on RPM Records, it reached #30 in the Billboard Hot 100. The song was featured on the soundtrack of the movie, Key Witness, starring Dennis Hopper.

Weird OHW Fact... Just on a personal level, I think this song would be a great hit for Scooby Doo, if the cartoon dog ever recorded.

OH SO CLOSE... BUT NO CIGAR...

JOHN D. LOUDERMILK - LANGUAGE OF LOVE

John D. Loudermilk, more known for his songwriting rather than his recordings is sometimes thought of as a one hit wonder... His recording, Language of Love, reached #32 in the Billboard Hot 100 in 1960.

But... folks forget his previous hit in 1957, Sittin' in the Balcony, which just squeaked into the Top 40 at #38.

JOHNNY KIDD & THE PIRATES – SHAKIN' ALL OVER

Led by singer/songwriter Johnny Kidd, they hit the big time in 1960 with their UK #1, Shakin' All Over. Some consider them a one hit wonder... but just the year before, they scored a #25 hit in the UK Chart with, Please Don't Touch.

1961...

As Ham the Chimp is rocketed into space aboard American Mercury-Redstone 2, the year begins...
John F. Kennedy is sworn in as the 35th President of the United States, Supercar, the first Gerry Anderson series filmed in Supermarionation debuts on TV, the Beatles perform for the first time at The Cavern Club in Liverpool, the Bay of Pigs Invasion of Cuba begins, the movie West Side Story is released, Catch-22 by Joseph Heller is published.

ADRIAN KIMBERLY - THE GRADUATION SONG... POMP AND CIRCUMSTANCE
Written by Elgar, with adaptation by Adrian Kimberly, aka Don Everly, recorded on Calliope Records (their own record label. It got to #34 in the Billboard Hot 100, but no other instrumental charted. Immediately following calliope's collapse, they joined the marines, and fell out of the limelight.

ANN-MARGRET - I JUST DON'T UNDERSTAND
Written by Marijohn Wilkin and Kent Westberry, it was released by Swedish-born singer/actress Ann-Margret Olsson It reached #17 in the US Billboard Hot 100, staying in the chart for 6 weeks.
Weird OHW Fact... The Beatles covered the song in 1963, on the album, Live at the BBC.

ARTHUR LYMAN - YELLOW BIRD
Written by Michel Mauléart Monton, this Haitian song took its original lyrics from an Oswald Durand poem. It has been covered extensively, but the most popular was Lyman's. It reached #4 in the Billboard Hot 100, and #2 in the Easy Listening Chart. His best-selling follow-up was, Love For Sale, (US #43, 1963).

BARRY MANN - WHO PUT THE BOMP (IN THE BOMP, BOMP, BOMP)
Written by Barry Mann and Gerry Goffin, it was recorded by Mann on ABC-Paramount Records, and backed by the Halos. It reached #7 in the Billboard Hot 100, staying in the chart for 12 weeks. The Viscounts had the hit in the UK, reaching #21 in the UK Chart.
Weird OHW Fact... Showaddywaddy had a minor hit with the song in 1982, reaching #37 in the UK.

THE BLUE JAYS - LOVERS ISLAND

Written by band members Leon Peels and Alex Manigeault, the Blue Jays, a doo wop ensemble from Venice, California, got a recording contract after winning a talent show. On Milestone Records, they released Lover's Island, reaching #31 in the Billboard Hot 100. Their follow-ups, Tears are Falling, and The Right to Love, failed to chart.

BOB MOORE AND HIS ORCHESTRA - MEXICO

Sold more than 2 million copies.
Written by Boudleaux Bryant, this instrumental was recorded by orchestra leader Bob Moore on Monument Records. Although he'd worked with many music greats, this was the only hit to have his name on it. The single reached #7 in the Billboard Hot 100, #1 in the Easy Listening Chart, #22 in the R&B Chart. It was also a hit in Australia and Germany.

BOBBY EDWARDS - YOU'RE THE REASON

Written by Bobby Edwards, Terry Imes-Fell and Fred Henley, it was recorded on Crest Records. It reached #11 in the Billboard Hot 100, and #4 in the Country Chart. The follow-up, What's the Reason, only reached #71.

BRUCE CHANNEL - HEY! BABY

Written by Margaret Cobb and Bruce Channel (pronounced like the perfume), it was recorded by Channel on LeCam Records. The song was a massive hit, reaching #1 in the Billboard Hot 100, and #2 in the UK Chart. Despite his follow-ups, Number One Man, (US #52), Come On Baby, (US #98), Going Back To Louisiana, (US #89), and Mr. Bus Driver, (US #90), he never charted in the USA again.
Weird OHW Fact... He is NOT a one hit wonder in the UK, however; in 1968, he scored a #12 in the UK with, Keep On.
Weird OHW Fact... Canadian country singer Anne Murray's version topped Canada's Country Chart, and reached #7 in the US Country Chart.
Weird OHW Fact... The song was featured in Dirty Dancing (the scene where they dance on the big log).

THE CAPRIS - THERE'S A MOON OUT TONIGHT

Italian Americans from Queens, this band's name came from a car; the Lincoln Capri. They recorded two songs on Planet Records, Indian Girl, and There's a Moon Out Tonight. The second song rose in the charts, finally reaching #3 in the Billboard Hot 100. They toured the song for a year but soon broke up.

CATHY JEAN AND THE ROOMMATES - PLEASE LOVE ME FOREVER
Written by John Malone and Ollie Blanchard in 1958, it was recorded by Cathy Jean and the Roommates on Valmor Records. Their version spent 12 weeks in the Billboard Hot 100, reaching #12, and #23 in Canada. Their follow-up, Glory of Love, (a Benny Goodman #1 hit in 1938), only reached #49 in the Billboard Hot 100.

CHRIS KENNER - I LIKE IT LIKE THAT, PART 1
Sold over 1 million copies.
Written by Chris Kenner and Allen Toussaint, it was first recorded by Louisiana's Kenner on Instant Records. The song reached #2 in the Billboard Hot 100, and #2 in the R&B Chart. He did not chart again.
Weird OHW Fact... The Dave Clark Five in 1965 released their version, which got to #7 in the Billboard Hot 100, and #12 in Australia.
Weird OHW Fact... The song is featured in 1987's Full Metal Jacket.

THE CLEFTONES - HEART AND SOUL
Written by Hoagy Carmichael and Frank Loesser in 1938, it was covered extensively before The Cleftones recorded it on Gee records. It reached #18 in the Billboard Hot 100, and #10 in the R&B Chart.
Weird OHW Fact... The song was featured on the American Graffiti soundtrack.

CURTIS LEE - PRETTY LITTLE ANGEL EYES
Written and recorded by Curtis Lee, produced by Phil Spector on Dunes Records, with backing vocals by the Halos, it spent 11 summer weeks in the Billboard Hot 100, peaking at #7, also hitting #15 in Canada, and #5 in New Zealand.
Weird OHW Fact... His 1961 follow-up, Under the Moon of Love, missed the chart, just reaching #46 in the Billboard Hot 100. Amazingly, the 1976 Showaddywaddy version (a UK #1) also just reached #46 in the Billboard Hot 100.
Weird OHW Fact... Although bands like Mud and Showaddywaddy revived Lee's songs in the 1970's, they were never a hit for Lee in the UK.

DAVE BRUBECK QUARTET - TAKE FIVE
Written by Paul Desmond, it was first recorded by the Dave Brubeck Quartet for the 1959 album Time Out. Re-issued two years later, after

the jazz success of Eddie Harris's Exodus (see entry below) it reached #25 in the Billboard Hot 100, #5 in Billboard's Easy Listening Chart, and #6 in the UK Chart.

Weird OHW Fact... At that date it was the best-selling jazz single.

Weird OHW Fact... On his death in 1977, Desmond bequeathed the royalties for the song to the Red Cross, about $100,000 per year.

DONNIE AND THE DREAMERS - COUNT EVERY STAR

Written by Sammy Gallup and Bruno Coquatrix, it was first released by Ray Anthony and His Orchestra, reaching #4 in 1950. Recorded by Donnie and the Dreamers, it reached #35 in the Billboard Hot 100. Despite many attempts, it was their only hit.

DON SHIRLEY - WATER BOY

Born in Pensacola, Florida, he composed 3 symphonies, piano concerti, a cello concerto, and many more, having his symphonies played by national orchestras, including the London Philharmonic. His one hit, however, was not his own composition. Water Boy stayed in the Billboard Hot 100 for 14 weeks, but just squeaked into the chart at #40.

Weird OHW Fact... His musical endeavors are far too numerous to mention here, recording 16 albums.

THE DREAMLOVERS - WHEN WE GET MARRIED

A doo wop group from Philadelphia, Pennsylvania, the Dreamlovers had been known as The Romancers and The Midnighters before hitting the big time on Heritage Records. When We Get Married, got to #10 in the Billboard Hot 100, but after changing record company, their follow-up, If I Should Lose You, peaked at #62.

Weird OHW Fact... One of the Dreamlovers compositions, You Gave Me Somebody to Love, was a UK hit for Manfred Mann in 1966.

THE DUALS - STICK SHIFT

A surf rock duo from Los Angeles, California, The Duals were led to Star Revue Records by H. B. Barnum. Stick Shift, the obvious single, was released nationally on Sue Records, and reached #25 in the Billboard Hot 100, with an album following the next year. Follow-up singles, Cha Cha Guitars, and, The Big Race, both did not chart, ending their music career.

Weird OHW Fact... Neither Star Revue Records nor The Duals received any royalties from (the well-named) Sue Records until 2004, just 43 years later.

EDDIE HARRIS - EXODUS

Sold over 1 million copies.

Jazz saxophonist, Eddie Harris, signed with Vee-Jay after leaving the army. He included Ernest Gold's theme from the movie Exodus on his first album (over 50 were recorded), and the single became his only hit. It reached #36 in the Billboard Hot 100 and #16 in the R&B Chart.

Weird OHW Fact... The single was the first jazz record ever to be certified with a gold award; selling more than 1 million copies.

THE EDSELS - RAMA LAMA DING DONG

Written by band member, George 'Wydell' Jones Jr. , it was recorded by doo-wop group, The Edsels, on Capitol Records. It was a real slow-burner, recorded in 1957, and being played 4 years later by a New York DJ. The song reached #21 in the Billboard Hot 100, but the band could not consolidate their success.

Weird OHW Fact... On its original release, it was wrongly labelled Lama Rama Ding Dong, perhaps contributing to its sinking without trace.

Weird OHW Fact... The song is the anthem of German soccer team, VFL Wolfsburg.

Weird OHW Fact... I'm not saying the group were petrol-heads, but the band were originally called, The Essos, after the oil company, then changed their name to, The Edsels, a popular Ford motor car.

ERNIE K-DOE - MOTHER-IN-LAW

Written by Allen Toussaint, it was recorded on Minit Records by flamboyant Ernie K-Doe, with the piano solo by Toussaint. It reached #1 in the Billboard Hot 100 and in the R&B Chart. He never charted mainstream again, but the follow-ups, Te-Ta-Te-Ta-Ta, (R&B #21, 1961) and, Later for Tomorrow (R&B #37, 1967) were minor hits.

Weird OHW Fact... In the recording studio, after many mistakes, Toussaint stormed out, vowing never to play the song again. He was coaxed back to the piano by Ernie and a backing singer, Willie Harper.

FARON YOUNG - HELLO WALLS

One of the first songs written by Willie Nelson, it was Faron Young's debut single on Capitol Records. It was a huge hit, staying on the Country Chart for 23 weeks, peaking at #1, and crossing over to the Billboard Hot 100 at #12.

Weird OHW Fact... Willie Nelson recorded the song on his own debut album, And Then I Wrote, the next year.

FREDDY KING - HIDEAWAY

Written by Freddie King and Sonny Thompson, this blues instrumental was first recorded by King, on Federal Records. It reached #29 in the Billboard Hot 100, and stayed 19 weeks in the R&B Chart, peaking at #5. **Weird OHW Fact...** It was covered by guitar greats Eric Clapton/John Mayall (1963), Jeff Healey (1983), and Stevie Ray Vaughn (1985).

H.B. BARNUM - LOST LOVE
Child actor, producer, arranger were some of his many titles, but he did release a couple of solo singles too. The instrumental, Lost Love, reached #35 in the Billboard Hot 100, but he did not chart again, turning to arranger.
Weird OHW Fact... He also recorded the first version of, Nut Rocker, credited to Jack B. Nimble and the Quicks, a UK one hit wonder for B. Bumble and the Stingers.

THE FLARES - FOOT STOMPIN'–PART 1
Written by Aaron Collins, and recorded by The Flares on Felstead Records. Formed in Los Angeles, this band went through many name (Debonaires, Flairs, Peppers, Ermines) and personnel changes. As the Flares, they achieved their only hit, reaching #25 in the Billboard Hot 100, and #20 in the Black Singles Chart.

THE HALOS - NAG
This Bronx doo wop group formed as session musicians. Their first single, L-O-V-E was under the name, The Craftys, but their second single charted. Nag reached #25 in the Billboard Hot 100, but despite singing on many other artists' hits, they never charted again.

JANIE GRANT - TRIANGLE
Written and recorded by sixteen year old Janie Grant (born Rose Marie Casilli) on Caprice Records, it spent 13 weeks in the Billboard Hot 100 and peaked at #29. Her two follow-ups did not climb so high; Romeo, (#75 in 1961) and, That Greasy Kid Stuff, (#74 in 1962).

THE JARMELS - A LITTLE BIT OF SOAP
Written by Bert Berns, it was recorded was a song, first sung in a bluesy soul style by The Jarmels, from Richmond, Virginia, on Laurie Records. The song reached #12 in the Billboard Hot 100, and #7 in the R&B Charts. Despite many attempts, they never charted again.
Weird OHW Fact... A 1963 version in Asia, by the Hong Kong-based, Cliff Foenander and The Fabulous Echoes, spent a staggering 25 weeks at number 1 in top ten charts in Asia.

Weird OHW Fact... In 1978, Showaddywaddy's version reached #5 in UK Chart.

JOE BARRY - I'M A FOOL TO CARE
Sold over 1 million copies.
Born Joseph Barrios, Louisiana's Barry struck 'gold' with his second release. Originally a hit for Les Paul and Mary Ford, it was recorded on Smash Records, reaching #24 in the Billboard Hot 100, #15 in the Black Singles Chart, and #49 in the UK Chart. The follow-up, Teardrops in My Heart, did not make the Top 40.

JØRGEN INGMANN AND HIS GUITAR - APACHE
Written by Jerry Lordan, and recorded originally by Bert Weedon, the Shadows had the international hit (Top 10 in ten countries, and #1 in four), but their version did not chart in the USA. Danish jazz guitarist Jørgen Ingmann's cover reached #2 in the Billboard Hot 100, #9 in the R&B Chart, and #2 in Canada. He had hits elsewhere, but never again in the USA.
Weird OHW Fact... Apache remains one of the worlds most covered instrumental tracks.

JOSE JIMENEZ (BILL DANA) - THE ASTRONAUT (PART 1 AND 2)
The Steve Allen Show introduced Bill Dana as a fictional Bolivian character, José Jiménez, who couldn't settle into one occupation. Eventually they found a job; astronaut. The sketch was put on vinyl and released, getting to #19 in the Billboard Hot 100.
Weird OHW Fact... An album, José Jiminez in Orbit (Bill Dana on Earth) followed.

KENNY DINO - YOUR MA SAID YOU CRIED IN YOUR SLEEP LAST NIGHT
From Queens, New York, Dino came in second in a Navy talent show in Iceland. He signed with Columbia Records, and this was his first single, and only hit. The song reached #24 in the Billboard Hot 100, and sung until his death in 2009.
Weird OHW Fact... On the record, the backing group were Lois Green, Leslie Smith and Alan Eichler, all students at Syosset High School at the time.
Weird OHW Fact... Dino was dogged by bad choices; he was offered an opportunity to record a duet with Paul Simon but turned it down. Later, he was offered the song, Suspicion, but his record company nixed the project.

Weird OHW Fact... In the UK, actor Doug Sheldon's version was the hit, reaching #29 in the UK singles chart.

Weird OHW Fact... Ex Led Zeppelin vocalist, Robert Plant recorded a version of the song for his 1990 album Manic Nirvana.

KOKOMO - ASIA MINOR

This was an instrumental recording by jazz pianist Jimmy Wisner, who used the pseudonym of 'Kokomo', not to distance his fan base. The rock 'n' roll version of Grieg's Piano Concerto in A Minor reached #8 in the Billboard Hot 100, and #35 in the UK Charts.

Weird OHW Fact... The recording was turned down by ten record companies, so Wisner released it on his own.

Weird OHW Fact... The recording was banned by the BBC, citing the record "distorted melody, harmony and rhythm".

LITTLE CAESAR & THE ROMANS - THOSE OLDIES BUT GOODIES (REMIND ME OF YOU)

Written by Nick Curinga and Paul Politi, this nostalgic tune was recorded by Los Angeles band on Del-Fi Records. It reached #9 in the Billboard Hot 100, and #28 in the R&B Chart. Their follow up only got to #101.

Weird OHW Fact... Occasionally the group's live show included wearing togas on stage and notably on Dick Clark's American Bandstand TV show.

Weird OHW Fact... Before settling on the name, Little Caesar & the Romans, the band was called, The Cubans, but changed their name briefly to The Upfronts after the Bay of Pigs Invasion.

THE MARATHONS – PEANUT BUTTER

Written by Hidle Brown Barnum, Martin Cooper, Fred Smith and Cliff Goldsmith, it was recorded on Arvee Records. The line-up at this stage was Jimmy Johnson (Lead), Carl Fisher (Ténor), Dave Govan (Baritone), and Carver Bunkum (Bass). It reached #20 in the Billboard Hot 100 in 1961. Supposedly, the Olympics were on tour so their manager secretly signed the Vibrations to record this song as 'The Marathons'. Unfortunately for the band, Chess Records discovered the fraud and stopped Arvee records from releasing further copies. It was also released on Argo records. (See featured spot above, The American One-Hit-Wonder Kings...)

Weird OHW Fact... The peanut bar, Snickers, was called 'Marathon' in the UK for many years.

THE MAR-KEYS - LAST NIGHT
Sold over 1 million copies.
Written by band members Charles Axton, Floyd Newman, along with Gilbert C. Caple, Jerry Lee Smith and Chips Moman, it was recorded on Satellite Records by Memphis band, The Mar-Keys. The song reached #3 in the Billboard Hot 100, and #2 in the R&B Charts. They released their last album in 1971.

PAUL DINO - GINNIE BELL
Written by Paul Dino, and recorded on Promo Records, it reached #38 in the Billboard Hot 100.

PHILIP UPCHURCH COMBO - YOU CAN'T SIT DOWN, PART 2
Sold over 1 million copies.
Co-written by two band members in 1959, and named, Can't Sit Down, it was re-vamped two years later and recorded on Parkway Records. You Can't Sit Down, Part 2, reached #29 in the Billboard Hot 100. The band did not chart again.
Weird OHW Fact... The following year a vocal version by the Dovells reached #3.

THE RAMRODS - (GHOST) RIDERS IN THE SKY
Written in 1948 by Stan Jones, and covered by many, Connecticut's The Ramrods' version on Amy Records used overdubbing and twangy guitars, taking the song to #30 in the Billboard Hot 100, and #8 in the UK Chart. Their follow-up, Loch Lomond Rock, an instrumental featuring twang guitar, sax and bagpipes, did not chart.

ROCHELL AND THE CANDLES - ONCE UPON A TIME
Written by Jimmy Johnson, it was recorded by this curiously-named all-male African American from Los Angeles on Swingin' Records. The group comprised Rochell Henderson, Johnny Wyatt, Mel Sasso and T.C. Henderson. The song reached #26 in the Billboard Hot 100.
Weird OHW facts... The high 'female' voice is actually Johnny Wyatt.

ROY DRUSKY - THREE HEARTS IN A TANGLE
Written by Ray Pennington and Sonny Thompson in 1958, it was first recorded by Pennington under the stage name 'Ray Starr', but withdrew it, dis-satisfied with the production. Roy Drusky's version on Decca Records got to #35 in the Billboard Hot 100, and #2 in the Country Chart.

Weird OHW Fact... In 1962, James Brown changed the time signature to 4/4 time, and his version got to #18 in the R&B Chart.

SHELBY FLINT - ANGEL ON MY SHOULDERS

Written by Shelby Flint in 1960 and recorded on Valiant Records, it reached #22 in the Billboard Hot 100. It was covered by three other artists, Jerry Wallace, Kathy Young, and Jimmy Young, but neither of them charted.

THE SHELLS - BABY, OH BABY

Written by Johnston, Bouknight, Coleman, and released on Johnson records, this Brooklyn doo-wop group scored a one hit wonder in 1957, reaching the Top 30. When the single was re-released in 1961, it got to #21 in the Billboard Hot 100. Subsequent singles were not so successful. They broke up a year later.

SHEP AND THE LIMELITES - DADDY'S HOME

Written by the three band members, James 'Shep' Sheppard, Clarence Bassett and Charles Baskerville and recorded on Hull Records. It reached #2 in the Billboard Hot 100, but the follow-up, Ready for Your Love, just skirted the Top 40 at #42.

THE STARLETS - BETTER TELL HIM NO

Written by Bernice Williams for his Chicago girl group, The Starlets, and recorded on Pam Records. The record reached #38 in the Billboard Hot 100, and they toured with Jackie Wilson, Mary Wells, and Gladys Knight & the Pips. Their follow-up single, My Last Cry, never charted. (Also see The Blue-belles entry, 1962)

THE STEREOS - I REALLY LOVE YOU

Written by Leroy Swearingen and first recorded by his Ohio vocal group, The Stereos, on Cub Records. It reached #29 in the Billboard Hot 100, and #15 in the U.S. Black Singles Chart.
Weird OHW Fact... In 1982 George Harrison covered the song on his album, Gone Troppo.

TROY SHONDELL - THIS TIME

Written by Chips Moman, it was first recorded by Thomas Wayne (see 1958 entry, Tragedy). Troy Shondell's version on Goldcrest Records was the biggest hit, spending 13 weeks in the Billboard Hot 100, and reaching #6. It also got to #4 in Norway and Canada, #8 in New Zealand, and #18 in the UK Charts.

THE VELVETS - TONIGHT (COULD BE THE NIGHT)

This is a strange one. The Velvets were a doo-wop group from Odessa, Texas. The members were Virgil Johnson, a high-school English teacher, and four of his students. Roy Orbison was responsible for getting them signed to Monument Records, and the song reached #26 in the Billboard Hot 100. Their follow-up, Laugh, just got to #90.

OH SO CLOSE... BUT NO CIGAR...

JIMMY DEAN – BIG BAD JOHN

Jimmy Dean was an American Country singer, and his biggest hit, Big Bad John reached #1 in the Billboard Hot 100, and #2 in the UK Chart. Most think he's a one hit wonder. But the readers of this book know better. In the US, he had other hits, PT-109 (US#8), but the 1962 hit, Little Black Book, keeps him out of every one hit wonder list. It reached #29 in the US and #33 in the UK.

1962...

As the Beatles audition for Decca Records, and are rejected, the year begins...
An avalanche in Peru kills an estimated 20,000 people, the Taco Bell restaurant chain is started, the 1962 FIFA World Cup is held in Chile, the first Walmart store opens in Rogers, Arkansas, President John F. Kennedy announces the space race at Rice University and the Cuban Missile Crisis stops the world.

ACKER BILK - STRANGER ON THE SHORE
Reached #1 in USA.
Sold over 1 million copies.
Written by Bernard Stanley 'Acker' Bilk for his daughter, the clarinet-led instrumental was a smash hit. It reached #2 in the UK, (one of many hits) then when released in the USA, went straight to #1 in the Billboard Hot 100, in the USA, where he is a one hit wonder.
Weird OHW Fact... It was the first UK hit to reach #1 since the launch of the Billboard Hot 100.
Weird OHW Fact... Acker got his nickname from the Somerset slang for 'friend' or 'mate'.

ARTHUR ALEXANDER - YOU BETTER MOVE ON
Written by Arthur Alexander, it was recorded at Muscle Shoals, Alabama on Dot Records. . It reached #24 in the Billboard Hot 100. Despite many releases, it would be his only chart hit. Bobby Vee also had a version in 1962, but it failed to chart.
Weird OHW Fact... The Rolling Stones recorded the song in 1964, on the album, December's Children (And Everybody's).

BARBARA GEORGE - I KNOW (YOU DON'T LOVE ME NO MORE)
Written by Eula Mae Jackson, it would be Barbara George's (born Barbara Ann Smith) debut single, and released on A.F.O. Records. It reached #3 in the Billboard Hot 100, and #1 in the R&B Chart. Her follow-ups, You Talk About Love, and, Send For Me (If You Need Some Lovin'), both hit the Billboard Hot 100, but not in the Top 40.
Weird OHW Fact... Eula Mae Jackson was in fact, Barbara George's mother.

BARBARA LYNN - YOU'LL LOSE A GOOD THING

Written by Barbara Lynn Ozen, and recorded on Jamie Records, her version was blues based, and it reached #8 in the Billboard Hot 100, and #1 in the R&B Chart. Her follow-up, Second Fiddle Girl, reached #63, her highest subsequent entry.

Weird OHW Fact... In 1975, Freddy Fender's country version of the song reached #1 in the Country Chart, and #32 in the Billboard Hot 100.

B. BUMBLE AND THE STINGERS – THE NUT ROCKER

Having already had US hits with rock versions of 'In The Mood', and 'Bumble Boogie', the band had a couple of mediocre singles, then recorded their spoof, rock version of the march from Tchaikovsky's, The Nutcracker, reaching #23 in the Billboard Hot 100. Released in the UK on Top Rank Records, the single went to #1 in the UK Chart, but it would be their only hit.

Weird OHW Fact... A version by Jack B. Nimble and the Quicks was released in the US in the same year, but was not a hit.

Weird OHW Fact... In 1972, Emerson, Lake & Palmer did their own version, reaching #19 in the UK Chart, and #70 in the Billboard Hot 100.

BENT FABRIC AND HIS PIANO - ALLEY CAT

Reached #1 in Australia.

Sold over 1 million copies.

In 1961, Bent Fabricius-Bjerre wrote the instrumental 'Omkring et flygel'... roughly translated as 'Around a Piano'. It was an instant hit in his native Denmark. Re-marketed as 'Alley Cat' it reached #1 in Australia, #7 in the Billboard Hot 100, and #49 in Germany. The follow-up, Chicken Feed, peaked at #63 in the Billboard Hot 100.

Weird OHW Fact... In 2003, after an absence of 40 years, Bent Fabric returned to the Danish charts, the single, Jukebox, reached #3, and, Shake, reached #10.

BILLY JOE AND THE CHECKMATES - PERCOLATOR (TWIST)

This was a novelty version of a Maxwell House advertising jingle, co-written by Billy Joe Hunter (born Lewis Joseph Bedinsky, but changed his name to Bedell) and some session musicians. The single reached #10 in the Billboard Hot 100, but despite writing and recording songs, the ensemble never charted again.

Weird OHW Fact... In 1955 Bedell formed Era records, and recorded Gogi Grant's The Wayward Wind, (see 1956 entry) and Chanson d'Amour, by Art and Dotty Todd (see 1958 entry).

THE BLUE-BELLES - I SOLD MY HEART TO THE JUNKMAN

Chicago's The Starlets have already been listed in the book (see 1961 entry), but in 1962, they were poached by Newtown Records for a one off recording. The single was released under the name, The Blue-Belles, rose in the charts. Reaching #15, a 'dummy' band was recruited to lip synch for TV shows, and this included Patti LaBelle.

Weird OHW Fact... The Starlets sued Newtown Records, and were awarded $5000 each.

BOB BRAUN - TILL DEATH DO US PART

Perhaps better known for, The Bob Braun Show, which he hosted from 1967 to 1984 five days a week, Braun also had a brief singing career. On Decca Records, he released, Till Death Do Us Part, which reached #26 in the Billboard Hot 100. Braun tried in vain many times for another hit.

Weird OHW fact... In 1969, Braun interviewed TV anchorman Nick Clooney and his young son, George. The 8 year old talked about his recent tonsillectomy. It was George Clooney's first time on TV.

BOBBY GREGG AND HIS FRIENDS - THE JAM–PART 1

Before Robert J. 'Bobby' Gregg was a member of The Band, with Bob Dylan, he fronted Bobby Gregg and His Friends for an instrumental single. The Jam - Part 1, on Epic Records, reached #29 in the Billboard Hot 100, and #14 in the R&B Chart. His follow-up, Potato Peeler, only reached #89.

Weird OHW Fact... He played drums on Bob Dylan's, Like A Rolling Stone, and Simon and Garfunkel's, The Sound of Silence.

BUNKER HILL - HIDE AND GO SEEK–PART 1

Born David Walker, and known as such for his gospel singing, in some circles he is better known by his R&B stage name, Bunker Hill. He only had one moment of chart joy, reaching #33 in the Billboard Hot 100, and #27 in the R&B Chart.

Weird OHW Fact... Despite changing his name for his R&B recordings, he was found out by his gospel choir, Mighty Clouds of Joy, and fired.

THE CASCADES – RHYTHM OF THE RAIN

Reached #1 in Canada and Ireland.

Sold more than 1 million copies.

Written by band member John Claude Gummoe, it was recorded on Valiant Records. It reached #3 in the Billboard Hot 100, and #1 in the Easy Listening Chart. Outside the US, it topped the Canadian and Irish Charts, and reached #3 in Australia, #5 in the UK, and #7 in Norway.

The band charted again, but their best effort was, Maybe the Rain Will Fall, (US#61 in 1969). (Yup, they had a thing about 'rain'.)

Billboard ranked the song as #4 of 1963.

Weird OHW Fact... The song was used in the soundtrack of the 1979 film, Quadrophenia.

Weird OHW Fact... The song was written some years earlier while standing watch in the US Navy, during a thunderstorm.

CHARLIE DRAKE - MY BOOMERANG WON'T COME BACK

Reached #1 in Australia.

British 'cheeky chappie' and comedian had a hit on both sides of the Atlantic on Parlophone and United Artists Records with this non politically correct song. Despite being temporarily banned by the BBC, it topped the Aussie chart, and reached #14 in the UK Chart, #3 in Canada, and #21 in the Billboard Hot 100.

Weird OHW Fact... It was banned in the UK until a reference to 'black in the face', was changed to 'blue in the face', a less obvious hit at the Aborigines 'apparently' on the record. Australia, however, had no such grievance against the 'black' mentioned in the song; it reached #1 there by December 1962. One source states the song stayed at #1 for 12 weeks.

CLAUDE KING - WOLVERTON MOUNTAIN

Written by Merle Kilgore and Claude King, it was a rewrite of an earlier song. Recorded on Columbia Records, it was an instant country hit, topping the chart for nine weeks. It also crossed-over to the Billboard Hot 100 at #6 and #3 in the Easy Listening Chart.

Weird OHW Fact... The song is based on a real person called Clifton Clowers who lived on 'Woolverton' Mountain, (the spelling is correct).

CLAUDINE CLARK - PARTY LIGHTS

Written by Claudine Clark, from Macon Georgia, it was recorded as her second single on Chancellor Records. The song reached #5 in the Billboard Hot 100, but her follow-up, the jauntily-named, Walkin' Through a Cemetery, did not chart.

THE CONTOURS - DO YOU LOVE ME

Written by Berry Gordy, the song was originally intended for the Temptations. When Gordy couldn't find them, The Contours recorded it on Gordy Records, taking it to #3 in the Billboard Hot 100, and #1 in the R&B Chart. It was The Contours only hit, and it was covered by a host of bands, including the Tremeloes who took it to #1 in the UK Chart. Other notable versions were the Dave Clark Five, The Sonics, The Kingsmen, Paul Revere & the Raiders, and Johnny Thunders and the Heartbreakers.

Weird OHW Fact... After being featured in Dirty Dancing, it shot back into the US chart, peaking at #11 in the Billboard Hot 100.

THE CORSAIRS - SMOKY PLACES

Consisting of the three Uzell brothers, Jay, James and Moses, and their cousin, George Wooten, this doo-wop group from La Grange, North Carolina recorded Smoky Places as their second single. It reached #12 in the Billboard Hot 100, and #10 in the R&B Chart. Their follow-up, I'll Take You Home, only reached #62, the best of their subsequent efforts.

DON AND JUAN - WHAT'S YOUR NAME?

Written by Claude 'Juan' Johnson, it was recorded by Don and Juan on Big Top Records. The song reached #7 in the Billboard Hot 100. Their follow-up, Magic Wand, did not chart.

DON GARDNER AND DEE DEE FORD - I NEED YOUR LOVING

Written by Bobby Robinson and Don Gardner, and recorded by Gardner and singer Dee Dee Ford. The song reached #20 in the Billboard Hot 100, and #4 in the R&B Chart. Their highest follow-up, Don't You Worry, only reached #66.

Weird OHW Fact... Don is not to be confused with the writer of, All I Want for Christmas Is My Two Front Teeth, that song written by Donald Yetter Gardner.

EDDIE HOLLAND - JAMIE

Before Edward 'Eddie' Holland Jr. became a huge songwriter and producer, with over 200 hits under his name, he tried his own hand at recording. Jamie reached #30 in the Billboard Hot 100, and #6 in the R&B Chart. He did not chart again, the closest was, Just Ain't Enough Love, which just reached #54. Holland is a huge player in the Motown Record label and sound.

EMILIO PERICOLI - AL DI LÀ

Sold over 1 million copies.

When Betty Curtis won the Sanremo festival Al di là, Italian singer, Pericoli recorded his own version of the song. It was worldwide hit, reaching #6 in the Billboard Hot 100, #3 in the Adult Contemporary Chart, and #30 in the UK Chart.

Weird OHW Fact... Pericoli entered Sanremo himself the next year, but his song, Quando, Quando, Quando, was not a hit in the US.

ERNIE MARESCA - SHOUT! SHOUT! (KNOCK YOURSELF OUT)

Written by Ernie Maresca and Thomas F. Bogdany, it was originally recorded by Maresca on Seville Records. The song reached #6 in the Billboard Hot 100, and #25 in the R&B Chart.

Weird OHW Fact... Maresca wrote, The Wanderer, for Dion (US #2, 1961)

Weird OHW Fact... Maresca also co-wrote many hits for Dion and other artists, including, Runaround Sue (US#1, 1961).

TELL HIM - THE EXCITERS

Reached #1 in France.

Written by Bert Berns (as Bert Russell), it was recorded by The Exciters on United Artists Records. Originally entitled 'Tell Her', and first recorded by Johnny Thunder, The Exciters' version, Tell Him, reached #4 in the Billboard Hot 100, #5 in the R&B Chart, #5 in Australia, and topped the French Chart.

Weird OHW Fact... In the UK, the Exciters' single reached #46, while a version by Billie Davis reached #10 in the UK Chart.

FRANK IFIELD - I REMEMBER YOU

Written in 1941 by Victor Schertzinger and Johnny Mercer, it was recorded by Australian yodeler, Frank Ifield, who had the song's biggest hit. His version reached #1 in the UK, and #5 in the Billboard Hot 100, and #1 in the Easy Listening Chart.

Weird OHW Fact... It was then covered by Slim Whitman, and the yodeling style is now a standard.

Weird OHW Fact... Johnny Mercer supposedly wrote the song for Judy Garland, giving it to her on the day she married David Rose.

GEORGE MAHARIS - TEACH ME TONIGHT

From Astoria, Queens, New York City, this actor/singer is better known for his film work, or as Buz Murdock in the TV series Route 66. He recorded many albums and singles, but just one charted, Teach Me Tonight, reaching #25 in the Billboard Hot 100.

Weird OHW Fact... In the July 1973 issue of Playgirl magazine, he posed nude for the magazine.

JACK ROSS - CINDERELLA

Jack Ross was a contemporary of Elvis Presley. In 1962 he released his first single, Cinderella, a spoof spoonerism rendition of the Cinderella story, reaching #16 in the Billboard Hot 100. His follow-ups, Margarita, and, Happy Jose [Ching Ching], did not chart.

JAMES RAY- IF YOU GOT TO MAKE A FOOL OF SOMEBODY
Written by Rudy Clark, it was recorded by African American R&B singer James Jay Raymond on Caprice Records. The song reached #22, in the Billboard Hot 100. His follow-up single was, Itty Bitty Pieces, which reached #41 in the Billboard Hot 100. So close, but he's a one hit wonder.
Destitute when he had the hit, his story, just goes downhill. He died in 1963 from a drug overdose.
Weird OHW Fact… The song was covered by the Beatles, and in the UK, Freddie and the Dreamers had the hit (UK#5, 1962).
Weird OHW Fact… James Ray also recorded the very first version of, Got My Mind Set on You, later a 1988, #1 hit for George Harrison, and a song also written by Rudy Clark.

JIMMY ELLEDGE - FUNNY HOW TIME SLIPS AWAY
Sold more than 1 million copies.
Written by Willie Nelson and first recorded by country singer Billy Walker in 1961, it was recorded by Jimmy Elledge on RCA Victor. Elledge's version reached #22 in the Billboard Hot 100. His follow-ups did not chart, and he remained a one hit wonder.

JIMMY MCGRIFF - I GOT A WOMAN, PART 1
Written by legend, Ray Charles, it was recorded by Jimmy McGriff on Sue Records. His version reached #20 in the Billboard Hot 100.
Weird OHW Fact… Dire Straits mention the song by name in their massive hit, Walk of Life, from the 1985 album, Brothers in Arms.

JIMMY SMITH - WALK ON THE WILD SIDE–PART 2
Written by Mack David and Elmer Bernstein as the lead song for the movie of the same name, it was recorded as an instrumental on the album, The Unpredictable Jimmy Smith. The single reached #21 in the Billboard Hot 100. It was his only hit.

JOANIE SOMMERS - JOHNNY GET ANGRY
Written by Edwards/David, it was recorded as her second single by singer/actress, Joanie Sommers on Warner Brothers records. It reached #7 in the Billboard Hot 100. She continued to record, but none charted.

Weird OHW Fact... Sommers' debut single, One Boy, from the musical, Bye Bye Birdie, reached #54 in the Billboard Hot 100.

JO ANN CAMPBELL - (I'M THE GIRL ON) WOLVERTON MOUNTAIN
Already having had a minor hit with, Motorcycle Michael, (US#41 1961), she followed up the song with a reply to Claude King's, Wolverton Mountain (see Claude King's entry above). The song reached #38 in the Billboard Hot 100. The best of her follow-ups reached US#88.

JOE HENDERSON - SNAP YOUR FINGERS
Written by Grady Martin and Alex Zanetis, it was originally recorded by gospel singer Joe Henderson on Todd Records. His version reached #8 in the Billboard Hot 100, and #2 in the R&B Chart. He had 3 minor hits after that, Big Love, The Searching Is Over, and, You Take One Step (I'll Take Two).
Weird OHW Fact... He died in 1964, from a heart attack, aged just 27.

KENNY BALL AND HIS JAZZMEN - MIDNIGHT IN MOSCOW
Sold more than 1 million copies.
Written by Vasily Solovyov-Sedoi and Mikhail Matusovsky in 1955, it was recorded by the British jazz group, Kenny Ball and his Jazzmen on Kapp Records. Their instrumental reached #2 in the UK Charts, then crossed the pond and landed in the #2 spot in the Billboard Hot 100, #1 in the Easy Listening Chart.
Weird OHW Fact... The song was originally called Leningradskie Vechera, (Leningrad Nights).

KETTY LESTER - LOVE LETTERS
Sold over 1 million copies.
Written by Victor Young and Edward Heyman, it was recorded by Ketty Lester (born Revoyda Frierson) on Era Records as her second single. Originally intended to be the B-side, it was played by DJ's and rose in the charts. It reached #5 in the Billboard Hot 100, #2 in the R&B Chart, and also #4 in the UK Chart.
Weird OHW Fact... She was extremely close to having a second hit; her follow-up, Gershwin's, But Not For Me, reached #41 in the US and #45 in the UK.
Weird OHW Fact... Lester is also is known for her acting role as Hester-Sue Terhune on TV series Little House on the Prairie.

KRIS JENSEN - TORTURE

Written by John D. Loudermilk Jr., it was recorded by Kris Jensen, from New Haven, Connecticut, on Hickory Records. The song reached #20 in the Billboard Hot 100, but despite recording many more songs, it would be Jensen's only hit.

Weird OHW Fact... Loudermilk originally wrote the song for The Everly Brothers, but only after witnessing Jensen's success did the Everly brothers record the song.

LARRY FINNEGAN - DEAR ONE
Reached #1 in Australia.
Sold more than 1 million copies.
Written by Larry Finnegan and Vincent Finneran it was recorded by New Yorker, Finnegan on Old Town Records. It reached #1 in Australia and #11 in the Billboard Hot 100. It would be his only hit, and never charted in the Hot 100 again.

Weird OHW Fact... In 1965 he moved to Sweden, setting up the record label SvenskAmerican. As well as promoting native singers, he also recorded his own songs in Swedish.

LITTLE JOEY AND THE FLIPS - BONGO STOMP
The band, from Philadelphia, Pennsylvania, recorded the song on Joy Records. Joey Hall's voice, (the only black member of the band) sounded like a young boy, but was actually 19 when the record was released. It reached #33 in the Billboard Hot 100. Their follow-ups, Bongo Gully, and, Fool, Fool, Fool, did not chart.

MARCIE BLANE – BOBBY'S GIRL
Sold more than 1 million copies.
Written by Gary Klein and Henry Hoffman, it was recorded by Brooklyn teenager, Marcie Blane (born Marcie Blank) on Seville Records. It shot into the Top 10, making Blane the hottest female singer in America. The song reached #3 in the Billboard Hot 100. However, despite the enormity of the hit, her follow-up, What Does A Girl Do?, only got to #82.

Weird OHW Fact... In the UK, the song was covered by Susan Maughan. (see entry below)

Weird OHW Fact... Blane originally only demo'd the song as a favor to a friend.

THE MAJORS - A WONDERFUL DREAM
The Majors, an R&B and Doo-wop group, hailed from Philadelphia, Pennsylvania. Their first single, A Wonderful Dream, on Imperial

Records reached #22 in the Billboard Hot 100, #23 in the R&B Chart. Their follow-up, She's A Troublemaker, only reached #63.

MIKE CLIFFORD - CLOSE TO CATHY

Written by Earl Shuman and Bob Goodman, the song was recorded as Clifford's first session with United Artists Records. The song reached #12 in the Billboard Hot 100, and stayed in the chart for 12 weeks. His follow-up, What To Do With Laurie, only reached #67.

Weird OHW Fact... Clifford had minor hits in Argentina, Brazil, Venezuela, Chile, the Philippines, Canada, Germany and Japan.

NATHANIEL MAYER AND THE FABULOUS TWILIGHTS - VILLAGE OF LOVE

From Detroit, Michigan, and originally released on Fortune Records, the song reached #22 in the Billboard Hot 100. His follow-ups, Leave Me Alone, and I Had A Dream, failed to chart.

Weird OHW Fact... Mayer literally disappeared for 30 years, re-surfacing to record again in 2002.

THE ORLONS - DON'T HANG UP

Written by Dave Appell and Kal Mann, it was released by The Orlons as a follow-up to their #2 Billboard Hot 100 hit, Wah-Watusi. Don't Hang Up got to #4 in the Billboard Hot 100, and charted at #39 in the UK Chart. The UK did not 'get' the Watusi song, and the band did not chart there again, making them one hit wonders in the UK.

PHIL MCLEAN - SMALL SAD SAM

Written by Sunny Skylar, Small Sad Sam was a parody of Jimmy Dean's #1 hit, Big Bad John. Phil Mclean was a DJ on WERE radio in Cleveland, and he recorded the song on Versatile Records. It reached #21 in the Billboard Hot 100

REX ALLEN - DON'T GO NEAR THE INDIANS

Rex Allen is a TV and movie star, famous for his voice-overs and narration. He even has his own star on Hollywood's sidewalk. His only hit single, Don't Go Near The Indians, reached #17 in the Billboard Hot 100, and Top 5 in the Country Chart.

Weird OHW Fact... Basically in the song, the man in love with an Indian cannot marry her because he was kidnapped as a baby and the girl is his sister.

Weird OHW Fact... Allen died in 1999 after being run over accidentally by his own care giver.

RONNIE & THE HI-LITES - I WISH THAT WE WERE MARRIED

Written by Weiss and Lewis, it was recorded on Joy records by the doo-wop group from Jersey City. It reached #16 in the Billboard Hot 100, and stayed in the chart 12 weeks, selling half a million copies.

Weird OHW Fact... Their lead singer was 12 year old Ronnie Goodson. His girlfriend, Eva Boyd would go on to record, The Locomotion (US#1, 1962)

THE ROUTERS - LET'S GO (PONY)

Written by Lanny and Robert Duncan, when members of The Starlighters, it was recorded on Warner brothers Records. It reached #19 in the Billboard Hot 100, and #32 in the UK Chart.

Weird OHW Fact... The song is remembered for its repetitious, clap clap clap-clap-clap clap-clap-clap-clap Let's Go! Chant.

Weird OHW Fact... The original Starlighters demo included guitars by Tony Valentino and Jody Rich, who went on to form The Standells, and a hit, Dirty Water. (One hit wonder in 1966, see entry)

THE SENSATIONS - LET ME IN

From Philadelphia, Pennsylvania, The Sensations had already had two R&B Chart hits in the late 50's before breaking up and starting families. Lead singer, Yvonne Mills wrote, Let Me In, and the band reformed, recording their new hit on Chess Records, reaching #4 in the Billboard Hot 100 and #2 in the R&B Chart. Their follow-ups were unsuccessful.

Weird OHW Fact... Yvonne Baker went solo, and recorded, You Didn't Say a Word, well known in Northern Soul circles.

THE SHERRYS - POP POP POP-PIE

Written by Johnny Madara and Dave White to cash in on a dance craze called, The Popeye, it was recorded on Guyden Records. It reached #35 in the Billboard Hot 100, and #25 in the R&B Chart. A follow-up, Slop Time, (cashing in on another dance, The Slop) failed to chart.

THE SPRINGFIELDS - SILVER THREADS AND GOLDEN NEEDLES

Reached #1 in Australia.
Sold over 1 million copies.
Written by Jack Rhodes and Dick Reynolds, it was first recorded by Wanda Jackson in 1956. However, it is better known as being recorded by newly-formed British trio, The Springfields (Including a young Dusty Springfield, her brother Tom Springfield, and Mike Hurst) as their third single. (Their first two singles had been hits in the UK, Breakaway,

UK#31, and bambino, UK#16) Silver Threads And Golden Needles was an international hit, reaching #20 in the Billboard Hot 100, the first single by a British group to reach the Top 20, announcing the beginning of the British Invasion. The trio had more hits in the UK before breaking up, including, Island of Dreams, (UK#5), and, Say I Won't Be There, (UK#5), but they are a one hit wonder in the US.

Weird OHW fact... The Springfields beat the Tornados', Telstar, by two months, (see entry below) and The Beatles by 15 months.

Weird OHW Fact... Dusty Springfield's real name is Mary Isobel Catherine Bernadette O'Brien, changed immediately prior to forming The Springfields.

Weird OHW Fact... Tom Springfield (born Dionysius 'Dion' P. A. O'Brien) became producer and songwriter for The Seekers. He wrote, I'll Never Find Another You, A World of Our Own, and, The Carnival is Over. He also co-wrote, Georgy Girl, with Jim Dale, nominated for an Academy Award for Best Original Song of 1966.

Weird OHW Fact... Mike Hurst formed the Methods, which included band members, Jimmy Page and Albert Lee. He discovered Marc Bolan and Cat Stevens, and produced The Move, Manfred Mann, and Spencer Davis, before discovering Showaddywaddy, Shakin' Stevens and Samantha Fox.

STAN KENTON - MAMA SING A SONG

Written and first recorded by Bill Anderson, the song reached #1 in the Country Chart. Stan Kenton's version, (featuring a narrative spoken by Kenton), reached #32 in the Billboard Hot 100, earning him a Grammy nomination in the Best Documentary or Spoken Word Recording category.

Weird OHW Fact... Although Anderson's version topped the Country Chart, and spent 27 weeks in the Country Top 40, its position in the Billboard Hot 100 (#US#*89) was dwarfed by other versions, Stan Kenton (US#35), actor Walter Brennan (US#38).

SUSAN MAUGHAN – BOBBY'S GIRL

Written by Gary Klein and Henry Hoffman, and originally a hit for Marcie Blane (see entry above), it was recorded by Susan Maughan from Birmingham, England. Her version reached #3 in the UK Chart, #6 in Ireland, #6 in Norway, and #5 in Israel. Obviously, being in this list, she's a one hit wonder.

Weird OHW Fact... However, she tried very hard to escape the one-hit-wonder tag; her follow-ups were, Hand a Handkerchief to Helen, (UK#41 1962), and, She's New To You, (UK #45 1963). So close!

THE TORNADOS - TELSTAR

Reached #1 in UK, USA, Belgium, South Africa and Ireland.

Sold more than 5 million copies.

Written by Joe Meek for the English band the Tornados, who recorded the song on Decca Records and London Records. It reached #1 in the UK Chart, #1 in the Billboard Hot 100, and #1 in Ireland, Belgium, and South Africa, $3 in Norway and Holland, and #6 in Germany. The song stayed at UK #1 for five weeks, and stayed in the chart for an amazing 25 weeks.

Weird OHW Fact... The single reached #5 in the Billboard Black Singles chart. This is weird, because, as far as I can determine, none of the group were remotely black.

Weird OHW Fact... Telstar was actually an AT&T communications satellite, launched into orbit on 10 July 1962.

Weird OHW Fact... Although Acker Bilk and Kenny Ball had US #1's in 1962, they were jazz in orientation, and not particularly part of the 'British Invasion'. If The Springfield's hit, Silver Threads And Golden Needles, (the first hit by a British band into the US Top 20) was the launch of the 'British Invasion', then Telstar announced that it had well and truly landed on the beaches!

(For details on all those songs, see above entries; they're all one hit wonders!)

Finally...

Weird OHW Fact... Meek was taken to court for plagiarism by a French composer, Jean Ledrut, and he did not receive one penny in royalties until the case would be concluded. Ledrut claimed Meek had gotten Telstar from a piece called, La Marche d'Austerlitz. The case was eventually decided in Meeks favor, but not until **three weeks after Meek's suicide**. A real tragedy.

TRADE MARTIN - THAT STRANGER USED TO BE MY GIRL

An American songwriter and producer, he also released a few solo singles. One of these, on Coed records, That Stranger Used to Be My Girl, reached #28 in the Billboard Hot 100.

Weird OHW Fact... Martin also released, We've Got To Stop The Mosque At Ground Zero in 2010. The ground intended for the mosque is now going to be a residential building.

VALJEAN - THEME FROM BEN CASEY

Valjean Johns was an American pianist, and is probably best known for the theme song from the TV show Ben Casey. The recording reached #28 in the Billboard Hot 100. The success of the single prompted an album, Theme from Ben Casey, which reached #113 in the Billboard Album Chart.

THE VOLUMES - I LOVE YOU

Written by the band's bassist, Ernest Newsom and their manager, Willie Ewing, it was recorded on Chex Records. It reached #22 in the Billboard Hot 100. Their follow-up, Come Back Into My Heart, did not chart, and the band broke up in 1965.

1963...

As Britain's pride and joy, the steam locomotive Flying Scotsman makes its final journey, the year begins...
Harold Wilson becomes Prime Minister of the UK, Alcatraz Federal Penitentiary closes, Alfred Hitchcock's film The Birds is released, General Hospital debuts on ABC, Coca-Cola introduces its first diet drink, Tab cola, the Great Train Robbery takes place in England, President John F. Kennedy is assassinated by Lee Harvey Oswald.

ALLAN SHERMAN - HELLO MUDDAH, HELLO FADDUH
Written by Allan Sherman, Amilcare Ponchielli, and Lou Busch, this novelty song was modelled on letters of complaint Sherman received from his son Robert while at Camp. The song reached #2 for three weeks in the Billboard Hot 100, and the follow-up, The Twelve Gifts Of Christmas, got to #5. However, in the UK, Hello Mudduh, Hello Fadduh, was his only charting hit.

BABY WASHINGTON - THAT'S HOW HEARTACHES ARE MADE
Jeanette (Baby) Washington was raised in Harlem, New York, was a soul singer, with two minor hits in her catalogue before she hit the 'big time'. The Time, (R&B #22) and, The Bells, (R&B # 20) established her as an up and coming talent. She joined Sue Records, and recorded, That's How Heartaches Are Made, reaching the pinnacle of #40 in the Billboard Hot 100, #10 in the R&B Chart. Although a regular in the R&B Chart, it would be her only mainstream hit.
Weird OHW Fact... Dusty Springfield described Washington as her 'all-time favorite singer', recording both this song, and, I Can't Wait Until I See My Baby's Face'.

BARRY & THE TAMERLANES - I WONDER WHAT SHE'S DOING TONIGHT
Written by band member and creator of Valiant Records, Barry De Vorzon, and offered to The Cascades. When they didn't record the song, De Vorzon's own trio did. It reached #21 in the Billboard Hot 100, spending 10 weeks in the chart, and got to #23 in the R&B Chart. De Vorzon went on to songwriting and production.
Weird OHW Fact... De Vorzon wrote Nadia's Theme, from the Young and Restless TV show, a one hit wonder in 1976.

Weird OHW Fact... De Vorzon also managed Dorsey Burnette, a one hit wonder in 1960, and he wrote, Hey Little One, recorded by her (#48) and Glen Campbell (#54).

Weird OHW Fact... Don't confuse this song with 1968's, I Wonder What She's Doing Tonight, written and recorded by Tommy Boyce and Bobby Hart (#8).

BETTY HARRIS - CRY TO ME

Written by Bert Berns, it was first recorded by Solomon Burke in 1961. Both Betty Harris and Dionne Warwick released the song in 1963; Harris's slower version (produced by Berns) reached #25 in the Billboard Hot 100, and #10 in the R&B Chart. Warwick's version did not chart. Three more singles followed, but were not successful.

Weird OHW Fact... The song was covered by the Pretty Things, Rolling Stones, and Tom Petty.

BIG DEE IRWIN (WITH LITTLE EVA) - SWINGIN' ON A STAR

Written by Jimmy Van Heusen and Johnny Burke, it was made famous by Bing Crosby in the 1944 film, Going My Way. Big Dee Irwin (with Little Eva, of Loco-Motion fame) reached #38 in the Billboard Hot 100, and #7 in the UK Chart, making him tour there for 9 month on the strength of its success.

Weird OHW Fact... Even with Little Eva's help, Irwin never charted again, the closest being the duet, Happy Being Fat.

BILL ANDERSON - STILL

Written by Bill Anderson, he recorded the song on Decca Records. It would be his second Country Chart #1 (topped the chart for 7 weeks), and crossed over to the Billboard Hot 100 at a very respectable #8. It would be his only mainstream hit.

Weird OHW Fact... Anderson hosted the game show, the Better Sex, with Sarah Purcell.

Weird OHW Fact... In 1963 it was covered by Al Martino, Bing Crosby, Karl Denver (UK#15), and Ken Dodd (UK#35).

BILL PURSELL - OUR WINTER LOVE

Written by Johnny Cowell, the instrumental piece was recorded on Columbia Records by Oakland's Bill Pursell. His version reached #9 in the Billboard Hot 100, #20 in the R&B Chart, #12 in Australia, and #25 in Canada. He never charted again.

Weird OHW Fact... Pursell worked hard as a session keyboardist, and played piano on many of Johnny Cash's albums.

BOOTS RANDOLPH - YAKETY SAX

Composed by James Q. 'Spider' Rich and Boots Randolph, it was recorded by saxophonist Boots Randolph (born Homer Louis Randolph III) firstly on RCA Victor, then on Monument Records, where it became a hit. It reached #35 in the Billboard Hot 100, and is considered his signature tune.

Weird OHW Fact... It is based on the 1958 song, Yakkity Yak, by The Coasters.

Weird OHW Fact... It is perhaps better known as the closing theme music for The Benny Hill Show. Benny Hill had his own one hit wonder in 1971, with Ernie (The Fastest Milkman In The West).

THE BRUISERS - BLUE GIRL

Written by lead singer Daniel Boone (born Peter Green) and the band's manager, Barry Mason, it was recorded by The Bruisers, and the single went to #31 in the UK Chart. The band did not chart again, and broke up in 1967.

Weird OHW Fact... Daniel Boone went on to write and record, Beautiful Sunday, a multi-million selling one hit wonder in 1972.

Weird OHW Fact... Barry Mason went on to write many hits, including, Love Grows (Where My Rosemary Goes), a one hit wonder for Edison Lighthouse in 1970.

THE BUSTERS - BUST OUT

Written by Dave Benjamin, it was recorded by Massachusetts band, The Busters, on Arlen Records. The guitar/sax instrumental reached #25 in the Billboard Hot 100. They never charted again. The B-side, Astronaut's, is also well worth a listen to.

THE CARAVELLES - YOU DON'T HAVE TO BE A BABY TO CRY

Written by Bob Merrill and Terry Shand, it was first a hit in the 50's for Ernest Tubb, Moon Mullican, and Tennessee Ernie Ford. Recorded by British duo (Lois Wilkinson and Andrea Simpson), they took it higher than ever before, #3 in the Billboard Hot 100, #6 in the UK Chart, and #48 in Australia. It was their only hit.

Weird OHW Fact... The Caravelles were named after the Sud Aviation Caravelle, a French aircraft.

THE CLASSICS - TILL THEN

Written by Eddie Seiler, Sol Marcus, and Guy Wood in 1944, the song had already charted before The Classics recorded it, The Mills Brothers

(US#8 1944), and The Hilltoppers (US#10 1954). Their version reached #20 in the Billboard Hot 100, and #7 in the Adult Contemporary Chart. Changing labels frequently, they split up in 1966.

THE CHANTAYS - PIPELINE
Written by band members Brian Carman and Bob Spickard, this is perhaps the biggest surf instrumental ever. Released on Downey Records, it reached #4 in the Billboard Hot 100, and became a signature tune of the age.
Weird OHW Fact... The tune was originally called 'Liberty's Whip', but was renamed after the band members watched a surfing movie, and the image of a surf 'pipeline' became marked in their minds.

THE DARTELLS - HOT PASTRAMI
From Oxnard, California, the group got together while teenagers, and recorded a demo of Hot Pastrami. They were signed by Dot Records, and the single reached #11 in the Billboard Hot 100, #15 in the R&B Chart. Their follow-up singles failed, the best being, Dance Everybody Dance, which got to #99.
Weird OHW Fact... The lyrics of Hot Pastrami are a lampoon of Nat Kendrick and the Swans, (Do The) Mashed Potatoes. (Actually recorded by James Brown and his band, but name changed due to contract difficulties)

DAVE DUDLEY - SIX DAYS ON THE ROAD
Written by Earl Green and Carl Montgomery in 1961, it was originally recorded by Paul Davis. Dave Dudley's version of this 'trucking song' reached #32 in the Billboard Hot 100, and #2 in the Country Chart. It is often revered as the first of all trucking road songs.

DIANE RAY - PLEASE DON'T TALK TO THE LIFEGUARD
Written by Sylvia Dee and George Goehring, it was recorded by North Carolina's Diane Ray for her expectation filled album, The Exciting Years. The single reached #31 in the Billboard Hot 100. She would not chart again.

DORIS TROY - JUST ONE LOOK
Reached #1 in Canada.
Written by Doris Troy and Gregory Carroll, it was a hit before the Hollies covered it in 1964. Doris Troy's original version topped the Canadian Chart, and reached #10 in the Billboard Hot 100, #3 in the R&B Chart, and #8 in New Zealand.

Billboard ranked the song as #81 in 1963.

Weird OHW Fact... The Hollies reached #2 in the UK Chart, and #98 in the Billboard Hot 100; it was their first US 'hit'.

THE EARLS - REMEMBER THEN

Written by Tony Powers and Beverly Ross, (some also give credit to producer, Stan Vincent) and first recorded by Bronx doo-wop vocal group The Earls, sometimes known as 'Larry Chance and the Earls'. It reached #24 in the Billboard Hot 100, and #29 in the R&B Chart. Their follow-ups, Never, and, Eyes, did not make the top 40.

Weird OHW Fact... Beverly Ross also wrote, Lollipop. (One hit wonder in 1958, see entry).

Weird OHW Fact... Larry Chance went to high school in Philadelphia with Chubby Checker and Frankie Avalon.

THE GLENCOVES - HOOTENANNY

Credited on the record to Deane, Goehring, and Horther, it was recorded on Select Records by Long Island folk group, The Glencoves. The single reached #38 in the Billboard Hot 100, but no other hits were recorded.

Weird OHW Fact... Band singer Bill Byrne became Mayor of Morgantown, West Virginia.

Weird OHW Fact... A 'Hootenanny', is a singalong party.

INEZ AND CHARLIE FOXX - MOCKINGBIRD

The lullaby was recorded by Inez Foxx and her brother Charlie on Sue Records. It was a hit, reaching #7 in the Billboard Hot 100, #2 in the R&B Chart, and #7 in the Black Singles Chart. It did not chart in the UK until its re-release in 1969.

Weird OHW Fact... Inez Foxx's best follow-up, Hurt By Love, reached #54 in the USA and #40 in the UK. Ironically that takes her out of the one-hit-wonder bin in the UK, but made her one in her native land.

JACK NITZSCHE - THE LONELY SURFER

Written by Bernard Alfred 'Jack' Nitzsche, his instrumental reached #39 in the Billboard Hot 100. A small detail in such an illustrious musical career, but a detail nevertheless. Nitzsche, born in Chicago, was a musical giant, Phil Spector's right hand man, music score writer (Exorcist and One Flew Over The Cuckoo's Nest) of over 30 films, and song writer for many of music's greats.

JAMES GILREATH - LITTLE BAND OF GOLD

Written by James William Gilreath from Prairie, Mississippi, the song was released on Statue Records in Tupelo, Mississippi. Released nationally on Joy Records, it reached #21 in the Billboard Hot 100, and #19 in the R&B Chart. It also got to #29 in the UK Chart. His follow-ups, Lollipops, Lace, and Lipstick, and, Keep Her Out of Sight, did not chart.

JAN BRADLEY - MAMA DIDN'T LIE
Written by Curtis Mayfield, it was recorded by Mississippian Jan, (born Addie) Bradley, on Midwest Records. Her first Mayfield song, We Girls, did not chart, but Mama Didn't Lie (now on Chess records) reached #14 in the Billboard Hot 100, and #8 in the R&B Chart.
Weird OHW Fact... Overshadowed by Mayfield and Chess disputing royalties, Bradley started writing her own songs and, I'm Over You, was a minor hit (R&B#24 1965).

THE JAYNETTS - SALLY GO 'ROUND THE ROSES
Written by Lona Stevens and Zell Sanders, the song was recorded on Chess Records by the newly formed girl singing group from the Bronx, New York. It reached #2 in the Billboard Hot 100, #7 in France, and #2 in New Zealand. The follow-up singles came close, Keep an Eye on Her, just missed the Hot 100, and, Dear Abby, reached #94.

JOE HARNELL AND HIS ORCHESTRA - FLY ME TO THE MOON–BOSSA NOVA
Joseph Harnell was an American composer and arranger, and had played with the Glen Miller band during the war. His only hit was his arrangement of, Fly Me To the Moon, on Kapp Records, which reached #14 in the Billboard Hot 100, and #4 in Adult Contemporary Chart.
Weird OHW Fact... Harnell recorded 20 albums in his musical career.

JOHNNY THUNDER - LOOP DE LOOP
This slow handclap version of the children's nursery song, Looby Loo,63, was initiated by record producer Teddy Vann, who had the idea, and suggested the new name, Johnny Thunder. On Diamond Records, it reached #4 in the Billboard Hot 100. Of all his follow-ups, Everybody Do The Sloopy, was the most successful at #67.
Weird OHW Fact... As well as changing his name for the recording, Vann released his age as ten years younger to appeal to the teenage market.

KAI WINDING - MORE

Danish trombonist and composer Kai Chresten Winding played with many of the big bands of the 40's and 50's, including Benny Goodman's. He recorded a version of, Time Is On My Side, before the Rolling Stones recorded it. He only had one solo hit, however, More, the theme from the movie, Mondo cane. It reached #8 in the Billboard Hot 100.

Weird OHW Fact... He recorded over 40 albums as band leader, and over 60 as a contributing artist.

KYU SAKAMOTO - SUKIYAKI
Reached #1 in USA.
Sold more than 13 million copies.
Written by Rokusuke Ei and Hachidai Nakamura, the song was recorded by 22 year old Japanese Actor and singer, Kyu Sakamoto. His worldwide hit, sung in Japanese, Ue o Muite Arukō, ('I look up when I walk') was known as 'Sukiyaki' to most of the world, and sold more than 13 million copies. It reached #1 in the USA Billboard Hot 100, and #6 in the UK Charts.

Weird OHW Fact... It was the first Japanese song to enter either the US or the UK chart.

Weird OHW Fact... Sakamoto died in the crash of Japan Airlines Flight 123 in 1985, aged just 43.

LES COOPER AND HIS SOUL ROCKERS - WIGGLE WOBBLE
From Norfolk, Virginia, Cooper sang in a few doo-wop groups, including The Empires and The Whirlers. His instrumental, Wiggle Wobble, was a surprise hit, reaching #22 in the Billboard Hot 100, and #12 in the R&B Chart. His follow-up, Let's Do the Boston Monkey, on Enjoy Records, did not chart.

LITTLE JOHNNY TAYLOR - PART TIME LOVE
Written by Clay Hammond this blues song was first recorded by Little Johnny Taylor on Galaxy Records, as his second single. It reached #19 in the Billboard Hot 100, and was #1 in the R&B Chart. His follow-ups, Since I Found A New Love, (#78 1964) and, Everybody Knows About My Good Thing Pt.1, (#60 1970) came close, but close enough.

Weird OHW Fact... Little Johnny Taylor is often confused with the more successful, Johnnie Taylor, mostly because Johnnie Taylor recorded a version of this song. Befuddling, huh?

LOS INDIOS TABAJARAS - MARIA ELENA
Sold over 1 million copies.

Written in Spanish in 1932 by Lorenzo Barcelata, English lyrics were added by Bob Russell. It was recorded in 1958 by Los Indios Tabajaras, Natalicio and Antenor Lima, guitar playing brothers from Brazil. It reached #6 in the Billboard Hot 100, #3 in the East Listening Chart, and #5 in the UK Chart.

Weird OHW Fact... The duo recorded over 50 albums in a 40 year career.

Weird OHW Fact... It was covered by The Shadows in 1967, and by Ry Cooder in 1972.

NED MILLER - FROM A JACK TO A KING

Written by country singer Ned Miller, it was first released in 1957, with limited success. Five years later the single was re-issued at Miller's urging, and it crossed over into the mainstream charts, reaching #6 in the Billboard Hot 100, #2 in the Country Chart, and #3 in the Adult Contemporary Chart. It also reached #1 in Ireland, and #2 in the UK Chart.

Weird OHW Fact... In the UK it was the sixth most-played single of 1963.

Weird OHW Fact... It has been covered many times, notably by Elvis, Jim Reeves, and Jerry Lee Lewis.

THE PASTEL SIX - CINNAMON CINDER (IT'S A VERY NICE DANCE)

Written by Russ Regan, it was released by The Pastel Six on Zen Records. It served as a promotional record for a chain of LA teen nightclubs in Los Angeles, California. It reached #25 in the Billboard Hot 100, but the band did not chart again.

Weird OHW Fact... If you took away the lyrics from the song, you could substitute Curtis Lee's 'Under The Moon Of Love, in their place. (See Curtis Lee's entry, 1961)

THE PIXIES THREE - BIRTHDAY PARTY

This girl trio of Midge Bollinger, Kaye McCool, and Debra Swisher were just 16, and still at high school when they were signed to Mercury records. Their first single grazed the Billboard Hot 100 at #40, but their follow up, 442 Glenwood Avenue/Cold, Cold Winter, only got to #56.

Weird OHW Fact... The trio toured with Bobby Goldsboro and The Rolling Stones, then, in 1965, eventually graduated from high school. They did not chart again.

THE RAINDROPS - THE KIND OF BOY YOU CAN'T FORGET

Married in 1962, Ellie Greenwich and Jeff Barry formed The Raindrops the following year. Their first single, What A Guy, reached #41, but their follow-up took them to #17 in the Billboard Hot 100. It would be their last charting single.

Weird OHW Fact... In 1963, a follow-up, That Boy John, bombed after the assassination of John F. Kennedy.

Weird OHW Fact... Press photographs of the group often showed them as a trio, using Greenwich's younger sister Laura, who did not sing on the records. Rarely performing live with the same line-up, sometimes a second female singer was used to fill the group on stage, (sometimes the younger sister), singing into a dead microphone.

THE RAN-DELLS - MARTIAN HOP

Written by band members John Spirit, Robert Lawrence Rappaport, and Steve Rappaport, this novelty song was recorded on Chairman Records. It reached #16 in the Billboard Hot 100, and #27 in the Black Singles Chart.

Weird OHW Fact... It may be the world's first ever 'sample'... The song's short introduction is an uncredited sample from the 1962 record, Moon Maid, by Tom Dissevelt and Dick Raaymakers.

RANDY & THE RAINBOWS - DENISE

Written by Neil Levenson, it was inspired by his childhood friend, Denise Lefrak. Recorded by doo-wop Randy & the Rainbows, from Queens, New York, it reached #10 in the Billboard Hot 100, #18 in the Black Singles Chart, and #5 in Canada. Their follow-up single, Why Do Kids Grow Up, just got to #97.

Weird OHW Fact... in 1977, a cover version (with the name changed to Denis) broke Blondie to the world, Netherlands #1, Belgium #1 and UK #2.

RAY BARRETTO - EL WATUSI

Ray Barretto, a conga player, had a brief moment of solo greatness. He recorded a version of the Latin dance craze, El Watusi on Columbia Records and took the song to #17 in the Billboard Hot 100.

Weird OHW Fact... Although he probably enjoyed the cash injection, he hated being typecast in this role and soon refused to play such music.

THE REBELS - WILD WEEKEND

Written by Tom Shannon and Phil Todaro, it was recorded in 1961 by the group from Buffalo, New York, but the single flopped. Re-released in 1963 on Swan records, it reached #8 in the Billboard Hot 100.

Weird OHW Fact... To avoid confusion with 'Duane Eddy and his Rebels', the Rebels soon changed their name to the Rockin' Rebels. Records can be found both names.

ROBIN WARD - WONDERFUL SUMMER
Sold over 1 million copies.
Written by songwriter/producer Perry Botkin and Gil Garfield, it was given to Robin Ward (Jackie Ward) to record a demo. To achieve a higher pitched voice, it was sped up, and a name change requested (to that of her daughter, Robin). The finished single reached #14 in the Billboard Hot 100, and because of the speed/name change, it is a one hit wonder.
Weird OHW Fact... However! Jackie ward has had her singing voice on over 800 movies and is heard on the theme songs dozens of others including Flipper, Batman, and one of the voices in The Partridge Family.

THE ROCKY FELLERS - KILLER JOE
Written by Bert Russell, Phil Medley, and Bob Elgin, the song was recorded by the American-born Filipino pop/rock band on Scepter Records. The song reached #16 in the Billboard Hot 100, but the follow-up, another Elgin song, Like the Big Guys Do, did not chart.
Weird OHW Fact... Killer Joe was inspired by the infamous 'King of the Discothèque', Killer Joe Piro.

ROLF HARRIS - TIE ME KANGAROO DOWN, SPORT
Written by Australian Rolf Harris in 1957, it became a hit around the world in two different years. In 1960, it was #1 in Australia, #2 in the UK, and Top 10 in many countries. It wasn't until a new recording (produced with Beatles guru, George Martin) in 1963 that Rolf Harris hit America, reaching #3 in the Billboard Hot 100, and topping the Easy Listening Chart for 3 weeks. Harris would have many hits worldwide, but never again in the USA where he remains a one hit wonder.
Weird OHW Fact... Harris originally offered his unknown Australian backing musicians 10% of the royalties, but they refused, having no confidence in the song, taking £28 ($40) to be divided equally among them instead.
Weird OHW Fact... the weird 'wobble' sound is from a 'wobble board, a 3ft by 2ft piece of hardboard (Masonite for you Americans).
Weird OHW Fact... In 1963, Harris sang the song on a BBC radio show, with the Beatles playing guitars and singing backing vocals, and the verses changed to include every Beatles' name.

Weird OHW Fact... The fourth verse has reference to Abo's, a slur on the Aboriginal people of Australia. In today's more politically correct times, Harris has expressed apologies for its use.

THE SECRETS - THE BOY NEXT DOOR
Written by Johnny Madara and David White, the song was recorded by the American girl group The Secrets (originally called The Sonnets) from Cleveland, Ohio on Philips Records. The song reached #18 in the US Billboard Hot 100, and although three singles followed the hit, none of them charted.

Weird OHW Fact... (See The Raindrops entry above) The JFK assassination interrupted another group's search for stardom...The Secrets were booked for American Bandstand on the weekend of November 22, 1963, but the show was cancelled due to coverage of the assassination.

SUNNY & THE SUNGLOWS - TALK TO ME
Written and recorded by Joe Seneca in 1958, it was covered by Sunny & the Sunglows from San Antonio, Texas on Tear Drop records. The song reached #11 in the Billboard Hot 100, #4 in the Adult Contemporary Chart, and #12 in the Black Singles Chart. It was covered by the Beach Boys in1976.

THE SURFARIS - WIPE OUT
Written by Bob Berryhill, Pat Connolly, Jim Fuller, and Ron Wilson, the instrumental is an iconic tune from the 'surf' era. It reached #2 in the Billboard Hot 100, #10 in the Hot R&B Chart, #5 in Canada, and #5 in the UK Chart.

Weird OHW Fact... In 1987, The Fat Boys & The Beach Boys did their own version, reaching #12 in the Billboard Hot 100, and #2 in the UK Chart.

Weird OHW Fact... The surfing term, 'wipeout', describes a surfer coming to a fall, usually violent, painful or turbulent.

THE SINGING NUN - DOMINIQUE
Sold over 2 million copies.
Jeanne-Paule Marie 'Jeannine' Deckers was a Belgian singer-songwriter who joined a religious order in 1959. When she continued to write and sing songs in the convent, it was decided to make an album to sell in the convent shop to raise funds. The single, Dominique, sung in Belgian on Philips Records, took the world by storm, reaching #1 in the Billboard Hot 100, and in many other countries.

Weird OHW Fact... Deckers and her lesbian lover committed suicide in 1985, citing financial worries as a contributing cause. They are buried together.

THEOLA KILGORE - THE LOVE OF MY MAN

From Shreveport, Louisiana, like so many singers, she began singing in church choir. She recorded a few demos, but her break came with an adaptation of, The Love of God, recorded by the Soul Stirrers. On Serock Records, the single reached #21 in the Billboard Hot 100, and #3 in the R&B Chart. Her follow-up, This Is My Prayer, peaked at just #60.

TOM GLAZER AND THE DO-RE-MI CHILDREN'S CHORUS - ON TOP OF SPAGHETTI

Written by Sharon Ruth and Philip Anders, the song is an adaptation of the old standard, On Top of Old Smokey. It was recorded by folk singer/songwriter Tom Glazer, (born Thomas Zachariah Glazer) on Kapp Records. The song reached #14 in the Billboard Hot 100. It was his only entry in the mainstream charts.

THE VILLAGE STOMPERS - WASHINGTON SQUARE

This Dixieland jazz group from Greenwich Village in New York City recorded Washington Square on Epic Records. It reached #2 in the Billboard Hot 100, and #1 in the Adult Contemporary Chart. Their follow-ups came close, From Russia with Love, (#81 1964) and, Fiddler on the Roof, (#97 1964) did not change their one hit wonder status.

VINCE GUARALDI TRIO - CAST YOUR FATE TO THE WIND

This instrumental selection was written and recorded by jazz pianist Vince Guaraldi (born Vincent Anthony Dellaglio) on Parkway Records. It reached #22 in the Billboard Hot 100, and would be his only charting hit.

Weird OHW Fact... In 1965 the British group, Sounds Orchestral, reworked the jazz out of the piece, and reached #5 in the UK Chart, #10 in the Billboard Hot 100, and spent 3 weeks at #1 in the Easy Listening chart.

1964...

As the 'British Invasion' of America takes a solid form with The Beatles, The Dave Clark Five, The Kinks, The Rolling Stones, Herman's Hermits, The Animals, Dusty Springfield and Sandie Shaw, the year begins...

Plans for the NYC World Trade Center are announced, the Beatles vault to the #1 in the Billboard Hot 100, and star on the Ed Sullivan Show, the game show Jeopardy debuts on NBC, Sidney Poitier is the first African-American to win an Academy Award, Nelson Mandela is sentenced to life imprisonment in South Africa, the Warren Commission publishes its report.

THE AD LIBS – THE BOY FROM NEW YORK CITY

Written by George Davis and John T. Taylor, it was originally recorded by soul group The Ad Libs on Blue Cat Records. It was their second single and reached #8 in the Billboard Hot 100. It was their only chart hit.

Weird OHW Fact... Elsewhere, there would be two versions of the hit to choose from, Darts (UK #2, and Ireland#3 in 1978), and Manhattan Transfer (New Zealand #2, US#8, Switzerland #3 and Canada #8 in 1981).

ASTRUD GILBERTO - THE GIRL FROM IPANEMA

Written by Antônio Carlos Jobim and Vinicius de Moraes in 1962, the English lyrics were added later, and an English version recorded. Gilberto's version reached #5 in the Billboard Hot 100, and spent two weeks at #1 in the easy Listening Chart. It charted all over the world, hitting #29 in the UK Charts.

In 1965 it won a Grammy for Record of the Year.

Weird OHW fact... Astrud Gilberto had never recorded before, and just happened to be at the recording studio with her husband. Everyone at the recording thought her voice perfect for the song, and it stayed.

THE CAREFREES - WE LOVE YOU BEATLES

This British group came together in 1964, and will always be known as the group who sang, We Love You Beatles. The song reached #39 in the Billboard Hot 100, but their follow-up did not chart. The band broke up within the same year they formed.

THE CHARTBUSTERS - SHE'S THE ONE

From Washington, D.C., this optimistically-named band recorded just one hit. She's The One was released on Mutual Records and reached #33 in the Billboard Hot 100. It stayed in the Hot 100 for 8 weeks. None of their follow-ups even made the chart.

Weird OHW Fact... The band's demo of the song had been turned down by 20 record labels before Mutual took them on.

CILLA BLACK - YOU'RE MY WORLD
Sold over 1 million copies.

Written and recorded in 1963 Umberto Bindi and Gino Paoli as 'Il Mio Mondo' ('My World'). English lyrics were added by Carl Sigman, and the song took off. Liverpool's Cilla Black's (born Priscilla Maria Veronica White) version was her second UK #1 hit and entered many of the world charts, Australia, New Zealand, Europe, South Africa and Canada, but it was her only US chart entry, hence its inclusion here. The single reached #26 in the Billboard Hot 100, and #1 in the UK Chart.

Weird OHW Fact... Burt Bacharach asked Cilla to record, Alfie, the theme song for the soon-to-be-released film. But even that couldn't break the US again, Cher's version reached #32 instead.

Weird OHW Fact... Cilla Black released 18 studio albums, and had 19 Top 40 hits in the UK.

Weird OHW Fact... She died in 2015, and the day after her funeral, a compilation album of her songs went to number one on the UK Albums Chart... It was Cilla Black's first number one album.

DALE WARD - LETTER FROM SHERRY
Written by Kenneth Moffitt, it was recorded by dale ward on Dot Records. The single reached #25 in the Billboard Hot 100, but none of his other singles charted.

DANNY WILLIAMS - WHITE ON WHITE
Although Danny Williams was a South African pop singer, he had the nickname, 'Britain's Johnny Mathis. With his smooth singing style, he topped the UK Chart with, Moon River, before Andy Williams did his version. White on White reached #9 in the Billboard Hot 100, and #9 in Canada, but the song bombed in the UK.

Weird OHW Fact... Williams appeared in the 1962 movie, Play It Cool (1962), starring Billy Fury as pop singer Billy Universe.

THE DEVOTIONS - RIP VAN WINKLE
From Astoria, Queens, New York, the doo wop group, The Devotions, took three releases to get their record into the charts. Released in

1961on Delta Records, then switching to Roulette Records in 1962 and in 1964, it finally reached #36 in the Billboard Hot 100. The Devotions are still performing as of 2016.

EARL-JEAN - I'M INTO SOMETHIN' GOOD

Written by husband and wife team Gerry Goffin and Carole King, it was recorded by Brooklyn's Earl-Jean 'Jeanie' Reavis (born Earl-Jean McCrea) on Colpix Records. Earl-Jean had been a member of the girl band, the Cookies and had two hits under their belts. Going solo for the first time, I'm Into Somethin' Good, reached #38 in the Billboard Hot 100. Her follow up song (Goffin/King), Randy You're Quite A Guy, failed to chart.

Weird OHW Fact... That same year, Herman's Hermits covered the song and reached #1 in the UK Charts, #13 in the Billboard Hot 100, and #7 in Canada.

Weird OHW Fact... The Cookies two hits were also penned by Goffin and King, Don't Say Nothin' Bad (About My Baby), (US #7), and Chains, (US# 17).

Weird OHW Fact... When Earl-Jean cut the record, she was pregnant with Goffin's baby. Goffin and King gave her financial support, but she retired from the music industry and became a early childcare specialist, opening a day care center.

GALE GARNETT - WE'LL SING IN THE SUNSHINE

Reached #1 in New Zealand.
Sold over 1 million copies.
Written and recorded by Gale Garnett on RCA Victor Records, it reached #1 in her native New Zealand, #4 in the Billboard Hot 100, #1 in the Easy Listening chart and #10 in Australia. Her follow-up, Lovin' Place, reached #54 in the Billboard Hot 100, but the rest did not chart. In the UK, The Lancastrians cover got highest, a disappointing #44. The song won the Grammy for Best Folk Recording in 1965.

Weird OHW Fact... Garnett turned to writing and acting, and had a supporting role in many films, including, My Big Fat Greek Wedding.

Weird OHW Fact... The Lancastrian version included guitars by Jimmy Page and Big Jim Sullivan.

GLORIA LYNNE - I WISH YOU LOVE

Written in French in 1942 by Léo Chauliac and Charles Trenet, English lyrics were added by Albert Askew Beach in 1957. Recorded by Harlem's Gloria Lynne on Everest Records, it reached #28 in the Billboard Hot 100, and #10 in the Easy Listening Chart. I Should Care, was her immediate follow-up, (US#64 1964), and, Watermelon Man, was her best attempt (US#62 1965)

Weird OHW Fact... Lynne's recording career spanned a staggering fifty years, from 1958 to 2007.

HELMUT ZACHARIAS – TOKYO MELODY

The theme, used by the BBC in the UK for its Winter Olympic coverage, was recorded by Helmut Zacharias, German violinist and composer. The record got to #9 in the UK Singles Chart. As far as I can tell, it was his only UK hit.

THE HONDELLS - LITTLE HONDA

Written by Beach Boys, Brian Wilson and Mike Love, it was recorded by them on their album, All Summer Long. Producer Gary Usher immediately assembled a group of session musicians (including Glen Campbell) for an album project, an album with songs all about the Honda motorcycle entitled, Go Little Honda. Called The Hondells, their first recording got to #9 in the Billboard Hot 100, and #21 in Australia. The project soon ran out of steam, their follow-up single, My Buddy Seat, only got to #87.

Weird OHW Fact... The song pays homage to the 'small' Honda 50 motorcycle.

Weird OHW Fact... After seeing the success of The Hondells version, Capitol Records released it as a single for the Beach Boys, reaching just #65 in the U.S. Billboard 100.

Weird OHW Fact... After hearing Glen Campbell's vocals on the record, he was snatched up by The Beach Boys to tour, sitting in for Brian Wilson, playing bass, and singing high harmonies.

THE HONEYCOMBS - HAVE I THE RIGHT?

Reached #1 in the UK, Australia and Canada.
Sold over 1 million copies.
Written by Ken Howard and Alan Blaikley, the song was given to London's The Sheratons, who changed their name for the release to The Honeycombs to cash in on their oddity; a female drummer called Honey Lantree. The song charted slowly, but soon hit #1 in the UK, #3 in Ireland, and #2 in the Netherlands. Overseas, it topped the Australian and Canadian charts, and reached #5 in the Billboard Hot 100. The band would go on to have another 3 Top 40 hits in the UK, but never charted in the USA again, their best attempt being, I Can't Stop, which got to #48.

Weird OHW Fact... Unusually for the time, The Honeycombs recorded their own German version of the song, 'Hab ich das Recht?', and both the English and the German versions reached #21 in the German charts.

Weird OHW Fact... The song was recorded in producer Joe Meeks apartment, the same place Telstar was recorded (One Hit Wonder in 1962, see entry).

IRMA THOMAS - WISH SOMEONE WOULD CARE

In a long hard working career, Irma Thomas scored only one mainstream chart hit. Wish Someone Would Care, on Imperial records reached #17 in the Billboard Hot 100, but her immediate follow-up, Anyone Who Knows What Love Is (Will Understand), just got to #52.

Weird OHW Fact... In a career spanning 50 years, she won the Grammy Award for Best Contemporary Blues Album for, After the Rain, in 2007.

J. FRANK WILSON AND THE CAVELIERS - LAST KISS

Sold over 1 million copies.

Written and first recorded by Wayne Cochran, who based the idea on a car accident near his home, it was not a hit. Recorded by The Caveliers on Josie Records, it was attempt #64 in the recording studio that made it onto the record. It was a smash hit, reaching #2 in the Billboard Hot 100.

Billboard ranked the song as #9 in 1964.

Weird OHW Fact... Ironically (considering the lyrics) while touring to promote the record, the manager fell asleep at the wheel, and crossed the centerline, going head-on into a trailer truck. He was killed outright, but the band survived with serious injuries. Wilson sang the song on crutches, and it propelled sales.

Weird OHW Fact... The song was a US Billboard one hit wonder for Canadian band, Wednesday, in 1974.

JACKIE ROSS - SELFISH ONE

Written by McKinley/Smith, it was recorded by hard-working Jackie Ross on Chess Records. The single reached #11 in the U.S. Billboard Hot 100 Chart, and #4 on the Cashbox R&B Chart. Her follow-up's tried hard, I've Got The Skill, reached #89 and in 1965, Jerk and Twine, only got to #85. Discovered by Sam Cooke in 1954, Ross recorded from 1954 to the 1970's.

JIMMY HUGHES - STEAL AWAY

Written by Jimmy J Hughes, (Percy Sledge's cousin), he recorded the ballad on Vee-Jay Records on the Fame label. It reached #17 in the

Billboard Hot 100, and when the follow-up, Try Me, reached # 65, Hughes signed an album deal. In 1966, Neighbor, Neighbor, reached #65 in the Billboard Hot 100, and #4 in the newly formed R&B Chart, but the rest of the follow-ups were not as successful.

THE JELLY BEANS - I WANNA LOVE HIM SO BAD
Written by Jeff Barry and Ellie Greenwich, it was recorded on Red Bird Records, by the vocal group from Jersey City, New Jersey. The single reached #9 in the Billboard Hot 100, and the follow-up came close... Baby Be Mine, peaked at #51. The bad were dropped by Red Bird Records by the end of the year and broke up in 1965.

JOE HINTON - FUNNY (HOW TIME SLIPS AWAY)
Sold over 1 million copies.
Written by Willie Nelson in 1961, it was first recorded by country singer Billy Walker. Mississippi's Joe Hinton's version crossed over from the Country Chart to mainstream, reaching #13 in the Billboard Hot 100, and spent 4 weeks at #1 in the Cash Box R&B Chart. I Want a Little Girl, his follow-up single, reached #34 in the R&B Chart, but did not chart mainstream.
Weird OHW Fact... Hinton died of skin cancer in 1968, at age 38.

JOEY POWERS - MIDNIGHT MARY
Written by Artie Wayne and Ben Raleigh, it was originally intended for the Everly Brothers, but they did not record it. Joey Powers (born Joseph S. 'Joe' Ruggiero, and called Joey Rogers on some 1958 songs) recorded the song on Amy Records, and it reached #10 in the Billboard Hot 100.
Weird OHW Fact... On the strength of the single he quickly recorded an album, Midnight Mary, in the same week J. F. Kennedy was shot. On the album were Paul Simon (then Jerry Landis) and Roger McGuinn.
Weird OHW Fact... Powers was later the manager of, Phantom's Opera, the band that included; Richie Sambora, Tico Torres and Alec John Such, who would form Bon Jovi in 1983.

JUMPIN' GENE SIMMONS - HAUNTED HOUSE
Morris Eugene Simmons was born in Itawamba County, Mississippi. He recorded as early as 1958, but his one hit came in '64, a cover of Johnny Fuller's, Haunted House, and would be his only chart hit. It reached #11 in the Billboard Hot 100.
Weird OHW Fact... He co-wrote, Indian Outlaw, a country hit for Tim McGraw in 1994.

Weird OHW Fact... Kiss bass player Chaim Witz chose Gene Simmons as his stage name as an homage to the singer.

LORNE GREENE - RINGO

Written by Don Robertson and Hal Blair, it became the only hit single for Canadian-born actor Lorne Greene on RCA Victor Records. It reached #1 in the Billboard Hot 100, #1 in the Easy Listening Chart, #21 in the Country Chart, and #1 in Canada.

Weird OHW Fact... The B-side was the song in French, it being Canada's second language.

Weird OHW Fact... It was the last ever spoken #1 in the Billboard Hot 100.

Weird OHW Fact... Lorne Green is better known for his role in the western TV show, Bonanza, and the 70's series, Battlestar Galactica.

MICKEY LEE LANE - SHAGGY DOG

Born in Rochester, New York, Mickey Lee Schreiber played piano for Neil Sedaka, and wrote songs for Bill Haley. He also released the odd single himself, and one made its way to #38 in the Billboard Hot 100, and #36 in Australia. His follow-up, Hey Sah-Lo-Ney, did not chart.

THE MURMAIDS - POPSICLES AND ICICLES

Written by David Gates (founder of Bread), it was recorded by teenage trio, The Murmaids. Sisters Carol and Terry Fischer and their friend Sally Gordon were recording back-up vocals when Kim Fowley from Chattahoochee Records offered them a contract. The single reached a staggering #3 in the Billboard Hot 100, and #12 in Australia, but did not chart in the UK. Two follow-up singles were released, Heartbreak Ahead, and, Wild And Wonderful, but they did not chart.

THE NASHVILLE TEENS - TOBACCO ROAD

Written and first recorded by John D. Loudermilk in 1960, this pop band from Surrey, England, recorded the song on Decca Records after being spotted by Mickey Most touring with Chuck Berry. With Most's production, it was an instant hit, reaching #6 in the UK Chart. It crossed the Atlantic well, getting to #14 in the Billboard Hot 100. They followed it up with another Loudermilk song, Google Eye, which reached #10 in the UK, but failed to chart in the USA, stalling at #117.

Weird OHW Fact... The Nashville Teens were producer Mickey Most's third acquisition, following The Animals, Herman's Hermits.

PATTY & THE EMBLEMS - MIXED-UP, SHOOK-UP GIRL

Written by Ralston McGriff and Leon Huff, it was recorded by Patty & the Emblems (from Camden, New Jersey) on Herald Records. It reached #37 in the Billboard Hot 100, and #13 in the R&B Chart. Recording until 1967, they would not have another hit.

Weird OHW Fact... from 1964 to 1998 Leon Huff wrote hundreds of songs, many of them big hit for well-known artists. This was his very first hit song.

PETER DRAKE AND HIS TALKING STEEL GUITAR - FOREVER

Sold over 1 million copies.

Peter Drake was a Nashville-based producer and pedal steel guitar player. He recorded one solo album, Still, on Smash Records, and the one hit single from it sold a million copies, reaching #25 in the Billboard Hot 100.

Weird OHW Fact... Drake put a tube in his mouth and with the aid of a 'talk box' mixed his words with the sounds of the steel guitar.

THE PREMIERS - FARMER JOHN

Written and first recorded by the duo Don 'Sugarcane' Harris and Dewey Terry in 1959, it was recorded by The Premiers (from San Gabriel, California) as their debut single. With dubbed cheers and party noises it reached #17 in the Billboard Hot 100. They quickly recorded an album full of cover versions of R&B standards, but the band would not chart again.

Weird OHW Fact... Searching for that elusive second hit, the band toured with The Crystals and Gene Pitney, and warmed up stages for the British invaders, The Rolling Stones, The Kinks, and The Dave Clark Five.

THE PYRAMIDS - PENETRATION

Written by S Leonard, it was recorded by The Pyramids on Best Records, and considered to be the final recording of the 'surf era'. It reached #18 in the Billboard Hot 100, but their follow-ups, Midnight Run, and Contact, did not chart.

Weird OHW Fact... In the 1964 movie, Bikini Beach, the band appeared on stage wearing Beatles wigs... they then removed them, revealing their newly shaved heads.

THE REFLECTIONS - (JUST LIKE) ROMEO AND JULIET

Written by Bob Hamilton and Freddie Gorman, it was recorded by doo-wop band, The Reflections, on Golden World Records. The song reached the giddy heights of #6 in the Billboard Hot 100, but the band never charted again.

Weird OHW Fact... Despite many cover versions, the song never charted until Aussie band, Mental As Anything's version in 1980 reached #27 in Australia.

RITA PAVONE - REMEMBER ME

At just 17, Rita Pavone became a star in her native Italy, her songs, La partita di Pallone, (The Soccer Game), and Cuore, (Heart) both sold over one million copies. Two years later she had her only American hit, Remember Me, reaching #26 in the Billboard Hot 100, and #16 in Canada.

Weird OHW Fact... Pavone became a star in many European countries having numerous Top 40 hits.

THE RIVIERAS - CALIFORNIA SUN

Written by Henry Glover in 1960, it was first recorded by Joe Jones without success. Recorded by new band, The Rivieras on Riviera Records, it was originally a B-side, but soon became a hit. It reached #5 in the Billboard Hot 100. The band's follow-ups never got anywhere near; Let's Have a Party, (#99), Little Donna, (#93), and, Rockin' Robin, (#96).

Weird OHW Fact... The song is considered to be the last American Rock and Roll song before the British Invasion. It reached #5 in the same week that the Beatles hit #1 with, I Want To Hold Your Hand.

Weird OHW Fact... The song was included in the soundtrack of the 1987 movie Good Morning, Vietnam.

ROBERT MAXWELL AND HIS HARP AND ORCHESTRA - SHANGRI-LA

Written by New York's Robert Maxwell, he recorded it himself in 1964 on Festival Records, taking it to #15 in the Billboard Hot 100. Maxwell plays the harp himself on the record. He never charted again.

THE SAPPHIRES - WHO DO YOU LOVE

From Philadelphia, Pennsylvania, The Sapphires recorded, Who Do You Love, on Swan Records as their second single. It reached #25 in the Billboard Hot 100, but none of their many follow-ups charted.

Weird OHW Fact... The band's backing singers were... Melba Moore, who peppered the R&B Charts for twenty years, and in the 1970's... and Valerie Simpson and Nick Ashford, who, as married duo Ashford & Simpson, had the smash hit, Solid, in 1984.

THE SWINGING BLUE JEANS - HIPPY HIPPY SHAKE

Written and recorded by Chan Romero (Robert Lee 'Chan' Romero from Billings, Montana), in 1959 when he was just 17 years old, the song reached #3 in Australia. Liverpool band, The Swinging Blue Jeans (originally called The Bluegenes) recorded the song on HMV Records, and got to #2 in the UK Charts, and #24 in the Billboard Hot 100. The follow-up, Good Golly Miss Molly, got close (UK#11, US#43) and, You're No Good, got to #3 in the UK Charts (US#97), but the band would not chart in the USA again, hence their one hit wonder tag.

Weird OHW Fact... The song was recorded by The Beatles before The Swinging Blue Jeans got to it, but they never released the song as a single. The song is hugely Beatle-esque in sound.

TOMMY TUCKER - HIGH-HEEL SNEAKERS

Written and recorded by Tommy Tucker on Checker Records, it reached #11 in the Billboard Hot 100, and #1 in the R&B Chart. In 2017, the song was inducted into the Blues Foundation Blues Hall of Fame.

OH SO CLOSE... BUT NO CIGAR...

PRETTY THINGS – DON'T BRING ME DOWN

Written by Johnny Dee (the manager of The Fairies), it first performed by the British rock band, The Pretty Things. It was a #10 hit in the UK Singles Chart, and #34 in Canada, and it is often thought of as a one hit wonder. However... in the UK, their follow-ups were, Honey I Need, (UK#13), and, Cry to Me, (UK#28).

Result? Not a one hit wonder in the UK, but they are a one hit wonder in Canada.

1965...

As the state funeral of World War 2 Prime Minister Sir Winston Churchill takes place in London, the year begins...
Sir Stanley Matthews, aged 50, plays his final First Division game, in Montgomery, Alabama, 1,600 civil rights marchers demonstrate, My Fair Lady wins 8 Academy Awards, Jim Clark wins the Indianapolis 500 and the Formula One title, the Post Office Tower opens in London, American troops in Vietnam to be increased to 400,000.

ADAM FAITH WITH THE ROULETTES - IT'S ALRIGHT
With nearly 20 UK Top 20 hits under his belt, it was time Adam Faith hit the USA. At the height of the British Invasion, he charted his only US hit on Amy Records, which was not released in the UK. The song went to #31 in the Billboard Hot 100, but his follow-up, Talk About Love, just reached #97.
Weird OHW Fact... To my generation who missed the 1060's music, Adam faith will be remembered as 'Budgie', from a UK TV drama.
Weird OHW Fact... He also managed singer Leo Sayer.

ALVIN CASH AND THE CRAWLERS - TWINE TIME
Born Alvin Welch in St. Louis, Missouri, he and three brothers moved to Chicago to get work as a dance act, The Crawlers. They were approached by One-der-ful Records to do a demo of Twine Time, and it was released as a single. It got to #14 in the Billboard Hot 100, and #4 in the R&B Chart. The follow-ups, Barracuda, got to #59 in the Billboard Hot 100, and, The Philly Freeze, got to #49, but after that the hits failed.
Weird OHW Fact... Although Alvin's brothers appeared as The Crawlers, they did not record a single note, the vocals being provided by local band, The Nightliters.

BARRY MCGUIRE - EVE OF DESTRUCTION
Reached #1 in USA.
Sold over 1 million copies.
Written by P. F. Sloan in 1964, it was recorded by ex-New Christy Minstrels Barry McGuire in the summer of 1965 on Dunhill Records. Born in Oklahoma City, McGuire took the single to #1 in the US Billboard Hot 100, and #3 in the UK Chart.
Weird OHW Fact... The gruff-sounding vocal track was not intended to be on the public version, but a copy of the early recording leaked out to a DJ who, of course, began playing it. McGuire's recording includes a

mumbled fluff where he forgot the words. The more polished vocal track was never issued commercially.

Weird OHW Fact... The single was banned by Radio Scotland.

BOBBY MCCLURE - DON'T MESS UP A GOOD THING

Born in Chicago, Illinois, he began his singing career in church in St. Louis. He recorded Don't Mess Up a Good Thing on Chess Records, and it made the Top 40, reaching #33 in the Billboard Hot 100, and #5 in the Black Singles Chart. His follow-ups were not so successful, You'll Miss Me (When I'm Gone), got to #91, and Peak of Love just made it at #97.

BUCK OWENS AND THE BUCKAROOS - I'VE GOT A TIGER BY THE TAIL

Written by Harlan Howard and Buck Owens, it was released just a week after recording it on Capitol Records. It soon became one of the signature songs on the Texan's live set list. The song reached #1 in the Hot Country Singles Chart, and crossed over to the Billboard Hot 100 at #25, and got to #12 in Canada.

Weird OHW Fact... As the B-side in the UK, Little Things went to #5 in the UK Chart for Dave berry.

Weird OHW Fact... Although regarded as a one hit wonder in non-country circles, Owens recorded 39 studio albums, and had 21 #1's in the Country Chart.

CANNIBAL & THE HEADHUNTERS - LAND OF A THOUSAND DANCES

Written and first recorded by Chris Kenner in 1962, it was recorded by the Mexican-American band from Los Angeles on Rampart Records. Their version reached #30 in the Billboard Hot 100, but it would be their only hit.

Weird OHW Fact... The now infamous, 'na, na na na na' chant in the song, was an improvisation by lead singer Frankie Garcia when he'd forgotten the words in the recording studio. When Wilson Pickett covered the song (US#6, UK#22) in 1966, he kept the chant in.

THE CASTAWAYS - LIAR, LIAR

Written by band members James Donna and Denny Craswell, it was recorded by the rock band from the Twin Cities in Minnesota on Soma Records. It reached #12 in the Billboard Hot 100, but none of the follow-up singles charted.

Weird OHW Fact... It was covered by Debbie Harry in 1988, and wa featured in two great movie soundtracks, Good Morning, Vietnam, and, Lock, Stock and Two Smoking Barrels.

THE DETERGENTS - LEADER OF THE LAUNDROMAT
Well known for recording novelty spoof songs, when the Shangri-Las', Leader of the Pack, was in full swing, the band swung into action. This was their only parody to become a hit, however, and it reached a very respectable #19 in the Billboard Hot 100.

Weird OHW Fact... Not surprisingly the composers of the original song sued, and the suit was settled out of court.

EDDIE RAMBEAU - CONCRETE AND CLAY
Written by Tommy Moeller and Brian Parker (Unit 4 + 2 band members, the original UK artists, UK#1), it was recorded by Eddie Rambeau and released just a week before the Unit 4 + 2 recording hit American stores. Both versions were successful, Unit 4 + 2's reaching #28, and Eddie Rambeau's getting to #35. His follow-up singles, My Name is Mud, and, The Train, did not chart.

Weird OHW Fact... Rambeau could also write songs; Navy Blue, co-written with Bob Crewe and Bud Rehak was a #6 hit for Diane Ray, and their follow-up, Kiss Me Sailor, got to #29.

THE FORTUNES - YOU'VE GOT YOUR TROUBLES
Reached #1 in Canada.
Written by songwriting legends, Roger Greenaway and Roger Cook, the song was recorded by English harmony group, the Fortunes. This, their fifth single, was a massive hit; Top 10 in the Billboard Hot 100, #2 in the UK, and #1 in Canada. Their next two singles were, Here It Comes Again, (UK #4), and, This Golden Ring, (UK #14), but they never scored in the USA again, hence the one hit wonder tag.

FRED HUGHES - OO WEE BABY, I LOVE YOU
From Compton, California, he formed his first band at high school, first the Cymbals, then the Creators. Signed to Vee-Jay Records, he recorded, Oo Wee Baby, I Love You, which reached #23 in the Billboard Hot 100, and #3 in the R&B Chart. His follow-up, You Can't Take It Away, only reached #96. When the record label folded, so did Hughes' career.

Weird OHW Fact... In the UK the song became a soul classic, and was re-released in 1976 by DJM Records to cash in on public demand.

THE GENTRYS - KEEP ON DANCING
Sold more than 1 million copies.
Written by Allen A. Jones and Willie David Young in 1963, and recorded by the Avantis, it was covered by The Gentrys on Youngstown Records.

The song reached #4 in the Billboard Hot 100, staying in the chart for 13 weeks. Their best follow-ups, from 1970 were, Why Should I Cry, (US#61), and, Cinnamon Girl, (US#52).

Weird OHW Fact... This was one of a fashion of hits of the time; a rock beat, mention a bunch of dance crazes that everyone knows, repeat after a short solo, and finish.

Weird OHW Fact... Being an Edinburgh boy myself, I would be ill not to mention that the song was covered by The Bay City Rollers in 1971 (UK#9).

GLENN YARBROUGH - BABY THE RAIN MUST FALL
Originally with the Limeliters, Glenn Robertson Yarbrough went solo in 1964. His first few singles flopped, but he recorded the theme from the Steve McQueen movie, Baby the Rain Must Fall, on RCA Victor Records, and it was a hit. It reached #12 in the Billboard Hot 100, and #2 in the Easy Listening Chart. His follow-up, It's Gonna Be Fine, was less successful, just peaking at #54.

Weird OHW Fact... In 1977, Yarbrough sang for the animated movie, The Hobbit, singing, The Greatest Adventure, and, The Road Goes Ever On. In the animated, The Return of the King, he sings, Frodo of the Nine Fingers.

GOLDIE & THE GINGERBREADS - CAN'T YOU HEAR MY HEARTBEAT
Written by John Carter and Ken Lewis it was recorded by Herman's Hermits for release only in the US, and got to #2. In a weird case of flip-flopping, US girl band, Goldie & the Gingerbreads, had the single in the UK, reaching #25 in the UK Charts. Weird how music goes, huh?

HEDGEHOPPERS ANONYMOUS - IT'S GOOD NEWS WEEK
Written by Jonathan King, who took over the Peterborough band's musical management in 1965, he changed their name to Hedgehoppers Anonymous (formerly called The Trendsetters, then The Hedgehoppers) and got them signed to Decca records. The song reached #5 in the UK Charts staying in the chart for 12 weeks, #8 in Australia, and a poor #48 in the Billboard Hot 100. Their follow-up, Don't Push Me, got to #28 in Australia.

HORST JANKOWSKI - A WALK IN THE BLACK FOREST
Sold over 1 million copies.
Written and recorded by the classically-trained German pianist (In German, Eine Schwarzwaldfahrt), on Mercury Records. It reached #12

in the Billboard Hot 100, #1 in the Easy Listening Chart, and #3 in the UK Chart.

Weird OHW Fact... It has become the song played at the end of every Plymouth Argyle F.C. home game, as the spectators leave the stadium.

IAN WHITCOMB AND BLUESVILLE - YOU TURN ME ON (TURN ON SONG)

Written by Ian Timothy Whitcomb, it was recorded by Whitcomb on Tower Records. It reached #8 in the Billboard Hot 100, but his follow-up, N-E-R-V-O-U-S, only got to #59. Technically he charted as part of the British Invasion, having never had a hit in his native UK.

Weird OHW Fact... In 1966, he released his last charting single, an old Al Jolson number, Where Did Robinson Crusoe Go With Friday On Saturday Night. It reached #101 in the Billboard Hot 100.

JEWEL AKENS - THE BIRDS AND THE BEES

Sold over 1 million copies.

The writing of this song is in dispute, some say it was written by the twelve-year-old son of Era Records' owner Herb Newman, some by Newman himself. But the label on the record states Barry Stuart, and I'll leave it there. Recorded on Era Records, it was a smash hit, reaching #3 in the Billboard Hot 100, #21 in the Black Singles Chat, and #29 in the UK Chart. His follow-up, Georgie Porgie, only reached #68.

Weird OHW Fact... Akens was with the group, the Turn-Arounds at the time they were offered the song, but Jewel Eugene Akens was the only one of the group to like the song, so he recorded it solo. That's the way the cookie crumbles.

JULIE ROGERS - THE WEDDING

Written by Chilean musician, Joaquin Prieto as, The Wedding (La Novia), it was recorded by many artists in the early 1060's. Julie Rogers' version, on Mercury Records, (with English lyrics by Fred Jay), was released in the UK, climbing steadily to #3 in the UK Chart. From there it went global, reaching #10 in the Billboard Hot 100, #1 in Australia, #2 in the Netherlands, #10 in Austria and #16 in Germany.

Weird OHW Fact... In the 1970's, it was calculated that between all the different versions of the song available, over seven million copies had been sold.

THE LARKS - THE JERK

1964 was a great year for jerking; with at least three songs vying for the title of king of the new dance craze. The Larks (originally the

Meadowlarks), from Los Angeles recorded The Jerk on Money Records, and it slid ceremoniously to #7 in the Billboard Hot 100, and #7 in the R&B Chart.

Weird OHW Fact... The other bands to capitalize on the dance's popularity were, The Miracles, Come on Do the Jerk, reaching #50, and The Capitols song, Cool Jerk, getting to #7.

LITTLE JIMMY DICKENS - MAY THE BIRD OF PARADISE FLY UP YOUR NOSE

Written by Neal Merritt, and performed by Little Jimmy Dickens, it was modelled on one of the put-downs from Johnny Carson on the Tonight Show. Recorded on Columbia Records, it rose to #15 in the Billboard Hot 100, and got to #1 in the Country Music Chart.

Weird OHW Fact... Little Jimmy Dickens peppered the Country Chart for thirty years in a long musical career.

LITTLE MILTON - WE'RE GONNA MAKE IT

No stranger to the R&B Chart or Blues Chart, James Milton Campbell refined his style to that of BB King, and had his only mainstream hit. We're Gonna Make It, a bluesy song, reached #25 in the Billboard Hot 100, and got to #1 in the R&B Chart, his only number one there. He followed the hit with, Who's Cheating Who, (R&B#4), but none had the same success.

THE MARVELOWS - I DO

Formed in Chicago in 1959, the band eventually got a contract with ABC-Paramount Records. Four tracks were recorded, A Friend, My Heart, Hey Hey Baby, and I Do. Although, I Do, was not meant as a single, it would be their only hit. It reached #37 in the Billboard Hot 100, and #7 in the R&B Chart. Four years later, their song, In the Morning, reached #24 in the R&B Chart, their last single.

Weird OHW Fact... It was covered twice by The J. Geils Band, in studio and live versions.

THE MCCOYS - HANG ON SLOOPY

Reached #1 in USA.

Written by Wes Farrell and Bert Berns, and originally titled, My Girl Sloopy, it was recorded by The McCoys from Union City, Indiana, on Bang Records. It reached #1 in the US Billboard Hot 100 and #5 on the UK Singles Chart. They charted with their follow-up, Fever, reaching #7 in the Billboard Hot 100, but unfortunately just #44 in the UK, where they are known as one hit wonders.

Weird OHW Fact... The same year, a cover in Spanish, Es Lupe, by the band, Los Johnny Jets, reached #1 in Mexico and stayed there for 13 weeks.

ROBERT GOULET - MY LOVE, FORGIVE ME (AMORE, SCUSAMI)
Written by Gino Mescoli and Vito Pallavicini, it was a John Foster hit in Italy, reaching #3 in the Italian Chart, and staying in the Top 10 for five months. Translated into English, and recorded by Robert Goulet, it reached #16 in the Billboard Hot 100, and #3 in the Middle-Road Singles Chart. His best follow-up was, Summer Sounds, which reached #58.
Weird OHW Fact... Born in Lawrence, Massachusetts, Goulet is better known for his film and TV work, with a huge stage and screen resume.

SAN REMO GOLDEN STRINGS - HUNGRY FOR LOVE
The Strings were a fusion group from Detroit, Michigan, some played in the Detroit Symphony Orchestra, the others... a Motown backing band called, The Funk Brothers. Their only US hit, on Motown Records, reached #27 in the Billboard Hot 100, and #3 in the Adult Contemporary Chart. Their best, 'also ran' was, I'm Satisfied, which peaked at #39.
Weird OHW Fact... However, they are also a one hit wonder in the UK! In 1971 they had a #39 entry in the UK Chart with, Festival Time.

SHIRLEY BASSEY - GOLDFINGER
Reached #1 in Japan.
Written by John Barry, Leslie Bricusse, and Anthony Newley, the song was used as the theme song for the second James Bond movie, Goldfinger, in 1964. It gave Bassey her only Billboard Hot 100 hit at #8, reaching #21 in the UK, #1 in Japan, #4 in Australia, and Top 10 in most of Europe.
Weird OHW Fact... The song almost didn't make it to the movie; Goldfinger's producer, Harry Saltzman, detested it, saying, 'That's the worst ### song I've ever heard in my ### life'.

THE SILKIE - YOU'VE GOT TO HIDE YOUR LOVE AWAY
Written by Beatles John Lennon and Paul McCartney, the Fab Four actively encouraged their folk singing friends from Hull University (The Silkie) to record the song. Lennon produced it, McCartney played guitar, and Harrison was also featured on the recording. The song reached #28 in the UK Chart, and #10 in the Billboard Hot 100. The band split up the next year.

SOUNDS ORCHESTRAL - CAST YOUR FATE TO THE WIND
Written and originally recorded by Vince Guaraldi in 1963, it won a Grammy Award for Best Original Jazz Composition. Words were written by Carel Werber. The British group, Sounds Orchestral, un-jazzed the original, and reached #5 in the UK Chart, #10 in the Billboard Hot 100, and three weeks at #1 in the Easy Listening chart.

Weird OHW Fact... American jazz pianist, Vince Guaraldi (born Vincent Anthony Dellaglio), is perhaps better known for his jazz piano recordings used in the Peanuts and Charlie Brown animated comic shows.

THE SPOKESMEN - THE DAWN OF CORRECTION
Written by band members John Medora, David White, and Ray Gilmore, it was a musical counter to Barry McGuire's protest hit, Eve Of Destruction, earlier in the summer of 1965. The single reached #36 in the Billboard Hot 100 chart, but subsequent attempts to cash in on its success failed.

TONY CLARKE - THE ENTERTAINER
Born in New York City, he was brought up in Detroit, Michigan, where he signed with Chess Records. The self-penned, The Entertainer, reached #31 in the Billboard Hot 100, and #10 in the R&B Chart. It would be his only hit.

Weird OHW Fact... He died in 1971, shot by his wife.

Weird OHW Fact... Clarke also wrote, Pushover, and, Two Sides to Every Story, both hits for Etta James.

UNIT 4 + 2 - CONCRETE AND CLAY
Written by band members Tommy Moeller and Brian Parker it was recorded by the band on Fontana Records. It reached #1 in the UK, and #21 in Australia. It was decided to release the record in the USA, but Eddie Rambeau released his own version just a week before the Unit 4 + 2 recording hit American stores. Both versions were successful, Unit 4 + 2's reaching #28, and Eddie Rambeau's getting to #35.

Unit 4+2's follow-up, (You've) Never Been In Love Like This Before, reached #14 in the UK and #38 in Australia. It never charted in the USA, where Unit 4+2 will always be known as a one hit wonder.

Weird OHW Fact... The band was called Unit 4+2 because they had six members, a 4-piece harmony unit, and 2 musicians who didn't sing. That makes sense, right?

THE WAIKIKIS - HAWAII TATTOO

Sold over 2 million copies.

Written by Michael Thomas in 1961, the Hawaiian-esque instrumental was recorded by Belgian band, The Waikikis, on Kapp records, and was an instant hit in Belgium, and reached #4 in Germany. It was a hit in Australia before ultimately hitting #33 in the Billboard Hot 100 three years after its original release.

Weird OHW Fact... The Waikikis made many Hawaiian albums, and their only hit single sold more than 2.5 million copies worldwide.

THE WONDER WHO? - DON'T THINK TWICE

Written by Bob Dylan, it was recorded by, The Wonder Who?, as their first single. The band name was actually a fake name for the band, The Four Seasons, and Frankie Valli, for their singles between 1965 and 1967. It was the only single of the 'fake' band to chart, reaching #12 in the Billboard Hot 100. Their highest follow-up was, On the Good Ship Lollipop, which reached #87.

OH SO CLOSE... BUT NO CIGAR...

JONATHAN KING - EVERYONE'S GONE TO THE MOON

Sold over 1 million copies.

Written by Jonathan King (born Kenneth George King), many people think this was the first of many of his one-hit wonders under different names. (but of course, they're wrong.) On Decca Records, it reached #4 in the UK Chart, then #17 in the Billboard Hot 100. It has been covered many times. Unfortunately King's illustrious musical career has been clouded by child sex abuse charges.

Weird OHW Fact... Prompted by Decca, King changed his name for the release of the single.

BUT... he's not a one hit wonder in his own name... in 1970, Jonathan King reached #26 in the UK Chart and #28 in the Dutch Chart with a cover version of, Let It All Hang Out.

1966...

As Indira Gandhi is elected Prime Minister of India, the year begins...

Winnie the Pooh and the Honey Tree is released, The Flintstones aired its last episode, albums Pet Sounds (Beach Boys) and Blonde on Blonde (Bob Dylan) are released, Star Trek debuts on NBC, Dr Who has its first regeneration; William Hartnell's face transforms into Patrick Troughton.

? & THE MYSTERIANS – 96 TEARS

Reached #1 in USA and Canada.
Sold over 1 million copies.
Written by 'Question Mark' (Rudy Martinez), it was recorded by the weirdly-titled garage rock band, ? and the Mysterians. It reached #1 in the Billboard Hot 100, #1 in Canada, and #37 in the UK. But it wasn't a US one hit wonder. Later that year, their follow-up song, I Need Somebody, reached #22. However, the follow-up didn't chart in the UK or Canada, making 96 Tears a one hit wonder there.

BARRY YOUNG - ONE HAS MY NAME (THE OTHER HAS MY HEART)

Written in 1948 by cowboy Eddie Dean, and Hal Blair, it was recorded by Barry Young on Dot Records. His short story is quite tragic; he started 1966 in January with his hit, getting to #13 in the Billboard Hot 100, and making an album of the same name which reached #37 in the Billboard Album Charts. Sadly he ended 1966 with a brain abscess, and died in December, aged 35.

BOBBY MOORE & THE RHYTHM ACES - SEARCHING FOR MY LOVE

Sold over 1 million copies.
Written by band leader Bobby Moore, he recorded the single on the Checker label. It reached #27 in the Billboard Hot 100, and #7 in the R&B Chart. The follow-up, Try My Love Again, peaked at #97, and the next one just featured in the R&B Chart. The band split up in 1969.

BOB KUBAN AND THE IN-MEN - THE CHEATER

Written by John Krenski, it was recorded by Bob Kuban and his band, on Musicland Records. The single reached #12 in the Billboard Hot 100, but the follow-ups did not have the same success, The Teaser (US #70), and the Beatles, Drive My Car' (US #97).

Weird OHW Fact... Ironically (considering the song's title), Walter Scott, who fronted the In-men, and sang the song's vocals, was murdered by his wife's lover in 1983. His wife hid the details, and the case went unknown for four years.

BOB LIND - ELUSIVE BUTTERFLY
Written by Bob Lind, from Baltimore, Maryland, this song reached cult status almost immediately. It reached #5 in the Billboard Hot 100, #5 in the UK Charts, #2 in Australia, and #4 in South Africa. In the UK Val Doonican had a version, also reaching #5, and #3 in his native Ireland, where Lind's version never charted. In South Africa Judy page's version vied with Lind's, but eventually just got to #5.
Weird OHW Fact... Other covers just in 1966 were, Petula Clarke, Jane Morgan, Cher, Carmen McRae, Billy Walker, Richard Anthony, The Batchelors, Hugh Masekela, Graham Bonnie, Lou Christie, Johnny Mathis and Bobby V.

BRIAN WILSON - CAROLINE, NO
Written by Beach Boy Brian Wilson and Tony Asher (with whom Brian wrote most of the songs on Pet Sounds), it was recorded by Brian alone and was meant to stamp Brian's leaving the group to work as a solo artist. The solo song reached #32 in the Billboard Hot 100.
Weird OHW Fact... Brian's message made little difference to the band. The song was included as the final track on the Beach Boys platinum album, Pet Sounds.

BUDDY STARCHER - HISTORY REPEATS ITSELF
Written by Buddy Starcher (born Oby Edgar Starcher) and Minnie Pearl, this spoken word recording describes familiar features between the assassinations of Lincoln and Kennedy, and ran over the music of, Battle Hymn of the Republic, and, America the Beautiful. The single reached #39 in the Billboard Hot 100, and #2 in the Country Chart. The follow-up, Day of Decision, just got to #131.

THE CAPITOLS – COOL JERK
Written by Donald Storball to cash in on the newest dance craze, it was recorded by Detroit, Michigan R&B group, The Capitols on Karen Records. It reached #2 in the R&B Singles chart, #7 in the Billboard Hot 100, and #9 in Canada. The song, like Chubby Checkers', 'The Twist', had its own dance moves, The Jerk. It worked for the novelty first single, but even that couldn't sell their subsequent releases.

CHICAGO LOOP - (WHEN SHE NEEDS GOOD LOVIN') SHE COMES TO ME

This rock group hailed from Chicago, Illinois, and their only hit single (on the DynoVoice label) reached #37 in the Billboard Hot 100. The guitarist on the recording was Michael Bloomfield (voted in the top 100 guitarists of all time) and keyboardist was Barry Goldberg, just at the start of his career.

COUNT FIVE - PSYCHOTIC REACTION

Written by the band during school hour, Psychotic Reaction took ages to get to the public. First they had to refine the more 'acid rock' style, still not well known. Then they had to find a record company willing to take a chance. Eventually Double Shot Records came along, but the first release flopped. Re-touched again a year later, the single shot straight to #5 in the Billboard Hot 100.

DARRELL BANKS - OPEN THE DOOR TO YOUR HEART

Written by Darrell Banks and Donnie Elbert, this song has been described as 'one of the finest non-Motown releases to emerge from Detroit'. It reached #27 in the Billboard Hot 100, and would be his only hit.

Weird OHW Fact... Banks was registered as the sole songwriter, and this was disputed by Elbert, who stated that Banks just changed the tempo. The two went to court.

DAVID AND JONATHAN – MICHELLE

Reached #1 in Canada.

Written by John Lennon and Paul McCartney, this recording was mainly at the behest of their manager, George Martin. Urged by Martin, the songwriting duo Roger Greenaway and Roger Cook recorded their version, which reached #18 in the Billboard Hot 100, #3 in the Adult Contemporary Chart, and #11 in the UK Chart. Their follow-up, Lovers of the World Unite, reached #7 in the UK Chart, but did not chart in the USA, making David and Johnathan a US one hit wonder.

Weird OHW Fact... The Beatles never released the song as a single in the UK or US, even though it reached #1 in Belgium, France, Netherlands and Norway, and won a Grammy in 1967.

DAVID HOUSTON - ALMOST PERSUADED

Written by Glenn Sutton and Billy Sherrill, and first recorded by hard working country star, David Houston. The song reached #1 in the

Country Chart, and crossed over successfully into the Billboard Hot 100 at #24. It would be his only mainstream hit.

The song won a Grammy Award for Best Country & Western Recording of 1966.

Weird OHW Fact... Houston is a Country legend, with an impressive 55 songs in the US and Canadian country charts, including 6 US #1's and 7 Canadian #1's.

DAVID MCCALLUM - COMMUNICATION

Scot David McCallum is probably best known for his acting roles in, The Man From Uncle, and recently in NCIS, but he does have a musical past. As a child he played the oboe, and after The Man From Uncle, he recorded four songs, one of which, Communication, made it to #32 in the UK Charts. While not up to William Shatner's 'best', it's worth a listen.

DEON JACKSON - LOVE MAKES THE WORLD GO ROUND

Written by Deon Jackson, from Ann Arbor, Michigan, this soul singer sang from his schooldays. His self-penned, You Said You Love Me, and, Come Back Home, were both small, regional hits. Singing in clubs, he released, Love Makes the World Go Round, on Carla Records, reaching #11 in the Billboard Hot 100, and #3 in the Black Singles Chart. The follow-ups did not hit the Top 40; Love Takes a Long Time Growing, (US #77), Ooh Baby, (US #65). Kiki Dee got to #87 in the Billboard Hot 100 with her version in 1971.

Weird OHW Fact... Although Jackson is a one hit wonder, his recordings are still popular in the Northern Soul circuit in the UK.

FRANK GALLOP - THE BALLAD OF IRVING

Frank Gallop is probably best remembered as a TV announcer and personality, but he also had a musical side. He recorded, The Ballad of Irving, (written by Dick Williams, Frank Peppiatt, and John Aylesworth) on Kapp Records, and the song got to #2 in the Adult Contemporary Chart and #34 in the Billboard Hot 100. The follow-up, The Son of Irving, did not chart.

Weird OHW Fact... The song was a parody of Lorne Greene's, Ringo.

JACKIE LEE - THE DUCK

After the success of Bob & Earl (a one hit wonder in 1966, but listed in this book as 1969, Harlem Shuffle) Earl Nelson released, The Duck, under the name Jackie Lee. The dance song got to #14 in the Billboard Hot 100.

Weird OHW Fact... Jackie was Nelson's wife's name, and Lee was his own middle name).

J. J. JACKSON - BUT IT'S ALRIGHT

Written by Jerome (J.J.) Louis Jackson and Pierre Tubbs, it was recorded on Jackson's debut album. The song reached #4 in the R&B Charts, and #22 in the Billboard Hot 100. It was also re-released in 1969, when it charted once more (#45). He did hit the R&B Chart regularly, but never the mainstream chart again.

Weird OHW Fact... Jackson's first writing credit was, The Lord Will Understand (And Say 'Well Done'), for Billy Williams. The record got banned by the BBC for 'religious overtones'.

JOHNNY SEA - DAY FOR DECISION

Born in Gulfport, Mississippi, John Allan Seay, Jr. was a country music singer. At the time of his only 'hit', he had already recorded five albums, and four Top 30 hits in the US Country Chart. Day for Decision, however was a spoken word song, and crossed over to #35 in the Billboard Hot 100, #14 in the Country Chart, and even #47 in Canada, his only chart entry there.

JUST US - I CAN'T GROW PEACHES ON A CHERRY TREE

Written by Chip Taylor (writer of another one hit wonder, Angel of the Morning, in 1968), and recorded as a duo with session musician, Al Gorgoni, they included the track on their only album together. The title track was a hit in the US, reaching #3 in the Adult Contemporary Chart and #34 in the Billboard Hot 100.

THE KNICKERBOCKERS - LIES

From Bergenfield, New Jersey, The Knickerbockers were the epitome of a hard working band. They were signed to Challenge records, recorded singles, pushed the music to the public, and appeared on Dick Clarke's show, Where The Action Is. One single hit the big time, #20 in the Billboard Hot 100. Their follow-up, All I Need Is You, was handled badly by the record company, and just reached #46.

Weird OHW Fact... The band's name comes from Knickerbocker Road that runs through their town.

THE LEAVES - HEY JOE

Just as Jimi Hendrix was singing the old blues favorite, and being discovered in a New York café, garage band, The Leaves, were recording it in California. Their up-tempo version beat Jimi's by six months, getting to #31 in the Billboard Hot 100, and #39 in Canada, staying in both charts for 9 weeks.

LOVE - 7 AND 7 IS
Written by Arthur Lee, it was recorded by his band Love on their second album, Da, Capo, on Elektra Records. It stayed in the chart for 10 weeks, peaking at #33 in the Billboard Hot 100.

Weird OHW Fact... The song finished with an atomic explosion, and for live performances, the sound was reproduced by kicking a nearby reverb unit.

LOS BRAVOS - BLACK IS BLACK
Reached #1 in Spain and Canada.
Sold more than 3 million copies.
Written by Michelle Grainger, Tony Hayes, Steve Wadey, it was recorded by the Spanish beat band from Madrid. It was their debut single, and hit Top 10 all over Europe, #1 in Spain, #2 in the UK, before going overseas, #4 in the Billboard Hot 100 (spending 12 weeks in the chart), and #3 in Australia. The band's follow-up, I Don't care reached #16 in the UK, but they were a one hit wonder everywhere else.

Weird OHW Fact... The German lead singer sounded like Gene Pitney, and many buyers were convinced he was.

MIKE DOUGLAS - THE MEN IN MY LITTLE GIRL'S LIFE
Michael Delaney Dowd Jr. is probably better known as a big show host, having his own national show on NBC. During this time, he recorded a few songs, one of which was picked up. The Men in My Little Girl's Life reached #6 in the Billboard Hot 100, but apart from singing it on his own show, he was too busy to promote it fully.

Weird OHW Fact... At the time, in 1966, he was earning half a million dollars a year as a variety show host.

NAPOLEON XIV - THEY'RE COMING TO TAKE ME AWAY, HA-HAAA!
Written by Jerry Samuels (aka Napoleon XIV), whilst he was a recording engineer at Associated Recording Studios in New York. Released on Warner Bros. Records, the song shot up the charts, reaching #3 in the Billboard Hot 100, and #4 in the UK Charts.

Weird OHW Fact... Under his son's name, Scott David, he wrote, The Shelter of Your Arms, for Sammy Davis Jr. (US #17) in 1964.

Weird OHW Fact... The song is based loosely on the Scottish pipe tune, The Campbells Are Coming.

NEAL HEFTI - BATMAN THEME

Written by Neal Hefti, who worked for Harry James's band from the late 1940's, the tune was released by the band on their album, Live At The Riverboat. The single, lifted from the album, reached #35 in the Billboard Hot 100.

Weird OHW Fact... Because he arranged the Ron Hicklin Singers to shout 'Batman', eleven times in conjunction with the trumpets, the album sleeve stated, 'words and music by Neal Hefti'.

THE NEW VAUDEVILLE BAND - WINCHESTER CATHEDRAL

Reached number 1 in USA and Canada.

Sold more than 3 million copies.

Written by Geoff Stephens (There's a Kind of Hush, and, The Crying Game), it was recorded by British novelty band, The New Vaudeville Band, who had been specifically gathered by Stephens to sing the song in a mock 1920's Vaudeville style. To his shock, the single took off in the UK and USA. It reached #1 in the Billboard Hot 100, #1 in Canada, and #4 in the UK Charts. Their follow-ups only charted in the UK, so they are considered an American one hit wonder.

Weird OHW Fact... The song won the Grammy Award in 1967 for Best Contemporary (R&R) Recording, despite it not being even close to a rock and roll song.

Weird OHW Fact... In 1967, while in his late 60's, singer Rudy Vallée, whose vaudeville voice and style the original recording had tried so hard to imitate, recorded his own version of the song. It did not chart.

NORMA TANEGA - WALKIN' MY CAT NAMED DOG

Written by Norma Tanega, the lyrics are based on an apartment complex where they didn't allow dogs, so she kept a cat, and took it for walks. The song reached #22 in the Billboard Hot 100, #22 in the UK Charts, and Top 10 in Canada. She later toured with Gene Pitney, and Bobby Goldsboro.

Weird OHW Fact... She had a relationship with Dusty Springfield, living with her for five years.

THE OVERLANDERS – MICHELLE

Originally a folk band, the Overlanders released many cover versions, but the only hit was Lennon McCartney composition, Michelle. The Overlanders' version reached #1 in the UK, staying there for 3 weeks, beating off the David and Johnathan version. They never charted again.

PINKERTON'S ASSORTED COLOURS - MIRROR, MIRROR

Written by band singer, Tony Newman, it was recorded by the pop band from Rugby, Warwickshire. It reached #9 in the UK Charts, and the follow-up, Don't Stop Loving Me Baby, only reached #50. They were labelled as one hit wonders, but some members went on to form The Flying Machine, another one hit wonder, this time in the USA (see listing in 1969).

RAY CONNIFF - SOMEWHERE, MY LOVE
Written by Maurice Jarre, and originally called, Lara's Theme, for inclusion in the movie, Doctor Zhivago. At the urging of Connie Francis, English lyrics were added by Paul Francis Webster. Ray Conniff, with The Ray Conniff Singers, recorded the song, taking it to #9 in the Billboard Hot 100. Connie Francis' version did not chart.
Weird OHW Fact... Maurice Jarre is the father of synthesizer icon, Jean Michel Jarre.

ROBERT PARKER - BAREFOOTIN'
Sold over 1 million copies.
Written by Robert Parker (from New Orleans, Louisiana), and recorded on Nola Records, it reached #2 in the R&B Charts, #7 in the Billboard Hot 100, and #24 in the UK Charts. He never charted again.

THE SHADES OF BLUE - OH HOW HAPPY
Written by Edwin Starr, the song was recorded by Detroit vocal group, The Shades of Blue. The song reached #12 in the Billboard Hot 100, #7 in the R&B Chart, and #9 in Canada. Their follow-ups, Lonely Summer, reached #72, and, Happiness, got to #78.

THE STANDELLS - DIRTY WATER
Written by Ed Cobb (and still disputed by band members Dodd, Valentino, and Tamblyn), and recorded by Los Angeles garage rock band, The Standells, the song is supposedly about the bad water in the Boston Harbor and Charles River. The single reached #11 in the Billboard Hot 100, and #8 in Cashbox. Their best of their other singles, The Boy Next Door, reached #102.
Weird OHW Fact... The Boston Bruins ice hockey team started playing the song after a win in 1991, with the Boston Red Sox baseball team following soon after.

THE STATLER BROTHERS - FLOWERS ON THE WALL
Reached #1 in Canada.

Written by band member, Lew DeWitt, it was recorded by country group, The Statler Brothers, on their first album of the same name. it reached #4 in the Billboard Hot 100, and #2 in the Country Chart, #1 in Canada, #2 in New Zealand, and #38 in the UK Charts.

The song won the Grammy Award in 1966 for Best Contemporary (R&R) Performance.

THE SWINGIN' MEDALLIONS - DOUBLESHOT (OF MY BABY'S LOVE)

Written by Don Smith and Cyril Vetter, it was originally recorded in 1964 by Dick Holler & the Holidays. From Greenwood, South Carolina, and originally known as the Medallions, they recorded the song as their second single. It reached #17 in the Billboard Hot 100, but the follow-up, She Drives Me Out of My Mind, only reached #71.

SYNDICATE OF SOUND - LITTLE GIRL

Written by band members Don Baskin and Bob Gonzalez, the song was recorded by the garage rock band from san Jose, California. Winning a recording contract in a talent contest, the band recorded Little Girl, and, You, the A and B sides of their debut single. It reached # 8 in the Billboard Hot 100, and #6 in Cashbox. Their follow-ups, Keep It Up, and, Mary, did not chart, and the subsequent, Brown Paper Bag, reached #73 in 1970. They split up soon afterwards.

THE T-BONES - NO MATTER WHAT SHAPE (YOUR STOMACH'S IN)

Reached #1 in Canada.

Written by Granville Sascha Burland, the instrumental was recorded by The T-Bones on their fourth album of the same name. It reached 33 in the Billboard hot 100 staying in the chart for 13 weeks, and reached #1 in Canada.

Weird OHW Fact... The T-Bones who recorded the song did not want to go on tour, so the record company simply got a bunch of session musicians to tour.

TOMMY MCLAIN - SWEET DREAMS

Written by Don Gibson in 1955, this country song had already been a minor hit for Gibson, Faron Young and Patsy Cline. Recorded by Tommy McLain from Jonesville, Louisiana, he took it into the Billboard Hot 100 at #15, the song's highest position. It didn't chart Top 40 in the UK, stalling at #49. It would later be covered by Emmylou Harris, Reba McEntire, Tammy Wynette, and Elvis Costello.

VERDELLE SMITH - TAR AND CEMENT

Reached #1 in Australia.

Originally an Italian song, Il ragazzo della via Gluck, written by Adriano Celentano, the English version was written by Lee Pockriss and Paul Vance. Verdelle Smith recorded the song with acoustic guitar and light strings for her album, Alone In My Room, the title track reaching #62 in the Billboard Hot 100. Tar and Cement reached #38 in the Billboard Hot 100, and probably a shock #1 in Australia.

THE VISCOUNTS - HARLEM NOCTURNE
Written by Earle Hagen and Dick Rogers in 1939, the tune is considered a jazz standard, and was released by The Viscounts twice. On the first release, in 1959, it reached #53, and later in 1966, it got to #39 in the Billboard Hot 100.

WALTER WANDERLEY - SUMMER SAMBA (SO NICE)
Written by Brazilian composer Marcos Valle, with English lyrics by Norman Gimbel, it was recorded by the Walter Wanderley Trio on their album, Rain Forest. The samba reached #26 in the Billboard Hot 100, and #3 in the Easy Listening Chart. Other versions were in the chart at the same time; Johnny Mathis, Vikki Carr, and Connie Francis were all beaten in the charts by the Wanderley version.

1967...

As the first 'Spaghetti Western', A Fistful of Dollars, starring Clint Eastwood, is released, the year begins...
Astronauts Gus Grissom, Ed White, and Roger Chaffee are killed in a fire on their Apollo spacecraft, the Pirates of the Caribbean ride opens in Disneyland, California, Glasgow Celtic win the European Cup, Israel's Six-Day War takes place, Elvis Presley and Priscilla Beaulieu are married, Captain Scarlet and the Mysterons broadcasts on ITV.

1910 FRUITGUM COMPANY - SIMON SAYS
Sold over 3 million copies.
Written by Elliot Chiprut, (the song is based on the old child's game), it was recorded by the New Jersey band on their debut album. It was a huge hit, reaching #4 in the Billboard Hot 100, #2 in the UK, and #2 in Australia. The band did continue to have hits in the USA and Australia, (1, 2, 3, Red Light, and, Indian Giver, were Top 10 in both countries, and 1 million sellers), but the band did not chart in the UK again, making them one-hit wonders there.

BILL COSBY - LITTLE OLE MAN (UPTIGHT–EVERYTHING'S ALRIGHT)
Written by Stevie Wonder, Sylvia Moy, and Henry Cosby, comedian Bill Cosby recorded a version on his first comedy album, Silver Throat: Bill Cosby Sings. The song reached an astonishing #4 in the Billboard Hot 100, one of the first comedians to get so high. He never charted again.
Weird OHW Fact... The song's co-writer, Henry Cosby, is no relation.

BLUES MAGOOS - (WE AIN'T GOT) NOTHIN' YET
Written by band members Ron Gilbert, Ralph Scala and Mike Esposito, and heavy on Vox organ sounds, it became the Bronx band's only chart hit, reaching #5 in the Billboard Hot 100. The best follow-up, ironically entitled, Pipe Dream, reached #60.
Weird OHW Fact... You cannot hear the opening riffs of this song to miss the 'steal' from Deep Purple on their worldwide hit, Black Knight.
Weird OHW Fact... In the UK, it was released by the band, The Spectres, who would become Status Quo.

BOB CREWE GENERATION - MUSIC TO WATCH GIRLS BY
Written by Tony Velona and Sidney Ramin, and hearing it first on a Pepsi commercial, it would be Bob Crewe's only hit using his own name.

The jazzy, 'groovy' tune got to #15 in the Billboard Hot 100, and #2 in the Easy Listening Chart.

Weird OHW Fact... In the same year, Star Trek's Leonard Nimoy recorded it on his album, Leonard Nimoy Presents Mr. Spock's Music from Outer Space, but under the new title, Music To Watch Space By.

BUFFALO SPRINGFIELD - FOR WHAT IT'S WORTH (STOP, HEY WHAT'S THAT SOUND)

Written by Stephen Stills, it was recorded on their debut album, Buffalo Springfield. The song reached #7 in the Billboard Hot 100 chart, but did not chart significantly anywhere else. Their highest charting follow-up was, Rock 'n' Roll Woman, reaching #44.

Weird OHW Fact... The song's title, For What It's Worth, was added after writing.

BUNNY SIGLER - LET THE GOOD TIMES ROLL/FEELS SO GOOD

Written by Shirley Goodman, and Leonard Lee in 1956, the medley was recorded by Walter 'Bunny' Sigler and became his first and only chart hit. It reached #22 in the Billboard Hot 100, and #20 in the R&B Chart. A further medley, Lovey Dovey/You're So Fine, hit the R&B Chart, but did not go mainstream.

CANNONBALL ADDERLEY - MERCY, MERCY, MERCY

Written by band pianist Joe Zawinul, the soul/swing jazz instrumental was recorded by saxophonist Julian Edwin 'Cannonball' Adderley and his band. This crossover hit reached #11 in the Billboard Hot 100. Adderley had worked with Miles Davis on the album, Kind of Blue, and was well respected on the jazz circuit.

Weird OHW Fact... His nickname came from the name 'cannibal', a high school name because of his huge appetite.

THE CASINOS – THEN YOU CAN TELL ME GOODBYE

Written by John D. Loudermilk, and first released as a country song in 1962 by Don Cherry, it was the doo-wop version by Cincinnati's the Casinos that many people remember. It reached #6 in the Billboard Hot 100 and #28 in the UK. Their subsequent singles did not chart.

CHRIS BARTLEY - THE SWEETEST THING THIS SIDE OF HEAVEN

Written by Van McCoy (Do the Hustle), it was recorded by Bartley as his first single from his debut (and only) album. The song reached #10 in the R&B Chart, #32 in the Billboard Hot 100, and #14 in Canada. Despite a US and UK tour, the follow-up, Baby I'm Yours, did not chart.

DAVIE ALLAN AND THE ARROWS - BLUE'S THEME

Three years before Easy Rider, the movie The Wild Angels, paired Peter Fonda with a Harley Davidson motorbike. Co-starring Nancy Sinatra, Bruce Dern and Diane Ladd, when it hit the screens, the music was paramount to the mood and action. The film's fuzz guitar opening, 'Blues' Theme, became Davie Allen's biggest hit. It reached #37 in the Billboard Hot 100, staying in the chart for 17 weeks. Although he went on to pen other soundtracks, none got into the charts.

THE EASYBEATS - FRIDAY ON MY MIND

Reached #1 in Australia.
Sold over 1 million copies.
Written by band members Harry Vanda and George Young, the single took the Easybeats from Australian obscurity to world domination. The song reached #1 in Australia (their second #1), #6 in the UK, and #16 in the Billboard Hot 100. Their subsequent singles were less worldly, with only, hello, How Are You, charting in the UK (#20). By 1969 they had broken up.
Weird OHW Fact... All 5 of the band came from immigrant families in Australia's poorest areas.
Weird OHW Fact... George Young's little brothers gained more fame than he did... Angus and Malcolm Young formed the guitar duo behind ACDC.
Weird OHW Fact... Vanda and Young wrote, Love Is In the Air, for fellow immigrant John Paul Young, a one hit wonder in 1978. They then went on to produce the first 6 ACDC albums.

EVERY MOTHER'S SON - COME ON DOWN TO MY BOAT

Written by Jerry Goldstein and Wes Farrell, the song was recorded by New York's sunshine band, Every Mother's Son, on their debut album. The song reached #6 in the Billboard Hot 100, #3 in Canada, and #29 in Australia. Their highest follow-up, Put Your Mind at Ease, reached #46 in the US, and #8 in Canada.
Billboard ranked the song as #22 of 1967.

THE FIFTH ESTATE - DING-DONG! THE WITCH IS DEAD

With whistle solos from Michael Praetorius's Terpsichore suite, The Fifth Estate took the Wizard of Oz song to #11 in the billboard Hot 100. It was the highest charting recording of any song from the Wizard of OZ.
Weird OHW Fact... In 2013, after UK Prime Minister Margaret Thatcher's death, the song reached a morbid #2 in the UK Charts.

THE FLOWER POT MEN - LET'S GO TO SAN FRANCISCO

Written by John Carter and Ken Lewis, it is the only charting single by the transition pop group, The Flower Pot Men. With lead vocals by Tony Burrows, it would be the first of his SIX one hit wonders. The song, in a rich Beach Boys style harmony, reached #4 in their native UK, #9 in Norway, and Top 20 in most of Europe.

THE HOMBRES - LET IT OUT (LET IT ALL HANG OUT)

Written by band members Jerry Lee Masters, John Will Hunter, Gary Wayne McEwen, and B. B. Cunningham, this garage band from Memphis, Tennessee, is best remembered for their one hit in 1967. The song reached #12 in the Billboard Hot 100, and #16 in Australia. Four subsequent singles failed to chart.

Weird OHW Fact... British one hit wonder (under different names), Jonathan King, had the UK hit in 1970.

JEFF BECK – HI HO SILVER LINING

Written by Scott English and Larry Weiss, it was first released by London band The Attack. Jeff Beck released his version days later, and it was his single that charted first, hence he got the hit. It reached #14 in the UK, #17 in Ireland, and #25 in Australia.

Weird OHW Fact... Although it launched his solo career, Beck has stated that the song is like having a "pink toilet seat hung around your neck for the rest of your life".

Weird OHW Fact... John Paul Jones (soon to form Led Zeppelin) played bass, and Rod Stewart sang backing vocals.

JERRY JAYE - MY GIRL JOSEPHINE

Jerry Jaye, from Manila, Arkansas, grew up as a country/rockabilly singer. He recorded the Fats Domino song, My Girl Josephine, on his debut album, and the single rose to #29 in the Billboard Hot 100. Four other singles taken from the album did not chart. In 1975, he had two minor hits in the Country Chart, but he never hit mainstream again.

JON AND ROBIN AND THE IN-CROWD - DO IT AGAIN A LITTLE BIT SLOWER

Written by Wayne Carson Thompson (he wrote The Box Tops' hit, The Letter', and the #1, Always On My Mind) for the duo, Jon Abdnor Jr., and Javonne (Robin) Braga. It was released on Abdnor's father's label, Abnak Records, and got to #18 in the Billboard Hot 100. The duo split up the next year. The 'In Crowd' were other Abnak artists.

KENNY O'DELL - BEAUTIFUL PEOPLE

Born Kenneth Gist Jr. in Oklahoma, and before becoming a successful country star, he wrote, Next Plane to London, a one hit wonder for Rose Garden (see entry below). His next penned song, released as a solo venture, Beautiful People, reached #38 in the Billboard Hot 100, much higher than his follow-ups. He turned to country in 1974, having hits in the Country Charts of USA and Canada.

Weird OHW Fact... O'Dell wrote the country hit, Behind Closed Doors, a hit for Charlie Rich, which won a Grammy in 1973.

KIM WESTON & MARVIN GAYE - IT TAKES TWO

Written by William 'Mickey' Stevenson and Sylvia Moy, it was recorded by Weston and Gaye on Tamla Records. The duet reached #14 in the Billboard hot 100, #4 in the Soul Chart, and #16 in the UK Charts.

Weird OHW Fact... Decades later, in 1990, Kim Weston recorded a duet with Frankie Gaye (the late Marvin Gaye's brother), to record a new version of the song.

LINDA JONES - HYPNOTIZED

Born in Newark, New Jersey, Jones was originally a gospel singer, discovered at a local club. Signed by Loma Records, her first single was their biggest hit, reaching #21 in the Billboard Hot 100, and #4 in the R&B Chart. Her best follow-up only reached #61, although she charted regularly in the R&B Chart.

MIRIAM MAKEBA - PATA PATA

Written by South African Miriam Makeba and Jerry Ragovoy, and first recorded in 1959 in her native South Africa by Makeba's girl group, The Skylarks. Re-recorded with a spoken part in English, it reached #12 in the Billboard Hot 100.

Weird OHW Fact... Pata Pata, means, Touch Touch.

Weird OHW Fact... She performed the song in Italy in 2008, just minutes before she collapsed on stage and died, aged 76.

THE MOJO MEN - SIT DOWN, I THINK I LOVE YOU

Written by Stephen Stills, and originally recorded by Buffalo Springfield the year before, it was a hit for the San Francisco group, The Mojo Men. Their 'Mamas and Papas' style recording reached #36 in the Billboard Hot 100, #39 in Cashbox, and #26 in Canada. They never charted again.

THE MUSIC EXPLOSION - LITTLE BIT O' SOUL

Sold over 1 million copies.
Written in 1964 by John Carter and Ken Lewis, and originally recorded by Coventry's, The Little Darlings, it was a US hit for Mansfield, Ohio's rock band, The Music Explosion. It reached #2, in the Billboard Hot 100, but their follow-up single, Sunshine Games, just got to #63.

THE MUSIC MACHINE - TALK TALK
Written by band member Sean Bonniwell, garage rockers, The Music machine, recorded the song for RCA Records. At under two minutes, it still had four timing charges. It reached #15 in the Billboard Hot 100, staying in the charts for 12 weeks. Their follow-up, The People In me, did not chart.

OSCAR TONEY, JR. - FOR YOUR PRECIOUS LOVE
Born in Selma, Alabama and raised in Georgia, Tomey was originally a gospel singer. After trying to break into the music industry, he signed to Bell Records, and his first single reached #23 in the Billboard hot 100, and #4 in the R&B Chart. His follow-up, Turn On Your Love Light, just reached #65.

PARADE - SUNSHINE GIRL
Written by Jerry Riopelle, Murray MacLeod, and Allen "Smokey" Roberds, musicians and actors, they showed the song to A&M Records, who immediately signed them up. Using studio musicians,
Sunshine Girl reached #20 in the Billboard hot 100. Their follow-up singles, She's Got the Magic, and, Frog Prince, did not chart.
Weird OHW Fact... Stuart Margolin, soon to be actor, co-wrote the B-side with the band.

THE PARLIAMENTS - (I WANNA) TESTIFY
Written by band leader George Clinton and Deron Taylor, it was the third single released by the Detroit group, The Parliaments. It reached #3 in the R&B Chart and #20 in the Billboard Hot 100. It would turn out to be their only charting hit.
Weird OHW Fact... The only band member to be on the recording was George Clinton, the rest could not make it to the studio.

ROBERT KNIGHT – EVERLASTING LOVE
Written by Buzz Cason and Mac Gayden, this Motown sound-alike was originally a B-side for Robert Knight. Luckily someone started to play it, and it became a hit. It reached #13 in the Billboard Hot 100, and #40 in

the UK Charts. It has been covered extensively, from Gloria Estefan to Ireland's U2.

Weird OHW Fact... Covered by the Town Criers in Australia, it reached #2 there.

THE ROSE GARDEN - NEXT PLANE TO LONDON

Written by Kenny O'Dell (see entry above), it was recorded by Los Angeles, California, folk/rock band who hit it big with their debut single. Next Plane to London, on Atco records, got to #17 in the Billboard Hot 100. Their follow-ups were unsuccessful.

SCOTT MCKENZIE - SAN FRANCISCO (BE SURE TO WEAR FLOWERS IN YOUR HAIR)

Reached #1 in the UK.

Sold more than 7 million copies.

The 66th biggest selling single of all time.

Written by John Phillips (Mamas & the Papas) who played guitars and sitar on the track, the song was recorded by Scott McKenzie for his album, The Voice of Scott McKenzie. It was an instant hit, reaching #4 in the Billboard Hot 100, and getting to #1 in the UK.

Weird OHW Fact... The Bee Gees song, Massachusetts, is an answer to McKenzie's single, about an easterner who goes to San Francisco, and is homesick for Massachusetts.

THE SEEDS - PUSHIN' TOO HARD

Written by band vocalist Sky Saxon (born Richard Elvern Marsh), it was recorded and released as, (You're) Pushin' Too Hard, in November 1965, and is an excellent example of a slow burner. It did not chart, then when the band released an album in April, 1966, one Los Angeles DJ began to play the single. Re-released in November, with the title changed slightly, it reached #36 in the Billboard Hot 100, spending 11 weeks in the chart, #40 in Cashbox.

Weird OHW Fact... Some radio stations banned the song, thinking that the lyric content referred to pushing illegal drugs.

SENATOR BOBBY - WILD THING

William 'Bill' Minkin is an American comedian, famous for his political satire. He recorded 'Wild Thing' on both sides of the single, one side mimicking Senator Robert Kennedy, the other Senator Everett Dirksen. The single got to #20 in the Billboard Hot 100.

SENATOR EVERETT MCKINLEY DIRKSEN - GALLANT MEN

Considering Senator Bobby's entry above, Republican Senator Dirksen himself recorded four spoken-word albums, and in one recorded his own poem, Gallant Men. Released as a single, it reached #29 in the Billboard Hot 100, then the oldest person to have done so. (This has since been eclipsed by Moms Mabley in 1969, and Gordon Sinclair in 1974; both one hit wonders).

Weird OHW Fact... In 1968, Dirksen won a Grammy for his recordings, Best Documentary Recording.

SOPWITH CAMEL - HELLO HELLO
Exceptional one hit wonders, America's psychedelic rockers Sopwith Camel made an album, had a hit single, and split up... all in just six months. The song reached #26 in the Billboard Hot 100 and #9 in Canada. Their best follow-up, Postcard From Jamaica, reached #88.

Weird OHW Fact... The Sopwith Camel is the name of a WW1 British biplane.

THE SUNSHINE COMPANY - BACK ON THE STREET AGAIN
From Los Angeles, California, they recorded the song on their debut album, Happy Is the Sunshine Company, on Imperial Records. It reached #36 in the Billboard Hot 100, but their best follow-up was, Look Here Comes The Sun, charting at #56. The band split up after 3 albums.

SPYDER TURNER - STAND BY ME
Born Dwight David Turner, this Detroit soul singer released a cover of Ben E. King's, Stand By me. The single reached #3 in the Billboard Black Singles chart and #12 in the Billboard Hot 100. He released an album, but the follow-up, I Can't Make it Anymore, only got to #95.

VICTOR LUNDBERG - AN OPEN LETTER TO MY TEENAGE SON
Sold over 1 million copies.
Victor Lundberg, from Grand Rapids, Michigan, was a radio presenter, and penned a 'letter' to his teenage son, spoken over the tune, Battle Hymn of the Republic. The patriotic urge for the young to fight for their country rose in just three weeks to #10 in the Billboard Hot 100, then vanished just as quickly. It sparked a plethora of similar recordings.

Weird OHW Fact... The identity of the actual 'son' in question was never released; Lundberg had at least one teenage son at the time.

WHISTLING JACK SMITH - I WAS KAISER BILL'S BATMAN
Written by Roger Cook and Roger Greenaway, who were one hit wonders themselves with Michelle in 1966, and wrote You've Got Your

Troubles, I'd Like to Teach the World to Sing, and Long Cool Woman in a Black Dress, among many other hits. This predominantly whistling song was originally called, Too Much Birdseed, and reached #5 in the UK Chart, staying in the chart for 12 weeks. Released in the US, it got to #20 in the Billboard Hot 100.

Weird OHW Fact... the artist's name, Whistling Jack Smith, is taken from Whispering Jack Smith, a well-known singer in the 20's and 30's.

THE YELLOW BALLOON - YELLOW BALLOON

Written by Gary Zekley for Jan & Dean's new album, the duos actual recording and arrangement were disliked by Zekley. He immediately passed it to other recording labels, and it was released by Canterbury Records by an ensemble of studio musicians named, The Yellow Balloon. Their recording reached #25 in the Billboard Hot 100. Although an album was hastily put together, the band did not chart again.

Weird OHW Fact... Jan & Dean's version only reached #111, vindicating Zekley's initial opinion.

Weird OHW Fact... With no B-side available for such a rushed job, the B-side was the song played backwards, and was entitled... Noollab Wolley.

1968...

As Martin Luther King Jr. is shot dead at the Lorraine Motel in Memphis, Tennessee, the year begins...
The Tet Offensive begins by Viet Cong forces in Viet Nam, Viet Cong soldiers attack the US Embassy in Saigon, the musical Hair opens on Broadway, the first International Special Olympics Summer Games are held in Chicago, Hawaii Five-O debuts on CBS, Richard Nixon wins the US presidential Election.

AMBOY DUKES - JOURNEY TO THE CENTER OF THE MIND
Written by Ted Nugent and Steve farmer (title is a novel by Irving Shulman) it was recorded on their second album of the same name. It reached #16 in the Billboard Hot 100, and was released in the UK as The American Amboy Dukes (amazingly a British band already had the name). Despite a few attempts, it was the band's only chart hit.

THE AVANT-GARDE - NATURALLY STONED
The Avant-Garde was a flash in the pan psychedelic pop group. They released three singles, having the narrowest success with the middle of the three. Naturally Stoned reached #40 in the Billboard Hot 100, but the follow-up, Fly With Me!, did not chart. The band broke up immediately afterwards.

THE BALLOON FARM - A QUESTION OF TEMPERATURE
The Balloon Farm from New Jersey, who took their name from a New York City nightclub, is best known for their single hit on Laurie Records. A Question of Temperature, reached #37 in the Billboard Hot 100. Their follow-up single, Hurry Up Sundown, did not chart, and not even an album was produced.

BARBARA ACKLIN - LOVE MAKES A WOMAN
Written by Eugene Record and Carl Davis it was recorded by the girl who had gone from receptionist at the record company to one of its stars. The song reached #15 in the Billboard Hot 100, #3 in the R&B Chart, and #15 in Canada. She turned to music writing, and had hits there too, but she never charted solo again.

BIG BROTHER AND THE HOLDING COMPANY - PIECE OF MY HEART
Sold over 1 million copies.

Written by Jerry Ragovoy and Bert Berns, and originally recorded by Erma Franklin in 1967, Janis Joplin's vocals carried it to #12 in the Billboard Hot 100. It would be Joplin's last single with the band before going solo.

Weird OHW Fact... Joplin was also a one hit wonder on her own merit. Amazingly just one of her solo singles, Me And Bobby McGee, got inside the Top 40 (#1 US), her nearest hits were, Kozmic Blues (#41 US), and Cry Baby (#43 US).

BLUE CHEER - SUMMERTIME BLUES

Written by Eddie Cochran and his manager Jerry Capehart in 1958, it was recorded by San Francisco rock band, Blue Cheer, on their debut album, Vincebus Eruptum. The single reached #14 in the Billboard Hot 100, and #3 in Canada. The follow-up, Just a Little Bit, reached #92, the last of their singles to break the Hot 100.

BOBBY TAYLOR & THE VANCOUVERS - DOES YOUR MAMA KNOW ABOUT ME

Co-written by Tommy Chong (yes, he's the other half of comedian duo Cheech & Chong) it was recorded by the Vancouver band on their debut album. The single reached #29 in the Billboard Hot 100, and #44 in their native Canada. Primed for stardom, the band's follow-ups came close, I Am Your Man, (US #85, US R&B #40, Canada #80) and, Malinda (US #48, US R&B #16, Canada #59).

The band broke up soon after.

Weird OHW Fact... At one point, the band was called Four Niggers & a Chink.

Weird OHW Fact... At their gigs, they were supported by a new local band... The Jackson 5.

BULL & THE MATADORS - THE FUNKY JUDGE

Not much known here... Bull & the Matadors were a funk group from East St Louis, Illinois. Their first single reached #39 in the Billboard Hot 100, and #9 in the R&B Charts, but their follow-ups, Move With the Groove, and, You Decide/Love Come Down, never charted.

CLIFF NOBLES AND CO. - THE HORSE

Sold over 1 million copies.

This is a strange one... Clifford James Nobles is a pop singer, who wrote a song... The Horse. On the B-side of the single is an instrumental of the song. The B-side got the airplay, and was the hit, reaching #2 in the Billboard Hot 100, #2 in the R&B Singles Chart, and getting a gold record. The band then released an album to cash in, mostly instrumentals. So, Nobles, the singer, got famous for not actually singing.

THE CRAZY WORLD OF ARTHUR BROWN - FIRE

Reached #1 in UK and Canada.
Sold over 1 million copies.
Written by Arthur Brown, Vincent Crane, Mike Finesilver and Peter Ker, it was included on their debut album. A surprise hit, it, reached #1 in the UK Chart and in Canada, #2 in the Billboard Hot 100, #3 in Germany, #4 in France, #6 in Netherlands, #7 in Austria, #8 in Ireland, #18 in Finland, and #19 in Australia.
Weird OHW Fact... Arthur Brown performed many times with parts of his attire on fire. He was burnt many times, and had to insure the act against damage to the stage. He also sang with a bowl of flaming methanol on his head, the bolt burnt his skull, and once when the bowl spilled onto his face, he was doused with beer to put the fire out.

DON FARDON - INDIAN RESERVATION

Sold over 1 million copies.
Don Fardon (born Donald Arthur Maughn), from Coventry, started his musical life as a singer for The Sorrows. Once he had gone solo, he recorded Indian Reservation (Written by John D. Loudermilk) and took the song to #3 in the UK Chart, #20 in the Billboard Hot 100, and #4 in Australia. His best follow-up, Follow Your Drum, reached #16 in Australia, but did not chart in the UK or USA.

THE EQUALS - BABY, COME BACK

Reached #1 in the UK, and Belgium.
Written by band leader Eddy Grant (born in British Guiana), and originally recorded by The Equals from North London, it is a classic example of a slow burner. Released in 1966, it stalled in the UK, but eventually hit Top 10 in Belgium and Netherlands, forcing a UK re-release. It reached #1 in the UK Chart (staying in the chart for 18 weeks), and Belgium, #2 in France and Ireland, #4 in Norway, #9 in Canada, #11 in Australia and Germany, and #32 in the Billboard Hot 100.
Weird OHW Fact... British fans will remember Eddy Grant's big 1983 hit, Electric Avenue. Bet you didn't know he'd had a number one 15 years before!

FOUR JACKS AND A JILL - MASTER JACK

Reached #1 in South Africa.

Written by David Marks, the song was recorded by folk rock band Four Jacks and a Jill on their fifth album, Master Jack. Already having a few hits in their native South Africa, it reached #1 there, #3 in the US Adult Contemporary Chart, #18 in the Billboard Hot 100, and #18 in Australia. The song did not chart in the UK. It would be their only international hit.

FRIEND & LOVER - REACH OUT OF THE DARKNESS

Written by Jim Post, it was recorded by Jim and his wife Cathy (the duo, Friend & Lover), on their debut and only album. The song reached #10 in the Billboard Hot 100, but the follow up, If Love Is in Your Heart, also from the album, only got to #86.

GENE AND DEBBE - PLAYBOY

Sold over 1 million copies.

Gene Thomasson and Debbe Neville were a husband and wife duo from Palestine, Texas. Their Everly Brothers style gave them just one hit, Playboy, reaching #17 in the Billboard Hot 100. Their follow-ups did not chart, and the duo stopped recording.

THE GUN – RACE WITH THE DEVIL

With brothers Adrian and Paul Gurvitz at the helm, The Gun was their second rock incarnation. From their debut album, the song, Race With The Devil, got to #10 in their native UK, and #35 in Australia. The band soon broke up with the Gurvitz brothers later forming the Baker Gurvitz Army.

Weird OHW Fact... Jon Anderson (Yes) was in the band at the time.

Weird OHW Fact... It was cover artist, Roger Dean's first album cover.

HENSON CARGILL - SKIP A ROPE

Country singer Henson Cargill's debut single from his debut album was, Skip a Rope. It got to #1 of both the US and Canadian Country Charts, then crossed over into #25 in the Billboard Hot 100, and #38 in Australia. He had many other Country hits, but never made the mainstream charts again.

THE HESITATIONS - BORN FREE

The Hesitations are R&B group from Cleveland, Ohio. Their first single, Soul Superman, grazed the Black Singles chart at #42, but their gospel-sounding version of the movie theme made it big. Born Free reached

#38 in the Billboard Hot 100, but the follow-up Climb Every Mountain, only got to #90.

Weird OHW Fact... After the fatal shooting of vocalist George "King" Scott, the group broke up.

HUGH MASEKELA - GRAZING IN THE GRASS

Reached #1 in the USA.

Written by Philemon Hou, the tune was first recorded by South African trumpeter Hugh Masekela on the album of the same name. The lazy jazz tune reached #1 in the Billboard Hot 100.

Billboard ranked the single as #18 of 1968.

Weird OHW Fact... Masekela lost the best pop instrumental Grammy to Mason Williams', Classical Gas.

Weird OHW Fact... On a connected side note, a copy editor changed the name of the song, originally called, Classical Gasoline.

HUGO MONTENEGRO - THE GOOD, THE BAD AND THE UGLY

Reached #1 in the UK.

Sold more than 1 million copies.

Hugo Mario Montenegro is best known for his interpretations from orchestral scores; he produced many albums of the same. The best example was Ennio Morricone's, The Good, the Bad and the Ugly. Montenegro's version went to #2 in the Billboard Hot 100, #3 in Canada, and #1 in the UK, where it remained at the top for 4 weeks.

Weird OHW Fact... Staying on the Clint Eastwood spaghetti idea, Montenegro's theme from, Hang 'Em High, hit #59 in Canada.

THE HUMAN BEINZ – NOBODY BUT ME

Written by Ronald Isley, Rudolph Isley, O'Kelly Isley, of (believe it or not) The Isley Brothers, the more successful version was recorded by Struthers, Ohio's garage band, The Human Beinz. Their version got to #8 in the Billboard Hot 100. The follow-up, Turn On Your Love Light, just reached #80 in the US, but staggeringly, got to #1 in Japan. The band broke up the next year, but due to contract obligations had to tour Japan anyway.

Weird OHW Fact... The song holds a weird record; the word, 'no', is said 100 times in two minutes, and is repeated 31 times in a row. The word, 'nobody', is said 43 times.

IRON BUTTERFLY - IN-A-GADDA-DA-VIDA

Written by band member Doug Ingle, the 17 minute track was recorded on their second album, taking up the whole of the album's B-side.

Despite its length, it reached #30 in the Billboard Hot 100. Other singles charted, but 1970's, Easy Rider (Let the Wind Pay the Way), was the closest to a hit (US #66). The band temporarily broke up in 1971.

Weird OHW Fact... In 2009, the song was named by VH1 as the 24th 'greatest hard rock song of all time'.

JEANNIE C. RILEY - HARPER VALLEY P.T.A.

Reached #1 in Australia, Canada, and USA.

Sold over 5 million copies.

Written by Tom T. Hall, it was first offered to Skeeter Davis, who passed it by. Unknown country singer Jeannie C. Riley from Stamford, Texas, recorded it, and it was released quickly as Billie Jo Spears was known to have recorded it. The song shot to #1 in the Billboard Hot 100, in Canada and in Australia, #12 in the UK, and #13 in New Zealand.

Weird OHW Fact... It was the first single to top both the Billboard Hot 100 and the US Country Chart. (Dolly Parton's 9 to 5, would be the second.)

Billboard ranked the song as #17 of 1968.

THE JIMI HENDRIX EXPERIENCE - ALL ALONG THE WATCHTOWER

Written by Bob Dylan, Jimi Hendrix recorded it at Olympic Studios in London, just a year after arriving in the UK. Hendrix was such a perfectionist that he was left to complete the bass part himself. The single reached #5 in the UK Charts, then #20 in the Billboard Hot 100, his highest US Chart position. Hey Joe (UK #6), Purple Haze (UK #3, US #65), and The Wind Cries Mary (UK #6, US #65)), all missed the US Top 40, making Jimi Hendrix a US one hit wonder. His last 'hit' was, Crosstown Traffic/Gypsy Eyes (UK #37, US #52).

Weird OHW Fact... Hendrix only recorded three studio albums, of which Electric Ladyland is considered the best.

JOHN FRED AND HIS PLAYBOY BAND - JUDY IN DISGUISE (WITH GLASSES)

Reached #1 in US, Germany and Switzerland.

Sold over 1 million copies.

Written by band members John Fred and Andrew Bernard, it was recorded on the Louisiana band's album, Agnes English. The song reached #1 in US, Germany and Switzerland, and #3 in the UK and Ireland. Their follow-up single, Hey, Hey, Bunny, just reached #57 on the Billboard chart.

Weird OHW Fact... The title is a play on the Beatles song, Lucy in the Sky With Diamonds, and it knocked another Beatles song, Hello, Goodbye, from the #1 spot for 2 weeks.

KASENETZ-KATZ SINGING ORCHESTRAL CIRCUS - QUICK JOEY SMALL (RUN JOEY RUN)

The whole idea of this bubblegum group was formed by record producers Jerry Kasenetz and Jeff Katz. They brought together some of the bands under their production company and formed a totally fictitious ensemble. It did not stop the single from selling, however, and it reached #25 in the Billboard Hot 100, #19 in the UK Charts, and #33 in Australia.

Weird OHW Fact... One of the bands was the, St. Louis Invisible Marching Band.

Yup.

LEAPY LEE - LITTLE ARROWS

Sold more than 3 million copies.

Written by Albert Hammond and Mike Hazlewood, it was recorded by Leapy Lee (born Graham Pulleyblank) on his debut album on Decca Records. It reached #2 in the UK Chart, #16 in the Billboard Hot 100, #11 in Hot Country, #8 in Canada, and #1 in the Canadian Country Chart. It was his third single, and made him a one hit wonder all over the world... except the UK, where a follow-up, Good Morning, reached #29.

Weird OHW fact... Leapy served three years in prison with his actor friend Alan Lake in1970, after being involved in a pub brawl.

THE LEMON PIPERS - GREEN TAMBOURINE

Reached number 1 in U.S.A.

Sold over a million copies.

Written by Paul Leka (and Shelley Pinz, it was recorded on debut album of the same name. It was the biggest hit by the Ohio rock group and reached #1 in the Billboard Hot 100 where it spent 13 weeks in the chart. Elsewhere it got to #2 in Australia, #3 in Canada, and #7 in the UK Charts. Their follow-ups, Rice Is Nice and Jelly Jungle, also written by Leka and Pinz, did not chart.

Weird OHW Fact... Paul Leka also wrote, Na Na Hey Hey Kiss Him Goodbye, a 1969 one hit wonder with band, Steam.

MADELINE BELL - I'M GONNA MAKE YOU LOVE ME

Written by Kenneth Gamble and Jerry Ross, the song was originally a minor hit for Dee Dee Warwick in 1966. In the UK, the song was offered to Dusty Springfield, who passed it onto bell, her American backing singer. Her version reached #3 in the UK Charts, then it hit America, reaching #26 in the Billboard Hot 100, #32 in the R&B Chart, prompting Bell to do a small tour in the USA.

Weird OHW Fact... The song's success prompted Diana Ross and the Supremes to make a version in the same year, hitting top ten everywhere; it is generally the version everyone remembers.

THE MAGIC LANTERNS - SHAME, SHAME

The Magic Lanterns were a typical example of success away from home. Formed as The Sabres in the Manchester area, they did have one minor UK hit after they changed their name, Excuse Me Baby, reaching #44 in the UK Charts. But it was not until their move to Atlantic Records that they struck stardom. Shame, Shame, reached #29 in the Billboard Hot 100, and #3 in Canada. It did not chart in the UK.

Weird OHW Fact... Notable members of the band were, Kevin Godley, Lol Creme (both of 10cc), Albert Hammond (a huge songwriter), and Steve Rowland.

Weird OHW Fact... The bassist was Mike 'Oz' Osborne, and he spent his life beating away fans trying to establish if Ozzy Osborne had ever played with the band before forming Black Sabbath.

MASON WILLIAMS - CLASSICAL GAS

Sold more than 1 million copies.

Mason Douglas Williams is a strange mix; first he wrote Classical gas, (3 times Grammy winner), and gold record, second he wrote comedy sketches for Smothers Brothers Comedy Hour, The Glen Campbell Goodtime Hour, and Saturday Night Live. The instrumental shot to #2 in the Billboard Hot 100, and #1 in the Easy Listening Chart. The tune won Grammys for Best Instrumental Composition, Best Contemporary-Pop Performance, Instrumental, and Best Instrumental Arrangement.

Weird OHW Fact... The tune was originally called, 'Classical Gasoline', but the title was shortened by a clerk of the record company.

Weird OHW Fact... He also co-wrote, Cinderella Rockefella, a supposed UK 'one hit wonder' for Esther and Abi Ofarim... see, 'Oh so Close... But no Cigar...' below.

MAX FROST AND THE TROOPERS - SHAPE OF THINGS TO COME

This is a complex one... probably written by Paul Wibier for the movie, Wild in the Streets, the actual 'Max Frost and the Troopers' were a band from the movie (the actual music was probably played by Dave Allen & The Arrows, a one hit wonder from 1966). The song was released and because of its success, an album was made. The single reached #22 in the Billboard Hot 100. Subsequent releases did not chart.

MERRILEE RUSH AND THE TURNABOUTS - ANGEL OF THE MORNING
Reached #1 in Canada, Australia and New Zealand.
Written by Chip Taylor, it took a while to get the right singer (The song refers to a one night stand) to perform it. Merilee Rush, then the opening act for Paul Revere and the Raiders, recorded the song and it was an immediate hit. It reached #7 in the Billboard Hot 100, and went on to be #1 in Canada, Australia and New Zealand.
Weird OHW Fact... It stalled in conservative Britain, just reaching #55. P. P. Arnold had a minor hit with it.
Weird OHW Fact... It was included on the soundtrack of the movie, Girl, Interrupted. Songwriter Chip Taylor's niece, Angelina Jolie, had the starring role.

THE O'KAYSIONS - GIRL WATCHER
Sold over 1 million copies.
Written by Ronald B. Killette and Wayne Pittman and recorded by The O'Kaysions from Wilson, North Carolina. Stalled under their small label, it was released from ABC Records, and reached #5 in the Billboard Hot 100, and #6 in the UK Chart. The follow-up, Love Machine, peaked at #76.
Billboard ranked the song as #45 of 1968.

PAUL MAURIAT - LOVE IS BLUE
Reached #1 in USA.
Sold over 1 million copies.
Written by André Popp and Pierre Cour, English lyrics were added by Brian Blackburn. Following Vicky Leandros's success with the song, Paul Mauriat's instrumental appealed to a different audience. It reached #1 in the USA, where it stayed for 5 weeks, the first performance by a French artist to top the chart. It also reached #12 in the UK Charts and topped the US Easy Listening Chart for 11 weeks.
Billboard ranked the record as the #2 song for 1968.

PEOPLE! - I LOVE YOU
Reached #1 in Japan, Israel, Australia, Italy, and South Africa.

Written by Zombies band member Chris White, it was first a hit for the Zombies in 1965. The San Jose rock band, People! recorded the song for their debut album. It only reached #14 in the Billboard Chart, but was a #1 in Japan, Israel, Australia, Italy, and South Africa. The band broke up in 1970 after a disagreement over Scientology.

PIGMEAT MARKHAM - HERE COMES THE JUDGE

Dewey 'Pigmeat' Markham was an all-round entertainer from Durham, North Carolina, best remembered as a comedian. He performed his comedy song, Here Comes the Judge, on Rowan and Martin's Laugh In, and was immediately encouraged to record it. The novelty song reached #4 in the R&B Chart, #19 in the Billboard Hot 100, #19 in the UK Charts, and #71 in Australia. His other releases did not chart, although he did record 19 albums.

RICHARD HARRIS - MACARTHUR PARK

Reached #1 in Australia and Canada.
Written by Jimmy Webb after a failed love affair, it was first recorded by Irish actor Richard Harris on his second album, A Tramp Shining. Fresh from the musical movie, Camelot, the song reached #1 in Australia and Canada, #2 in the Billboard Hot 100, #4 in the UK Chart, and #9 in Ireland.
The song won the 1969 Grammy Award for Best Arrangement Accompanying Vocalist(s).
Weird OHW Fact... It has also been described as 'the worst song ever written'. Go listen to him singing it live...!
Weird OHW Fact... The most notable version of the song was Donna Summer's disco version in 1978.

THE SANDPEBBLES - LOVE POWER

Written by Luther Vandross, Marcus Miller, and Teddy Vann, it was recorded by R&B group, The Sandpebbles, on Calla Records. It reached #14 in the Black Singles chart and #22 in the Billboard Hot 100.
Weird OHW Fact... It was revived by Luther Vandross in 1991, taking it to #4.

SHORTY LONG - HERE COMES THE JUDGE

Written by Shorty Long, Billie Jean Brown, and Suzanne de Passe, after hearing a similar song by comedian Pigmeat Markham, on Rowan and Martin's Laugh In. This new song was recorded by Birmingham, Alabama's Long and it reached #4 in the R&B chart and #8 in the

Billboard Hot 100, staying in the chart for 11 weeks. It also charted in the UK at #30.

Weird OHW Fact... Pigmeat Markham's own (different) song using the same title, Here Comes the Judge, charted just two weeks after Long's did (see listing above), reaching #19.

STATUS QUO - PICTURES OF MATCHSTICK MEN

Written by band leader Francis Rossi, it was their debut single, and taken from their album, Picturesque Matchstickable Messages from the Status Quo. It was a worldwide success, reaching #7 in the UK, Germany, Ireland, Sweden, and New Zealand, 38 in Canada, #12 in the Billboard Hot 100, and #19 in Australia. Status Quo tried for years to duplicate their US Success, to no avail; they will always be remembered as a USA one hit wonder.

Weird OHW Fact... Rossi wrote the song sitting on the toilet waiting for his mother in law to leave.

Weird OHW Fact... The lyrics refer to the 'matchstick' paintings of Salford's L. S. Lowry (Brian and Michael had a one hit wonder with the same subject matter in 1978 - Matchstalk Men And Matchstalk Cats And Dogs).

STEPPENWOLF – BORN TO BE WILD

Reached #1 in Canada.

Written by Canadian Dennis Edmonton (born Dennis Eugene McCrohan), best known by his stage name, Mars Bonfire. Briefly in the band, he specifically wrote Born To Be Wild for Steppenwolf, and continued to write for them during his solo career. The single, the second from their debut album, reached #1 in the band's native Canada, #2 in the Billboard Hot 100, #13 in New Zealand, #16 in Belgium, #20 in Germany and Austria, #30 in the UK, and #32 in the Netherlands.

It was their only hit in the UK and Netherlands, hence their inclusion here.

Billboard ranked the song as #31 of 1968.

Weird OHW Fact... It was the first mention of 'heavy metal' in any song lyrics, although the term was already loosely used.

THE SWEET INSPIRATIONS - SWEET INSPIRATION

R&B group, The Sweet Inspirations, had weighty credentials... Emily Houston was mother of Whitney Houston, and sister of Lee Warrick. Their only chart success, however, came with their recording of Sweet Inspiration, which reached #18 in the Billboard Hot 100.

Weird OHW Fact... The Sweet Inspirations were the backing vocals on Van Morrison's classic hit, Brown Eyed Girl.

TINY TIM - TIP TOE THRU' THE TULIPS WITH ME
Written in 1929 by Al Dubin, and Joe Burke, it had been used in cartoons until Manhattan Tiny Tim (born Herbert Buckingham Khaury) began to play the song at his gigs. In 1968 after appearing in a couple of feature films, he recorded it on his first album, God Bless Tiny Tim. The single got to #17 in the Billboard Hot 100, and became his signature song.
Weird OHW Fact... Tiny Tim was actually 6 feet one, and was married three times.

VICKY LEANDROS - L'AMOUR EST BLEU (LOVE IS BLUE)
Written by André Popp, and Pierre Cour, Greek singer Vicky Leandros sang it as the Luxembourg entry to the Eurovision Song Contest in 1967. It took a while, but it eventually reached #1 in the Billboard Hot 100, making it the only French hit to ever do so.
Weird OHW Fact... Vicki also has a mention in the 'Oh so close... But no cigar...' section in 1972, having two hits in the UK)

OH SO CLOSE... BUT NO CIGAR...

ESTHER AND ABI OFARIM - CINDERELLA ROCKEFELLA
Written by Mason Williams (Classical Gas) and Nancy Ames, most people remember the duo's version as a one hit wonder, but they're wrong. Cinderella Rockefella did indeed get to #1 in the UK, and was a hit in some European countries, but the Israeli husband and wife duo had already had a hit in the UK... One More Dance, reached #13 in the UK Chart months before.
Weird OHW Fact... Abi Ofarim won the Eurovision Song Contest for Switzerland in 1963, after a controversial vote change.

TOMMY JAMES AND THE SHONDELLS - MONY MONY
From Niles, Michigan, this rock band had two US singles, and many other hits, but there are scores of people in the United Kingdom that consider them a one hit wonder. Hanky Panky, Mony Mony, Crimson and Clover, and, Crystal Blue Persuasion were all big hits in the US, but not in the UK.
Many consider Mony Mony to be their only UK hit, however, they're wrong. Hanky Panky got to a tenuous #38 in 1966. So close...

1969...

As Led Zeppelin release their first album, and the Beatles play live for the last time on the roof of Apple Records, London, the year begins...

The Allende meteorite explodes over Mexico, the supersonic passenger jet, Concorde, has its first test flight, Prince Charles is invested as Prince of Wales at Caernarfon Castle, Apollo 11's lunar module Eagle lands on the moon's surface, the Woodstock Festival is held in New York state.

THE ARBORS - THE LETTER

Written by Wayne Carson, and first recorded by the Box Tops in 1967, the song is best known for its first line... "Give me a ticket for an aeroplane". The Arbors (from Ann Arbor, Michigan) had already grazed the chart with, A Symphony for Susan (#51), and Graduation Day (#59), but their cover version reached #20 in the Billboard Hot 100. The follow-up, I Can't Quit Her, got to #67, but they never charted again.

Weird OHW Fact... When the hits stopped, they shifted their focus, successfully writing music for commercials.

THE ARCHIES - SUGAR SUGAR

Reached #1 in Austria, Belgium, Canada, Germany, Ireland, Norway, Spain, UK and USA.

Written by Jeff Barry and Andy Kim, and performed by studio musicians for the TV cartoon series, The Archie Show. It reached #1 in the Billboard Hot 100 (for 4 weeks), in the UK (for 8 weeks) and in 8 other countries. It also reached #2 in Denmark, Switzerland, and #3 in Netherlands.

Weird OHW Fact... In 1970, Wilson Pickett covered the song, and it became a hit all over again.

BOB & EARL - HARLEM SHUFFLE

Written by Bobby Relf and Earl Nelson, the song was arranged by Barry White, and released in 1963. The first release almost made it, getting to #44 in the Billboard Hot 100. Later, in 1969, it was given a re-release, and climbed to #7 in the UK Chart, #7 in the Netherlands, #8 in Belgium.

Weird OHW Fact... George Harrison called it his favorite song of all time.

BROOKLYN BRIDGE - THE WORST THAT COULD HAPPEN

Sold over 1 million copies.

Written by Jimmy Webb, it was first recorded by The 5th Dimension in 1967, but is better known for its 1969 recording by Johnny Maestro & the Brooklyn Bridge. It reached #3 in the Billboard Hot 100.

Weird OHW Fact... Never have a band tried harder to rid themselves of the one hit wonder badge... the follow-ups in 1969 were, Blessed Is The Rain (#46), Welcome Me Love (#48), Your Husband, My Wife (#46), and You'll Never Walk Alone (#51).

Weird OHW Fact... It was listed after the 9-11 events on a list of inappropriate songs.

BUBBLE PUPPY - HOT SMOKE & SASAFRASS

From San Antonio, Texas, Bubble Puppy recorded the song on their debut album, A Gathering Of Promises. The single, Hot Smoke & Sasafrass, got to #14 in the Billboard Hot 100, #15 in Canada, and #39 in Australia. The band changed its name to Damian in 1970, and broke up in 1972.

THE BUCHANAN BROTHERS - MEDICINE MAN

Written by Terry Cashman (born Dennis Minogue), Gene Pistilli and Tommy West, it was recorded by the trio under the name, The Buchanan Brothers. The trio had already had a one hit wonder in 1967, Sunday Will Never Be the Same, under the name Spanky and Our Gang. Technically the song was a follow-up of, Son of a Lovin' Man, (#50 in Canada), but Medicine Man reached #22 in the Billboard Hot 100 and #15 in Canada. Cashman and West produced all Jim Croce's work.

CAT MOTHER & THE ALL NIGHT NEWS BOYS - GOOD OLD ROCK AND ROLL

Founded by Roy Michaels and Bob Smith in New York, they played with Stephen Stills and many other prominent musicians. They are best remembered for their medley of rock n' roll hits from their debut album, The Street Giveth and the Street Taketh Away, produced by Jimi Hendrix. The single got to #21 in the Billboard Hot 100. The song was ranked #35 in the top 50 songs of the summer of 69.

CHARLES RANDOLPH GREAN SOUNDE - QUENTIN'S THEME

Charles Randolph Grean was an American composer and musician and had already written a couple of hits. As a performer, however, he only charted once, his version of Robert Cobert's, Quentin's Theme, from the movie Dark Shadows reached #13 in the Billboard hot 100.

THE CHECKMATES, LTD. - BLACK PEARL

Written by Phil Spector, Toni Wine, and Irwin Levine, it was recorded by The Checkmates, Ltd, on their first studio album, Love Is All We have To Give. It reached #8 in the R&B Chart, #13 in the Billboard Hot 100, and #31 in Australia. The best of their follow-ups, Proud Mary, only reached #69 in the US, but did chart at #30 in the UK Chart, making them a US one hit wonder. The band broke up in 1970.

Billboard ranked the song as #66 of 1969.

CLARENCE REID - NOBODY BUT YOU BABE

Of Cochran Georgia's Clarence Henry Reid, we must ask ourselves a question... is it better to be remembered for a one hit wonder, or not remembered at all? Later known as 'Blowfly', and known for his explicit lyrics, his one hit got to #40 in the Billboard Hot 100. With 30+ albums, he certainly was prolific.

CLIQUE - SUGAR ON SUNDAY

Written by band member Gary Zekley, The Clique began life as the Roustabouts, from Beaumont, Texas. Sugar on Sunday was their second single, and it reached #22 in the Billboard Hot 100. Subsequent releases did not chart.

Weird OHW Fact... The B-side, Superman, was recorded by R.E.M. on their album Life's Rich Pageant, in 1986.

CRAZY ELEPHANT - GIMME GIMME GOOD LOVIN'

Written by Joey Levine and Ritchie Cordell, the song was recorded by this changing bubblegum ensemble on their debut album. It reached #12 in the Billboard Hot 100, and #12 in the UK Chart, making them only one of a few that did this (Zager and Evans, 2525, being another). Subsequent singles did not chart on either side of the Atlantic.

Billboard ranked the song as #89 of 1969.

Weird OHW Fact... Lead singers and band members changed with every single release, future 10cc member Kevin Godley sang on their last single, There Ain't No Umbopo.

THE CUFF LINKS - TRACY

Reached #1 in Canada.

Sold over 1 million copies.

Written by Paul Vance and Lee Pockriss, the song was recorded by singer Ron Dante, and a bunch of studio musicians. Tracy quickly reached #9 in the Billboard Hot 100, #4 in the UK, #9 in Australia, and a staggering #1 in Canada. The follow up, When Julie Comes Around, reached #10 in the UK, #13 in Australia #24 in Canada, but only #41 in the Billboard Chart, making them a US one hit wonder.

Weird OHW Fact... The success of Tracy prompted an album, Tracy, which was recorded in just two days.

THE DELLS - I CAN SING A RAINBOW/LOVE IS BLUE

From Harvey, Illinois, formed in High School in 1952, and had an illustrious career, with 26+ albums and many hits. However in the UK, there was only one; a medley of, I Can Sing A Rainbow, and, Love Is Blue. It reached #22 in the Billboard Hot 100, and #9 in Canada, both frequent resting places for The Dells' singles. It also hit the charts in the UK at #15, and in the Netherlands at #10, becoming a one hit wonder in both countries.

DESMOND DEKKER AND THE ACES - ISRAELITES

Reached #1 in the UK, Netherlands, Jamaica, South Africa, Canada, Sweden and West Germany.

Sold over 1 million copies.

Written by Desmond Dekker and Leslie Kong, it became his signature song. It's difficult to find a harder-working musician, kicking out singles from 1963 until 1993. Apart from topping many major charts, Israelites reached #9 in the Billboard Hot 100, a landmark first Jamaican US hit. Decker moved to the UK where he charted regularly. He will, however be remembered as a US one hit wonder.

THE ELECTRIC INDIAN - KEEM-O-SABE

A Philadelphia ensemble put together by Bernie Binnick, who was co-founder of Swan Records. This 'native Indian' instrumental soon gained national interest and reached #16 in the Billboard Chart, #6 on Easy Listening, and #19 in Canada. An album was made of similar tunes, but no further releases reached the charts.

THE FAMILY DOGG - A WAY OF LIFE

British harmony group, based on the lead singers of Los Flaps and Diamond Boys, Steve Rowland,
Albert Hammond and Mike Hazlewood. The title track from their debut album reached #5 in the UK Chart. The follow-ups did not chart, and the three singers above went on to have illustrious musical careers.

Weird OHW Fact... These singers were held in high esteem; Elton John, and Jimmy Page, John Bonham and John Paul Jones of Led Zeppelin were all guest musicians on the album.

THE FLIRTATIONS - NOTHING BUT A HEARTACHE
Written by Wayne Bickerton and Tony Waddington (the team behind The Rubettes success), it was released by the South Carolina trio, The Flirtations, on Deram records. It reached #34 in the Billboard Hot 100, staying in the chart for 14 weeks, and #34 in the Netherlands. In the UK, it hit #51, in Australia, #97.

THE FLYING MACHINE - SMILE A LITTLE SMILE FOR ME
Sold over 1 million copies.
Written by Tony Macaulay and Geoff Stephens, it was recorded by British pop group The Flying Machine, who were formed from the bones of Pinkerton's Assorted Colours (one hit wonder in 1966). The song reached #5 in the US Billboard Hot 100 and Cashbox, and got to #4 in Canada. The follow-up, Baby Make It Soon, only peaked at #87. The band broke up the next year.
Billboard ranked it as the #76 song of 1969.

GARLAND GREEN - JEALOUS KIND OF FELLA
Sold over 1 million copies.
Written by Green, R. Browner, M. Dollinson and J. Armstead, the song was recorded by Garland Green (from Dunleith, Mississippi) on MCA Records. It reached #20 in the Billboard Hot 100, #5 in the R&B Chart and #2 in Cashbox. The follow-up, Don't Think That I'm a Violent Guy, peaked at a disappointing #113. He continued to hit the R&B Charts for the next 20 years, but never had another mainstream hit.
Weird OHW Fact... Green was the tenth of eleven children.

HARLOW WILCOX AND THE OAKIES - GROOVY GRUBWORM
Sold over 1 million copies.
Written by session musician Harlow Wilcox and music producer Bobby Warren, it was recorded by Wilcox as Harlow Wilcox & the Oakies to give it a country sound. This crossover single reached #30 in the U.S. Billboard Hot 100, and #20 in Canada. It also made the #1 spot in the Canadian Country Chart. It was also nominated for a Grammy award.

HUMBLE PIE - NATURAL BORN BUGIE
Fresh from the break-up of the Small Faces, Steve Marriott got together with Peter Frampton to form one of the first Super-groups; Humble Pie. Their first single, Natural Born Bugie, reached #4 in the UK and #19 in Australia. The band issued many singles, like I Don't Need No Doctor (US #73) and Hot n' Nasty (US #52), but they never charted again, and did not break into the US Top 40.

THE ILLUSION - DID YOU SEE HER EYES

From Long Island, New York, The Illusion was a hard working psychedelic hard rock band, supporting acts like The Who, Jimi Hendrix, and The Allman brothers. Their only hit, Did You See Her Eyes, reached #32 in the Billboard Hot 100. The best follow up, Together, just topped out at #80.

THE INTRIGUES - IN A MOMENT

This Philadelphia soul trio recorded, In A Moment, on their debut album, produced by Van McCoy. It would be their only hit, reaching #31 in the Billboard Hot 100 and #10 in Black Singles. The best mainstream follow-up, I'm Gonna Love You, reached just #86.

JANE BIRKIN & SERGE GAINSBOURG - JE T'AIME... MOI NON PLUS

Reached #1 in Austria, Norway, Switzerland and UK.

Written by Serge Gainsbourg, for Brigitte Bardot in 1967, Gainsbourg recorded it two years later with Jane Birkin. The resultant single was banned in many countries (including the BBC) for explicit sexual tones, but it did nothing to stop the record's success. It topped four charts, #2 in Ireland and Netherlands, #3 in Germany, #5 in Mexico, a surprising #58 in the Billboard Hot 100, and hit Top 10 in most others.

Weird OHW Fact... "Je t'aime... moi non plus", is French for "I love you... me neither". Yeah, doesn't make much sense.

Weird OHW Fact... The original recording with Gainsbourg and Bardot was not released until 1986.

JOE JEFFREY GROUP - MY PLEDGE OF LOVE

From Arkansas via Cleveland, Ohio, this rhythm and blues band has two connections with the one hit wonder story. Their only hit, My Pledge of Love , reached #14 hit in the Billboard Hot 100 and #6 in Canada. They never charted again. However, the band released a version of, My Baby Loves Lovin', at the same time as the White Plains version. White Plains got to #4 in Canada, #9 in UK, and #13 in the USA. The Joe Jeffrey Group's version just reached #115 in the Billboard hot 100.

JOE SOUTH - GAMES PEOPLE PLAY

Written by Joe South, from Atlanta, Georgia, this protest song was recorded on South's debut album, Introspect, and when released as second single from the album, was an immediate hit. It reached #12 in the Billboard Hot 100, #7 in Canada, #6 in the UK Chart, and won Grammy's for Best Contemporary Song and Song of the Year. Despite hits in the USA (Walk a Mile in My Shoes, #10 US and #12 Canada), he never charted in the UK again.

Weird OHW Fact... South also wrote another huge one hit wonder; Lynn Anderson's, (I Never Promised You a) Rose Garden.

JOHNNY ADAMS - RECONSIDER ME

Written by Margaret Lewis and Mira Smith, the country/soul ballad was recorded by New Orleans' Johnny Adams. He had already had a couple of hits on the R&B Chart, but this one broke through to mainstream. It reached #28 in the Billboard Hot 100, #8 in the R&B Chart. His follow-up, I Can't Be All Bad, only reached #89.

KAREN YOUNG - NOBODY'S CHILD

Written by Cy Coben and Mel Foree in 1949, it was included in Karen Young's debut album. The singer, from Sheffield, England, took the song to #6 in the UK Charts, but it would prove her only Top 40 hit.

KEITH BARBOUR - ECHO PARK

Written by Buzz Clifford (himself a one hit wonder in 1960), it was recorded by New York's Keith Barbour as the title track of his only album on Epic records. It reached #40 in the Billboard Hot 100, but the follow-up, My God and I, did not chart.

Weird OHW Fact... He was married to Days of Our Lives TV soap actress Deidre Hall from 1971 to 1978.

Weird OHW Fact... He was a member of The New Christy Minstrels before going solo.

LAWRENCE REYNOLDS - JESUS IS A SOUL MAN

Written by Lawrence Reynolds and Jack D. Cardwell, it was the title track of Reynolds' debut album. Born in Mobile, Alabama, Reynolds was a country singer, and Jesus is a Soul Man crossed over to the mainstream charts, reaching #28 in the Billboard Hot 100. It was his only single release.

MARMALADE - REFLECTIONS OF MY LIFE

Sold over 2 million copies.
Written by band members Junior Campbell and Dean Ford, it was recorded on their first Decca album. In this power ballad, the Scottish band from Glasgow would have their greatest hit. It reached #3 in their native UK, #6 in Canada, #10 in the Billboard Hot 100, #8 in Norway, #9 in Netherlands and Belgium, and #20 in New Zealand.

Weird OHW Fact... The band was awarded a special award for over 1 million airplays in the US alone.

Weird OHW Fact... In the UK, they might be better remembered for their 1968 #1 Beatles cover, Ob-La-Di, Ob-La-Da.

MAX ROMEO – WET DREAM

Jamaican reggae singer Max Romeo had a huge list of single releases, but on just his second attempt, he struck gold. Despite its explicit lyrics getting the single banned, it became a instant hit in his native Jamaica, and reached #10 in the UK, and #11 in the Netherlands where the title was changed to The Dream.

Weird OHW Fact... Once the record was a hit, British DJ's were told to drop the title and only introduce the record as... 'a record by Max Romeo'.

MERCY - LOVE (CAN MAKE YOU HAPPY)

Sold over 1 million copies.

Written by Jack Sigler, Jr. it was recorded by Florida pop band, Mercy, as the title track on their debut album. It was an instant hit, reaching #2 in the Billboard Hot 100, Adult Contemporary, and Easy Listening Charts. It also reached #2 in Canada. The follow-up, Forever, disappointed, just reaching #79.

Billboard ranked the song as #42 of 1969.

MOMS MABLEY - ABRAHAM, MARTIN AND JOHN

Written by Dick Holler and a hit by Dion a year earlier, comedienne Loretta Mary Aiken (Moms Mabley) covered the song in a serious recording, reaching #35 in the Billboard Hot 100 and #18 in the R&B Charts.

Weird OHW Fact... It made her the oldest living person (aged 75) to have a US Top 40 hit.

MOTHERLODE - WHEN I DIE

Reached #1 in Canada.

From London, Ontario, Canada, this pop rock group hit the charts with their debut single from their first album. When I Die reached #1 in Canada, and #18 in the Billboard Hot 100, and #12 on Cash Box. Their biggest follow-up hit, Memories Of A Broken Promise, got to #40 in Canada, but did not chart in the US.

THE NEON PHILHARMONIC - MORNING GIRL

This ensemble was led by songwriter Tupper Saussy and singer Don Gant. Featuring the Nashville Symphony Orchestra, their only hit was Morning Girl, which reached #17 in the Billboard hot 100, #15 in the Cash Box Chart, and #6 in Canada.

NOEL HARRISON - THE WINDMILLS OF YOUR MIND
Written by French composer Michel Legrand with lyrics by Americans Alan and Marilyn Bergman, it was recorded by Noel John Christopher Harrison on his second album in 1968. The song was featured as the theme song from the movie, The Thomas Crown Affair, winning the Academy Award for Best Original Song in 1968, and reaching #8 in the UK Charts. Harrison, busy filming on location, did not sing at the Academy Award ceremony, the song being sung by Jose Feliciano.
Weird OHW Fact... Noel is the son of actor Rex Harrison.
Weird OHW Fact... Perhaps best known for his acting roles (as Mark Slate in 29 episodes of the NBC series The Girl from U.N.C.L.E.), also was a singer and British Olympic skier.

OLIVER – GOOD MORNING STARSHINE
Written by James Rado, Gerome Ragni, Galt MacDermot for the musical, Hair, it was recorded by William Oliver Swofford, (from North Wilkesboro, North Carolina) officially known as Oliver. It was his debut single, and #1 in Canada, #2 in New Zealand, #3 in the Billboard Hot 100, #6 in the UK, and #10 in Australia. The follow-up, Jean, got to #2 in the Billboard Hot 100, but did not chart in the UK.
Billboard rated the song as #43 of 1969.

THE PEPPERMINT RAINBOW - WILL YOU BE STAYING AFTER SUNDAY
From Baltimore, Maryland, this group were originally called, New York Times. Signed to Decca Records they charted with their second single, Will You Be Staying After Sunday, reaching #32 in the U.S. Billboard Hot 100, #21 on Cashbox, and #19 in Canada. The best follow-up reached #54... so near yet so far. The band broke up the next year.

RENÉ Y RENÉ - LO MUCHO QUE TE QUIERO (THE MORE I LOVE YOU)
This Latin duo from Laredo, Texas, had already a minor hit back in 1964 (Angelito (Little Angel) #43) when they were the first Mexican/American act to appear on American Bandstand. So when their second hit rocked the charts, it came as no surprise for the hard working team. The single got to #14 in the Billboard Hot 100. They released their last single the next year.

ROY CLARK - YESTERDAY, WHEN I WAS YOUNG

Written by Charles Aznavour, and originally entitled, Hier Encore, (Only Yesterday), English-language lyrics were written by Herbert Kretzmer. Roy Linwood Clark is probably best known for hosting the country variety TV show, Hee Haw. His version of the song crossed over at #19 in the Billboard Hot 100, #9 in the Country Chart, and #7 in Canada.

Weird OHW Fact... he was the first to have his own theatre in Branson Missouri, now filled with such venues.

THE RUGBYS - YOU, I

Louisville rock band, The Rugbys had tried to break into the limelight. It happened suddenly. After achieving local success, national stations began to play one of their B-side, You I. It quickly got to #24 in the Billboard Hot 100, #22 in Cashbox Chart. The follow-up, Wendegahl the Warlock, did not chart.

SMITH - BABY IT'S YOU

Sold more than 1 million copies.

Written by Burt Bacharach, Luther Dixon and Mack David, it was a minor hit for both the Shirelles and the Beatles. Recorded on their debut album, A Group Called Smith, the Los Angeles Rock band took it to its highest charting position. Reaching #5 in the Billboard Hot 100. The band broke up after two unsuccessful albums.

SPIRAL STARECASE - MORE TODAY THAN YESTERDAY

Sold over 1 million copies.

Written by band guitarist, Pat Upton, the song was recorded on the Sacramento, California band's debut album of the same name. The song reached#7 in Cashbox, #12 in the Billboard Hot 100, and #6 in Canada. It did not chart in the UK. The follow-up, No One for Me to Turn To, just reached #52, so they only just make it into the one hit wonder family. Billboard ranked it as the #50 song of 1069.

SPIRIT - I GOT A LINE ON YOU

Written by band singer/guitarist Randy Craig Wolfe (stage name Randy California), and recorded by Los Angeles rockers, Spirit, the single was a chart surprise as the band were better known as an 'album band'. It reached #25 in the Billboard Hot 100 and #28 in Canada. Their best follow-up, 1984, reached #69 in 1969.

THUNDERCLAP NEWMAN - SOMETHING IN THE AIR

Written by Speedy Keen, Thunderclap Newman were a project by the Who's Pete Townsend to combine the talents of Speedy (Drums) Jimmy McCulloch (guitar) and Andy Newman (piano), but he left them to work on Tommy. Their one hit single got to #1 in the UK Charts for three weeks, and to #37 in the Billboard Hot 100. Their follow-up single, Accidents, charted in the UK at #44, but not the USA. The band broke up soon afterwards.

TONY JOE WHITE - POLK SALAD ANNIE
Written by Tony Joe White, it tells of the rough life of a southern girl (Poke salad is a cooked dish of greens, similar to spinach). It reached #8 in the Billboard Hot 100, #10 in Canada, and #8 in Australia.
Billboard ranked it as the #77 song of 1969.

UNDERGROUND SUNSHINE - BIRTHDAY
From Montello, Wisconsin, Underground Sunshine was a psychedelic rock band. Their only hit was a Beatles cover, Birthday, which reached #19 in Cashbox, and #26 in the Billboard Hot 100. Their follow-up single, written by the Byrds David Gates, Don't Shut Me Out, did not chart.

THE UPSETTERS - RETURN OF DJANGO/DOLLAR IN THE TEETH
This Jamaican reggae band were destined for a heady future. Originally a house band for Jamaican reggae producer Lee 'Scratch' Perry, they soon became The Upsetters. Their instrumental hit, reached #5 in the UK Singles Chart. The band would have no other commercial success, but they would go on to form the basis of The Wailers, Bob Barley's band.

VIK VENUS - MOONFLIGHT
Jack Spector was an American DJ. Working in New York, he recorded a novelty single to commemorate the moon landing; a reporter interviewing the astronauts. It reached #38 in the Billboard Hot 100.
Weird OHW Fact... Spector was the first New York DJ to airplay the Beatles, I wanna Hold Your Hand.

WIND - MAKE BELIEVE
Before hitting the big time with Dawn, and tying ribbons round old oak trees, Tony Orlando had been working hard for a decade. In one of his incarnations, Wind, he scored only once, the single, Make Believe, reached #28 in the Billboard Hot 100. Their follow-up, I'll Hold Out My Hand, did not chart.

THE WINSTONS - COLOR HIM FATHER

Written by Richard Lewis Spencer, it was recorded by the six piece Washington D. C. funk/soul group. It reached #2 in the R&B Chart, and #7 in the Billboard Hot 100. It was awarded the Grammy for best R&B song in 1970.

Weird OHW Fact... At 1.26 on the B-side, Amen, Brother, is the most sampled drum solo ever.

THE YOUNGBLOODS - GET TOGETHER

Written by Chet Powers, and first charted by the Kingston Trio in 1964, it was released by the Youngbloods in 1967, but it just reached #62 in the Billboard hot 100. In 1969 it was used as an anthem for the National Conference of Christians and Jews. Re-released to cash in on the free airplay, it soared to #5 in the US.

Weird OHW Fact... Youngbloods leader, Jesse Colin Young, (born Perry Miller) was raised in Queens and was in fourth grade with Art Garfunkel.

ZAGER AND EVANS - IN THE YEAR 2525 (EXORDIUM AND TERMINUS)

Reached #1 in USA, UK, New Zealand, Ireland, Canada, Switzerland. Sold over 4 million copies.

Written by Rick Evans in 1964, it took the Nebraska band four years to even record it. Of course, it was a massive hit, reaching #1 in the Billboard Hot 100 for six weeks, #1 in the UK for 3 weeks, Canada 1 week, Ireland 2 weeks, and New Zealand for 2 weeks. It also charted top 10 in most other major charts. Their follow-up, Mr. Turnkey, (about a rapist who nails his wrist to his jail cell) was unsurprisingly not a hit. The band broke up in 1971.

Weird OHW Fact... The song was #1 in the USA when men first walked on the moon, and when Woodstock took place.

So Close... But No Cigar...

PETER SARSTEDT – WHERE DO YOU GO TO MY LOVELY

Reached #1 in the UK.

Written by Peter Sarstedt, the song was recorded in a accordion waltz style beat. It was his biggest hit, sitting atop the UK charts for four weeks. He is often considered a one hit wonder, but his signature song never charted high in the US; he peaked at #70. Most people forget that in the UK, he followed up the song with, Frozen Orange Juice, which reached #10 the same year.

Weird OHW Fact... Sarstedt was born in India, his parents working for the British Administration.

Weird OHW Fact... Twenty years later, in 1989, he was still receiving more than 60,000 pounds per year from royalties from the one song.

THE SEVENTIES...
1970...

As London Council announces its plans for the Thames Barrier at Woolwich, the year and the decade begins...
Black Sabbath release their first album, the Weathermen plant a bomb in New Jersey, Paul McCartney says he's leaving the Beatles, Apollo 13 breaks down, and limps back to earth, the Movie Kelly's Heroes is released, Elvis tours for the first time since 1958, Pope Paul VI ends his world tour.

100 PROOF (AGED IN SOUL) - SOMEBODY'S BEEN SLEEPING
Sold over 1 million copies.
100 Proof was a Detroit Michigan soul act set up for new label, Hot Wax/Invictus. Joe Stubbs, formerly of Motown groups The Contours and The Originals, was co-lead singer, along with Steve Mancha. This was 100 Proof's second single, and their only hit.
It reached #8 in the US Pop Charts, and #6 on the R&B Charts.

1970 ENGLAND WORLD CUP SQUAD - BACK HOME
Written by Bill Martin and Phil Coulter, it was the first of many football songs to chart mainstream. It reached #1 for three weeks in the UK Charts, and #2 in Ireland. Meant to encourage the team to win the Mexico World Cup, England was knocked out in the quarter finals.

ALIVE N KICKIN' - TIGHTER, TIGHTER
Written by Bob King and Tommy James for their debut album, Alive N Kickin'. It reached #7 on the Billboard Hot 100 and peaked at #5 in the Canadian charts.
Billboard ranked the record as the #47 song of 1970.

ASSEMBLED MULTITUDE - OVERTURE FROM TOMMY (A ROCK OPERA)
The Assembled Multitude was an instrumental collective of studio musicians in Philadelphia, Pennsylvania. They released a self-titled album on Atlantic Records which included instrumental versions of many modern classics; Woodstock, Ohio, MacArthur Park, While My Guitar Gently Weeps, and Tommy Overture, amongst others.
The Overture from Tommy reached #16 on the US Billboard Singles chart.

BLUES IMAGE - RIDE CAPTAIN RIDE

American rock band Blues Image wrote and recorded the song on their album, Open.

When a shorter version was released as a single, it was an immediate success, reaching #4 in the USA and Canadian charts; Blues Image's first (and only) Top 40 chart hit.

BOB & MARCIA - TO BE YOUNG, GIFTED AND BLACK

Written by Nina Simone and Weldon Irvine, their release reached #5 in the UK Singles Chart and #15 in Ireland. The song was a treasure trove for cover artists, even Elton John had a go.

Weird OHW Fact... The song was written in memory of Simone's friend, Lorraine Hansberry, author of the play A Raisin in the Sun, who died in 1965, aged just 34.

BOBBY BLOOM - MONTEGO BAY

Reached #1 in New Zealand.

Co-written and performed by Bobby Bloom, the song was a Top 10 hit on both sides of the Atlantic. It reached #3 in the UK, #5 in Canada, #7 in Australia and #8 on the US Billboard Hot 100.

The song appeared in the film The Ice Storm.

Weird OHW Fact... In the original tapes and album version, Bloom sings Oh, What a Beautiful Morning at the end of the song. On the issued single recording, this is faded out, supposedly to avoid paying Rodgers & Hammerstein royalties. However, DJ's began to play the album track anyway.

THE BROTHERHOOD OF MAN - UNITED WE STAND

Written by Tony Hiller and Peter Simmons, it was the band's first and only international hit, peaking at #13 in the Billboard Hot 100, #9 in Canada, #8 in Australia, and #10 in the U.K.

The song has become an anthem in times of disunity, used as a football chant and by various political themes.

Billboard ranked the record as the #64 song of 1970.

Weird OHW Fact... The song was used as the closing credits of the TV show The Brady Bunch Hour.

CHRISTIE - YELLOW RIVER

Reached #1 in UK, Ireland, Finland, and Norway.

Written by band leader Jeff Christie, it was first offered to The Tremeloes, who recorded it in early 1970. When they did not release it

as a single, their voices were taken off the recording, and Christie's added.
It was an international hit, reaching #1 in the UK for one week. In the US, it reached #23 on the Billboard Hot 100.

CRABBY APPLETON - GO BACK
Crabby Appleton was an American rock band fronted by singer-songwriter Michael Fennelly. Their first single and only hit, Go Back, reached #36 on the Billboard Hot 100 chart. Despite their disappointing chart success, the band toured extensively, opening for the Doors, Sly and the Family Stone, Three Dog Night, Guess Who, ABBA, and George Carlin.

CROW - EVIL WOMAN (DON'T PLAY YOUR GAMES WITH ME)
Written and recorded by Minneapolis-based band Crow, the song appeared on their 1969 album Crow Music. It reached #19 on the US Billboard Hot 100 Pop chart.
In 1970, it was covered by Black Sabbath and released as their first single; Evil Woman. The song also appeared on the UK version of the band's debut album, Black Sabbath, later that year, but not the USA release.

EDISON LIGHTHOUSE - LOVE GROWS (WHERE MY ROSEMARY GOES)
Reached #1 in UK, New Zealand.
The single hit #1 in the UK Singles Chart for a total of five weeks, #2 in Australia, #3 in Canada and South Africa.
English pop band Edison Lighthouse may be classed as a one-hit wonder, but their lead singer at the time, Tony Burrows, leads the race for the most one-hit wonders. In 1970, he hopped from one band to the next, and had five charting hits with five different groups (Edison Lighthouse, The Pipkins, White Plains, Brotherhood of Man, and The First Class), an achievement unmatched.
Billboard ranked the record as the #40 song of 1970.

ERNIE - RUBBER DUCKIE
Muppet Ernie (voice by Jim Henson) had a hit named after Ernie's toy, a rubber duck called (amazingly) Rubber Duckie. Written by Jeff Moss and arranged by Joe Raposo, it became a shock mainstream hit, reaching #16 on the Billboard Hot 100.

FREE - ALRIGHT NOW

Reached #1 in Austria, Denmark, Netherlands, Norway, and Sweden. Although they scored top-ten hits in the UK with My Brother Jake, and Wishing Well, these songs did not chart anywhere else, making Free a USA one hit wonder. From the Island Records album, Fire and Water, the song hit #2 on the UK singles chart and #4 on the US Billboard Hot 100 singles chart.

In 2006, the BMI London awarded a Million Air award for 3 million air plays of All Right Now in the USA.

FIVE FLIGHTS UP - DO WHAT YOU WANNA DO
An American R&B ensemble including Geneva Crawford, Blanton McFarlin, Carlnetta Kelly, Charles Termell and J.B. Bingham, had a hit with the song "Do What You Wanna Do", written by J.B. Bingham. The song reached #37 on the US Billboard Hot 100.

THE FIVE STAIRSTEPS – O-O-H CHILD
Considered by many to be the first family of soul, the Chicago family group only had one top 40 song. O-o-h Child got to #8 in the Billboard Hot 100.

Billboard ranked the record as the #21 song of 1970.

FRIJID PINK - THE HOUSE OF THE RISING SUN
#1 in Germany and Norway.

Sold more than 1 million singles.

Frijid Pink is a Detroit rock band, best known for their international hit of "House of the Rising Sun".

In the USA charts the song debuted at #29 and rose to #7 a month or so later, #2 in Poland and Switzerland, #3 in Austria, Canada, Denmark, and Netherlands, #4 in Israel and UK. Selling a million copies in the USA, it was their only major hit, and gave the song a better worldwide success than the Animals version in 1964.

HOTLEGS - NEANDERTHAL MAN
Sold 2 million copies worldwide.

Hotlegs, consisting of Eric Stewart, Kevin Godley, and Lol Creme (soon to be called 10cc) was an English band best known for its hit single "Neanderthal Man", reaching #2 in the UK, and #22 in the US.

IDES OF MARCH – VEHICLE
Written and sung by band member Jim Peterik, this funk brass-filled single was the one hit for the Chicago-based band. The single rose to #2 on the Billboard Hot 100. It has been used and covered many times.

Weird OHW Fact... It is said to be the fastest selling single in the history of Warner Bros. Records.

JACK BLANCHARD & MISTY MORGAN - TENNESSEE BIRD WALK

A novelty single by the country music husband-and-wife duo Jack Blanchard & Misty Morgan. Their second release, the single went to #1 on the country charts for two weeks and crossed over to the Billboard Hot 40 reaching #23.

THE JAGGERZ - THE RAPPER

Reached #2 in USA and #3 in Canada.
Sold over 1 million copies.
Written by band member Dominic Ierace (Iris), the song rose to #2 on the Billboard Hot 100, certified Gold by the RIAA in 1970.

JOHN PHILLIPS – MISSISSIPPI

John Edmund Andrew Phillips, affectionately known as Papa John, was the leader of the vocal group The Mamas & the Papas. From his second solo album John, the Wolf King of L.A. the minor hit "Mississippi", dipped inside the Billboard Hot 40. It would be his only solo hit.
Phillips withdrew from the limelight as his use of drugs increased.

KENNY ROGERS & THE FIRST EDITION - SOMETHING'S BURNING

Written by Mac Davis, it was recorded by Rogers before he went solo. There was only one hit from his 'Edition' days; Something's Burning went to #11 in the Billboard Hot 100, and #8 in the UK.

LEE MARVIN - WAND'RIN' STAR

Reached #1 in Ireland, and UK.
The gritty movie star sang the song on Paint Your Wagon. The released single was a hit in the UK and Ireland, topping both charts.
Weird OHW Fact... Lee Marvin's stay at UK #1 kept The Beatles at #2 with Let It Be.
Weird OHW Fact... It was covered by Shane MacGowan and The Popes on their 1997 album The Crock of Gold. (Yup, the spelling is correct; this was after leaving the Pogues).

LIZ DAMON'S ORIENT EXPRESS - 1900 YESTERDAY

Liz Damon's Orient Express is a Hawaiian R&B band, taking its name from the fact that every back-up singer had Asian roots. The song spent 12 weeks on the Billboard Hot 100 chart, reaching #33. It also reached #15 in Canada.

LYNN ANDERSON – ROSE GARDEN
Reached #1 in Australia, Belgium, Canada, Finland, Germany, New Zealand, Norway, and Switzerland.
Written by Joe South, and first released by Billy Joe Royal in 1967, Anderson's release topped the U.S. Billboard country chart for five weeks. It would prove to be one of the biggest country crossovers in history, reaching #2 in Netherlands, #3 in UK and USA Billboard Hot 100..
Anderson got a Grammy Award for Best Female Country Vocal Performance in 1971.

MARMALADE - REFLECTIONS OF MY LIFE
Sold 2 million copies worldwide.
A hit single for Scottish band, Marmalade, it was written by their lead guitarist Junior Campbell, and singer Dean Ford (born Thomas McAleese).
The song charted worldwide, reaching #3 in the UK in 1969, and #10 in the US in 1970 on the Billboard Hot 100. Despite their success in the UK, it was their only American hit.
In 1998 the writers were awarded a Special Citation of Achievement by the BMI for radio plays in excess of one million in the USA.

MASHMAKHAN - AS THE YEARS GO BY
Reached #1 in Canada and Japan.
Sold over a million copies.
The rock fusion band recorded this track for their debut album. It topped the Canadian singles chart, and reached #31 in the Billboard Hot 100.

MATTHEWS SOUTHERN COMFORT – WOODSTOCK
A hit in the UK thanks to Radio 1 DJ's Tony Blackburn's sponsorship, it topped the chart after a month's slow moving traffic. The single also reached #2 in Ireland, Norway, Sweden, and Poland, #3 in South Africa, #4 in New Zealand, #15 in Austria, and #9 in Denmark. Since the song had already been a hit in 1970 by Crosby, Stills, Nash & Young, (#11 USA, #3 Canada) it took an edict in Canada to play more home based music to raise sales in the USA, but four months later in 1971 the Matthews version reached #23 in the Billboard Chart, #5 in Canada.
Weird OHW Fact... MCA Records only released the Matthews version in the UK after they were certain that the Crosby, Stills, Nash & Young version was not going to chart.

MCGUINESS FLINT - WHEN I'M DEAD AND GONE

Written by Scots Benny Gallagher and Graham Lyle, this heavily mandolin accented song was released as a debut single by McGuinness Flint. It reached #2 in the UK charts, and #34 in Canada (where they are the 'one hit wonder'), but failed to Chart the US Top 40 (#47). Gallagher & Lyle would chart later. A follow-up single, Malt and Barley Blues, was a UK #5 hit the following year.

Weird OHW Fact... The song was about the life of bluesman Robert Johnson.

MICHAEL NESMITH AND THE FIRST NATIONAL BAND – JOANNE

The First National Band released three albums in the country rock genre between 1970 and 1971.   Their first album contained five songs from Nesmith's Monkees days, including Joanne. Much to everyone's surprise, it rose to #21 on the Billboard Hot 100. It would be Nesmith's last chart entry.

MICHAEL PARKS - LONG LONESOME HIGHWAY

A career actor, Parks recorded the theme song for the show, Long Lonesome Highway, which charted at #20 in the Billboard Hot 100. It was his only hit.

MIGUEL RÍOS - A SONG OF JOY (HIMNO A LA ALEGRIA)

Reached #1 in Australia, Canada, Germany and Switzerland.
Sold over 4 million copies.
Spanish singer and actor Miguel Ríos recorded this song set to Beethoven's Ninth Symphony.
A #1 worldwide, it reached #14 in the USA and #16 in the UK.
In Germany, it is the most successful hymn ever.

MOUNTAIN – MISSISSIPPI QUEEN

Written by band members Leslie West, Corky Laing, Felix Pappalardi and lyricist David Rea, the American Long Island (new York) rock band recorded this rock classic, which was their most successful single. It reached #21 in the Billboard Hot 100 record chart. It has been covered by W.A.S.P., Sam Kinison, Amanda Ayala, and Ozzy Osbourne.

MUNGO JERRY – IN THE SUMMERTIME

Reached #1 in Australia, Austria, Belgium, Canada, Denmark, France, Germany, Ireland, Italy, Netherlands, New Zealand, Norway, South Africa, Sweden, Switzerland, and UK.

Sold more than 30 million copies.

The consummate one hit wonder, the debut single by British rock band Mungo Jerry reached #1 in charts all around the world. It became one of the best-selling singles of all-time.

Billboard ranked the record as the #53 song of 1970.

Weird OHW Fact... The song's lyrics "have a drink, have a drive, go out and see what you can find" led to the song's use in a UK campaign Drinking and Driving Wrecks Lives.

Weird OHW Fact... The band's name comes from the TS Elliot poem, Mungojerrie and Rumpleteazer, from Old Possum's Book of Practical Cats.

Weird OHW Fact... When they got suddenly booked onto Top of the Pops, the band leader, Ray Dorset, had to ask his boss for time off work.

THE NEIGHBORHOOD - BIG YELLOW TAXI

Although written, composed, and originally recorded by Canadian Joni Mitchell, the original recording only reached #67 in the Billboard Charts. The cover version by The Neighborhood broke the Billboard Hot 40 in the same year reaching #24.

Weird OHW Fact... A subsequent re-release of a live version by Joni Mitchell also peaked at #24.

NICKY THOMAS - LOVE OF THE COMMON PEOPLE

A folk ballad written by John Hurley and Ronnie Wilkins, it has been covered by a myriad of artists. Nicky Thomas' version sold over 175,000 copies in the UK, reaching #9 in the UK Singles Chart. It was famously covered by Paul Young in 1984, giving him a worldwide #1.

NORMAN GREENBAUM - SPIRIT IN THE SKY

Reached #1 in Australia, Canada, Ireland, Germany and UK.

Written and recorded by Norman Greenbaum, he released it in late 1969 on the album of the same name.

The single became an almost instant gold record, selling two million copies from 1969 to 1970, reaching #3 on the US Billboard Hot 100 chart. As well as chart-topping, it reached top ten in most major music charts.

Billboard ranked the record as the #22 song of 1970.

Weird OHW Fact... Cover versions by Doctor and the Medics and Gareth Gates have also hit #1 in the UK.

THE ORIGINAL CASTE - ONE TIN SOLDIER

Reached #1 in Canada.

Recorded for the TA label in late 1969, the song reached #34 on the American pop charts in 1970.

In 1971, Coven had a hit with a cover version, and Skeeter Davis hit the Canadian Country chart with it in 1972.

PACIFIC GAS AND ELECTRIC - ARE YOU READY?

Pacific Gas & Electric was an American blues rock band, led by singer Charlie Allen. From their second album, their only hit was the gospel-tinged "Are You Ready?". It reached #14 in the Billboard Hot 100.

THE PIPKINS - GIMME DAT DING

Written and composed by Albert Hammond and Mike Hazlewood on EMI Columbia, the gimmick single reached #6 in UK, #9 in USA, and #7 in Canada.

The original version of the song, performed by Freddie Garrity, was released on the album Oliver in the Overworld.

Weird OHW Fact... Gimme Dat Ding was used (as Gimme Dat Ring) by Coca-Cola to advertise their new Ring Pull Cans in the early 1970's.

THE PRESIDENTS - 5-10-15-20 (25-30 YEARS OF LOVE)

This was the title track and first release from the album. The song was produced by Van McCoy (1975 one hit wonder, The Hustle). It reached #11 on the US Billboard Hot 100. The song was nominated for a Grammy Award for Best R&B Performance by a Duo or Group with Vocals.

R. DEAN TAYLOR - INDIANA WANTS ME

Written, composed, and recorded by Canadian R. Dean Taylor on the Rare Earth label, a subsidiary of Motown Records. It was a top ten hit in both the USA and UK, #3 in Canada.

Taylor's only hit in the US, it rose to #5 on the Billboard Hot 100. He had already hit the UK charts with minor hit, Gotta See Jane, but Indiana Wants Me stayed his only US hit.

RARE EARTH – GET READY

Reached #1 in Canada.

Written by Smokey Robinson, this version by American band Rare Earth reached #4 in the Billboard Charts, but it is significant in that it is the only Rare Earth single to chart in Canada, where it topped the charts.

THE RATTLES – THE WITCH

Sold over 1 million copies.

The Rattles, a multi-hit German band, performed at the same venues as The Beatles in the sixties. The Witch, was their only international hit, #4 in Germany, #8 in the UK, #20 in Austria, and a distant #79 in the USA.

ROBIN MCNAMARA - LAY A LITTLE LOVIN' ON ME

Written by Robin McNamara, Jeff Barry and Jim Cretecos, and taken from the album of the same name, the song reached #11 on the Billboard Hot 100 and was McNamara's only hit.

SHOCKING BLUE – VENUS

Reached #1 in Australia, Belgium, Canada, Denmark, France, Italy, Spain, Switzerland, and USA.
#2 in Austria, Germany, Japan.
Sold 8 million copies worldwide.
Written by Dutch band member Robbie van Leeuwen, he took the song to #1 in nine countries.
Weird OHW Fact... As a cover in 1986, Bananarama returned the song to #1 in seven countries.

STEAM - NA NA HEY HEY KISS HIM GOODBYE

Sold over 6.5 million copies.
Written by Paul Leka, Gary DeCarlo and Dale Frashuer, and recorded by their fictional band, Steam, they took the single to #1 in the USA; it was the last Billboard #1 of the sixties. It also reached #6 in Canada.
Weird OHW Fact... The catchy chorus was sung as; na na na na, na na na na, etc, just waiting on lyrics to fill in the notes... they were never added.

THE STREET PEOPLE - JENNIFER TOMKINS

Rupert Holmes and Ron Dante recorded the song for release on their second album, The Cuff Links, but due to contractual difficulties, Dante pulled out of the project. Holmes released the single under a new band name, and another one hit wonder was born.
It reached #36 in the Billboard Hot 100, but his follow-up single flopped.

TEEGARDEN AND VAN WINKLE - GOD, LOVE AND ROCK AND ROLL

American musical duo, Skip Knape, and David Teegarden formed in Tulsa, Oklahoma. The song, which had roots in the gospel song, Amen, reached #22 in the Billboard Hot 100.

TEE SET - MA BELLE AMIE

Sold over one million singles.

Tee Set, a pop rock band from Delft, Netherlands, originally released this as a single from their album, Ma Belle Amie in Holland, selling over 100,000 singles.

Signed by Colossus Records, they re-released the single, and the song reached #5 on the Billboard Hot 100 in 1970.

Their next single got banned in the USA, making them a one hit wonder.

TEN YEARS AFTER - LOVE LIKE A MAN
In 1971 they would have their 'American' one hit wonder, but in 1970, they had their only charting UK hit. The song was on the band's fifth album, Cricklewood Green, and it reached #10.

TODD RUNDGREN - WE GOTTA GET YOU A WOMAN
Written, performed and recorded by Todd Rundgren from the album Runt. The single reached #20 in US and Canada. The Four Tops covered this song in 1972.

VINCENT BELL - AIRPORT LOVE THEME
Sold over 1 million copies.

American Vinnie Bell was a session guitarist, inventor, and pioneer of electronic musical effects.

He invented the first electric 12-string guitar, and the electric sitar. His rare solo release, the theme from the movie Airport, reached #31 on the Billboard Hot 100.

It won a Grammy Award for Best Instrumental Composition.

WHITE PLAINS - MY BABY LOVES LOVIN'
Written by Roger Cook and Roger Greenaway, and released on Decca records, the British pop group White Plains had their one and only hit. It reached #4 in Canada, #9 in UK, and #13 in the USA.

The lead vocalist is session singer Tony Burrows, who also sang lead for Edison Lighthouse, The Pipkins, and the Brotherhood of Man, singing in four different one hit wonders in 1970.

OH SO CLOSE... BUT NO CIGAR...

SUGARLOAF - GREEN EYED LADY/ DON'T CALL US, WE'LL CALL YOU
A lot of people consider Sugarloaf to be a one hit wonder; guess what? They're wrong.

213

Green Eyed lady, written by band member Jerry Corbetta with J.C. Phillips and David Riordan, from their first album, Sugarloaf, topped the Canadian Charts and peaked at #3 in the Billboard Hot 100 in 1970. This was their biggest hit.

However, Don't Call Us, We'll Call You reached #5 in Canada, and #9 in the Billboard charts.

So close...

1971...

As 66 football fans die on the staircase at Ibrox Stadium in Glasgow, the year begins...

Charles Manson is pronounced guilty, Apollo 14 lands on the moon, Led Zeppelin sings Stairway to Heaven in public for the first time, Scot Jackie Stewart becomes Formula One champion, Disney World opens in Orlando, Florida, and Ricky Martin is born.

ASHTON, GARDNER AND DYKE - RESURRECTION SHUFFLE

Ashton, Gardner and Dyke were a power rock trio, best remembered for this one song. Their success was short lived, the single was their only hit, dipping into the Billboard Hot 100 at #40. It fared better in the UK, reaching #3.

THE BEGINNING OF THE END - FUNKY NASSAU

Written by Ray Munnings and Tyrone Fitzgerald, and recorded on the album Funky Nassau, the song reached #15 in the Billboard Hot 100, and #31 on the UK Singles Chart.
Billboard ranked it as #75 single of 1971.

THE BELLS - STAY AWHILE

Reached #1 in Canada.
Sold 4 million copies.
A Canadian rock band from Montreal, Quebec, had minor hits, but only one big hit single. Stay Awhile, written by Ken Tobias, became a worldwide hit, going to #1 in Canada, and reaching #7 in the Billboard Hot 100 chart.
Billboard ranked it as #75 single of 1971.

BENNY HILL - ERNIE (THE FASTEST MILKMAN IN THE WEST)

Written by English comedian Benny Hill, the song was first written as a reference to Hill's own experiences as a milkman. The song shot to the top of the UK Charts, and stayed at #1 for 4 weeks, all through Christmas.

BLOODROCK - D.O.A.

An American hard rock band out of Fort Worth, recorded this track on the album Bloodrock 2. DOA reached #36 on the Billboard Hot 100 chart. Their other singles did not chart.

Weird OHW Fact... The song was inspired by a childhood friend crashing a small aircraft, killing him outright.

BREWER & SHIPLEY - ONE TOKE OVER THE LINE
Brewer & Shipley's third album included the track One Toke Over The Line, which, although they charted 3 times in USA, became their only Canadian hit, hence their inclusion in the OHW list. It reached #5 in Canada, and #10 in USA.

THE BUOYS – TIMOTHY
Written by Rupert Holmes, Timothy is the grisly story of three men trapped down a mine. Two men survived, having eaten poor Timothy. The song reached #17 in the U.S. Billboard Hot 40, #9 in Canada.
Weird OHW Fact... The song was written purposefully graphic in order to be banned; any publicity is good, etc.

C. COMPANY FEATURING TERRY NELSON - BATTLE HYMN OF LT. CALLEY
Sold nearly 2 million copies.
Terry Nelson Skinner, a DJ from Russelville, Alabama, put together a band for this single. The narration and song (to the tune The Battle Hymn of the Republic) tell the story of the My Lai massacre in Viet Nam, and the subsequent court marshalling of Lieutenant William Calley Jr.
Weird OHW Fact... This single sold over one million copies in just four days.

CHASE - GET IT ON
Jazz-rock brass-inspired band, Chase was the debut album by Bill Chase, a veteran trumpeter. Get It On spent 13 weeks in the Billboard Chart, topping out at #22.
Weird OHW Fact... The band literally died in 1974 when Chase's small plane crashed, killing him and three other band members.
Weird OHW fact... T Rex retitled their song Get It On, to Get It On (Bang a Gong), to avoid any confusion.

CLIVE DUNN – GRANDAD
Written by Herbie Flowers and Kenny Pickett, at Clive Dunn's request, Dunn was still starring in British sitcom Dad's Army when the single was released. It hit the charts in January, topping the UK charts for 3 weeks, and staying in the chart for a staggering 27 weeks. His follow-up singles did not chart.

Weird OHW Fact... Although he acted a man in his 70's, Dunn turned just 51 while the song was at #1.

COVEN - ONE TIN SOLDIER (THE LEGEND OF BILLY JACK)

Jinx Dawson of the band, Coven, recorded the track for the movie Billy Jack. The single reached #26 on Billboard's Hot 100, but was pulled from release by the movie's producers citing doubts over the recording's rights.

Weird OHW Fact... Jinx Dawson asked, that although she had recorded the version on her own, that the band be credited with the performance.

CYMARRON - RINGS

Written by songwriters Eddie Reeves and Alex Harvey, American band Cymarron's recording turned out to be their only hit. It reached #17 in the Billboard charts, and the song has been covered many times.

Weird OHW Fact... The band was named after Cimarron Strip - a TV western show from 1967.

DADDY DEWDROP - CHICK-A-BOOM (DON'T YA JES' LOVE IT)

Written by Janice Lee Gwin and Linda Martin, the song was recorded for his namesake album, Daddy Dewdrop. The song reached #9 on the U.S. Billboard Hot 100, #2 in Canada, and #4 in Australia.

Billboard ranked the song #34 of 1971.

DAVE AND ANSELL COLLINS - DOUBLE BARREL

Reached #1 in UK and Jamaica.

Kingston Jamaica's session singer Dave Barker and keyboardist Ansell Collins got together for this smash hit. It topped the charts in the UK and Jamaica, reaching #22 in the Billboard Hot 100; it would be their only USA hit.

DENISE LASALLE - TRAPPED BY A THING CALLED LOVE

Sold over 1 million copies.

Co-produced and written by Denise LaSalle, Trapped By a Thing Called Love was a crossover hit from the R&B charts to #13 on the Billboard Hot 100.

FREDDIE HART - EASY LOVIN'

Written by country music's Freddie Hart, this crossover hit became his breakout single. It reached #1 on the US Country Chart, and soon broke into the mainstream Hot 100 at #17. Although he continued to record, it became his only Billboard hit.

FREDDIE NORTH - SHE'S ALL I GOT
Written by Gary U.S. Bonds and Jerry Williams Jr, Nashville DJ Freddie North included the track on his album, Friend, on Mankind Records. It reached a lowly #39 in the Billboard Chart, and was covered many times.
Weird OHW Facts... Johnny Paycheck's version was a #2 U.S. country hit the same year, and Tracy Byrd's version reached #4 on the U.S. and Canadian country charts.

THE FREE MOVEMENT - I'VE FOUND SOMEONE OF MY OWN
Written by Frank F. Robinson, the single reached #5 in the Billboard Hot 100.
Billboard ranked the song #27 of 1971.

THE FUZZ - I LOVE YOU FOR ALL SEASONS
Written by Sheila Young, and performed by American female vocal trio from Washington, D.C., it reached #10 on the U.S. R&B chart and #21 on the Billboard Hot 100 .
Billboard ranked the song #45 of 1971.

THE GLASS BOTTLE - I AINT GOT TIME ANYMORE
Written by Gary Criss, this song peaked at #36 on the Billboard Hot 100.
The band's next single charted weakly, then the band split.

JACKIE MOORE - PRECIOUS, PRECIOUS
Sold over 1 million copies.
This song just clears the hurdles needed to get into the book. From Jacksonville, Florida, Moore is best known for Precious, Precious, which peaked at #30 on the Billboard Hot 100.
Another 'hit' in 1973 reached #42 in the Canadian chart.
Her 1979 disco hit, This Time Baby, hit #1 on the Hot Dance Music/Club Play chart, and reached #49 in the UK, but did not chart on Billboard.

JANIS JOPLIN - ME AND BOBBY MCGEE
#1 in Australia, and USA.
Amazingly, the lofty Janis Joplin achieves OHW status, as the best of her other singles reached #41, thus not in the top 40. Her biggest hit apart from Me and Bobby McGee, (Piece of My Heart), was recorded by band, Big Brother and the Holding Company, so not technically Janis Joplin. The single went to #1 in USA and Australia, #6 in Canada, #11 in New Zealand.

Billboard ranked the song #11 of 1971.

JEAN KNIGHT – MR. BIG STUFF
Sold over 2 million copies.
American singer Jean Knight only had one hit, but what a cracker! Stax Records publisher pushed it to the company, and it soon reached #2 in the Billboard Hot 100.
Billboard ranked it as the #18 song for 1971.
It was nominated for Best Female R&B Vocal Performance at the 1972 Grammy Awards.

JONATHAN EDWARDS – SUNSHINE
Sold more than 1 million copies.
Written by Jonathan Edwards, and released as the first single from his debut album Jonathan Edwards, the single reached #4 in the Billboard Hot 100 chart.
Weird OHW Fact… Sunshine was not planned for release, but a recording blip erased Please Find Me from the master tape, and it was replaced by Sunshine on the album.

LAURA LEE - WOMEN'S LOVE RIGHTS
Having had a string of low chart entries in the late '60's, Lee moved to the new Hot Wax label. One of her initial recordings, Women's Love Rights, became her biggest hit, reaching #11 on the R&B chart and #36 in the Billboard Hot 100.

LES CRANE - DESIDERATA
For his album of the same name, Les Crane's spoken-word recording of Ehrmann's epic poem, Desiderata, ran up to a surprise #8 on the Billboard chart, #4 on the Canadian RPM Magazine chart, #6 on the UK Melody Maker's chart, and #4 on the Australian singles chart.
Weird OHW Fact… Everyone involved in the project assumed the poem too old to still be in copyright; they were wrong, Ehrmann's ownership was confirmed, and he received royalties.

THE MIXTURES - THE PUSHBIKE SONG
Reached #1 in Australia and New Zealand.
Written by Idris and Evan Jones in the same breathy beat style as Mungo Jerry's In the Summertime, Australian band The Mixtures took this round the world. Topping the Aussie and Kiwi charts, it also reached #2 in the UK, #31 in Canada, and #44 in USA.

THE NITE-LITERS - K-JEE
From Louisville, Kentucky, the band would change its name to The New Birth after releasing this single. It reached #39 in the Billboard Hot 100.

OCEAN - PUT YOUR HAND IN THE HAND
A gospel pop song composed by Gene MacLellan, it became a hit single for the Canadian band Ocean, as the title track to their debut album.
The single reached #10 in Canada, and peaked at #2 on the U.S. Billboard Hot 100, going on to be the 22nd best-seller of 1971.
Ocean charted in Canada again, but failed to break any other markets.
The song was used in the 2013 film, Prisoners.

PAUL HUMPHREY AND THE COOL AID CHEMISTS – COOL AID
Paul Nelson Humphrey from Detroit, Michigan, was as a session drummer in the 1960s for many of the big jazz names. In 1971, he formed the band, and had one hit; Cool Aid reached #29 in the Billboard Hot 100.

PAUL STOOKEY - THE WEDDING SONG (THERE IS LOVE)
A member of Peter, Paul and Mary, Stookey first performed the song at the wedding of his band-mates in 1969.
He recorded it for his solo album Paul and, on release reached #24 on the Hot 100 in Billboard, and #31 in Canada.

PETER NERO - THEME FROM SUMMER OF '42
Peter Nero is a pianist and by 1971 had many albums under his belt. He moved to Columbia records, and the result was an album of movie themes. The above single sold over a million copies.

THE PIGLETS - JOHNNY REGGAE
This Jonathan King song is credited to The Piglets. The single cover states clearly that the single was "conceived, created, produced and directed by Jonathan King". It reached #3 in the UK Charts.

RAY PRICE - FOR THE GOOD TIMES
Written by Kris Kristofferson, Ray Price's version topped the US country music chart. It won "Song of the Year" by the Academy of Country Music. It crossed over into the Billboard chart, reaching #11, the only Ray price recording to be a hit outside the country charts. It also reached #13 in Canada, and #39 in Australia.

REDBONE - THE WITCH QUEEN OF NEW ORLEANS

A native American band, they charted a few hits in the USA, but this was their only UK hit. It reached #2, and #21 in USA. The better known, Come and Get Your Love, would be their biggest US hit.

REDEYE - GAMES
An American rock band from Los Angeles, California, they released two albums on Pentagram Records and had one hit single; Games.
Games reached #27 in the Billboard Hot 100. The follow-up single, Red Eye Blues, trickled in at #78.
A true one hit wonder.

RICHIE HAVENS - HERE COMES THE SUN
Richie holds the medal for being the first performer at Woodstock in 1969. Playing for three hours as many of the subsequent acts were held up in traffic, he later covered the George Harrison song, Here Comes the Sun, giving him his only top 40 Billboard hit.
The single got to a lofty #16.
Weird OHW Facts... The song was recorded by Steve Harley & Cockney Rebel, who took it to #10 in the UK, #7 in Ireland.

SAMMI SMITH - HELP ME MAKE IT THROUGH THE NIGHT
Written by Kris Kristofferson, Smith's recording was the song's most well-known version. In sales, popularity, and radio airplay, it is one of the most successful country singles of all time, topping the country singles chart. It was also a successful crossover hit, reaching #8 in the Billboard hot 100, #4 in Canada, and #7 in Australia.
Sammi Smith won the Grammy Award for Best Country Music Female performance.

SOUNDS OF SUNSHINE - LOVE MEANS (YOU NEVER HAVE TO SAY YOU'RE SORRY)
Three American brothers from Los Angeles formed this group. The title track of their only album was a minor U.S. hit, reaching #39 on the Billboard Hot 100. The title of the song was taken from a line in the 1970 film Love Story.

ST CECELIA - LEAP UP AND DOWN (WAVE YOUR KNICKERS IN THE AIR)
Written by Keith Hancock and produced by Jonathan King, it reached #12 in the UK Charts, and remained in the chart for 17 weeks.

SWEATHOG – HALLELUJAH

A California rock band, they released two albums on CBS Records, on which was their only hit, Hallelujah, which peaked at #33 on the Billboard Hot 100 chart.

TEN YEARS AFTER – I'D LOVE TO CHANGE THE WORLD
Written by band leader, Alvin Lee, it was the first single from the British Rockers album A Space in Time. It is the band's only Top 40 hit, reaching #40 on the Billboard Hot 100. Although the band sold millions of albums, they never charted again.

TIN TIN - TOAST AND MARMALADE FOR TEA
Written by Steve Groves and produced by Maurice Gibb of the Bee Gees for Australian band Tin Tin, this song reached #20 in the US Billboard Hot 100, #10 in Australia.
Weird OHW Fact... Gibb played bass on the single with a broken arm.

TOM CLAY - WHAT THE WORLD NEEDS NOW IS LOVE/ABRAHAM, MARTIN AND JOHN
DJ, Tom Clay remixed the 1965 David/Bacharach song to create What the World Needs Now is Love/Abraham, Martin and John. It contains spoken commentary from many sources, a boy, a drill sergeant, and excerpts of JFK's speeches.
It peaked at #8 in the Billboard Hot 100 and was Clay's only Top 40 hit.

THE UNDISPUTED TRUTH - SMILING FACES SOMETIMES
Written by Norman Whitfield and Barrett Strong for the Motown label, it was originally recorded by the Temptations in 1971. The Undisputed Truth recorded and released it immediately rising to #3 in the Billboard Hot 100. It was the only Top 40 single by the band.
Weird OHW Fact... Ironically, the temptations got their revenge; the Undisputed Truth's next single, Papa Was a Rollin' Stone reached only #63. The temptations released it and it went straight to the top, earning them Grammy Awards too.

WADSWORTH MANSION - SWEET MARY
American rockers from Providence, Rhode Island, released their first single, and it became their only hit. The song got to #7 on the US Billboard Hot 100.

OH SO CLOSE... BUT NO CIGAR...

BLACKFOOT SUE – STANDING IN THE ROAD

Twin brothers Tom and David Farmer and Eddie Golga made up this British band. They are usually seen as a one hit wonder... but we know better.

Standing in the Road reached #4 on the UK Singles Chart.

Sing Don't Speak reached #36 in December 1972, taking them out of the one hit wonder bin.

(WHERE DO I BEGIN?) THEME FROM LOVE STORY - HENRY MANCINI, FRANCIS LAI, ANDY WILLIAMS

This is a story about a movie theme/tune, which was given lyrics, then set free.

With music by Francis Lai and lyrics by Carl Sigman, the song was first recorded by Henry Mancini as an instrumental. It reached #13 in the Billboard Hot 100.

Released as a song by its lyricist, Francis Lai, it reached #31.

When recorded and released by Andy Williams later that year, it rose to #9 in the USA and #4 in the UK.

NEIL YOUNG - HEART OF GOLD/HARVEST MOON

Never considered a one hit wonder in the US, Neil Young did not chart well elsewhere, in the UK, he kept himself from the One Hit Wonder Club by the thinnest of margins.

Heart of Gold reached #10 in the UK Chart, Harvest Moon limped in as a lowly #36.

1972...

As un-surrendered Japanese soldier Shoichi Yokoi is discovered in Guam after just 28 years in the jungle, the year begins...
Bloody Sunday sees 14 killed by British Soldiers in Derry, Mariner 9 sends pictures of Mars, The Godfather premiers, Hurricane Agnes kills 117, Jane Fonda tours North Vietnam, Olympics in Munich, M*A*S*H begins on CBS, Apollo 17 lands on the moon... the last men to walk there.

APOLLO 100 FEATURING TOM PARKER – JOY
The British instrumental studio-based group only recorded one album. Their first single was their only hit, inspired by Bach's Joy of Man's Desiring. It rose to a lofty #6 in the Billboard hot 100. The band broke up the next year.

ARGENT - HOLD YOUR HEAD UP
Sold over 1 million copies.
Recorded on the third Argent album, All Together Now, English rockers got their first and only US hit. The single reached #5 in both the US and UK.
Billboard ranked it as the #50 song for 1972.

ARLO GUTHRIE - CITY OF NEW ORLEANS
Son of Woody Guthrie, although Arlo is best known for his 18 minute debut, Alice's Restaurant Massacre, his only top-40 hit was this cover of Steve Goodman's song, reaching #18 in the Billboard Hot 100.
Weird OHW Fact... Guthrie's song, Massachusetts, was named the official folk song of the state where he lived most of his life.

BILLY PAUL – ME AND MRS. JONES
Reached #1 in USA.
Written by Kenny Gamble, Leon Huff, and Cary Gilbert, and originally recorded by Billy Paul, it was a smash hit worldwide, topping the Billboard Hot 100, and staying there for 3 weeks.

BRENDA LEE EAGER - AIN'T UNDERSTANDING MELLOW
Sold over a million copies.
From Mobile, Alabama, she later moved to Chicago, Illinois, and was soon the lead singer in Jerry Butler's backup group. Her first single with

Butler, Ain't Understanding Mellow, was her biggest chart hit, reaching # 3 on the Billboard R&B chart and # 21 on the Billboard Hot 100.

She never fully charted again; although their duet recording (They Long to Be) Close to You, reached # 6 on the R&B chart, it only peaked at # 91 on the pop chart.

BRIGHTER SIDE OF DARKNESS - LOVE JONES

American R&B/soul group formed at Calumet High School in Chicago, Illinois. Their lead vocalist, Darryl Lamont, was only 12 years old. Love Jones reached #16 in the Billboard Hot 100. It was their only hit.

Weird OHW Fact... Cheech and Chong released a parody, Basketball Jones, in 1973, which reached #15.

BULLET - WHITE LIES, BLUE EYES

Roget Pontbriand and his American rock band had their only hit with this song, reaching #28 in the Billboard Hot 100 chart. Pontbriand went on to play with K.C. and the Sunshine Band and Wild Cherry.

COMMANDER CODY AND HIS LOST PLANET AIRMEN - HOT ROD LINCOLN

Written by Charlie Ryan, and first released in 1955, Commander Cody included this track on their album, Lost in the Ozone. Their only hit single, Hot Rod Lincoln, reached #9 on the Billboard Hot 100, and #7 in Canada.

CASHMAN AND WEST - AMERICAN CITY SUITE

Before founding Lifesong Records in 1975, Cashman & West's song reached #27 on the Billboard chart and #25 on the Canadian RPM chart. The Cashman-West duo also produced all the hits of singer-songwriter Jim Croce.

THE CHAKACHAS – JUNGLE FEVER

Sold over 1 million copies.

Written by Bill Ador on Polydor Records, the Belgian group's song reached #8 in the Billboard Hot 100 and topped at #29 in the UK. The song was banned by the BBC, who thought the song's heavy breathing and moaning were too explicit for UK audiences.

Billboard ranked it as the #51 song of 1972.

CHARLEY PRIDE - KISS AN ANGEL GOOD MORNING

Pride was already an established country star when, in 1971, he released his biggest hit, Kiss an Angel Good Mornin'. It quickly became a huge crossover single, reaching #21 in the Billboard Hot 100. The song's success won him Country Music Association's Entertainer of the Year award, and Top Male Vocalist.

The song was Pride's only career pop top-40 hit.

CHI COLTRANE - THUNDER AND LIGHTNING
A pianist from Racine, Wisconsin, her only hit was on Columbia records, which reached #17 on the Billboard Hot 100. Moving to Europe, she never charted in the USA again.

CLIMAX - PRECIOUS AND FEW
Sold over 1 million copies.

Formed in Los Angeles, California, they are most remembered for their only hit which peaked at #3 on the Billboard Hot 100 singles chart. Their follow-up single, Life and Breath only reached #52, making them one hit wonders.

CROSBY & NASH - IMMIGRATION MAN
Written by Graham Nash, recorded by Nash and Dave Crosby, it was the lead single for the duo's debut album, Graham Nash David Crosby. It reached #36 in the Billboard Hot 100; their only Top 40 hit as that duo.

DANIEL BOONE - BEAUTIFUL SUNDAY
Reached #1 in Germany.

Sold over 2 million copies worldwide.

Born Peter Green, he changed his name, and wrote the song with Rod McQueen. The result was his only USA hit. It peaked at #12 in the UK Singles Chart, and #15 in the USA Billboard Hot 100. It charted worldwide, and is still the biggest hit in Japan by an international artist.

Weird OHW Fact... A madcap football fan, he supports Scottish team Dundee United. He and McQueen also wrote Blue is the Colour, the Chelsea FC anthem.

DANNY O'KEEFE - GOOD TIME CHARLIE'S GOT THE BLUES
Written by Danny O'Keefe in 1967, but not released. Re-recorded with a slower arrangement for his second album, the new version reached #9 on the Billboard Hot 100 singles chart, and #19 in Canada.

THE DELEGATES - CONVENTION '72
This novelty song group charted with a spoof political hit.

The embodiment of one-hit-wonder-ness, it peaked at #8 on the Billboard Hot 100.

DEREK AND THE DOMINOS – LAYLA
Reached #1 in France and Puerto Rico
Written by Eric Clapton and Jim Gordon, the single was released in 1971, achieving limited success. Re-released the next year, it shot to fame around the world. Considering it's longevity, and being included in so many rock classic lists, the song only reached #10 in the US Billboard Hot 100, and #7 in the UK.
Weird OHW fact... 21 years later, the acoustic version won the 1993 Grammy Award for Best Rock Song.

THE ENGLISH CONGREGATION - SOFTLY WHISPERING I LOVE YOU
Reached #1 in South Africa and New Zealand.
Written by David and Jonathan in 1968, this version peaked at #4 in the UK, and #29 in the Billboard Hot 100 chart.

FLASH - SMALL BEGINNINGS
This English prog rock band contained Yes guitarist Peter Banks and vocalist Colin Carter. They recorded three albums, but only scored one minor hit, Small Beginnings, getting to #29 in the Billboard Hot 100 chart. Their other releases did not even chart the 100.

FREDERICK KNIGHT - I'VE BEEN LONELY FOR SO LONG
Written by his wife, Posie Knight, the single was released by Stax records and reached #27 in the Billboard Hot 100, and #23 in the British Chart. It would be his only hit.

GODSPELL CAST - DAY BY DAY
Sold one million copies.
With Robin Lamont on lead vocals, this release charted at #13 on the Billboard Hot 100. It was the only hit from the original album.

THE HILLSIDE SINGERS - I'D LIKE TO TEACH THE WORLD TO SING (IN PERFECT HARMONY)
Sold 1 million copies.
Did you think the Coca Cola single was done first by the New Seekers? You're wrong.
After the New Seekers announced their schedule too full to fit it in, the Hillside Singers were assembled by advertising agency McCann Erickson to sing the song in the Coke television commercial. Producer Al Ham then re-wrote the lyrics for a single, and it peaked at #13 on the Billboard Hot 100 chart.

Weird OHW Fact... The success of the song prompted the New Seekers to record the song too; their version became the standard, hitting #1 in UK and New Zealand, #7 in USA.

HOT BUTTER – POPCORN
Reached #1 in Australia, France, Germany, Netherlands, Norway, and Switzerland.
Sold over 2 million copies.
The moog song was first written and recorded by Gershon Kingsley in 1969. The Hot Butter version became an international hit, selling a million copies in France alone. Although it just reached #5 in UK, and #9 in USA, it topped the charts in many countries.

J. J. CALE - CRAZY MAMA
American guitarist, singer, and songwriter, he wrote After Midnight and Cocaine, recorded by Eric Clapton, and Call Me the Breeze, recorded by Lynyrd Skynyrd. Crazy Mama was his only solo single to chart, reaching #22 on the U.S. Billboard Hot 100 chart.

JOEY HEATHERTON – GONE
A sex symbol of the 1960/70s, she released her first album, The Joey Heatherton Album, in 1972. The first single, covering Ferlin Husky's 1957 hit, reached #24 in the Billboard Hot 100. The second single, I'm Sorry, charted weakly at #87.

JO JO GUNNE - RUN RUN RUN
A rock band in Los Angeles, California, the group's name is derived from Joe Joe Gun, a 1958 Chuck Berry song that peaked at #83. Their only hit, Run Run Run, charted at #6 in the UK Singles Chart and reached #27 in U.S. charts.

KING HARVEST - DANCING IN THE MOONLIGHT
French-American rock group King Harvest's Wurlitzer electric piano hit reached #13 on the Billboard Hot 100. The band's other singles never charted. The hit was covered by a variety of artists. Most noted, UK's Toploader, who charted in the UK and Australia in 2000.

LITTLE JIMMY OSMOND - LONG HAIRED LOVER FROM LIVERPOOL
Reached #1 in UK.
Released as "Little Jimmy Osmond", at 9 years old, the youngest Osmond brother became the youngest ever UK #1, sitting at the top

spot for 5 weeks over Christmas. It peaked at #2 in Australia, but just charted in the USA at #38.

MALO – SUAVECITO
Think Santana was the first band to chart with a hit called Smooth? You're wrong.
Written by Richard Bean, Malo's (a Latin rock and roll band) only hit single, "Suavecito," ("soft" or "smooth" in Spanish) reached #18 in the Billboard Hot 100. The song was originally written as a poem for a high school sweetheart.

MICKEY NEWBURY - AN AMERICAN TRILOGY
As the title suggests, the track is actually an arrangement of three songs, Dixie, All My trials, and The Battle Hymn of the Republic.
The original Mickey Newbury version reached #26 in the Billboard Hot 100. Elvis Presley's cover only peaked at #66, but is probably the better known version.
Weird OHW Fact... Wikipedia states that "over 465 versions of "An American Trilogy" have been recorded by different artists."

MOTT THE HOOPLE - ALL THE YOUNG DUDES
Written by David Bowie after the band refused Suffragette City, it was first recorded and released by Mott the Hoople. Considering it is now considered an iconic song, it reached #3 in the UK charts, and a lowly #37 in the USA.

MOUTH & MACNEAL - HOW DO YOU DO
Reached #1 in Netherlands, Belgium, Denmark, Switzerland, and New Zealand.
Sold over 1 million copies.
Dutch duo Mouth & MacNeal had this international hit, charting worldwide. It rose to #8 in the Billboard Hot 100 and stayed in the chart for 19 weeks. A year later, a Die Windows cover version reached #1 in Germany.

NEIL REID - MOTHER OF MINE
Sold over 2.5 million copies.
Written by Bill Parkinson, this song is best remembered by the Neil Reid version. Released in December 1971, after the young Scot won Opportunity Knocks singing it, it reached #2 in the UK Charts.
Weird OHW Fact... The song was the B-side to Jimmy Osmond's Long-Haired Lover from Liverpool.

Weird OHW Fact... The associated album reached #1, making Reid the youngest artist to chart that high. He was 12 years old.

Weird OHW Fact... Two years later, his voice broke; he never sang again.

PYTHON LEE JACKSON - IN A BROKEN DREAM

Written by band keyboardist, Dave Bentley, the Australian band from Sydney recorded the song in 1969, with a young studio singer Rod Stewart on vocals. After breaking up, and a short hiatus, they reformed in 1972 and released the single, it reached #3 in the UK Charts, and #56 in USA. The band broke up immediately after the hit.

Weird OHW Fact... In 1969 Rod Stewart was an unknown, and got a new set of seat covers for his car for his vocals for the single.

Weird OHW Fact... Stewart re-recorded the song in 1992 with Pink Floyd's David Gilmour and Led Zeppelin's John Paul Jones.

ROYAL SCOTS DRAGOON GUARDS - AMAZING GRACE

Reached #1 in UK, Ireland, Australia, New Zealand, Canada and South Africa.

Sold over 7 million copies.

Bringing the sound of the mass pipes and drums to the world, the regimental band toured extensively, playing in competitions, concerts and parades. Their recording of Amazing Grace reached #1 in charts all over the world, and #11 in the Billboard Chart.

SAILCAT - MOTORCYCLE MAMA

The American rock band signed with Elektra Records, but only charted once. While their album reached #38, their sole hit single, Motorcycle Mama, peaked at a creditable #12 in the Billboard singles chart.

SHAG - LOOP DI LOVE

First recorded in 1971 by J. Bastós, the new version by English musician/entrepreneur Jonathan King, released it on his UK record label under the pseudonym Shag. King's version reached #4 in the UK Singles Chart.

T. REX - BANG A GONG (GET IT ON)

Reached #1 in UK and Ireland.

Although considered to be one of the best bands of the '70's, T. Rex only had one USA hit, giving them one-hit-wonder status, reaching #10 in the Billboard Charts. It was the only one of four UK #1 hits to chart in the USA.

TERRY DACTYL AND THE DINOSAURS – SEASIDE SHUFFLE

Written by 'John Lewis', this English novelty band released a handful of singles in the early 70's, but only one would be a hit. With the help of Johnathan King, this Mungo Jerry-esque single got to #2 in the UK Chart. The follow-up, On a Saturday Night, got to #45.

Weird OHW Fact... John Lewis was actually Jona Lewie, (You Always Find Me In the Kitchen At parties)

THINK - ONCE YOU UNDERSTAND

A studio group put together for the single on Laurie Records, the record was banned in some countries for the heroin mentions. It reached #23 in the U.S. Billboard Hot 100 chart, and was a minor hit in the UK and Germany.

URIAH HEEP - EASY LIVIN'

Although the English rock band have sold 40 million albums, their only US hit was Easy Livin'.

Slipping into the Billboard Hot 100 at #39, it was a minor hit worldwide.

ON SO CLOSE... BUT NO CIGAR...

LOOKING GLASS - BRANDY (YOU'RE A FINE GIRL)/JIMMY LOVES MARY-ANNE

Reached #1 in USA, and Canada.

Although not exactly achieving one hit wonder status, this band is worth a mention... they got so close. Written and composed by Elliot Lurie (who had a second OHW (Cherry baby) with band Starz; see 1977) and recorded on their debut album Looking Glass. The single reached #1 in the Billboard Hot 100.

Billboard ranked it as the 12th song of 1972.

Jimmy Loves Mary-Anne charted at #33, dashing their one-hit-wonder aspirations.

HAWKWIND - SILVER MACHINE/URBAN GUERILLA

Hawkwind, my favorite teenage band, hit the limelight in 1972, with Silver Machine, which reached #3 in the UK Charts. They would have gotten a one hit wonder mention, if a later single, Urban Guerrilla, didn't chart at #39. Blah.

VICKY LEANDROS – COME WHAT MAY

Sold over 6 million copies.

Represented Luxembourg at Eurovision, she won the contest, and the translated single got to #2 in the UK Singles Chart. One hit wonder? Nope. The same year she released The Love in Your Eyes, which reached #40 in the UK Charts. Very close, but no cigar.

1973...

As U.S. President Richard Nixon announces the suspension of offensive action in North Vietnam, the year begins...
Rowe v. Wade, the US Supreme Court overturns bans on abortion, comet Kohoutec is discovered, The Young and the Restless debuts on CBS, Motorola make the first cellphone call, Pablo Picasso dies, Watergate begins, Soviet Mars 5 probe launched, Yom Kippur war ends, movie The Sting opens in Manhattan.

ANN PEEBLES - I CAN'T STAND THE RAIN
Written by Ann Peebles, Don Bryant and Bernard "Bernie" Miller, it was a minor hit for Peebles. The single reached #38 on the US Chart but only #41 on the UK singles chart. It was Peebles only hit.

B. W. STEVENSON - MY MARIA
Written by B. W. 'Buck Wheat' Stevenson and Daniel Moore, the country/rock song reached #9 in the Billboard Chart and stayed in the top 40 for 12 weeks, and #7 in Canada.

BARBARA FAIRCHILD - THE TEDDY BEAR SONG
Written by Don Earl and Nick Nixon, this country 'classic' reached #1 on the Billboard magazine Hot Country Singles chart. It got to #32 in the mainstream Billboard Hot 100, #42 in Canada.

BLUE HAZE - SMOKE GETS IN YOUR EYES
British conductor and composer, arrangement specialist, Johnny Arthey, had worked with the greats in the music world. In 1972, he formed studio group Blue Haze and their reggae cover version of the 1933 song reached #32 in the UK Singles Chart. It was their only hit.

BOBBY 'BORIS' PICKETT AND THE CRYPT-KICKERS – THE MONSTER MASH
First written and recorded in 1962, this song has charted on the Billboard three times. Originally banned by the BBC for being 'too morbid', in 1973 it hit #10 in the Billboard Chart and #3 in the UK.

CLINT HOLMES - PLAYGROUND IN MY MIND
Reached #1 in Canada.
Sold over 1 million copies.
Born in Bournemouth, England, he was raised in Buffalo, New York.

Written by Paul Vance with Lee Pockriss, and featuring Vance's son on the chorus, the song soared to #2 on the Billboard Hot 100 chart, and topped the Canadian charts for 3 weeks.

CROSS COUNTRY - IN THE MIDNIGHT HOUR
From Brooklyn, New York, the group released one self-titled album on the Atco Records label featuring a more psychedelic version of Wilson Pickett's classic. It reached #30 in the US Billboard Hot 100.

DR. JOHN - RIGHT PLACE WRONG TIME
From his sixth album, In the Right Place, this song reached #9 in the U.S. Billboard Hot 100, and #6 in Canada.
Billboard ranked it as the #24 song of 1973.

ERIC WEISSBERG AND STEVE MANDELL - DUELING BANJOS
The Arthur "Guitar Boogie" Smith tune was arranged and recorded for the movie, Deliverance, by Eric Weissberg and Steve Mandell, this tune reached #2 in the Billboard Hot 100, and #2 in Canada.
It was nominated for the 30th Golden Globe Awards in the Best Original Song category.

EUMIR DEODATO - ALSO SPRACH ZARATHUSTRA (2001)
This Brazilian musician scored a worldwide hit with this jazz/funk version. It reached #2 in the Billboard Hot 100, #3 in Canada, and #7 in UK.
It won the 1974 Grammy Award for Best Pop Instrumental Performance.

FIRST CHOICE - ARMED AND EXTREMELY DANGEROUS
This American girl group charted from the album of the same name. It reached #16 in the UK, #28 in the USA, and #55 in Canada.

FOCUS - HOCUS POCUS
Although Sylvia was a bigger worldwide hit, (#4 in UK) Hocus Pocus is the Dutch band's only USA chart entry.
The keyboard classic reached #9 in UK, and #20 in the Billboard Hot 100.

FOSTER SYLVERS - MISDEMEANOR
American singer, songwriter and producer, he scored his only solo hit from his first release from his first album.
Written by his brother, Leon, it reached #7 in the Billboard Hot 100.

The follow-up, a cover of Dee Clark's 1959 hit, Hey Little Girl, charted at lowly #63.

FRED WESLEY AND THE J.B.'S - DOING IT TO DEATH
Written by James brown, this funk song featured Brown on vocals, but he wasn't listed on the single sleeve. It reached #22 in the Billboard Chart, and #1 in the Soul singles chart.

GOLDEN EARRING – RADAR LOVE
Reached #1 in Netherlands.
These Dutch rockers were huge in their own country, and had a few hits in the USA too, (Twilight Zone, Quiet Eyes) but in the UK, from their massive hit album, Moontan, this was their only hit, topping out at #7 in the UK charts. It reached #13 in USA, #5 in Germany, #6 in Belgium. The follow-up, Instant Poetry, reached #51 in the UK charts, their only other chart entry.

GREGG ALLMAN – MIDNIGHT RIDER
The Allman Brothers wrote and recorded the song back in 1971; it was the second single from their second studio album, Idlewild South. It did not chart, but the track was covered by Gregg Allman on his solo album, Laid back. It got to #19 in the Billboard Hot 100, #17 in Canada.
Weird OHW Fact... Gregg Allman and roadie Robert Payne broke into Capricorn Studios to make a demo of the song.

GUNHILL ROAD - BACK WHEN MY HAIR WAS SHORT
From Mount Vernon, New York, they are best known for their only chart hit, produced by Kenny Rogers. They reached #40 on the US Billboard Hot 100, where it spent 15 weeks in the chart. In Canada it only reached #53.

THE HOTSHOTS - SNOOPY VS. THE RED BARON
Written by Phil Gernhard and Dick Holler, it was a hit in 1966 by American band The Royal Guardsmen. The Hotshots' ska version reached #4 in the UK Singles Chart.

HURRICANE SMITH - OH, BABE, WHAT WOULD YOU SAY?
Norman 'Hurricane' Smith engineered for the Beatles, and produced many albums for Pink Floyd, the Pretty Things and Barclay James Harvest.

His first solo single, Don't Let It Die, reached #2 in the UK, but his second reached over the Atlantic, hitting #3 in the Billboard chart, #3 in Canada, and #4 in the UK.

Weird OHW Fact... Smith served as a glider pilot during WW2, he didn't fly Hurricanes.

THE INDEPENDENTS - LEAVING ME
Sold over 1 million copies.
Written and produced by Chuck Jackson and Marvin Yancy, Leaving Me was a R&B crossover single hitting #1 on the R&B charts. The song reached #21 on the Billboard Hot 100, their only hit.

JEANNE PRUETT - SATIN SHEETS
Written by John Volinkaty, this song got to the top of the country charts, and #3 in the Canadian country scene. The song reached #28 in the Billboard Hot 100, and was her only hit.

JOE STAMPLEY - SOUL SONG
Into the book by the skin of his teeth comes American country singer Joe Stampley. The song reached #37 in the Billboard Hot 100, while hitting high in the country charts in USA and Canada.

JOHN & ERNEST - SUPERFLY MEETS SHAFT
This American novelty group comprising John Free and Ernest Smith, recorded their only hit single reaching #31 on the Billboard Hot 40. Their follow-up single, Soul President Number One, did not chart.

JUD STRUNK AND THE MIKE CURB CONGREGATION - DAISY A DAY
Reached #1 in Australia.
This much covered song was written and performed by Jud Strunk and The Mike Curb Congregation. It was an international hit, reaching #14 on the Billboard Hot 100, #3 in Canada, and a shock #1 in Australia. Billboard ranked the song #89 of 1973.

LOUDON WAINWRIGHT III - DEAD SKUNK
A novelty song written by Wainwright, it took a few months to chart fully, but rose to #16 in the Billboard Hot 100 chart, #8 in Canada, and #12 in Australia.

LOU REED - WALK ON THE WILD SIDE
Taken from the classic album, Transformer, the song was produced by David Bowie and Mick Ronson. Released as a double A-side with Perfect

Day, there may never have been a more influential low-charting single. It made top 40 in most countries, but never cracked below top 10; its highest positions were #39 in the UK, and #10 in the US Billboard Hot 100.

MANU DIBANGO - SOUL MAKOSSA

Cameroon saxophonist, Manu Dibango, released this early disco hit and peaked at #35 on the US Billboard Hot 100 chart. The song became an international hit with cover versions everywhere.

Weird OHW Fact... Since the song was slow to be produced, more than 23 cover versions were vying for sales at the same time.

MARIE OSMOND - PAPER ROSES

Written by Fred Spielman and Janice Torre, it was first a top five hit in 1960 for Anita Bryant. Marie took her version to higher heights; a quick #1 in the Country charts, it soon crossed over, #2 in the UK, #5 in the Billboard Chart, #13 in Canada.

Weird OHW Fact... Fans of Scottish Football club, Kilmarnock, have adopted Paper Roses as the club's anthem.

NEW YORK CITY - I'M DOIN' FINE NOW

The band, New York City, originally called the Tri-Boro Exchange, caught the limelight on their first single release. It reached #17 on the Billboard Hot 100, #26 in Canada, and #20 on the UK Singles Chart.

Billboard ranked the song #46 of 1973.

British band, Pasadenas, covered the song in 1991 song which reached #4 in the UK.

SIMON PARK ORCHESTRA – EYE LEVEL

Reached #1 in UK.

Sold over 1 million copies.

The theme tune for the Netherlands based detective series, Van der Valk, the single failed in its first release in 1972. A year later upon re-release, it shot straight to the top of the UK charts, #3 in Ireland. It spent over 24 weeks on the UK chart.

SKYLARK - WILDFLOWER

Written by Doug Edwards and Dave Richardson, it was first performed by the Canadian band Skylark, who took it to #9 in the Billboard Chart, and #10 in Canada.

It has been covered by many artists sampled in a few hip hop songs.

STEALERS WHEEL - STUCK IN THE MIDDLE WITH YOU
Sold over 1 million copies.
Written by Scot Gerry Rafferty and Joe Egan, it was recorded for their first album. It reached #2 in Canada, #8 in the UK, and #6 in the US Billboard Hot 100 chart.
Billboard ranked the song #30 of 1973.

STORIES - BROTHER LOUIE
Reached #1 in USA and Canada.
Written by Errol Brown and Tony Wilson of Hot Chocolate, it had already been a UK Top 10 hit but failed to chart in the USA. Covered by the Stories six months later, it reached #1 in the Billboard Hot 100 in the US, and in Canada.

SYLVIA - PILLOW TALK
Written by Sylvia for Al Green, he turned it down as too risqué. Sylvia recorded it herself, and it reached #3 in the Billboard Hot 100. It also reached #3 in Canada and #14 in the UK.
Billboard ranked the song #22 of 1973.

TIMMY THOMAS - WHY CAN'T WE LIVE TOGETHER
Sold over 2 million copies.
American R&B singer, keyboardist, songwriter and record producer, reached #3 on the Billboard Pop Singles, and #12 in the UK. It was his only hit in either the USA or UK.

VICKI LAWRENCE - THE NIGHT THE LIGHTS WENT OUT IN GEORGIA
Reached #1 in USA and Canada.
Written by husband Bobby Russell, the Carol Burnett Show star Vicki Lawrence, American singer, actress, and comedian recorded it on debut album. It was a smash hit, immediately topping the USA and Canadian charts.
Billboard ranked the song #11 of 1973.

OH SO CLOSE... BUT NO CIGAR...

THE STRAWBS – LAY DOWN/PART OF THE UNION
Yes, the Strawbs actually had another single. But, on a real stretched lifeline, they are a one hit wonder in the Netherlands.
Lay Down reached #12 in the UK Charts.

Part of The Union, got to #2 in the UK, but also charted at #20 in Netherlands, thus making them not a one hit wonder in the UK, but they are a one hit wonder in the Netherlands.

1974...

As the F-16 makes its first flight over California, the year begins...
Heiress Patty Hearst, is kidnapped, the Terracotta Army is discovered in China, ABBA's Waterloo wins the Eurovision Song Contest, Juan Perón, President of Argentina, dies, Turkey invades Cyprus for the second time, the Rumble in the Jungle takes place in Zaire...

ANDY KIM – ROCK ME GENTLY
Reached #1 in USA and Canada.
Born Andrew Youakim, he is a Canadian pop rock singer and songwriter. His biggest solo hit was Rock Me Gently, which topped the US and Canadian singles charts. Elsewhere, it reached #2 in the UK, #10 in Ireland, and #31 in Australia.
Billboard ranked it as the #29 song for 1974.
Weird OHW Fact... Andy co-wrote Sugar Sugar for The Archies.

BACHMAN–TURNER OVERDRIVE - YOU AIN'T SEEN NOTHING YET
Reached #1 in USA, Canada, Denmark, and New Zealand.
If ever there was a break-out song for an 'album band', this was it. Written by Randy Bachman, from the hit album Not Fragile, it took seven weeks to slide up to the top the USA Charts. It topped major charts, and hit top ten almost everywhere else, #2 in UK, #3 in Netherlands, #4 in Ireland and Australia. They never charted in the UK again, making them a one hit wonder.
Billboard ranked it as the #94 song for 1974.

BAD COMPANY – CAN'T GET ENOUGH
As I mentioned in my introduction, sometimes I find a way to include songs just because I like them, sometimes I list songs just to show the idiosyncrasies of the pop market. This song is an example of the latter. Although Bad Company, with mega-star Paul Rodgers vocals, is a super group in its own right, this is the only Bad Company single to chart in Australia, reaching #22. The closest other chart single down under is Everything I Need, which just didn't make the top 40, topping at #41.

BILLY SWAN – I CAN HELP
Reached #1 in USA, Canada, Norway, Austria, Switzerland, Belgium, Netherlands, Germany, Australia, New Zealand, Sweden, Denmark and France.

Written and performed by Billy Swan, this country/pop crossover release charted worldwide. It only peaked in the UK charts at #6, and was ranked #43 on Billboard's Year-End Hot 100 singles of 1975.

BLACK OAK ARKANSAS – JIM DANDY.

Lead singer James Mangrum, known as Jim Dandy, recorded this cover on their most successful album, High on the Hog. The single peaked at #25 in the Billboard charts, and became their only hit.

Mangrum shares vocals with Ruby Starr, born Constance Henrietta Mierzwiak.

BYRON MACGREGOR/GORDON SINCLAIR – AMERICANS (A CANADIAN'S OPINION)

These pair of dueling Canadian newsmen go together in one story. On CFRB in Totonto, Gordon Sinclair recorded a patriotic commentary about America over the song, America the beautiful. When the piece was broadcast by US News, unsurprisingly, he got requests for copies. So, a recording of Sinclair's commentary was sold with profits funneled to the financially struggling American Red Cross. The 73 year old's recording shot to #24 on the Billboard Hot 100, making Sinclair the second-oldest living person ever to have a Billboard U.S. Top 40 hit. The single also trickled in at #42 in his native Canada.

However...

In nearby CKLW in Ontario, another recording was already being made by Byron MacGregor. Quicker on the draw, his version charted first, soaring to #4 in the Billboard Hot 100. The angry Sinclair had been beaten to the punch, and to make matters worse, MacGregor's version charted in Canada at #30.

CANDLEWICK GREEN - WHO DO YOU THINK YOU ARE?

Winning UK talent show Opportunity Knocks, Candlewick Green signed to Decca Records. Their first single reached #21 on the UK Singles Chart.

Weird OHW Fact... Bo Donaldson and The Heywoods covered the song, making a hit in the USA. (They also covered Billy Don't be a Hero, making another USA hit)

CARL DOUGLAS - KUNG FU FIGHTING

Reached #1 in UK, Australia, Austria, Belgium, Canada, France, Germany, Ireland, Netherlands, Norway, South Africa, USA.

Sold eleven million copies.

An epic one hit wonder, this single topped the charts all over the world, but it wasn't overnight; the disco hit charted slowly, gaining momentum as it hit the clubs. He never charted again.

CLIFF DEYOUNG - MY SWEET LADY
Actor and musician, Cliff starred in a TV movie, Sunshine using some of the songs of John Denver. The song "My Sweet Lady" from the movie peaked at #17 on the Billboard Hot 100. It was his only hit.

DAVE LOGGINS - PLEASE COME TO BOSTON
American singer-songwriter Dave Loggins released this track from his album Apprentice (In a Musical Workshop). It reached #5 in the Billboard Hot 100 chart, and #4 in Canada. The song has been covered many times.
It was nominated for a Grammy Award in the category Best Male Pop Vocal performance.

DAVID ESSEX – ROCK ON
Reached #1 in Canada.
Written by English singer David Essex, it became an international hit, reaching #3 in the UK Singles Chart. Overseas it reached #1 in Canada, $5 in the U.S. Billboard Hot 100, Essex's only USA top 40 hit, making him a one hit wonder.

EDDIE HOLMAN - HEY THERE LONELY GIRL
Sold over 1 million copies.
This was originally recorded as, Hey There Lonely Boy, in 1963. American R&B artist, Holman's version reached #4 in the UK Singles Chart.

GENE REDDING - THIS HEART
Gene Redding from Anderson, Indiana, released just one album, on Capitol Records. This Heart, the album's only hit, reached #31 in the Billboard Hot 100.
Weird OHW Fact... He was 'discovered' in Alaska by Etta James.

THE FIRST CLASS - BEACH BABY
Reached #1 in Canada.
Written by London husband and wife team John Carter and Gillian Shakespeare, the song hit USA at #4, and #13 in their native UK.
Weird OHW Fact... The band broke up before any promotion was done, so the new musicians who mimed on pop shows never recorded a note.

Billboard ranked it as the #94 song for 1974.

GORDON SINCLAIR/BYRON MACGREGOR – AMERICANS (A CANADIAN'S OPINION)

These pair of dueling Canadian newsmen go together in one story. On CFRB in Totonto, Gordon Sinclair recorded a patriotic commentary about America over the song, America the beautiful. When the piece was broadcast by US News, unsurprisingly, he got requests for copies. So, a recording of Sinclair's commentary was sold with profits funneled to the financially struggling American Red Cross. The 73 year old's recording shot to #24 on the Billboard Hot 100, making Sinclair the second-oldest living person ever to have a Billboard U.S. Top 40 hit. The single also trickled in at #42 in his native Canada.

However...

In nearby CKLW in Ontario, another recording was already being made by Byron MacGregor. Quicker on the draw, his version charted first, soaring to #4 in the Billboard Hot 100. The angry Sinclair had been beaten to the punch, and to make matters worse, MacGregor's version charted in Canada at #30.

THE HUES CORPORATION - ROCK THE BOAT

Reached #1 in Canada, USA.

Written by Wally Holmes for the American trio, it was released as the second single from the album Rockin' Soul. It was slow to chart, taking months to reach #1 in the Billboard Charts. It reached #6 in the UK, #8 in New Zealand, and #18 in Australia.

Billboard ranked it as the #43 song for 1974.

IAN THOMAS - PAINTED LADIES

Recorded by much-covered Canadian singer-songwriter Ian Thomas, it was released from his self-named debut album. It reached #4 on the Canadian charts and #34 in the Billboard Hit 100.

JIM WEATHERLY - THE NEED TO BE

American singer songwriter James Dexter Weatherly wrote hit songs for others (the Gladys Knight & the Pips hits; Midnight Train to Georgia, and Best Thing That Ever Happened to Me, are his songs) but he did have one solo hit, reaching #11 in US and #13 in Canada.

Weird OHW Fact... Weatherly played quarterback at the University of Mississippi and had to choose between music and football.

JOHNNY BRISTOL - HANG ON IN THERE BABY

Written by Johnny Bristol, it is the title track from his first album. It was a minor hit worldwide, and reached #8 in the Billboard Hot 100, and #3 in the UK. A cover by British band, Curiosity, also reached #3 in the UK.

THE KIKI DEE BAND - I'VE GOT THE MUSIC IN ME
Written by band keyboardist Bias Boshell, it reached #19 in the UK charts, where it stayed for 8 weeks. In the USA it reached #12. It has been covered by Heart, Tina Turner & Cher, Aretha Franklin, Céline Dion and Jennifer Lopez to mention a few.

LIEUTENANT PIGEON – I'LL TAKE YOU HOME AGAIN, KATHLEEN
Yes, they're a one hit wonder... but not for the song you think.
Written by front-man Rob Woodward, Mouldy Old Dough got to #1 in UK in 1972, and the follow up, Desperate Dan, charted at #17, destroying their one hit wonder chance in the UK. But! They did have a hit in Australia with I'll Take You Home Again, Kathleen, getting to the heady heights of #3 in the Australian Charts.
Weird OHW Fact... Keyboard plonker, Hilda Woodward (mother of Rob) was 60 when the band recorded the song. It makes her one of the oldest female UK number ones.

MARILYN SELLARS - ONE DAY AT A TIME
Written by Marijohn Wilkin and Kris Kristofferson, this song will appear in this book more than once. Sellars' version hit the US charts at #37. It was her only hit.

MARVIN HAMLISCH - THE ENTERTAINER
Sold over 2 million copies.
Not only is this American composer and conductor one of only twelve people to win Emmy, Grammy, Oscar and Tony awards (called an EGOT), he's one of only two people to have won those four prizes AND a Pulitzer Prize. However, he might be better known as the guy who did The Sting theme tune on ragtime piano. The recording hit #3 on the Hot 100, and charted all over the world.
He won an Academy Awards for the title song.

MELBA MONTGOMERY - NO CHARGE
Written by songwriter Harlan Howard, the most well-known version in America is by country singer Melba Montgomery. Her song was a #1 country hit in both the US and Canada, and charted in the mainstream Billboard chart at #39. (See the 1976 J.J. Barrie entry for the British OHW)

MERLE HAGGARD - IF WE MAKE IT THROUGH DECEMBER

Written and recorded by American country singer Merle Haggard, it topped the US and Canadian country charts. It is also his only Billboard chart hit, reaching #28, and #30 in Canada. It has been one of his trademark songs.

MFSB - TSOP (THE SOUND OF PHILADELPHIA)

Sold more than 1 million copies.
Written by Kenneth Gamble and Leon Huff, it was used as the theme for the television show, Soul Train, showcasing music from African American performers. The ensemble MFSB (Mother, Father, Sister, Brother)'s song reached #1 in the US Billboard Hot 100. It is seen as an example of the birth of disco music.

MIKE OLDFIELD - TUBULAR BELLS

Despite selling millions of albums, and having 25 charting singles worldwide, Mike Oldfield will always be known as a one hit wonder in the USA. A special mix of Tubular Bells was released as the movie, The Exorcist hit America. The song, used extensively in the movie, charted at #3 in the Billboard Hot 100.
Weird OHW Fact... Mike Oldfield also wrote Family Man, covered and made a hit by US band, Hall & Oates.

MOCEDADES - ERES TU (TOUCH THE WIND)

From the Basque region of Spain, the Eurovision Song Contest runners-up had a worldwide hit on their hands. One of the only Spanish language songs to reach the USA top 10, the song peaked at #9 in the Billboard Hot 100, and #30 in Australia.

NATURAL FOUR - CAN THIS BE REAL

American R&B group from Oakland, California, had many hits in the R&B category, but their 1973 release was their only mainstream Billboard chart entry. Topping out at #31, they disbanded after their third album.

PAPER LACE - THE NIGHT CHICAGO DIED

Written by Peter Callander and Mitch Murray, the song reached #1 on the Billboard Hot 100 for one week, in 1974, #3 in the UK charts, and #2 in Canada. The follow-up single, Black-Eyed Boys, just failed (US #41) making Paper Lace a one hit wonder in the USA.

Weird OHW Fact... Paper Lace sang Billy, Don't Be a Hero, a UK #1, but the song was ignored in the USA. Bo Donaldson and the Heywoods had the hit with the song in USA, selling 3 million copies. Flying on the coat-tails of others...

PAUL DA VINCI – YOUR BABY AIN'T YOUR BABY ANYMORE
Born Paul Leonard Prewer, in Greys, Essex, he is best known as the lead singer on Sugar Baby Love. He released just one solo hit single, despite many attempts, reaching #20 in the UK charts.
Weird OHW Fact... Paul sang lead vocals on the massive hit Sugar Baby Love by the Rubettes. He missed being in the band due to contractual reasons. So close...

PILOT – MAGIC
Reached #1 in Canada.
Sold over 1 million records.
Written by band members Billy Lyall and David Paton. Scottish pop rock band Pilot's breakout single was their only hit in North America. It topped the charts in Canada, #5 in USA, #6 in Ireland, #11 in UK, and #12 in Australia. Their follow-up single, January, topped the UK, Irish and Australian charts, but just went to #87 in USA.
Billboard ranked it as the #31 song for 1974.

PRELUDE - AFTER THE GOLD RUSH
Working on the folk scene, they had a hit with Neil Young's song, singing it A Cappella. It was a worldwide hit, #21 in the UK, #22 in the Billboard Chart, staying in the chart for 13 weeks.
Weird OHW Fact... The recording's idea took place at a bus stop, where the band just started singing the song. They included it in their stage show, and the rest is history.

REUNION - LIFE IS A ROCK (BUT THE RADIO ROLLED ME)
Written by Paul DiFranco and Norman Dolph, the lyrics are a fast-rate of late century icons, broken by the chorus and guitar solo. It reached #8 in the Billboard Hot 100 chart, #2 in Canada, and #33 in the UK.

RICK DERRINGER - ROCK AND ROLL, HOOCHIE KOO
Written by band member Rick Derringer, it was first recorded by Johnny Winter's band in 1970, although it did not chart. Derringer's solo version, three years later became a US hit, reaching #23 on the Billboard Hot 100.

RUBETTES - SUGAR BABY LOVE

Reached #1 in UK, Germany, Switzerland, the Netherlands, Austria, Belgium and Australia.

Unable to get a band to record the song, (Showaddywaddy and Carl Wayne both refused it) it was eventually released by the session band who first recorded it. Sugar Baby Love became a UK #1, #2 in South Africa, and #37 on the US Billboard Hot 100, where it became the Rubettes only hit.

Weird OHW Fact... Paul Da Vinci sang lead vocals on the massive hit, but he missed being in the actual band due to contractual reasons. So close to fame...

SAMI JO - TELL ME A LIE

Born Jane Annette Jobe, in Batesville, Arkansas, the country singer is best known for this crossover single, which reached #21 on the Billboard Hot 40. Her follow-up single, It Could Have Been Me, almost took her out of this book, but it only reached #46. She had many country hits.

SHIRLEY BROWN - WOMAN TO WOMAN

Sold over 1 million copies.

Written by James Banks, Eddie Marion and Henderson Thigpen, it was the last hit for STAX Records. It crossed from the soul chart to the mainstream Billboard Chart, reaching #22.

SISTER JANET MEAD - THE LORD'S PRAYER

Sold more than 3 million copies.

With music by Arnold Strals, this Australian nun used rock music to celebrate her faith. First charting in Australia (#3), it charted in many countries, including Canada, Japan, Brazil, Germany, and USA. It topped out at #4 in the Billboard Hot 100 chart, and stayed in the chart for 13 weeks.

Weird OHW Fact... This song made Sister Janet the first nun to have a hit in the US since Jeanine Deckers, the Singing Nun, hit (#1 with Dominique in 1963).

Weird OHW Fact... The song is also the only Top 10 hit whose complete lyrics come direct from the bible.

Weird OHW Fact... The song is also the only hit whose lyrics can be attributed to Jesus Christ.

THE SOUL CHILDREN - I'LL BE THE OTHER WOMAN

A Stax Records signing, The Soul Children had a few hits on the Billboard R&B Charts, but their only mainstream hit was the ballad, I'll Be the Other Woman. This recording reached #36 in the Billboard Hot 100.

THE SOUTHER, HILLMAN, FURAY BAND – FALLIN' IN LOVE
The Souther-Hillman-Furay Band is a reckoned super-group, formed by Asylum Records. Released from their debut album, Fallin' in Love reached #27 in the Billboard Hot 100.

SWEET SENSATION - SAD SWEET DREAMER
Reached #1 in the UK.
Written by David Parton (see 1977 listing), the song by British soul group (and New Faces winners) got to #1 in the UK Charts for just one week. It peaked at #14 on the Billboard Hot 100, and charted in Canada, but both not until the spring of 1975.

TERRY JACKS - SEASONS IN THE SUN
Reached #1 in Australia, Austria, Belgium, Canada, Denmark, France, Germany, Ireland, Norway, South Africa, Switzerland, New Zealand, UK and USA.
Sold more than 10 million copies.
Originally written by Belgian Jacques Brel, new English lyrics were added by Rod McKuen. The result was a worldwide hit for Canadian Terry Jacks. A Christmas hit, it would probably be easier to list the countries it didn't top the chart in.
Weird OHW Fact... Terry Jacks version is in the top 40 selling singles of all time.

TOM T. HALL – I LOVE
Written and recorded by country music artist Tom T. Hall, the song was released as the only single from the album, For the People in the Last Hard Town. Although the song was his fourth #1 in the US Country chart, it would be his first and last Billboard hit, at #12. It stayed in the mainstream chart for 15 weeks.
Billboard ranked it as the #83 song for 1974.

WEDNESDAY - LAST KISS
From Oshawa, Canada, this pop group scored their biggest Canadian hit, reaching #2 in their home charts. Last Kiss also reached #34 in the U.S. Billboard Hot 100 chart, making them a one hit wonder in the USA. They continued to chart in Canada.

WILLIAM DEVAUGHN - BE THANKFUL FOR WHAT YOU GOT
Sold over 2 million copies.
Written and first performed by William DeVaughn, the song features members of the MFSB ensemble (see entry above), and reached #4 in the Billboard Hot 100.

OH SO CLOSE... BUT NO CIGAR...

OZARK MOUNTAIN DAREDEVILS - JACKIE BLUE/IF YOU WANNA GET TO HEAVEN
Unfortunately for this book, both of the Ozark Mountain daredevils singles were hits in US.
Jackie Blue, #3 US, #2 in Canada.
If You Wanna Get to Heaven, reached #25 in USA.

1975...

As Stevie Nicks and Lindsey Buckingham join Fleetwood Mac, the year begins...
Space Mountain opens at Disney World in Florida, Charlie Chaplin is knighted, The Khmer Rouge start the genocide, Apollo &Soyuz dock together, comedy sitcom Fawlty Towers airs on BBC 2, the Queen single "Bohemian Rhapsody" is released, the term "Micro-soft" is used by Bill Gates.

ACE - HOW LONG?
Written by lead singer Paul Carrack, the single was released from their album Five-A-Side. It reached #3 in the US and Canada, and a lowly #20 in their homeland UK.
Weird OHW Fact... Although the lyrics heavily suggest that the song's subject matter is infidelity/adultery, this is not the case. Carrack had found out that his bassist, Terry Comer, had been playing with another band; Sutherland Brothers and Quiver. A somewhat forgiven Comer still played on the recording.

AMAZING RHYTHM ACES - THIRD RATE ROMANCE
Reached #1 in Canada.
Written by Russell Smith for the album, Stacked Deck, the band's debut single charted immediately. It reached #11 on the U.S. country singles charts and #14 on the Billboard Hot 100. The follow-up single, The End is Not in Sight, did not chart in the top 40.

BAZUKA – DYNOMITE
Written by Tony Camillo and performed by Bazuka, an American instrumental R&B group, which Camillo put together for the album project. The single reached #10 on the Billboard Hot 100, and #28 on the UK Singles Chart.
The single ranked #51 on Billboard's Year-End Hot 100 singles of 1975.

BENNY BELL - SHAVING CREAM
Originally recorded in 1946, Dr. Demento began to play the novelty song on his radio show in 1975 (each verse ends with a muffled rhyme of the word, 'shit'). Due to the renewed interest, Vanguard Records re-released the song, and it was a hit, reaching #30 on the Billboard Hot 100 chart.

BILLY HOWARD – KING OF THE COPS
An English comedy impressionist, Billy Howard hit the chart with his cop impression version of King of the Road. It reached #6 in the UK, and is well worth a look at the multi-impressions on the video.

BOOMER CASTLEMAN – JUDY MAE
Formerly with Michael Martin Murphey in The Lewis & Clarke Expedition, he became a solo artist, becoming, of course, a one-hit wonder. Judy Mae dipped into the charts at #33.
Weird OHW Fact... In 1968 Boomer Castleman was the inventor of the palm pedal, commonly now known as the Bigsby.

CAROL DOUGLAS - DOCTOR'S ORDERS
Reached #1 in Canada.
This disco track was a worldwide hit, reaching into many dance and mainstream charts. It topped at #7 in the UK, #11 in the US Billboard chart, #6 in Belgium, #4 in Ireland and #10 in New Zealand.

GWEN MCCRAE - ROCKIN' CHAIR
Born in Pensacola, Florida, Gwen McCrae has one hit to her name. The song rose to #1 on the R&B chart, and #9 on the Billboard Hot 100. The follow-up did hit the R&B chart, but got nowhere else.

GRAHAM CENTRAL STATION - YOUR LOVE
On Warner Bros records, Your Love went to #1 on the Hot Soul Chart for one week and reached #38 on the Billboard Hot 100.
Weird OHW Fact... The band's name is a word-play on New York City's Grand Central Station.

JASPER CARROT – FUNKY MOPED
Born Robert Norman Davis in Birmingham, England, he started as a folk musician, then turned to comedy. His only UK hit was a song written by Chris Rohmann, and produced by ELO's Jeff Lynn. It reached #5 in the UK Charts.

JESSI COLTER - I'M NOT LISA
Written and recorded by the American country artist, the country crossover single was released by Capitol Records. Reaching #1 in both USA and Canada's country charts, it reached #4 in the Billboard Hot 100, and #6 in Canada.
Billboard ranked it as the #40 song for 1975.

JIM GILSTRAP – SWING YOUR DADDY

Born James Earl Gilstrap, he sang backing vocalists for Stevie Wonder. His only solo hit was Swing Your Daddy, which reached #4 in the UK Singles Chart, #10 in the U.S. Billboard Black Singles chart.

KAMAHL - THE ELEPHANT SONG

Reached #1 in Netherlands and New Zealand.

This supposed kids song was written by Roger Woddis, Gregor Frenkel-Frank and Hans van Hemert. Recorded by Kamahl as part of a World Wildlife Fund TV Documentary, it shot to the top of the Netherlands and New Zealand Charts, getting into top 40 in Belgium.

Weird OHW Fact... Born Kandiah Kamalesvaran, he changed his name to Kamal for his first stage show, but was introduced as 'Camel'. He altered the name's spelling after that.

KRAFTWERK - AUTOBAHN

Although German electronic wizards Kraftwerk are considered to be a major worldwide phenomenon, they do have one hit wonder status in the USA and Canada. Autobahn was a smash hit all over the globe, #4 in New Zealand, #9 in their native Germany, and #11 in UK. Autobahn was their only North American hit, reaching #25 in the USA, and #12 in Canada.

LAUREL & HARDY WITH THE AVALON BOYS FEATURING CHILL WILLS - THE TRAIL OF THE LONESOME PINE

From their 1937 film Way Out West, it was originally recorded by the Avalon Boys and was lip-synced by laurel & Hardy. The deep bass part was sung by Chill Wills. It reached #2 in the UK Singles Chart.

LEON HAYWOOD - I WANT'A DO SOMETHING FREAKY TO YOU

Born Otha Leon Haywood in Houston, if you consider the recording as the one hit wonder part, he had two! In 1975, he had a USA hit with I Want'a Do Something Freaky to You, which reached #15 in the Billboard Hot 100, and in 1980, he broke into the UK charts (#12) with Don't Push It Don't Force It, which just missed the USA top 40.

MAJOR HARRIS - LOVE WON'T LET ME WAIT

Sold over 1 million copies.

Written by Vinnie Barrett and Bobby Eli, the single is ranked highly in soul playlists. Major Harris, formerly of The Delfonics, hit #5 on the Billboard Chart, and #1 on the soul chart.

Billboard ranked it as the #24 song for 1975.

MICHAEL MARTIN MURPHEY - WILDFIRE
Sold over 2 million copies.
Written by Michael Martin Murphey and Larry Cansler for the album, Blue Sky – Night Thunder. This serious song country crossover reached #3 on the Billboard Hot 100 chart. Despite many other albums, he never crossed over again.

MIKE BATT WITH THE NEW EDITION - SUMMERTIME CITY
The writer behind all the Womble music, and Steeleye Span's, All Around My Hat, Batt had his only 'solo' hit; Listed as Mike Batt with the New Edition, he recorded the theme to a BBC Show, Summertime Special. The song reached #4 in the UK Charts.

MINNIE RIPERTON - LOVIN' YOU
Sold over 1 million copies.
Minnie died just 4 years after her one and only hit. It reached #1 in the Billboard Hot 100, #2 in the UK. It was one of several songs to top the U.S. chart with no percussion.
It was ranked #13 on Billboard's Year-End Hot 100 singles of 1975.
Weird OHW Fact... Fellow 1975 one hit wonder Van McCoy; (The Hustle), died 4 years later in the same month, July, 1979.

MOMENTS & WHATNAUTS – GIRLS
The Whatnauts were a Baltimore band, and The Moments were from Hackensack, New Jersey. They teamed up for a single which went to #3 in the UK. It charted in the Disco and R&B Billboard Charts, but missed out on the Hot 100.

MORRIS ALBERT - FEELINGS
With lyrics written by Brazilian singer Morris Albert, and set to the tune of "Pour Toi," it was recorded for his debut album. Feelings reached #6 in the Billboard Charts, #4 in the UK, #5 in South Africa. There were lots of cover versions.
Weird OHW fact... Credited to Albert only, French songwriter Loulou Gasté, the composer of the tune sued, and won damages. They now share the credits.

NAZARETH – LOVE HURTS
Reached #1 in Belgium, Canada, Netherlands, Norway, South Africa
Written by Boudleaux Bryant, and first recorded by The Everly Brothers in 1960, this version is a chart beater all around the world.

Scottish band Nazareth, took the song to #10 in the USA, and a disappointing low of #40 in their native UK.

It was ranked #23 on Billboard's Year-End Hot 100 singles of 1975.

Weird OHW Fact... It became Norway's biggest ever hit single, spending 61 weeks on the chart, and 14 weeks at #1.

PETE WINGFIELD - EIGHTEEN WITH A BULLET

Wingfield is an English record producer, and musician who charted with this massive hit, taken from his album, Breakfast Special. It reached #15 in the USA, and #7 in the UK Charts.

POLLY BROWN - UP IN A PUFF OF SMOKE

An English singer from Birmingham, Polly is no stranger to one hit wonder-ism. Before her solo hit, she sang with Sweet Dreams on their Abba cover, Honey, Honey, a #10 hit in UK.

Although her solo hit, Up In a Puff of Smoke, did not chart in the UK, it reached #16 on the Billboard Hot 100, and #11 in Canada.

PURE PRAIRIE LEAGUE - AMIE

Written by band member Craig Fuller, it was originally recorded on their 1972 album Bustin' Out, but not released as a single until 1973. But it had two years to wait to chart properly, reaching #27 in the US Billboard Chart, #40 in Canada.

Weird OHW Fact... The band was dropped by their record company after the single did not chart. When it eventually became a hit, RCA had to re-sign them.

RALPH MCTELL - STREETS OF LONDON

Written by Ralph McTell, and first recorded for his 1969 album Spiral Staircase, it was released in Netherlands in 1972 (#9 one hit wonder) and again in the UK in 1974, where it rose to #2 in the UK Chart, selling 90,000 copies per day. It also won an Ivor Novello Award for Best Song.

ROGER WHITTAKER - THE LAST FAREWELL

Reached #1 in USA and in 11 other countries.

Sold over 11 million copies.

This chart hit is one of the slowest climbers ever. Released back in 1971, it was heard four years later and played in a radio station in Atlanta, Georgia. The listeners liked it, requested it again, and it soon began selling. It reached #19 in the Billboard Hot 100, and #1 in the contemporary chart.

The success in America rocketed sales all over the world; #2 in UK, and #1 in eleven countries.

SAMMY JOHNS - CHEVY VAN
Sold over 1 million copies.
Written and sung by Sammy Johns with instrumentals by members of the Wrecking Crew, the song reached #5 on the Billboard Hot 100 chart.

SHIRLEY & COMPANY - SHAME, SHAME, SHAME
Reached #1 in Austria, Belgium, and Netherlands.
Written by Sylvia Robinson and performed by American disco band Shirley & Company, this smash hit came out of the blue. Received well in Europe, the single reached #3 in Canada, #12 in the USA, and #6 in the UK.

TANYA TUCKER - LIZZIE AND THE RAINMAN
Written in 1971 by Kenny O'Dell and Larry Henley, the song has been recorded by Bobby Goldsboro, Alex Harvey, and The Hollies. Although Tucker had hits on the Country Charts, this was her only single to break into the Billboard Chart, reaching #37.

TELLY SAVALAS – IF
Written and first recorded by band Bread, Savalas did a spoken version, which shot to #1 in the UK and Ireland.
Weird OHW Fact... Savalas was an accomplished poker player, getting to #21 in 1992's WSOP main Event.

TRAVIS WAMMACK - (SHU-DOO-PA-POO-POOP) LOVE BEING YOUR FOOL
Born in Walnut, Mississippi, this American rock and roll guitarist was a child prodigy, recording his first record when he was twelve. In 1975 he released a solo album on which Shu-Doo-Pa-Poo-Poop) Love Being Your Fool, was featured. It reached #38 in the Billboard Hot 100.

TYPICALLY TROPICAL – BARBADOS
Reached #1 in UK, Ireland, and South Africa.
This summer reggae hit too five weeks to hit #1 in the UK, but stayed in the charts (and our heads) for eleven weeks. Follow-ups Rocket Now and The Ghost Song did not chart.
Weird OHW Fact... The Vengaboys version of the song, We're Going to Ibiza, also became a UK #1.

VAN MCCOY - THE HUSTLE

Reached #1 in USA and Canada.

This disco hit was written by McCoy, and went straight to #1 on the Billboard Hot 100.

and Hot Soul Singles charts during the summer of 1975. It also reached #3 in the UK, Belgium and Germany, #9 in Australia.

It won the Grammy Award for Best Pop Instrumental Performance for 1975.

Billboard ranked it as the #21 song for 1975.

Weird OHW Fact... Fellow 1975 one hit wonder Minnie Ripperton, (Lovin' You), died 4 years later in the same month, July, 1979.

WIGAN'S CHOSEN FEW – FOOTSIE

Northern Soul was rising as a musical force, and at the forefront was this single, reaching # 9 on the UK Singles Chart.

Weird OHW Fact... When the song was on BBC's Top of the Pops, dancers gave a demonstration of the Northern Soul style of dancing.

WINDSOR DAVIES AND DON ESTELLE - WHISPERING GRASS (DON'T TELL THE TREES)

Reached #1 in UK.

Written by Fred Fisher and his daughter Doris, and recorded by the Ink Spots in 1940, the song was covered by unlikely duo Davies and Estelle as their characters from the sitcom, It Ain't Half Hot Mum. It topped the British charts, and stayed at #1 for three weeks.

OH SO CLOSE... BUT NO CIGAR...

5000 VOLTS - I'M ON FIRE/DOCTOR KISS KISS

Nope, not ever close, really.

I'm on Fire was in the top 10 in Australia and #26charted in the United States.

Doctor Kiss Kiss reached #8 in the United Kingdom, and #6 in South Africa.

PETER FRAMPTON – SHOW ME THE WAY/DO YOU FEEL LIKE WE DO

So close Peter. You almost got in the one hit wonder bin.

Show Me The Way, got to #6 in the USA and #10 in the UK.

Do You Feel Like We Do, got to #10 in the USA, and just broke the chart in the UK, at #39.

1976...

As the first Concorde flight takes place, 1976 begins...
Harold Wilson resigns as Prime Minister of the UK, Patty Hearst is found guilty of bank robbery, Apple Computers is started by Steve Jobs and Steve Wozniak, the UK and Iceland end the Cod War, the summer Olympics are held in Montreal, Nadia Comăneci becomes a household name, Viking 1 lands on Mars, the Muppet Show is broadcast, The Band holds its last concert; the Last Waltz, Hotel California is released.

BARRY DEVORZON AND PERRY BOTKIN, JR. - NADIA'S THEME (THE YOUNG AND THE RESTLESS)
In the summer of 1976, ABC's sports program Wide World of Sports ran a montage of Romanian gymnast Nadia Comăneci's routines to the music of Cotton's Dream; composed by Barry De Vorzon and Perry Botkin. The public cried out for copies, and a hit was born.
The music, now lengthened and called Nadia's Theme (The Young and The Restless), reached #8 in the Billboard Charts.
It won a Grammy Award for Best Instrumental Arrangement, 1978.
Weird OHW Fact... ABC never credited DeVorzon as a composer. He sued and won damages of $240,000.
Weird OHW Fact... Although the video is ingrained into USA viewers' minds, it is often forgotten that Nadia Comăneci never actually performed to the tune.

BRASS CONSTRUCTION- MOVIN'
This Brooklyn, New York R&B/disco band charted in the UK three times, but this song was their only hit in the USA (#14), Netherlands (#10) and Belgium (#20).
The single hit most dance charts, but the band would never reach such dizzy heights again.

BROTHERHOOD OF MAN - SAVE ALL YOUR KISSES FOR ME
Reached #1 in UK, Belgium, France, Ireland, Netherlands, Norway, and Spain.
Sold more than 6 million copies.
Eurovision Song Contest winner , this worldwide hit brought Brotherhood of Man to superstar status. It charted worldwide, and was the #1 single for the year in the UK.

CATE BROS - UNION MAN

Earl and Ernest Cate from Fayetteville, Arkansas, join an august band of twins having one hit wonders. Their debut album contained the hit, Union Man, which reached #24 in the Billboard Hot 100, staying in the charts for 20 weeks.

CLEDUS MAGGARD & THE CITIZEN'S BAND - THE WHITE KNIGHT

Jay Huguely (writing as Cledus) is a novelty CB crossover country song. It reached #1 in the Billboard Hot Country Singles, and #19 in the mainstream Billboard Hot 100. He never charted again.

CW MCCALL – CONVOY

Reached #1 in USA, Canada, Australia and New Zealand.
Written by McCall and Chip Davis, this crossover novelty song was a worldwide hit. Top of the charts in USA and Canada, and reached #2 in the UK and Ireland.
Weird OHW Fact... Rather than be made for the movie, the song was actually the inspiration for the Sam Peckinpah film, Convoy, in 1978.

CYNDI GRECCO - MAKING OUR DREAMS COME TRUE

Once again, Cyndi Grecco is the quintessential one hit wonder. Her only hit was used as the theme song for the hit TV show, Laverne & Shirley. It reached #25 on the U.S. Billboard Hot 100, spending 16 weeks on the chart, and reached #16 in Canada.

ELTON JOHN/KIKI DEE - DON'T GO BREAKING MY HEART

Reached #1 in UK, USA, Australia, Canada, France, Ireland, Italy, New Zealand, South Africa, and Zimbabwe.
Sold more than 2 million copies.
Written by the John/Taupin team, the song was originally meant for Dusty Springfield, but she was too sick to record. The song was a worldwide smash hit, #1 in many countries, and charting in most.
Weird OHW Fact... Despite already having hits like, Your Song, Rocket Man, Daniel, Candle in the Wind, etc, it was Elton John's first UK #1.
It was ranked by Billboard, and in the UK, as the #2 song from 1976.

ELVIN BISHOP - FOOLED AROUND AND FELL IN LOVE

Elvin Richard Bishop was an American blues and rock musician. His one big hit shot to #3 in the US Billboard Hot 100 chart, #3 in New Zealand, #16 in Australia, #22 in Canada, and #34 in the UK charts.
Billboard ranked it as the #56 song for 1976.
Weird OHW Fact... Elvin Bishop never sang on the recording, the vocals were supplied by Mickey Thomas.

259

ENGLAND DAN AND JOHN FORD COLEY - I'D REALLY LOVE TO SEE YOU TONIGHT

Written by Parker McGee, from their album, Nights Are Forever. It reached #2 on the Billboard Hot 100 chart, and #26 in the UK.
Billboard ranked it as the #21 song for 1976.

FLASH CADILLAC & THE CONTINENTAL KIDS - DID YOU BOOGIE (WITH YOUR BABY)

An American retro rock 'n' roll band, they played the group Herbie and the Heartbeats in the film American Graffiti. Their only top 40 hit was Did You Boogie (With Your Baby).
The single reached #29 in the Billboard Hot 100.

GHEORGHE ZAMFIR - (LIGHT OF EXPERIENCE) DOINA DE JALE

The pan-pipe expert got his first big break as a BBC religious program featured his recording Doina De Jale. A single followed which rose to #4 in the UK charts. With the gateway open, he made many more pan-pipe albums.

HENRY GROSS – SHANNON

Reached #1 in Canada, and New Zealand.
Sold over 1 million copies.
Although reaching lofty heights elsewhere, and while charting at #6 in the USA, it only reached #32 in the UK.
Billboard ranked it as the #47 song from 1976.
Weird OHW Fact... The song was written about the death of Beach Boy Carl Wilson's Irish Setter.

SHERBET – HOWZAT

Reached #1 in Australia and New Zealand.
The Australian rock band had hits galore in their own country, but the smash hit, Howzat, broke them worldwide. It topped the charts, down under, reached #4 in UK, #6 in the Netherlands, and #8 in Norway. It did not chart in the USA, just hitting #61 in the Billboard Hot 100.

J.J. BARRIE – NO CHARGE

J. J. Barrie, Canadian songwriter and singer, recorded a version of Harlan Howard's country song, and it cringingly reached #1 in the UK Singles Chart, #2 in South Africa, #16 in New Zealand, #29 in Australia, and #39 in his native Canada. (The song had been a US country hit in 1974 by Melba Montgomery; see her 1974 OHW entry)

Billy Connolly spoofed it with a top 40 hit in the same year; No Chance (No Charge).

JOHN MILES – MUSIC
Reached #1 in Netherlands.
British musician John Miles gets two mentions in this book, the second is in 1977. Taken from his album Rebel, (Alan Parsons producer). As well as topping the Dutch Charts, it made #3 on the UK Singles Chart, #10 and on the German Singles Chart. It reached #88 in USA.

JOHN SEBASTIAN - WELCOME BACK
Written and recorded by former Lovin' Spoonful frontman John Sebastian, the theme song of the 1970s American television sitcom, Welcome Back, Kotter, was always going to be a hit record.
It reached #1 on the Billboard Hot 100, and #2 in Canada.
Billboard ranked it as the #58 song from 1976.

JOHN VALENTI - ANYTHING YOU WANT
Born John LiVigni in Chicago, after a spell with Puzzle, he went solo. From his one Ariola Records album, he released Anything You Want. It peaked at #37 on the Billboard Hot 100.

KEITH CARRADINE - I'M EASY
Written and performed by Keith Carradine, it reached #17 on the Billboard Hot 100 chart.
Featured in the movie, Nashville, it won the Academy Award in 1976 for Best Original Song, and the Golden Globe for Best Original Song.
Billboard ranked it as the #71 song from 1976.

LADY FLASH - STREET SINGIN'
Written and arranged by Barry Manilow, American trio, Lorraine Mazzola, Monica Pege and Debra Byrd, were Manilow's back-up singers. Their one solo hit, Street Singin', reached #27 on the Billboard Hot 100 record chart.

LARRY GROCE - JUNK FOOD JUNKIE
A novelty song about binge eating, it spent 15 weeks on the U.S. charts, reaching #9 on the Billboard Hot 100. It reached #48 in Canada.

LARRY SANTOS - WE CAN'T HIDE IT ANYMORE

Written by Barry Murphy, it is on Larry Santos's album, Casablanca. The single reached #36 on Billboard Hot 100 chart. It was also covered by Ritchie Havens.

MANUEL & THE MUSIC OF THE MOUNTAINS - RODRIGO'S GUITAR CONCERTO DE ARANJUEZ

Manuel, AKA Jeff Love, was a household name in the UK. The single, which got to #3 in the UK Charts, stayed in the chart for 10 weeks, and was one of the big hits of the year.

NORMAN CONNORS - YOU ARE MY STARSHIP

A tenuous entry if ever there was one... Pennsylvania jazz drummer Norman Connors released the song on Buddah Records, and it charted at #27 on the Billboard Hot 100.

Weird OHW Fact... The boat on his album's front cover belonged to actor John Wayne.

PRATT & MCCLAIN - HAPPY DAYS

Written by Norman Gimbel and Charles Fox, it is the theme song of TV hit show Happy Days. It reached #5 on the Billboard Hot 100, and #31 in the UK.

Weird OHW fact... The theme for Happy Days changed regularly; Rock Around the Clock for opening credits of seasons 1 and 2, (A Jim Haas Happy Days was used as closing credits). Pratt & McClain's version was used for opening and closing credits on seasons 3-10, and Bobby Arvon recorded a new version for the final season 11.

RED SOVINE – TEDDY BEAR

Released by country music singer Red Sovine, it shot to #1 in both the USA and Canadian Country Charts. After a few weeks, it became obvious that the song was a crossover hit, peaking at #40 on the Billboard Hot 100, and #4 in the UK Charts.

RICK DEES AND HIS CAST OF IDIOTS - DISCO DUCK

Reached #1 in USA, and Canada.
A disco novelty, this recording shot to #1 in USA and Canada, charting top ten worldwide, UK (#6), Australia (#4), and many more.
Billboard ranked it as the #99 song from 1976.

THE ROAD APPLES - LET'S LIVE TOGETHER

From Cambridge, Massachusetts, American pop rock group charted two singles on the Billboard Hot 100. Their first single rose to #35 on that chart. The follow-up release charted at a lowly #77, making them one hit wonders.

ROBIN SARSTEDT – MY RESISTANCE IS LOW
Written by legend Hoagy Carmichael, Robin (Brother of Peter Sarstedt), this song gave Robin a hit, after many, many tries. It reached #3 in the UK Charts. It was his only UK hit, although he did chart in Sweden, Belgium, and the Netherlands.

ROXY MUSIC - LOVE IS THE DRUG
From the album Siren, and already a #2 hit in the United Kingdom, it gave the UK supergroup its first hit in the United States, reaching #30 in the US Billboard Hot 100.
Despite their many world hits, it remains their only US hit.

SILVER - WHAM BAM
Written by country songwriter Rick Giles, this single reached #16 on the US Billboard Hot 100, and #27 in Canada. The song appears in the movie soundtrack of the 2017 Marvel Studios Guardians of the Galaxy Vol. 2.
Billboard ranked it as the #70 song from 1976.

STARLAND VOCAL BAND - AFTERNOON DELIGHT
Reached #1 in Canada and USA.
Sold over 1 million copies.
Written by band member Bill Danoff, this sexually suggestive song reached #1 in the U.S. Hot 100. It charted worldwide, #5 in New Zealand, #6 in Australia, and #18 in UK.
Billboard ranked it as the #12 song from 1976.

SUTHERLAND BROTHERS & QUIVER – ARMS OF MARY
Reached #1 in Ireland, Belgium, and the Netherlands.
Written by Scot, Iain Sutherland, and released on the album Reach for the Sky, the combination's debut album. The song disappointed in the USA (#48), but it was a hit worldwide; #3 in South Africa, #5 in UK, #17 in Germany, #28 in Australia, #33 in New Zealand.
Weird OHW Fact... This song may have been a one hit wonder in many countries, but not in their native UK. A future single, Secrets, got to #35 in the UK chart.

THELMA HOUSTON - DON'T LEAVE ME THIS WAY
Reached #1 in USA, and South Africa.

Written by Kenneth Gamble, Leon Huff and Cary Gilbert, and charted first by Harold Melvin & the Blue Notes, Houston's version was a worldwide hit. As well as topping the US Charts, it reached #4 in Canada and Sweden, #5 in Germany, #6 in Australia, and #13 in the UK.

Weird OHW Fact... The unreleased Harold Melvin & the Blue Notes version, was released on the strength of Houston's hit, and it reached #3 in the Disco Chart.

Billboard ranked it as the #7 song from 1977.

THIN LIZZY - THE BOYS ARE BACK IN TOWN

This is one of a few one hit wonders that shocked me.

Despite millions of plays on US rock radio stations, despite 33 single releases and 58 albums, this song was their only USA hit. From the album, Jailbreak, it reached #1 in Ireland, #8 in the UK and Canada, and a #12 hit in the Billboard Hot 100.

Billboard ranked it as the #97 song from 1976.

VICKI SUE ROBINSON - TURN THE BEAT AROUND

Written by Gerald Jackson and Peter Jackson, this debut album track reached #10 on the Billboard pop charts, also charting in Australia, Belgium, and Netherlands.

Robinson won a Grammy nomination for best female pop vocal.

Billboard ranked it as the #38 song from 1976.

WALTER MURPHY AND THE BIG APPLE BAND - A FIFTH OF BEETHOVEN

Reached #1 in USA, and Canada.

Sold over 1 million copies.

Arranged by Walter Murphy from Beethoven's Fifth Symphony, and included on the Saturday Night Fever soundtrack, this tune got to #1 on the Billboard Charts and in Canada.

Billboard ranked it as the #10 song from 1976.

Weird OHW fact... Walter Murphy played almost every note on the recording, but this fact was withheld, considering the audience would buy better from a group.

WILD CHERRY - PLAY THAT FUNKY MUSIC

Reached #1 in USA.

Sold over 3 million copies.

Written by band front man Rob Parissi, the single was the first release on the new Sweet City label.

It reached #1 in USA, #2 in Canada, #4 in Netherlands and New Zealand, and top 10 in other countries.

Billboard ranked it as the #5 song from 1976.

Weird OHW Fact... The song was allegedly written after an African American audience member asked, "Are you white boys gonna play some funky music?"

WING AND A PRAYER FIFE AND DRUM CORPS - BABY FACE

An American disco group put together by Harold Wheeler, they reached #14 on the Billboard Hot 100, and #12 in the UK Singles Chart.

YVONNE FAIR – IT SHOULD HAVE BEEN ME

Born Flora Yvonne Coleman, in Richmond, Virginia, Fair sang with the Chantels and James Brown.

Her cover of, It Should Have Been Me, just squeezed into the Billboard Hot 40, but hit a respectable #5 in the UK, her only UK hit.

SO CLOSE... BUT NO CIGAR...

THE BELLAMY BROTHERS LET YOUR LOVE FLOW/IF I SAID YOU HAD A BEAUTIFUL BODY WOULD YOU HOLD IT AGAINST ME

A one hit wonder? Yeah, in Canada, and in Germany. But in the UK and USA, and in most other world charts, they had two hits. Sorry.

BLUE OYSTER CULT – DON'T FEAR THE REAPER

This band is the closest to the cusp that this list gets. Don't Fear the Reaper reached #12 in the USA, #16 in the UK, and #7 in Canada, surely prime targets for the one hit wonder tag?

But a US follow-up, Burnin' For You, got to #40... blah.

And a UK follow-up, Goin' Through the Motions, ALSO got to #40... double blah.

Thankfully, Burnin' For You only reached #47 in Canada, making Blue Oyster Cult one hit wonders there.

1977...

As Alex Haley's Roots begins its run on TV's all over the world, the year begins...
Gary Gilmore is executed by firing squad, first test flight of Space Shuttle, two 747's collide over Tenerife, killing 583, Red Rum wins his record third Grand National, Star Wars opens in cinemas worldwide, Elvis Presley performs his last concert, and Marc Bolan dies in a car crash.

ALAN O'DAY - UNDERCOVER ANGEL
Reached #1 in USA, and Canada.
Sold over 1 million copies.
Written by Day, (who had already written a #1; Helen Reddy's, Angie Baby) the song went straight to the top of the Billboard Chart. It also reached #4 in New Zealand, and #9 in Australia.
Billboard ranked it as the #9 song for 1977.

BELLE EPOQUE - BLACK IS BLACK
Reached #1 in Australia.
French trio, Belle Epoque, had only one hit, but it did get to #1 in Australia. Their version of the Los Bravos song also reached #2 in the UK, and Top Ten in most of Europe.

BILL CONTI - GONNA FLY NOW
Reached #1 in USA.
Sold over 1 million copies.
Yup, it's the tune played as a sweaty Sylvester Stallone runs up the72 steps on the movie Rocky. Conti's orchestral version has a certain disco influence, and his recording reached the top of the Billboard Chart, and #8 in Canada.
Billboard ranked Conti's version as the #21 song of 1977
Weird OHW Fact... Presidential Candidate Walter Mondale used Gonna Fly Now as his campaign song in 1984. Yeah, that worked out well.

BRIGHOUSE AND RASTRICK BRASS BAND - THE FLORAL DANCE
A brass band favorite, this version was recorded by the band and released in time to chart before Christmas. It reached #2 in the UK Singles Chart, and sold half a million copies.

CAROLE BAYER SAGER – YOU'RE MOVIN' OUT TODAY

Reached #1 in Australia.

Written by Carole Bayer Sager (a prolific songwriter), Bette Midler and Bruce Roberts, the song was a #1 hit in Australia, and it reached #6 in the UK. This is her only solo hit, although she penned hits for many others.

CERRONE - LOVE IN C MINOR
Sold more than 3 million copies.

Born in Paris, Marc Cerrone is considered a musical great in Europe, with influences in disco and dance music for decades; worldwide, he has sold more than 30 million records. His biggest US hit, the highly suggestive single Love in C Minor, reached #3 on the Billboard Chart. Supernature, a bigger European hit, did not chart in the US.

C.J. AND CO. - DEVIL'S GUN
A disco group based out of Detroit, Michigan, their only hit was Devil's Gun, which reached #36 in the Billboard Hot 100, spending an incredible 29 weeks in the Top 100. It also reached #43 in the UK. Billboard ranked it as the #9 song for 1977.

DAVE MASON-WE JUST DISAGREE
Written by Jim Krueger, and released as the second single from Mason's album, Let It Flow, this country crossover reached #12 on the Billboard Hot 100. It was also covered by Billy Dean.

DAVID DUNDAS - JEANS ON
Reached #1 in Germany.

British musician David Dundas (Lord David Paul Nicholas Dundas) released this single from his debut album. The single eventually became Dundas's biggest hit, peaking at #3 on the UK, Australia, Ireland, and South Africa, while charting at #17 on the U.S. Billboard Hot 100. The single was used in a Brutus jeans commercial.

DAVID PARTON - ISN'T SHE LOVELY
Born David Eric Stanley Parton, this English singer-songwriter-producer recorded Stevie Wonder's hit single, finding his own fifteen minutes of fame. The song reached #4 in the UK Charts, staying in the chart for nine weeks.

Weird OHW Fact... Parton wrote, Sad Sweet Dreamer, a UK #1 single for Sweet Sensation (see listing for 1974).

DAVID SOUL - DON'T GIVE UP ON US

Reached #1 in USA, UK, Ireland, Canada and New Zealand.
Sold over 2 million copies.
Written by Tony Macauley, this Starsky/Hutch song was a worldwide hit, four weeks at Billboard #1, and ending up as the #2 for the year in the UK.
Billboard ranked it as the #29 song for 1977.
Weird OHW Fact... No matter if you love or hate this song, it's still one more hit than Starsky ever had!

THE DEAD END KIDS – HAVE I THE RIGHT
Reached #1 in Ireland.
Originally recorded by the London band, The Honeycombs (a UK #1 in 1964), Scottish boy band, The Dead End Kids, recorded this song, and had their only chart hit. It reached #1 in Ireland, and #5 in the UK Charts.

DEAN FRIEDMAN - ARIEL
Written and performed by Dean Friedman, and released from his debut album, it soon reached #26 in the U.S. Billboard Hot 100, and #19 in Canada. The song spent 22 weeks on the US Charts, while scoring #19 in New Zealand. This is his USA one hit wonder. Subsequent European hits, Lucky Stars, and Lydia, did not chart in the USA.

DEBBY BOONE - YOU LIGHT UP MY LIFE
Deborah Anne "Debby" Boone, American singer, author, and actress, is best known for her only hit, You Light Up My Life, which spent ten weeks at #1 on the Billboard Hot 100. Boone won the Grammy Award for Best New Artist, then re-focused her career on country music.

DR. BUZZARD'S ORIGINAL SAVANNAH BAND - WHISPERING/CHERCHEZ LA FEMME/SE SI BON
On their debut RCA album by disco group Dr. Buzzard's Original Savannah Band, released the single, reaching 327 in the Billboard Hot 100. The band did not chart again.

FACTS OF LIFE - SOMETIMES
American soul/disco group's (signed to Kayvette Records) second single was a remake of country singer Bill Anderson's hit. Their version reached #3 on the US Black Singles chart, and #31 in the mainstream Billboard Hot 100. The group did not chart again.

THE FLOATERS - FLOAT ON

Reached #1 in UK, and New Zealand.

An R&B/soul group from Detroit, Michigan, they had a hit with the first single. Float On soared to #2 in the US Billboard Charts, topping the charts in New Zealand and UK, #2 in the Netherlands, and charting well elsewhere. They released four albums, but never charted again.

Weird OHW Fact... Float On was used to advertise Cadbury's Crème Eggs in the 1990's.

HENHOUSE FIVE PLUS TOO - IN THE MOOD

Did you know Ray Stevens was a one hit wonder? Well, he was... under the pseudonym Henhouse Five Plus Too, he released a clucking chicken version of Glenn Miller's In The Mood. This annoying song got into the top 40 in both UK and USA. (Actual chart positions not known)

HIGH INERGY - YOU CAN'T TURN ME OFF (IN THE MIDDLE OF TURNING ME ON)

Written by Pam Sawyer and Marilyn McLeod, the four piece girl group hit #12 on the Billboard Hot 100 in 1978. Their follow-ups charted in the R&B charts, but not the mainstream ones.

HOT - ANGEL IN YOUR ARMS

Sold over 1 million copies.

Written by Herbert Clayton Ivey, Terrence Woodford and Herbert Tom Brasfield, the Hot version was a worldwide hit, reaching #6 in the Billboard Chart, #3 in Canada, #27 in Australia, and #3 in New Zealand.

JOHN MILES - SLOW DOWN

British rock musician John Miles, is perhaps better known for his bigger-selling hit, Music, but that song only charted at #88 in USA. This funky disco song was Music's follow up, and it charted at #34 on the Billboard Chart (#2 in the Disco Chart). It also reached #10 in the UK.

JULIE COVINGTON _ DON'T CRY FOR ME ARGENTINA

Sold over 1 million copies.

Reached #1 in Australia, Belgium, Netherlands, Ireland, new Zealand and the UK.

Fresh from her stint with TV show, Rock Follies, Julie Covington joined the cast of Evita. The biggest single from the show got to #1 all over the world, and was covered by Madonna in the movie.

LEBLANC & CARR – FALLING

Lenny LeBlanc and Pete Carr were seasoned professionals. When they released their only album, Falling was an immediate hit. The single reached #13 on the Billboard Hot 100, staying on the chart for 28 weeks.

Weird OHW Fact... LeBlanc and Carr were meant to be on the flight which crashed, killing the band members of Lynyrd Skynyrd. The bands were touring together, but a last minute change caused LeBlanc and Carr to miss the flight.

MAC MCANALLY - IT'S A CRAZY WORLD
Born in Red Bay, Alabama, Mac McAnally followed the classic OHW route; his self-titled debut album held the single that reached #37 on the Billboard Hot 100. His later albums held no further success.

MARY MACGREGOR - TORN BETWEEN TWO LOVERS
Reached #1 in USA and Canada.

Like so many one hit wonders, MacGregor charted her debut single, then hit nothing afterwards. As well as hitting #1 in the Billboard and Canada, it reached #4 in the UK.

The song was not a one hit wonder in USA, as a later single reached #39, but it was a one hit wonder in Canada and the UK.

MAYNARD FERGUSON - GONNA FLY NOW
Composed by Bill Conti, Gonna Fly Now is also known as the Theme from Rocky. It was nominated for an Academy Award for Best Original Song.

The version performed by Conti with an orchestra, hit #1 on the Billboard Hot 100, while this version, by jazz trumpeter Maynard Ferguson reached #22.

MERI WILSON - TELEPHONE MAN
Sold over 1 million copies.

Wilson was born in a US base in Nagoya, Japan, and raised in Marietta, Georgia. Her novelty risqué song was a surprise hit for everyone concerned. It reached #6 in the UK Singles Chart, and #18 in the Billboard Hot 100 chart.

Weird OHW Fact... Wilson's Telephone Man and Electric Light Orchestra's telephone Line, sat next to each other for two weeks on the US Chart.

PAUL NICHOLAS - HEAVEN ON THE 7TH FLOOR
Reached #1 in New Zealand.

Sold over 1 million copies.
Heaven on the 7th Floor was British singer's only hit in USA. From his debut album, it reached #6 in the Billboard Chart where it stalled for three weeks. It reached a lowly #40 in the UK, and #49 in Canada, but it topped the charts in New Zealand.

PETER MCCANN - DO YOU WANNA MAKE LOVE
Written and performed by American songwriter Peter McCann from his debut, self-titled album, the single reached #5 on the Billboard Hot 100. Billboard ranked it as the #17 song for 1977.

Q - DANCIN' MAN
A disco group from Beaver Falls, Pennsylvania, they were a one hit wonder from the first single from their debut album. Dancin' Man reached #23 in the Billboard Charts, but failed to chart anywhere else. Their follow-up single, Sweet Summertime did not chart.
Weird ONW Fact... Q are one of two bands to have a one hit wonder, and have their band name be a single letter. The other being M with Pop Musik (1979)

RAM JAM - BLACK BETTY
An African-American working song, taken into hard rock genre by New York rockers Ram Jam. Band member Bill Bartlett's arrangement was a hit, reaching #18 in the USA, #4 in the Netherlands, and top ten in UK, And Australia.
And I can remember actually buying this single in Edinburgh... great stuff.

RONNIE MCDOWELL - THE KING IS GONE
Sold more than 5 million copies.
Written and performed by American country artist Ronald Dean "Ronnie" McDowell. A committed Elvis fan, he wrote this after hearing of the star's death. Although a prodigious writer, none of his other recordings sold near as well. Despite huge sales, this song reached #13 in the Billboard Hot 100.

SAMANTHA SANG – EMOTION
Reached #1 in Canada, New Zealand.
Written by Barry and Robin Gibb, and recorded by Australian singer Samantha Sang, it was her only hit. The song went to #3 in the Billboard Charts, and #11 in the UK. It has been covered by many artists, the Bee

Gees themselves, and by Destiny's Child, who took the song to #5 in the US.
Billboard ranked her version as the #14 song for 1978. (It was released in December 1977)

THE SANFORD-TOWNSEND BAND - SMOKE FROM A DISTANT FIRE
The United States rock band reached #9 on the Billboard Hot with this song. It also hit Australia at #44. They would not chart again.
Ed Sanford co-wrote I Keep Forgettin' with Michael McDonald.

SILVETTI - SPRING RAIN
Written by Bibu Silvetti, the instrumental single was released in 1975, but it did not chart until it became popular in clubs and discos. Retitled from Lluvia De Primavera to Spring Rain for the American release, it finally reached #39, getting into our OHW list by the thinnest margin.
Weird OHW Fact... Silvetti was born in Argentina, moving to Mexico in his 30's.

SLAVE - SLIDE
Following the usual OHW criteria, Ohio funk/rock band Slide was a hit song released from their self-named debut album. It reached #32 on the Billboard Hot 100 singles chart. Despite peppering the R&B chart for years, this was their only mainstream hit.

SMOKIE - LIVING NEXT DOOR TO ALICE
Reached #1 in Austria, Germany, Ireland, The Netherlands, Norway and Switzerland.
Written by hit-makers Nicky Chinn and Mike Chapman, British band Smokie's version was the biggest hit. It reached #25 on the Billboard Chart, #5 on the UK Singles Chart, and, hit the top of the charts in many countries.
Weird OHW Fact... Everyone in the UK remembers the bawdy Chubby Brown version, and it scored better than the original in the UK, #3. However, Chubby's was just a copy of Dutch band Gompie's version which charted high all over Europe... thanks to both of them, it's now difficult to sing the original chorus without adding "Alice? Alice? Who the f#*k is Alice?"

SPACE – MAGIC FLY
The French keyboard band recorded their debut album, and released Magic Fly as their first single. The tune/song reached #2 in the UK, #3 in Ireland and #20 in the Netherlands.

STALLION - OLD FASHIONED BOY (YOU'RE THE ONE)

A somewhat typical OHW entry, this American pop rock group came from Denver, Colorado, having their only hit from the first single from their debut album.

The song charted at #37 in the Billboard Hot 100 chart.

STARZ - CHERRY BABY

Elliot Lurie at last gets a proper mention for a one hit wonder. After leaving Looking Glass (A 'So Close' entry with hit Brandy (You're a Fine Girl) in 1972) Lurie formed Fallen Angels, then Starz. From their album, Violation, Cherry baby was a minor hit, reaching #33 in the Billboard Hot 100.

TED NUGENT - CAT SCRATCH FEVER

Written by Ted Nugent, the recording is on the album of the same name. The iconic song is now played extensively on rock stations, although it only reached #30 in USA, and #37 in Canada. As a rock classic, it has been covered many times.

WILLIAM BELL - TRYIN' TO LOVE TWO

Sold over 1 million copies.

From his album, Comin' Back for More, it was an R&B crossover single, reaching #10 in the Billboard Hot 100. It would eventually sell over a million singles.

WILTON PLACE STREET BAND - DISCO LUCY (I LOVE LUCY THEME)

A group of disco musicians formed just for the single, the Wilton Place Street Band recorded a disco version of the I Love Lucy television show theme. It reached #24 on the Billboard Hot 40. They released 2 other singles, but the novelty had worn off and they did not chart.

OH SO CLOSE... BUT NO CIGAR...

AL STEWART - YEAR OF THE CAT

Scottish born singer-songwriter Al Stewart released the song from the album of the same name. It was a worldwide hit, #8 in USA, #3 in Canada, and top ten elsewhere. This probably should have been in the book as a one hit wonder...

But... his follow-up song, Time Passages, also charted in Australia, Canada and USA.

Weird OHW Fact... In 1945, Al's father, a RAF Flight Lieutenant, after impregnating his mother with Al, was killed in a plane crash when a practice flight went wrong. Such a shame.

THE BABYS - ISN'T IT TIME/EVERY TIME I THINK OF YOU
These British rockers are sometimes thought of as one hit wonders, but it simply isn't the case. (Both songs were written by Jack Conrad and Ray Kennedy.)
Isn't It Time (1977) was a chart-topper in Australia, and reached #13 in the U.S. Billboard Hot 100 and #8 in Canada.
Every Time I Think of You (1979) reached #13 in the U.S. Billboard Hot 100, #6 in Australia, and #8 in Canada.
Weird OHW Fact... Just in case you didn't notice; both their hits reached #13 in the USA and #8 in Canada; quite a coincidence.

MR. BIG – ROMEO
Who can forget the Queen-esque video. "That's a one hit wonder!" I hear you cry. Nope. As far as I can see, they didn't chart anywhere but the UK, and their follow up single got to #35 in the UK charts.

1978...

As film director Roman Polanski skips bail and flees to France, the year begins...
Charlie Chaplin's remains are stolen, the first episode of The Hitchhiker's Guide to the Galaxy, is transmitted on BBC Radio, the movie, Grease, is released, Pope John Paul I dies after only 33 days as Pope, and Ford initiates a recall for the Pinto, and the Space Invaders arcade game is released by Taito.

ACE FREHLEY - NEW YORK GROOVE
Written by Englishman, Russ Ballard, it was a UK hit for Hello (1975), and a USA hit for Ace Frehley(1978). Frehley, Kiss lead guitarist, recorded it on his first solo album, Ace Frehley. The song reached #13 on the Billboard Hot 100, his best charting single.

ALICIA BRIDGES - I LOVE THE NIGHTLIFE (DISCO 'ROUND)
Written by Alicia Bridges and Susan Hutcheson, I Love the Nightlife (Disco 'Round) went to #2 in the US Disco chart, then 'crossed over' to the mainstream chart, hitting a respectable #5, #3 in Canada, and a hit in Europe and Australia.
Billboard ranked it as the #64 song for 1978.

ALTHEA & DONNA - UPTOWN TOP RANKING
Reached #1 in UK.
Written by Jamaican teenager singers Althea Forrest and Donna Reid, they had a huge surprise hit on their hands. The song reached the top of the UK chart, staying in the chart for 11 weeks.
Weird OHW Fact... The recording was played by mistake by BBC DJ John Peel. He then got asked for it so many times, he ended up championing it.

BOBBY CALDWELL - WHAT YOU WON'T DO FOR LOVE
Caucasian Caldwell's promoters tried hard to hide his ethnicity, due to the African American-ness of both the groove and the vocals. When the video was released, his sales figures actually went up.
His soon-to-be signature song reaching #9 on the Billboard Hot 100.
Weird OHW Fact... When Valentine's Day approached, they printed a heart-shaped pressing. Priced at $7.98 (the cost of an album) it still quickly sold out, causing a further pressing of 50,000 to keep up with demand.

BONEY M - RIVERS OF BABYLON

Reached #1 in Australia, Austria, Belgium, France, Germany, Ireland, Netherlands, New Zealand, Norway, South Africa, Sweden, Switzerland, and the UK.

Sold over 4 million copies.

Written and recorded in 1970 by Brent Dowe and Trevor McNaughton (Jamaican reggae group The Melodians, #1 in Jamaica). The lyrics are paraphrased from Psalms 19 and 137. Boney M gave it a more disco beat, stuck Brown Girl in the Ring on the B-side, and their fame was assured. It reached #30 in USA, but topped charts all over the world. Their follow-up singles failed to chart in the US, making them a one hit wonder in USA.

Weird OHW Fact... In the UK, when the #1 hit had fell back to #20, DJ's began to play the B-side, Brown Girl in the Ring; the single shot back up the charts to #2.

BRIAN AND MICHAEL - MATCHSTALK MEN AND MATCHSTALK CATS AND DOGS

Reached #1 in UK.

The British music duo comprised Michael Coleman and Kevin Parrott. Their only charting hit, it was a song about the English artist, L.S. Lowry, who's style of painting was rather childlike and simple, hence the song's title. It reached #1 in the UK.

Weird OHW Fact... Coleman had to borrow £1000 to record/produce the record.

Weird OHW Fact... The brass band used was the Tintwistle Brass Band.

CELEBRATION FEATURING MIKE LOVE - ALMOST SUMMER

Written by Mike Love and Beach Boys band mates Al Jardine and Brian Wilson. Fronted by Beach Boys lead singer Mike Love, and incorporating members of the King Harvest (see 1972), Celebration released three albums. From the first album and movie soundtrack, the track Almost Summer, reached #28 in the Billboard hot 40.

CHERYL LADD - THINK IT OVER

More known for her acting work in movies like Millennium, and TV's Charlie's Angels, Cheryl Ladd had a decent singing voice. The single (on Capitol Records) reached #34 in the Billboard Hot 100, giving her a solitary hit.

Weird OHW Fact... Cheryl Ladd was the singing voice of Melody from the animated Hanna-Barbera's Josie and the Pussycats series.

CHERYL LYNN – GOT TO BE REAL

Sold over 1 million copies.

Written by Cheryl Lynn, David Paich and David Foster, the American disco singer charted with her first single from her debut album. She'd never reach the mainstream charts again. The song reached #12 in the Billboard Hot 100, #16 in Canada, but topped the Soul Chart. Billboard ranked it as the #69 song for 1978.

CHRIS REA - FOOL (IF YOU THINK IT'S OVER)

Born in Middlesbrough, England) is best known in Europe for his album Road To Hell, and hit singles, On the Beach, Let's Dance and Auberge. But in USA he remains a one hit wonder, Fool (If You Think It's Over) reached #12 in the Billboard Hot 100, #30 in his native UK.

CITY BOY - 5.7.0.5.

From Birmingham, England, City Boy's only hit single came from their Book Early album. 5705 reached #8 in the UK Top 10, selling 200,000 copies. It reached #17 in the USA, but their subsequent singles failed to chart. The follow-up, The Day the Earth Caught Fire, charted in the UK at #39, but it wouldn't change their USA one hit wonder moniker.

CLOUT - SUBSTITUTE

Reached #1 in South Africa, Australia, New Zealand, Germany, France, the Netherlands, Sweden, Austria, Denmark and Belgium.

This all-female South African rock group had one of the biggest one hit wonders of them all. First recorded by the Righteous Brothers, Johannesburg band, Clout, reached #1 in 10 countries. It reached #2 in the UK Singles chart, staying in the chart for 15 weeks. It only got to #67 in USA.

DAN HILL - SOMETIMES WHEN WE TOUCH

Canadian singer Daniel Grafton "Dan" Hill IV, had two international hits; Sometimes When We Touch, and Can't We Try, a duet with Vonda Shepard. In the UK, however, only the first song was a hit, reaching #13 in the UK charts, making him a UK one hit wonder. It topped the charts in his native Canada, and #3 in USA.

DEE D. JACKSON - AUTOMATIC LOVER

Reached #1 in Argentina, Italy, France, Spain, Turkey and Japan

Born Deirdre Elaine Cozier, in Oxford, England, she worked with the likes of Giorgio Moroder and Keith Forsey. Hitting top gear on her second release, it made #1 all over the world. Elsewhere, it reached #4 in the UK, #5 in Germany, and high in South America.

Weird OHW Fact... In Brazil, the media cashed in and released another single by a lookalike, even changed her name to D. Dee Jackson.

ERUPTION - I CAN'T STAND THE RAIN
Reached #1 in Belgium, Australia.

Written by Ann Peebles, Don Bryant, and Bernard "Bernie" Miller, and already a one hit wonder for Peebles (see 1973), Eruption's version was punchier and charted all over the world. It reached #2 in Norway, #3 in Italy, #4 in New Zealand and Austria, #5 in UK and France, #6 in Ireland, #7 in Germany; the list just goes on and on. Hitting in the dance, disco and R&B charts, it also reached #18 in the mainstream Billboard Chart; their only American hit.

FATHER ABRAHAM & THE SMURFS – THE SMURFING SONG
This novelty song, chained to the TV series, hit #1 in over 16 countries, although for the life of me I can't find details (Even though my daughter had the album). It got to #2 in the UK, held off by John Travolta and Olivia Newton John.

FRANKIE MILLER – DARLIN'
Reached #1 in Norway.

Written in 1970 by Stewart Oscar Blandamer, Scot Frankie Miller's Blues version topped the chart in... Norway, so, definitely a one hit wonder there. The song topped out in the UK at #6... but he had already charted earlier that year with Be Good To Yourself, reaching #27. So no OHW luck in UK.

FUNKADELIC - ONE NATION UNDER A GROOVE
New Jersey Funkers followed the now-familiar one hit wonder pattern; one hit single from their first album, followed by nothing else. One Nation Under a Groove reached #1 in the US Soul Chart, and #28 on the Billboard Hot 100. It is ranked in many 'best song' lists.

GERRY RAFFERTY – BAKER STREET
Reached #1 in Australia and Canada.

Okay, this is a stretch, but Gerry Rafferty is Scottish, so lay off. This release is included in the OHW list to show how idiosyncratic the music charts can be. This massive hit was an Aussie and Canadian #1, a US #2, and a UK #3.

However, despite hit other hits, Right Down the Line, Night Owl, and get It Right Next Time, all worldwide hits, none of them charted in Australia, making Baker Street and Gerry Rafferty an Aussie One Hit Wonder.

JAMES GALWAY – ANNIE'S SONG
Written by Jon Denver, the tune was recorded by Belfast native James Galway, 'Golden Flute'. The song and it got to #3 in the UK Charts.
Weird OHW Fact... He recorded the song for his second wife, Annie Renggli.

JILTED JOHN – JILTED JOHN
English comic musician Graham David Fellows is Jilted John. Their only hit (where John explains why he was jilted) got to #4 in the UK Charts, but their follow-up, Gordon the Moron, didn't make it.

JIMMY "BO" HORNE - DANCE ACROSS THE FLOOR
Having some success in the US R&B charts, Jimmy Horne's only mainstream hit came from his song, Dance Across the Floor. It slipped into the Billboard Chart at #38. Despite being a regular single R&B releaser, it would be his only mainstream charting single.

JOHN PAUL YOUNG - LOVE IS IN THE AIR
Written by George Young and Harry Vanda, the song became an immediate worldwide hit. It reached #2 in Norway, Sweden and South Africa, #3 in Austria, Australia and Germany, #5 in UK, and #7 in the Billboard Chart.
Weird OHW Fact... Like the boys from AC/DC Young was born in Scotland then his family emigrated to Australia.
Weird OHW Fact... John Paul Young has appeared on TV quiz show, Countdown, many times.

JUSTIN HAYWARD - FOREVER AUTUMN
I write this one gingerly, as I remember a follow-up single, Eve of the War, but I can't find a chart listing for it; perhaps I just remember the album. However, from Jeff Wayne's classic concept album sprang one great single; Forever Autumn. Sung by ex-Moody Blues singer/guitarist, Justin Hayward, it got to #5 in the UK Chart. America was slow to react to the new phenomenon, #47 in the US, #73 in Canada.
Weird OHW Fact... The album sat in the UK charts for 290 weeks; that's over five years!

LINDISFARNE - RUN FOR HOME
This Newcastle outfit was already a big band in Britain, with top 10 hits, Meet Me On the Corner, and Lady Eleanor, this was their only USA Chart entry. From their fourth album, Back and Forth, it reached #10 in the UK, and a lowly #33 in the Billboard hot 100.

LOVE & KISSES - THANK GOD IT'S FRIDAY
A disco ensemble, Love & Kisses is the theme song of the movie of the same name. Written by Alec R. Costandinos, it reached #1 on Billboard's Disco charts, #23 R&B and #22 in the mainstream Billboard Hot 100.

MARSHALL HAIN – DANCING IN THE CITY
Written by the British duo comprising Julian Marshall and Kit Hain, it shot to #1 in Australia and South Africa. The song reached #3 in the UK charts, but did not break America (#43 in the Billboard Charts).
Weird OHW Fact... Marshall went on to be another own hit wonder with Flying Lizards (1979).

MICHAEL ZAGER BAND - LET'S ALL CHANT
Sold over 5 million copies.
Written by Michael Zager and Alvin Fields, it was based on the idea that disco dancers wanted to chant along with the music. The single unexpectedly reached #1 on the disco chart and crossed over to the Soul Singles chart, at #15, and Billboard Hot 100, #36. In Europe, the single hit top 10 in many countries, #8 in UK, #2 in Belgium, #4 in Netherlands and Switzerland.
It is recognized as one of the biggest disco singles ever.

MOTORS - AIRPORT
Written by band member Andy McMaster, the single was released by London band, The Motors. It reached #4 in the UK Singles Chart.
In July '78, it was recognized at having sold over 250,000 copies.

NICK GILDER - HOT CHILD IN THE CITY
Reached #1 in USA, Canada.
Sold over 2 million copies.
English-Canadian musician Nick Gilder released this as a single from the album City Nights. It topped both the USA and Canadian charts, #3 in New Zealand, #9 in Australia.
He tried hard to get rid of his one-hit-wonder status in USA; Here Comes the Night got to #44 US, and (You Really) Rock Me reached #57US.

ODYSSEY - NATIVE NEW YORKER
Written by Sandy Linzer and Denny Randell, the song was first recorded by Frankie Valli in 1977. Covered by disco band, Odyssey, it reached #21 on the Billboard Hot 100, #5 in UK.
It was further covered by Black Box and Esther Phillips.

PATTI SMITH GROUP - BECAUSE THE NIGHT
Written by Bruce Springsteen and Patti Smith, and released from the Patti Smith Group album Easter. It reached #13 on the Billboard Hot 100 chart, and #5 in the UK, #9 in Sweden, #13 in Canada, and #15 in Australia.
Billboard ranked it as the #72 song for 1978.

PLASTIC BERTRAND - ÇA PLANE POUR MOI
Reached #1 in France, and Switzerland.
Written by Lou Deprijck and Yvan Lacomblez, the song reached #8 in the UK Charts, top ten in most of Europe; #2 in Netherlands and Australia, #4 in Ireland, #6 in Germany, and only #11 in his native Belgium. It reached #47 in the Billboard Chart.
Weird OHW Fact... The vocals were actually provided by the record's producer, Lou Deprijck.
Weird OHW Fact... Ça plane pour moi, does not mean 'Your plan For Me, but more idiomatic; 'Everything's going good'.

RAFFAEL CARRÀ – DO IT, DO IT AGAIN
Born in Italy, she was a film star for many years, often turning her talents to singing. With a few minor hits under her belt, she recorded the song in many languages, in English, Do it, Do it Again, it got to #9 in the UK Charts.

RANDY NEWMAN - SHORT PEOPLE
Sold over 1 million copies.
From his album, Little Criminals, it reached at #2 on the Billboard Hot 100 and stayed there for 3 weeks. Charting worldwide, it reached #2 in Canada, #12 in Australia, and #21 in New Zealand.

RUBICON - I'M GONNA TAKE CARE OF EVERYTHING
California funk rock band only released two albums. The first, entitled Rubicon, held their only hit, reaching #28 in the Billboard Hot 100, and spending 11 weeks in the chart. Band members Keagy, Gillis and Blades formed the highly successful Night Ranger. Johnny Colla became a original member of Huey Lewis and the News.

SANTA ESMERALDA - DON'T LET ME BE MISUNDERSTOOD

Written by Bennie Benjamin, Gloria Caldwell and Sol Marcus, the song is best known for the version by the Animals in 1965. This lively disco/flamenco/salsa version reached #15 on the Billboard Hot 100.

Weird OHW Fact... NBC Sports would sample the song, especially during coverage of the World Series.

SARAH BRIGHTMAN & HOT GOSSIP – I LOST MY HEART TO A STARSHIP TROOPER

This song was written by Jeff Calvert and Geraint Hughes, from the group, Typically Tropical, who are already in this book (1975). Sung by an 18-y-o Sarah Brightman and the sexy dance troupe Hot Gossip, the song shot to #6 in the UK Charts, #5 in Ireland, and #26 in Germany. Its sci-fi double entendre lyrics are well remembered, and the song was first performed on The Kenny Everett Video Show.

SCOTT FITZGERALD & YVONNE KEELY – IF I HAD WORDS

Netherlands singer Yvonne Keeley is best known for her duet with Scott Fitzgerald. The song reached #3 in the UK Singles Chart, #9 in Ireland, and #24 in Australia. It was a minor hit in New Zealand, Belgium, the Netherlands, Norway and Sweden.

Weird OHW Trivia... Yvonne was the girlfriend of Steve Harley (Cockney Rebel), and actually sang on the 1975 hit, Make Me Smile (Come Up and See Me).

STARGARD - THEME SONG FROM WHICH WAY IS UP

Written by Norman Whitfield, this song was the main theme to the Richard Pryor movie, Which Way Is Up? The song, sung by Stargard, reached #1 on the R&B Charts, and #21 in the Billboard Hot 100 singles chart.

STEVE MARTIN - KING TUT

Sold over 1 million copies.

Steve Martin and the Toot Uncommons (who were actually members of the Nitty Gritty Dirt Band), released the single after a Saturday Night Live performance. It reached #17 on the Billboard Hot 100, and #23 in Canada.

STONEBOLT - I WILL STILL LOVE YOU

From Vancouver, Canada, the band was first known as Perth Amboy. They soon changed their name to Stonebolt, and released a self-titled album in 1978. Their only hit single, I Will Still Love You, reached #29 in the Billboard Hot 100. The follow up came close, but no cigar... Love Struck just hit #70.

STREETBAND – TOAST
Soon to be called the Q-Tips, and featuring Paul Young on vocals, they had a novelty hit in the UK with Toast. It got to #18 in the UK charts and spent 5 weeks in the Top 40. When the Q-Tips split up, Paul Young would go on to a great solo career.

SWITCH - THERE'LL NEVER BE
From their first album, two singles headed towards the US charts. Unfortunately only one made it, making this R&B group a one hit wonder. There'll Never Be got to #37 in the US Billboard Hot 100.

TERRY WOGAN AND THE HANWELL BRASS BAND – THE FLORAL DANCE
Wogan's version of the song had him singing the lyrics, but for some reason did not include the last verse. His version got to #21 in the UK Singles Chart.

TOBY BEAU - MY ANGEL BABY
Written by band members Danny McKenna and Balde Silva, the single, included on their self-titled debut album, reached #13 on the Billboard Hot 100.
Weird OHW Fact... Toby Beau is the name of the old wooden shrimp boats once used on the Gulf Coast.

TUXEDO JUNCTION - CHATTANOOGA CHOO CHOO
Originally a Glenn Miller number, written by Mack Gordon and Harry Warren. Studio band Tuxedo Junction recorded a disco version that reached #32 in the Billboard Hot 100.

WALTER EGAN - MAGNET AND STEEL
Written and performed by Walter Egan, the single was released from Egan's second album, Not Shy. The song reached #8 in the U.S. Billboard Hot 100, #7 in New Zealand, #9 in Canada and #32 in Australia. With distinctive backing vocals by Fleetwood mac's Stevie Nicks and Lindsey Buckingham, it spent 22 weeks on the American charts.
Billboard ranked it as the #40 song for 1978.
Weird OHW Fact... Stevie Nicks, a beautiful blonde, was Egan's inspiration for the song. I wonder if he told Buckingham?

WARREN ZEVON - WEREWOLVES OF LONDON

Written by LeRoy Marinell, Waddy Wachtel, and Warren Zevon, on Asylum Records, the single reached #21 in the Billboard Hot 100, where it stayed for 6 weeks, and #15 in New Zealand.

Weird OHW Fact... Fleetwood Mac's drummer Mick Fleetwood and bassist John McVie played on the recording which was produced by Jackson Browne.

OH SO CLOSE... BUT NO CIGAR...

KANSAS – DUST IN THE WIND

Okay, this is a tenuous one, but since I now live in Kansas, I have to include their namesake rock band. However, the claim still exists.

Carry On My Wayward Son, was only a hit in US (#11) and Canada (#5). Elsewhere, it only charted in the UK, but at #51, outside the one hit wonder parameters.

But... Dust in the Wind charted #6 in the USA, #3 in Canada, and #36 in New Zealand of all places. So... because of Dust in the Wind, rock band Kansas are a one hit wonder in New Zealand.

Weird OHW Fact... Out of 30 album releases, Kansas albums only charted in three countries; USA, Canada, and... Sweden.

1979...

As the Dukes of Hazard debuts on CBS, 1979 begins...
Scotland fails in its first attempt at devolution, Voyager 1 passes Jupiter's rings, McDonalds introduces the Happy Meal, ESPN is launched, Carter freezes Iranian assets, Star Trek; The Motion Picture is released, and the USSR invades Afghanistan.

ALTON MCCLAIN AND DESTINY - IT MUST BE LOVE
All is not roses and champagne in the music world. An American disco girl group from Los Angeles, California, they formed in 1978, and signed to Polydor. Their first album did not sell, their first single, It Must Be Love, slipped into the Billboard Chart at #32. They were dropped a year later.

AMII STEWART - KNOCK ON WOOD
Reached #1 in Canada, USA.
Written by Eddie Floyd and Steve Cropper, this song has been covered many times. None, however reached the heights of Amii Stewart's version. The disco version hit charts worldwide, topping the tree in USA and Canada, and reaching #2 in Australia, France, Italy, and Switzerland, and #6 in the UK.
Billboard ranked it as the #22 song for 1979.

ANITA WARD - RING MY BELL
Reached #1 in USA, Canada, New Zealand, Spain, and UK.
Sold over 1 million copies.
Written by Frederick Knight, the song was originally meant for 11 year old Stacy Lattisaw. When she changed labels, Anita Ward got the single. Ward's single hit #1 on the disco and top ten in mainstream charts all over the world.
Billboard ranked it as the #9 song for 1979.

BARBARA MANDRELL - (IF LOVING YOU IS WRONG) I DON'T WANT TO BE RIGHT
Written by Homer Banks, Carl Hampton and Raymond Jackson, for The Emotions, it has been covered many times. The one I remember is Rod Stewart, from his Foot Loose & Fancy Free album.
Barbara Mandrell's cover topped the Country charts, and hit #31 on the Billboard Hot 100, and #23 in the UK.

BELL AND JAMES - LIVIN' IT UP (FRIDAY NIGHT)
Sold over 1 million copies.
Typical one hit wonders, this Philadelphia soul group recorded three albums, but never got past the success of their first single. Livin' It Up (Friday Night) got to #15 in the Billboard Hot 100, and a disappointing #59 in the UK Singles Chart.

BRAM TCHAIKOVSKY - GIRL OF MY DREAMS
Born Peter Bramall, in Lincolnshire, Bram is a British vocalist and guitarist. He has also the honor of being a one hit wonder three times over. (He was in the Motors (Airport) in 1978, and in the Netherlands, Sarah Smiles, reached #32 in 1979). Girl of My Dreams reached #37 in the Billboard chart; a one hit wonder in USA.

BROOKLYN DREAMS - HEAVEN KNOWS
Brooklyn Dreams, an R&B singing group were best known for their work with Donna Summer. The single was hers, and featured the group on back up.
It reached #4 in the Billboard Hot 100. The band continued to support Summer after the single's success.

THE BUGGLES - VIDEO KILLED THE RADIO STAR
Reached #1 in UK, Australia, Austria, France, Italy, Ireland, Japan, Spain, Sweden, Switzerland, and many more.
Written by Trevor Horn, Geoff Downes and Bruce Woolley, this iconic song was first recorded by Bruce Woolley with Thomas Dolby on keyboards. It was covered soon after by Horn and Downes, as The Buggles, on their debut album, The Age of Plastic.
The song was a worldwide hit, topping the charts in sixteen countries.
It only reached #40 in the Billboard Chart.

CHANSON - DON'T HOLD BACK
An American studio-based disco group on the Ariola label, they reached #21 on the Billboard Hot 100, and #33 in the UK Singles Chart.

CHUCK BROWN AND THE SOUL SEARCHERS - BUSTIN' LOOSE, PART 1
Charles Louis Brown, American guitarist, bandleader and singer, has the nickname 'The Godfather of Go-Go'. It does not reflect in his chart prowess, however, this single hit #34 in the Billboard Chart, and was his only chart entry.

THE CRUSADERS - STREET LIFE

Their only success was the 1979 album, Street Life, from which the title track was released as a single. With Randy Crawford on vocals, it dipped into the Billboard Charts at #36. Randy Crawford went on to a decent solo career.

Weird OHW Fact... Despite hits like, One day I'll Fly Away (#1 in Belgium and Netherlands, #2 in UK), You Might Need Somebody (#4 in UK), and Almaz (#2 in Ireland, #4 in UK), Randy Crawford never had another US Billboard hit. Her success was limited to Europe.

DAVID NAUGHTON - MAKIN' IT

Sold over 1 million copies.

Actor David Walsh Naughton starred in An American Werewolf in London, and in the sitcom Makin' It. He recorded and sang the show's theme song, peaking at #5 and staying in the Billboard chart for 16 weeks, #44 in the UK.

Billboard ranked it as the #14 song for 1979.

DRIVER 67 - CAR 67

Written by Paul Phillips and Pete Zorn, this novelty song revolves around a taxi driver's dashed love story. The song stayed in the UK for 12 weeks, and considering the artist, Driver 67, and the song, Car 67, it reached #7.

THE FLYING LIZARDS – MONEY (THAT'S WHAT I WANT)

Written by Barrett Strong in 1959, English band, The Flying Lizards, recorded the song, taking their version to #5 in the UK Charts. It also got to #50 in the USA.

FRANCE JOLI - COME TO ME

Recorded at the age of fifteen, this disco hit on Prelude Records reached #15 on the Billboard Hot 100, and topped the Billboard Hot Dance Club chart. It was to be the beginning of the end for disco... a new wave was about to hit the music scene.

FRANK MILLS - MUSIC BOX DANCER

Written by Frank Mills in 1974, it was not until 1979 that it made the charts. It made the top ten of many charts over Christmas, and was re-released in the USA in January.

It peaked at #3 in the Billboard Hot 100, #2 in New Zealand, #14 in Australia, and #47 in Canada.

Weird OHW Fact... A mistake by DJ five years later caused its success; he played the B-side of Mills most recent release, found Music Box Dancer, and played it often. The rest is pop history.

GIORGIO MORODER – (THE) CHASE
Despite being an international recording artist, this single, taken from his Academy Award winning soundtrack album, Midnight Express, is the Italian star's only USA Top 40 hit.
It reached #33 on the Billboard Hot 100, and #48 in the UK.

GONZALEZ - HAVEN'T STOPPED DANCING YET
A British R&B and funk band, they are best known for their worldwide disco hit, the Gloria Jones song, I Haven't Stopped Dancing Yet. It reached #26 on the Billboard Hot 100 and #15 in the UK Singles Chart.

HERMAN BROOD - SATURDAY NIGHT
Although already recognized in Europe, Saturday Night was the Ariole record label's attempt to push Dutchman Brood into America. The single reached #35 in the Billboard Hot 100, but that was both the beginning and end of his USA career.

IAN GOMM - HOLD ON
Ian Gomm played and toured with so many British greats, I don't have room to do the list justice, co-writing Cruel To Be Kind with Nick Lowe. However, in 1978, he released his first solo album, Summer Holiday. From the album, a single rose... Hold On reached #18 in the US, and #44 in Canada, missing his native UK entirely.

IAN MATTHEWS - SHAKE IT
After the success of Ian Matthews Southern Comfort, the lead singer went solo. This is his only charting single, reaching #13 in the Billboard Chart, #6 in Canada, and #17 in new Zealand.
Billboard ranked it as the #73 song for 1979.

INSTANT FUNK - I GOT MY MIND MADE UP (YOU CAN GET IT GIRL)
The disco band Instant Funk recorded widely in the late 1970/80's, but their only hit outside the USA R&B Charts was this 1979 release. It reached #20 in the Billboard Hot 100, while #13 in Canada, #16 in Belgium, and #20 in Netherlands.
It stayed outside the UK chart at #46.

IRONHORSE - SWEET LUI-LOUISE

Formed by ex- Bachman-Turner Overdrive member, Randy Bachman, Ironhorse was a Canadian rock band from Vancouver. Their only hit single was Sweet Lui-Louise, which reached #36 in the Billboard Hot 100 chart, and #26 in Canada. The single flopped in the UK, just reaching #60. Follow-up singles failed to chart.

JONES GIRLS - YOU GONNA MAKE ME LOVE SOMEBODY ELSE
Sisters Brenda, Valorie, and Shirley Jones, were backup singers for Aretha Franklin, Diana Ross, and many more. Their biggest solo hit was You Gonna Make Me Love Somebody Else, which trickled inside the Billboard Hot 100 at #38. It was an R&B hit, and a gold record. Their follow up efforts hit the R&B charts, but not the mainstream ones.

KERMIT THE FROG - RAINBOW CONNECTION
Written by Paul Williams and Kenneth Ascher, the song was 'performed' by Kermit the Frog (Jim Henson's voice) in the film, The Muppet Movie. It reached #25 on the Billboard Hot 100, remaining in the chart for 7 weeks. Kermit's, It's Not easy being Green, never charted.
Williams and Ascher won an Academy Award nomination for Best Original Song.
Weird OHW Fact... In New Zealand, 1996, a man burst into the Star FM radio station, taking the manager hostage, and demanded that Kermit's Rainbow Connection be played.

THE KNACK - MY SHARONA
Reached #1 in Australia, Canada, Italy, and USA.
Sold over 2 million copies.
Written by band members Berton Averre and Doug Fieger, this was the only major hit by Los Angeles punk band The Knack. It reached #1 on the Billboard Hot 100 singles chart, and stayed there for 6 weeks.
Billboard ranked it as the #1 song for 1979.
Weird OHW Fact... The single was the quickest to 1 million sales since the Beatles', I Want to Hold Your Hand, in 1964.

LAUREN WOOD - PLEASE DON'T LEAVE
A duet with Michael McDonald, this song rose quickly to #24 on the Billboard Hot 100. It was her only hit, despite many attempts with in different guises.

LENA MARTELL – ONE DAY AT A TIME
Written by Marijohn Wilkin and Kris Kristofferson, this song has been covered by over 200 artists.

Scottish singer Lena Martell took the song to #1 in the UK Charts, (for three weeks) crossing over to the pop charts successfully.

M - POP MUZIK
Reached #1 in Australia, Canada, Denmark, Germany, South Africa, Sweden, Switzerland, and the USA.
Sold over 2 million copies.
M is a project by English musician Robin Scott. From their debut album New York - London - Paris – Munich, they released their only hit; but it was a smash.
Pop Musik reached #1 in more than eight countries, and top ten in many more, making it one of the biggest hits of the year.
Billboard ranked it as the #40 song for 1979.
Weird OHW Fact... It only reached #2 in the UK, being firmly kept off the top spot by Art Garfunkel's, Bright Eyes.

MCFADDEN & WHITEHEAD - AIN'T NO STOPPIN' US NOW
Sold over 2 million copies.
Written (with keyboard player jerry Cohen) and performed by McFadden & Whitehead, from their debut album of the same name, McFadden & Whitehead, it was released and reached #13 on the Billboard Hot 100, #25 in Canada, and #5 in the UK.

MCGUINN, CLARK AND HILLMAN - DON'T YOU WRITE HER OFF
Byrds members Chris Hillman, Roger McGuinn and Gene Clark, got together in 1978, penning two albums together. The one hit was Don't You Write Her Off. Rising to #33 in the Billboard Charts, it would be their only hit in that particular partnership.

MOON MARTIN - ROLENE
Born in Oklahoma, John David Martin, he wrote many songs including, Bad Case of Loving You (Doctor, Doctor), recorded by Robert Palmer. Martin only had one solo hit; Rolene, which charted at #30 Billboard Hot 100.
Weird OHW Fact... Martin got the nickname "Moon" because lots his songs had the word "moon" in the title or lyrics.

NEW ENGLAND - DON'T EVER WANNA LOSE YA
New England is the Infinity Records debut album by the American rock band of the same name. From the album, their only hit, Don't Ever Wanna Lose Ya, dipped into the Billboard Hot 40.

NICK LOWE - CRUEL TO BE KIND
Written by Lowe and a bandmate from previous band Brinsley Schwartz, Ian Gomm.
Weird OHW Fact... Straight out of the gate, Cruel To Be Kind is a bit of a weird one... It peaked at #12 in SIX different charts. The song hit #12 in the USA, the UK, Canada, Australia, and New Zealand. Now if that weren't enough it also reached #12 in U.S. Cash Box Top 100.
Now, that's weird, yeah?

NITEFLYTE - IF YOU WANT IT
American disco group on Ariola Records, released the single, "If You Want It", which hit #37 on the U.S. Billboard Hot 100 chart. It would be their only hit.

PATRICK HERNANDEZ - BORN TO BE ALIVE
Reached #1 in Australia, Austria, Canada, Denmark, France, Germany, Italy, Mexico, New Zealand, Norway, Portugal, Spain, and Sweden.
Sold more than 4 million copies.
The French singer had a worldwide hit, and never needed to work again. Born To Be Alive hit too many charts to list, and reached #1 in over 15 countries.
Although it peaked at #16 in the Billboard Hot 100, it still sold over a million records stateside. In France it reached #1 and stayed there for 3 months, becoming the top French single of 1979.
In 1979, Hernandez received fifty-two gold and platinum record awards from more than fifty countries.
Weird OHW Fact... The song was recorded at Waterloo, Belgium, just a few yards from the 1815 battlefield.
Weird OHW Fact... When Patrick Hernandez was preparing for his 1979 US tour, he sent his producer to audition dancers to tour with him. Madonna was one chosen and you can see her in some of the official videos.

PINK LADY - KISS IN THE DARK
Kiss in the Dark was the band's first single released in America, by Japanese duo Pink Lady. The song reached #19 in the Japanese Oricon chart, and #37 in the American Billboard charts.
Pink Lady was the first Japanese recording act to chart in USA since Kyu Sakamoto ("Sukiyaki") 16 years earlier, and the first to have a hit sung in English.

QUANTUM JUMP - THE LONE RANGER

Singing the longest word in the world as the first line, (a hill in Hawke's bay,   New   Zealand; Taumatawhakatangihangakoauauotamateapokaiwhenuakitanatahu) the funk-based song was released in 1976, but didn't chart until 1979, two years after the band had split. It reached #7 in the UK.

THE RAMBLERS – THE SPARROW
The kids from Abbey Hey Junior School, Gorton, Manchester recorded this song on Decca Records for the Christmas market. It stayed in the UK Chart for 15 weeks and reached #11.

ROBERT JOHN - SAD EYES
Written and recorded by American singer Robert John, this song reached #1 in the Billboard Hot 100, and just slid inside the UK Top 40 at #31. This makes Robert John a one hit wonder in the UK.
The single also charted in Australia and Canada.

THE ROCKETS - OH WELL
An American rock band from Detroit, Michigan, they recorded five studio albums, including the 1979 Turn Up The Radio. From this album, they released one single, the Peter Green/Fleetwood Mac classic, Oh Well. It just slipped into the Billboard Hot 100 at #40.

ROGER VOUDOURIS - GET USED TO IT
Reached #1 in Australia.
Written by Michael Omartian and Roger Voudouris, performed by Voudouris, the single reached #1 in Australia, #21 on the Billboard Hot 100, and #45 in Canada.
Billboard ranked it as the #83 song for 1979.

RANDY VANWARMER - JUST WHEN I NEEDED YOU MOST
Written by Randy VanWarmer, this single was the pinnacle of his short career.
It reached #8 on the UK Singles Chart, and #4 on the Billboard Hot 100 chart.
It has been covered several times, notably by Smokie Robinson and Dolly Parton.
Randy VanWarmer died of Leukemia in 2004.

SNIFF 'N' THE TEARS - DRIVER'S SEAT

British band Sniff 'n' the Tears debut album included the track Driver's Seat. It reached #15 on the American Billboard Pop Singles chart, and reached #4 in the Netherlands, #17 in Canada, and #20 in New Zealand.

SPYRO GYRA - MORNING DANCE
Jazz Fusion band Spyro Gyra released this track from their second album, and it rose steadily to #24 on the Billboard Hot 100 chart, #17 in UK. Although Spyro Gyra has sold millions of albums worldwide, this single is the band's sole U.S. top 40 hit.

THE SUGARHILL GANG – RAPPER'S DELIGHT
Reached #1 in Canada and Netherlands.
Sold over 3 million copies.
The first single in the UK to be available as a 12" only, although it only peaked at #36 in the U.S. Billboard Hot 100 chart, it made #1 in Canada and Netherlands, #2 in Belgium, France, Norway, Sweden, and Switzerland, #3 in the UK.

SUZI QUATRO - STUMBLIN' IN
Written by songsters Mike Chapman and Nicky Chinn, and despite the bubblegum star's early 70's hits, this was Quatro's only US Top 40 hit, peaking at #4. The song did not chart in Quatro's stomping ground, UK, a dismal #41. It topped the Canadian charts and reached #2 in Australia, Germany, and New Zealand.
Billboard ranked it as the #23 song for 1979.

TUBEWAY ARMY – ARE FRIENDS ELECTRIC?
This London electronic band was led by the charismatic Gary Numan. Taken from their second album, Replicas, this song got to #1 in the UK, #3 in Ireland, #8 in New Zealand, and #9 in the Netherlands. It charted Top 40 in many other countries.
Weird OHW Fact... Newman dropped the Tubeway Army name for his next album, but kept the musicians as his band.

TYCOON - SUCH A WOMAN
Their bio is short. New Yorkers Tycoon released two albums on Arista Records. Such a Woman reached #26 in the U.S. Billboard Hot 100, and was produced by Robert "Mutt" Lange.

OH SO CLOSE... BUT NO CIGAR...

THE TOURISTS – I ONLY WANNA BE WITH YOU

Written by Mike Hawker and Ivor Raymonde, the Tourists' version got to #4 in the UK, #6 in Australia, and #13 in Ireland. It was a one hit wonder in Australia, but just failed in the Ireland, having one other minor hit, and in the UK; having another two minor hits.

THE EIGHTIES...
1980...

As the Rubik's Cube enters the life of millions of young people worldwide, the year begins...
The Winter Olympics take place in Lake Placid, New York, the Soviet Union allows its first rock concert, Iron Maiden release their first album, Mount St Helens erupts, AC-DC record Back in Black, Ronald Reagan defeats Jimmy Carter, Led Zeppelin's drummer, John Bonham, dies, and ex-Beatle John Lennon is shot.

AIR SUPPLY - ALL OUT OF LOVE
Written by Graham Russell and Clive Davis; the Australian duo, Air Supply. It reached #2 in the Billboard Hot 100, #2 in Canada, #3 in France, #9 in their native Australia and Ireland, and #11 in the UK, their only charting single in that country.
Billboard rated the song as #55 of 1980.

ALI THOMSON - TAKE A LITTLE RHYTHM
Written by Scottish singer-songwriter, from the album of the same name, Glasgow born Ali took the single to #15 in the Billboard Hot 100. His follow-up, Live Every Minute, did not chart. Ali has written songs for Gary Wright (Really Wanna Know You), A1, Steps, and Lisa Stansfield.
Weird OHW Fact... Ali first worked for Mountain Records as an office helper.
Weird OHW Fact... His brother is Doug Thomson, of Supertramp.

AMY HOLLAND - HOW DO I SURVIVE
Written by Paul Bliss, American pop singer Amy Holland recorded a version for her debut album, produced by Michael MacDonald. The song got to #22 in the Billboard Hot 100, but her subsequent singles did not chart that high.

AZYMUTH - JAZZ CARNIVAL

Although Brazilian jazz-funk band recorded many albums, the had only one hit, Jazz Carnival. It reached #19 in the UK Chart.

Weird OHW Fact... Azymuth title their music; *Samba Doido*, which translates to Crazy Samba.

BENNY MARDONES - INTO THE NIGHT

Self-penned, and from the album Never Run, Never Hide, the song reached #11 in the Billboard Hot 100. Then it got re-discovered, and rose again, this time to #20. In all, it spent 37 weeks in the chart. It charted in Canada at #12, Australia at #19, and New Zealand at #29. Billboard rated the song as #20 of 1980.

Weird OHW Fact... The song is one of only 10 recordings to ever get into the Billboard Top 20, TWICE!

BERNADETTE PETERS - GEE WHIZ

Tony and Golden Globe winner, actor and singer Peters had her only Billboard hit from her debut album, just tipping into the Top 40. She is well-known in the acting world on stage, television, and film, currently working on The Good Fight.

Weird OHW Fact... Multi-talented peters is also a children's book author.

BILLY PRESTON & SYREETA - WITH YOU I'M BORN AGAIN

Written by Carol Connors and David Shire, the song is a duet from the movie Fast Break. The song was a worldwide hit, charting initially in Europe reaching #2 in the UK charts. It topped out at #4 in the Billboard Charts.

Billboard rated the song as #21 of 1980.

BLACK SLATE - AMIGO

This was UK reggae band Black Slate's only hit, reaching #9 in the UK Charts. They toured Europe and New Zealand on the strength of the single, but didn't chart again.

BRUCE COCKBURN - WONDERING WHERE THE LIONS ARE

From the 1979 album Dancing in the Dragon's Jaws, this became Canadian Bruce Cockburn's only Billboard Top 40 hit, reaching #21. It charted in Canada, where it was named #29 in the Top Canadian song list.

CAPTAIN BEAKY & HIS BAND – CAPTAIN BEAKY
Two albums of poetry by Jeremy Lloyd were set to music by Jim Parker, narrated by celebrities. The project spawned one hit single; the title track, Captain Beaky, (vocals by Keith Michell) which reached #5 in the UK Charts.

CHANGE - A LOVER'S HOLIDAY
Written by Davide Romani and Tanyayette Willoughby, this soul crossover hit was taken from the album, The Glow of Love. Although the single was a successful soul and dance chart hit, it only reached #40 in the mainstream Billboard Chart. Overseas, it reached #14 in UK, 15 in the Netherlands, and #24 in New Zealand.

CHARLIE DORE - PILOT OF THE AIRWAVES
With it's a Capella beginning, who can forget this one… English singer-songwriter Charlie Dore fronted the band, and the song reached #13 on the US Billboard Hot 100, #3 in Canada, #12 in New Zealand, #28 in Australia.
Weird OHW Fact… This song was the last single played on Radio Caroline before it went dark.
Billboard rated the song as #77 of 1980.

DARA AND PAUL SEDAKA - SHOULD'VE NEVER LET YOU GO
Written by Paul Sedaka and Phil Cody, the song is a father/daughter duet. The song reached #19 in the Billboard Hot 100.
Weird OHW Fact… The single was Paul Sedaka's last charting single.

DENNIS WATERMAN BAND - I COULD BE SO GOOD FOR YOU
Gerard Kenny and Patricia Waterman wrote the theme tune to the ITV show, Minder, which Dennis Waterman sang. It reached #3 in the UK charts and Waterman toured with Gerard Kenny, and Sheena Easton as a result.

DEVO - WHIP IT

Written by band members Mark Mothersbaugh and Gerald Casale, and on the American New wave band's Freedom of Choice album, it was the band's only top 40 Hit in the USA. Topping at #14, it reached higher in Canada (#11) and New Zealand (also #11). Their follow up, Working in the Coal Mine actually charted in Canada and NZ, so they're not one hit wonders there.

Billboard rated the song as #94 of 1980.

DON WILLIAMS - I BELIEVE IN YOU
Written by Roger Cook and Sam Hogin, it was released from Don Williams' album of the same name. Although it was Williams' 11th Country number one, it was his only crossover hit, reaching #24 in the Billboard Chart. It reached #4 in New Zealand, #20 in Australia, #21 in Belgium, and #23 in the Netherlands.

FELIX CAVALIERE - ONLY A LONELY HEART SEES
Felix Cavaliere is best known for his time with the Young Rascals in the 60's. He only had one solo hit, Only a Lonely Heart Sees, which reached #36 on the Billboard Hot 100.

FERN KINNEY - TOGETHER WE ARE BEAUTIFUL
Reached #1 in the UK.

Written by Ken Leray, it was recorded by Steve Allan in 1978, reaching #67 in the UK Chart. Fern Kinney's version got to #1 in the UK, #2 in Ireland and top 40 in many other countries.

GARY NUMAN – CARS
Reached #1 in UK and Canada.

Written by Numan, Cars was a one hit wonder in USA and Canada. Despite a string of UK hits, he never quite got it right again for the trans-Atlantic audience. Cars topped the charts in UK and Canada, #5 in Ireland, and #9 in Australia. It peaked at #9 in the USA, and spent an amazing 17 weeks in the top 40.

Probably because of that chart longevity, Billboard rated the song as #12 of 1980.

JIMMY HALL - I'M HAPPY THAT LOVE HAS FOUND YOU

Best known as the front man with Alabama band Wet Willie, hall released a solo album, and charted with just one single. The song got to #27 in the Billboard Chart.

JOHNNY LEE - LOOKIN' FOR LOVE
Sold over 1 million copies.
Written by Wanda Mallette, Bob Morrison and Patti Ryan, the song was released by American country music singer Johnny Lee. From the soundtrack to movie, Urban Cowboy, this crossover song reached #5 in the Billboard Hot 100.
It was released in June 1980 as part of the soundtrack to the film Urban Cowboy, released that year. Marcy Levy was one of the female singers who provided backing vocals on the track.

KELLY MARIE - FEELS LIKE I'M IN LOVE
Reached #1 in the UK.
Written by Ray Dorset of Mungo Jerry in the '70's, Kelly Marie's version was a slow-charter, but it reached #1 in the UK, #2 in Belgium, #3 in Netherlands and Ireland, #5 in Germany, #6 in Austria and #7 in Australia.
Weird OHW Fact... Dorset meant to pitch the song to Elvis, but the American superstar died before Dorset got a chance.

THE KORGIS - EVERYBODY'S GOT TO LEARN SOMETIME
Written by lead singer James Warren and from the British band's second album, Dumb Waiters, the song reached #5 on the UK Singles Chart, #1 in France and Spain, #5 in Ireland, #6 in Switzerland, #11 in The Netherlands, #11 in Australia, #12 in New Zealand, and #14 in Belgium. It topped out in USA at #18 in the U.S. Billboard Hot 100 chart.
Weird OHW Fact... buzzy instrument after each chorus is a guzheng; an 18 string Chinese zither.

LARRY GRAHAM - ONE IN A MILLION YOU
Sold over 1 million copies.
Written by the prolific Sam Dees, the crossover song was recorded by slap bass guitar pioneer, Larry Graham. Larry played for Sly & the Family Stone and was the front man for Graham Central Station. The

song reached #9 in the US Billboard Hot 100, and as the title suggests, sold over 1 million copies.

LEON HAYWOOD - DON'T PUSH IT DON'T FORCE IT
Born Otha Leon Haywood, this Houston Texas singer is best known for his 1975 hit, I Want'a Do Something Freaky to You. In 1980, he had his only UK hit with, Don't Push It Don't Force It, reaching #12.

LIPPS INC. - FUNKYTOWN
Reached #1 in 28 countries.
Sold over 3 million copies.
(Better to tell where it didn't; #2 in UK and Sweden, #3 in Ireland, and #5 in Italy and South Africa.)
Written by their originator and producer, Steven Greenberg, Funkytown held the record for most countries at number one (28)... until Madonna's Hung Up (41).
Billboard rated the song as #8 of 1980.
Weird OHW Fact... Australian band Pseudo Echo, covered the song in 1986, hitting #1 in Australia and New Zealand, and charting worldwide (See 1986 entry).

MARTHA AND THE MUFFINS - ECHO BEACH
Written by band member Mark Gane, Canadian band, Martha and the Muffins, had a few hits in their native land, but their breakout single turned out to be a one hit wonder. It reached #5 in Canada, #6 in Australia, #10 in the UK Charts.

MASH - THEME SONG FROM M*A*S*H (SUICIDE IS PAINLESS)
Reached #1 in UK and Ireland.
Written by Johnny Mandel with lyrics by Mike Altman, this was the theme song for the movie and TV series M*A*S*H. and topped the charts in the UK and Ireland. #4 in the Netherlands.
Weird OHW Fact... Mike Altman is the son of the movie's director, Robert Altman, who was only 14.
Weird OHW Fact... Robert Altman made $70,000 for directing the movie; his son earned more than $1 million for co-writing the song.

MICKEY GILLEY - STAND BY ME
Written by King, Jerry Leiber and Mike Stoller, and made famous by Ben E. King, this version was included on the soundtrack of the movie Urban Cowboy. It rose to #22 in the Billboard Hot 100, reaching #1 in the US Country charts.

NIELSEN/PEARSON - IF YOU SHOULD SAIL
Once hailed as the next great super group, Reed Nielsen and Mark Pearson only recorded three albums. Their only charting single, If You Should Sail reached #38 on the Billboard Hot 100. They did not chart again.

NICK STRAKER BAND - A WALK IN THE PARK
From London, England, the single swept through Europe in late 1979 before charting in their native UK. It reached #20 in the UK Singles Chart. The follow-up, A Little Bit of Jazz, hit the dance chart #1 in US, but failed to chart in the Billboard Hot 100.

REGENTS – 7 TEEN
The British new wave band only had one hit. 7 teen got to #11in the UK Singles Chart. The follow-up, See You Later, only reached #55.

ROCKY BURNETTE - TIRED OF TOEIN' THE LINE
Reached #1 in Australia.
Written by Rocky Burnette and Ron Coleman (bass player of The Everly Brothers). It was a worldwide hit, reaching #8 in USA, #3 in South Africa and New Zealand, and #4 in Canada.
Billboard rated the song as #48 of 1980.
Weird OHW Fact... Burnette's only US hit, it reached #8 in USA. His father was an artist in the sixties, and his biggest hit, You're Sixteen also peaked at #8.

RODNEY CROWELL - ASHES BY NOW
Despite knowing the song Elvira (#95 US Country) and having heard it many times on the radio, this is actually Crowell's only US Billboard chart hit. This was actually Elvira's B-side, and recorded on the next

album, But What Will the Neighbors Think. Ashes by Now got to #37 in the US charts.

RODNEY FRANKLIN – THE GROOVE
From Berkeley, California, jazz pianist Rodney Franklin had one hit. From his CBS album, You'll Never Know, came the track, The Groove. It reached #7 in the UK Charts, but none of his follow-ups had any success.

ROGER DALTREY - WITHOUT YOUR LOVE
From the 1980 movie, McVicar, and written by Billy Nicholls (produced by Jeff Wayne of ELO) this was the highest chart hit for the Ex-Who lead singer. It reached #20 in the USA, although Free Me from the same album edged the contest in the UK. Despite many hits in the Top 100, he never broke the Billboard Top 40 again.

SKY - TOCCATA
Wonder group Sky, comprising the very best in classical artists, (guitarist John Williams, bassist Herbie Flowers, guitarist Kevin Peek, drummer Tristan Fry & Francis Monkman on keyboards) only had one charting hit. It reached #5 in the UK Charts, and got them a spot on Top of the Pops.

SPIDER - NEW ROMANCE (IT'S A MYSTERY)
New York rock band, Spider, have the most tenuous grasps on the one hit wonder moniker. Their sole hit, New Romance (It's a Mystery), reached #39 in the US Charts. Tina Turner covered their track, Better Be Good to Me, making it a hit.

SPLIT ENZ - I GOT YOU
Reached #1 in Australia, New Zealand.
Written by Neil Finn (later in Crowded House) from the album True Colours, this was New Zealand band, Split Enz's, widest success. It topped both the charts down under, and reached #12 in the UK, and #13 in Canada. It stayed outside the US Top 40 at #53, but was a one hit wonder in the UK.

STACY LATTISAW - JUMP TO THE BEAT

Written by Narada Michael Walden and Lisa Walden, reaching #1 in the US Dance Charts, but curiously it failed to show in the mainstream chart. It hit #3 in the UK, and top 40 in most of Europe. Although she would hit the billboard with later singles, it would be her only UK hit.
Weird OHW Fact... She was only 13 when she had the hit.

ST WINIFRED'S SCHOOL CHOIR - THERE'S NO ONE QUITE LIKE GRANDMA
Reached #1 in the UK and Ireland.
Written by Gordon Lorenz, this child's choir song was a Christmas #1. In the UK it knocked John Lennon to #2, and stopped Jona Lewie's Stop The Cavalry at #3.

STEVE FORBERT - ROMEO'S TUNE
From Meriden, Mississippi, American pop music singer-songwriter's song, Romeo's Tune, reached #11 in the U.S. Billboard Hot 100, #8 in Canada, and #13 in Australia. Keith Urban covered the song.
Billboard rated the song as #60 of 1980.

STYX – BABE
Reached #1 in USA and Canada.
Amazing though it may be to all American Rock fans, this was Styx's only UK hit. (Best of Times got to #42) Written by band member Dennis DeYoung for his wife Suzanne, the song hit the top of the chart in US and Canada. It reached #3 in Australia and New Zealand, #6 in the UK.

TERI DESARIO - YES I'M READY
Written by Barbara Mason in 1965, DeSario enlisted the help of Harry Wayne Casey (KC, of KC and the Sunshine Band) for her version. It reached #2 in the Billboard Hot 100, only kept from #1 by Queen's, Crazy Little Thing Called Love. Her follow-up work charted low, not reaching the Top 40.

TOM BROWNE - FUNKIN' FOR JAMAICA (N.Y.)
Queens (NY) jazz trumpeter Tom Browne recorded this on his second album, Love Approach. It hit #1 in the U.S. R&B chart and #9 on the

dance chart, but did not make the mainstream Hot 100. It reached #10 in the UK singles chart.

TOM JOHNSTON - SAVANNAH NIGHTS
Charles Thomas Johnston is one of those 'unknown' greats. He's the lead singer of the Doobie Brothers, and wrote their hits; Listen to the Music (#11), and Long Train Runnin' (#8). This is his only solo hit, reaching #34 in the Billboard Hot 100.

THE VAPORS – TURNING JAPANESE
Reached #1 in Australia.
Based in Surrey, England, The Vapors released the single from their album New Clear Days. As well as topping the Aussie charts, it reached #3 in the UK, #4 in Ireland, #6 in Canada, #9 in New Zealand, and a paltry #36 in the Billboard Hot 100.
Weird OHW Fact... Knowing they had a potential hit on their hands, and fearing one-hit-wonder-ship, the band waited until they had a follow-up single before releasing Turning Japanese... the follow-up didn't chart.

UTOPIA - SET ME FREE
Originally members of his own band, Utopia became a Todd Rundgren group in its own right. They only had one Billboard top 40 hit, peaking at #27, from the album Adventures in Utopia.

OH SO CLOSE... BUT NO CIGAR...

DONNIE IRIS - AH! LEAH!
Born Domenic Ierace, Donnie played with the Jaggerz and Wild Cherry, both one hit wonders. However, he's NOT a one hit wonder; his solo single, Ah! Leah!, hit #29, and the follow-up, Love Is Like a Rock, reached #37.

JONA LEWIE - YOU'LL ALWAYS FIND ME IN THE KITCHEN AT PARTIES/STOP THE CAVALRY

Yeah, he had two hits. Jona Lewie might be a one hit wonder in Switzerland (he is), but not much else...

You'll Always Find Me In The Kitchen At Parties reached #16 and stayed in the UK charts for 11 weeks.

Stop the Cavalry reached #3 in the UK, and was a major hit all over Europe.

Sorry, Jona, you don't make the list.

1981...

As Iran releases 52 American hostages held for 444 days, the year begins...

The first London Marathon is run, US President Reagan is shot, Pope John Paul is shot, the movie Raiders of the Lost Ark is released, Postman Pat is first shown on BBC1, Muhammed Ali fights his last fight, Paris Hilton is born, Bill Haley dies.

THE AFTERNOON DELIGHTS - GENERAL HOSPI-TALE

This Boston group comprised, Rebecca Hall, Janet Powell, Robalee Barnes, and Suzanne Boucher.

Their comedy/parody song reached #33 on the Billboard Hot 100. After their follow-ups did not chart, the ensemble disbanded.

ANEKA (MARY SANDEMAN) – JAPANESE BOY

Reached #1 in Belgium, Finland, Ireland, Sweden, Switzerland and the UK.

Sold more than 5 million copies.

Written by Bob Heatlie, the song was recorded by Scottish folk singer Mary Sandeman. A relative 'freak' hit, it was a world-wide smash, topping 6 charts and hitting Top 40 in most others. It did not chart in USA.

Weird OHW Fact... It did not chart in Japan... they thought it 'too Chinese'.

Weird OHW Fact... The producers got the name, Aneka, from the telephone directory.

BALANCE - BREAKING AWAY

These New York City hard rockers charted with a track from their debut album. It reached #22 in the Billboard Hot 100, their follow-up, falling in Love, only reached #58, relegating the band to their one-hit-wonder status.

BARABARA GASKIN (WITH DAVE STEWART) - IT'S MY PARTY

Reached #1 in the UK and New Zealand.

Barbara Gaskin, a folk singer and vocalist with Spirogyra, recorded many albums with Stewart. Their only hit got to #1 for four weeks in the UK, #3 in Austria, South Africa and Germany, #6 in Switzerland, #20 in the Netherlands. They expected big things from their follow-ups, but the highest was The Locomotion, reaching #71 in the UK.

CAROLE BAYER SAGER - STRONGER THAN BEFORE
Already a one hit wonder in Australia and the UK with Moving Out Today, this song came from her third and last album, Sometimes Late at Night. The song got to #30 in the Billboard Hot 100, her only USA solo hit.

Weird OHW Fact... Sager co-wrote Stronger Together, which was played behind Hilary Clinton at the 2016 Democratic Convention

CHAMPAIGN - HOW 'BOUT US
Reached #1 in Belgium and the Netherlands.

Named after their home town in Illinois, the American R&B band are best known for the hit single, How 'Bout Us. A one hit wonder in most countries other than the USA, their hit got to #5 in the UK Charts, #2 in New Zealand, #12 in the Billboard Charts.

Billboard rated the song as #45 of 1981.

Weird OHW Fact... Debunking their US one hit wonder status, they charted in the USA with their #23 aptly titled follow-up, Try Again.

CHRIS CHRISTIAN - I WANT YOU, I NEED YOU
This American songwriter has supplied many artists with great songs. However, his solo career was OHW short, his single just reaching #37 in the Billboard Chart. Cheryl Ladd, herself a one hit wonder, sings back-up on the song.

DIESEL - SAUSALITO SUMMERNIGHT
Reached #1 in Canada.

Dutch band, Diesel, released the single, Sausalito Summernight, from their album, Watts in a Tank. It reached #25 in the Billboard Hot 100, but topped the chart in Canada. Their next album, Unleaded, was not considered a success.

DELBERT MCCLINTON - GIVING IT UP FOR YOUR LOVE

Texan blues rock singer-songwriter, and Grammy winner had many hit blues albums, but he broke over to the mainstream charts only once. The song got to #8 in the Billboard Hot 100, #10 in Canada. However, he is not a one hit wonder in Canada; his follow-up, Every Time I Roll The Dice, got to #40 in the Canadian charts.

DOTTIE WEST - WHAT ARE WE DOIN' IN LOVE

Written by Randy Goodrum, the song features Kenny Rogers although he is not credited (The duo had recorded two other hit singles). The song got to #1 in the US country chart, and #14 in the Billboard Hot 100.
Billboard rated the song as #55 of 1981.

EMMYLOU HARRIS - MISTER SANDMAN

This entry surprised me, but it's true... Emmylou Harris is a one hit wonder. This single is the only one to break into the Billboard Top 40. Although she released 29 albums, and hit the top of the country charts in USA and Canada many, she never 'crossed over'. She did hit the top 40 with collaborations, but never again solo. Mister Sandman got to #37 in the Billboard Chart.

FRANKIE SMITH - DOUBLE DUTCH BUS

Written by Frankie Smith and Bill Bloom, their strange 'skipping' song got to #30 in the Billboard Hot 100, hitting #1 in the Soul chart for 4 weeks.
Weird OHW fact... Smith refused to pay his taxes, claiming WMOT Records had not paid him his royalties for the song. After investigation, WMOT was found to be laundering money for Larry Lavin, (Dr. Snow), a dentist/cocaine dealer.

FRED WEDLOCK - THE OLDEST SWINGER IN TOWN

With many folk albums under his belt, Fred Wedlock reached #6 in the UK Singles Chart, with his only hit, The Oldest Swinger in Town. In folk scene, he is best remembered for his parodies.

FUREYS WITH DAVEY ARTHUR - WHEN YOU WERE SWEET SIXTEEN

Written by James Thornton in 1898, this song has been a folk favorite for over a century. While Irish band, The Fureys, version contained nothing new, it still hit #1 in Ireland, #9 in Australia, and #14 in the UK.
Weird OHW Fact... At the turn of the century, before records, the sheet music sold over a million copies.

GET WET - JUST SO LONELY

A slim entry into the list, Get Wet only had one hit in America; the Boardwalk/Columbia single, Just So Lonely, which reached at #39 in the Billboard Hot 100. In Australia, it reached #15.

GRAHAM BONNET - NIGHT GAMES

From Skegness, England, Bonnet is one of rock's most potent vocalists. After leaving rainbow, he launched a solo album, charting just one single, Night Games. It reached #6 in the UK Charts. The follow-up, Liar, just trickled at #51.
Weird OHW Fact... The 'band' for the album comprised Mick Moody, Cozy Powell, Jon Lord, Francis Rossi and Rick Parfitt.

GROVER WASHINGTON JR. – JUST THE TWO OF US

Written by Bill Withers, William Salter and Ralph MacDonald, it was recorded on Washington's album Winelight. It reached #2 in the Billboard Hot 100.
The song won the Grammy Award for Best R&B Song.

JESSE WINCHESTER - SAY WHAT

American singer-songwriter James Ridout Winchester moved to Canada in 1967 to avoid the draft for the Vietnam. He had many hits in Canada, but just one charted in his native USA. It got to #32 in the Billboard Hot 100.

JIM STEINMAN - ROCK AND ROLL DREAMS COME THROUGH

Written by Jim Steinman, the musical genius behind the hits of Meatloaf, Bonnie Tyler and many others, released this track from a solo album, Bad For Good. It was also recorded by Meat Loaf on the album Bat Out of Hell II: Back into Hell. Steinman's version got to #32 in the Billboard Hot 100, #6 in New Zealand.

JOE DOLCE MUSIC THEATRE - SHADDAP YOU FACE

Reached #1 in Australia, Belgium, France, Germany, Ireland, new Zealand and the UK.

Sold more than 5 million copies.

Written by American, moved to Australia, Joe Dolce, the song depicts an ungrateful rebel Italian boy, being rebuked by his parents. Released in 1980, it hit #1 in the Australian charts and stayed there for 8 weeks. Growing around the world, it got to #1 in the UK Chart for 3 weeks, and many other European countries. In Canada it reached #2, and in the USA, just #53.

Weird OHW Fact... Just for those who don't know, it kept Ultravox's, Vienna, from reaching #1 in the UK.

Weird OHW Fact... A modest investment, Dolce just paid $500 for the recording and $1000 on the music video.

JOEY SCARBURY - THEME FROM THE GREATEST AMERICAN HERO (BELIEVE IT OR NOT)

Written by Mike Post and Stephen Geyer, it was the theme for the TV series, The Greatest American Hero. The series ran for 3 seasons, and the song got to #2 in the Billboard Hot 100, spending 18 weeks in the chart.

JOHN O'BANION - LOVE YOU LIKE I NEVER LOVED BEFORE

Born in Kokomo, Indiana, the American actor and singer's only hit went to #24 in the Billboard Hot 100. O'Banion starred in many movies, including Borderline, with Charles Bronson.

JOHN SCHNEIDER - IT'S NOW OR NEVER

John Richard Schneider is probably better known as the blond guy from the TV series, The Dukes of Hazzard. But he did have quite a stellar country music career, hitting the top of the US and Country charts many times. His only US crossover hit, however, was his first ever single. It reached #14 in the Billboard Chart, and #5 in Canada.

KATE ROBBINS AND BEYOND - MORE THAN IN LOVE

From Margate, Kent, Robbins is an actress, comedian, singer and songwriter, and the voice of most of Spitting Image's females. She only had one hit, but it was a good one; More Than in Love got to #2 in the UK Charts.

Weird OHW Facts... Robbins is a first cousin of Beatle, Paul McCartney.

KIM CARNES - BETTY DAVIS EYES

Reached #1 in Australia, France, Germany, Italy, Norway, South Africa, Spain, Switzerland, USA, and another 13 countries.

Written by Donna Weiss and Jackie DeShannon in 1974, Kim Carnes' version is the best known. It spent a staggering 9 weeks at #1 in the Billboard Chart, and won 2 Grammy Awards. Apart from the #1's, it reached #2 in Austria, New Zealand, #4 in Sweden, #5 in Ireland and #10 in the UK.

Billboard rated the song as #1 of 1981, and the #15 of all time.

Weird OHW Fact... It was a #1 in 21 countries; that's huge.

LAURIE ANDERSON - O SUPERMAN

American multi-level artist Laurie Anderson had a surprise hit from her project, United States Live. O Superman rose to #2 in the UK charts, #10 in the Netherlands, #11 in Ireland, #19 in Belgium, and #21 in New Zealand.

LEE RITENOUR - IS IT YOU

American session guitarist, Lee Mack Ritenour contributed to over 3000 songs in his life. His only solo chart entry got to #15 in the Billboard Hot 100. He added rhythm guitar to Funkin' For Jamaica and worked on Pink Floyd's Run Like Hell and One of my Turns.

LOOK - I AM THE BEAT

From Ely, England, they released I Am the Beat from their first album. It got to #6 in the UK Chart, but their follow-up just reached #50, the next one did not chart.

MOTÖR HEADGIRL SCHOOL - ST. VALENTINE'S DAY MASSACRE

The two band merge was the idea of producer Vic Maile; both bands were under the same label, bronze records. It was a #5 hit in the UK, and is obviously a one hit wonder.

PHIL SEYMOUR - PRECIOUS TO ME
In typical one hit wonder fashion, Phil Seymour got his only hit from his first single from his first album. The song reached #22 on the Billboard Hot 100, and an incredible #3 in Australia. The follow-ups, however, did not chart.

POINT BLANK - NICOLE
Hard working Texas rockers, Point Blank, released 6 albums. From their fifth album, American Exce$$, came their only charting single, Nicole. It reached #39 in the Billboard Hot 100. The group disbanded in 1984.
Weird OHW Fact... The band did over 200 gigs in one year; that's a lot of live music.

RACHEL SWEET - EVERLASTING LOVE
From Akron, Ohio, Sweet actually had hits in the UK and Australia, but her only chart hit in her native country was Everlasting Love. It got to #32 in the Billboard Hot 100, #35 in the UK, and #41 in Australia.
To stop her one-hit-wonder status in the UK and Australia, B-A-B-Y reached #35 in the UK, and I Go To Pieces, got to #36 in Australia.

ROBBIE PATTON - DON'T GIVE IT UP
Written by English singer/songwriter Robbie Patton, I feel this recording has many undertones of other songs. It is his only charting hit, reaching #26 in the Billboard Hot 100.
Fleetwood Mac's Bob Weston, Christine McVie, Bob Welch, and Lindsey Buckingham performed in the recording.

ROSANNE CASH - SEVEN YEAR ACHE
Taken from her second album of the same name, Seven Year Ache was her crossover hit which spawned a career of number ones and hits in the Country charts. Reaching #22 in the mainstream charts, she is considered a one hit wonder.

SILVER CONDOR - YOU COULD TAKE MY HEART AWAY

Silver Condor had a hit from their first self-named album. You Could Take My Heart Away reached #32 in the Billboard Hot 100, but no follow-up's charted.

SNOWMEN - HOKEY COKEY

Everybody knows one version of the dance, the Hokey Cokey. Its roots go back to folk songs of the early 1800's. One hit wonders, The Snowmen, got to #18 in the UK Chart, becoming a dance hit once again for a whole new generation.

SOFT CELL - TAINTED LOVE

Reached #1 in the UK, Australia, Germany, France, Belgium, Canada, South Africa, and another 10 countries.

Written by Ed Cobb of the Four Preps in the sixties, Soft Cell's version was a #1 hit in 17 countries. It peaked at #8 in the Billboard Chart in 1982; although the band had numerous hits in Europe, they never charted in the US again.

Despite its position in the US charts, Billboard still rated the song as #11 of 1982.

Weird OHW Fact... The song set a Guinness World Record for the longest stay on the Billboard Hot 100, staying in the chart for 43 weeks.

Weird OHW Fact... It took 19 weeks of worldwide airplay for the song to chart in the USA.

STANLEY CLARKE AND GEORGE DUKE - SWEET BABY

From California and Philadelphia, the duo released the single from their first album together. It reached #19 on the U.S. Billboard Hot 100, #6 on the R&B Chart. The electric sitar is prominent on the song.

SUSAN ANTON - KILLIN' TIME

Better known for her screen and Television acting work, Farrah Fawcett lookalike Susan had her own variety show. Of her many recordings, her duet with Fred Knoblock was her only hit. It reached #28 on Billboard's Hot 100.

Weird OHW Fact... Among other TV roles, Susan had a recurring role on Baywatch.

T.G. SHEPPARD - I LOVED 'EM EVERY ONE

Written by Phil Sampson, the song was recorded by country singer T.G. Sheppard. Although it was Sheppard's seventh #1 on the Country Charts, it was his one and only crossover hit. It reached #37 on the mainstream chart.

TERRI GIBBS - SOMEBODY'S KNOCKIN'

Blind country artist, Gibbs, has recorded 11 studio albums. However, her first single was her only crossover. It reached #13 on the Billboard Hot 100, and got to #20 in Canada. It was also nominated for a Grammy.

TIERRA - TOGETHER

From Los Angeles, California, Latin R&B band, Tierra had their only hit with a 1967 Intruders song, Together. It reached #18 on the Billboard Hot 100. It did not chart elsewhere.

TOMMY TUTONE – 867-5309/JENNY

Tommy Tutone is a power pop band, led by singer/guitarist, Tommy Heath. They are best known for their smash hit, 867-5309/Jenny, which reached #4 in the Billboard Hot 100. Elsewhere it got to #2 in Canada, #22 in Australia, and #32 in New Zealand.

Weird OHW Fact... Prank calls hit the number after the single's release... it was actually the number of the daughter of the police chief in Buffalo, New York.

TOM TOM CLUB - GENIUS OF LOVE

Founded by Tina Weymouth and Chris Frantz, (Husband/wife, also members of Talking Heads), they are better known in the UK for their #7 hit Wordy Rappinghood. However, only in the US are they one hit wonders. The song reached #31 in the Billboard Hot 100, #26 in Belgium, and #28 in New Zealand.

TONY CAPSTICK - THE SHEFFIELD GRINDER / CAPSTICK COMES HOME

Born Joseph Anthony Capstick, English comedian, and musician recorded many folk albums. In 1981, he found fame with this hit with the Carlton Main Frickley Colliery Band. It got to #3 in the UK Charts.

Weird OHW Fact... Tony is also known as one of the policemen in the TV sitcom, Last of the Summer Wine.

THE TWEETS - THE BIRDIE SONG (BIRDIE DANCE)

Composed in the 1950's by Swiss accordionist Werner Thomas as an oompah tune, it was released by The Tweets in 1981. The song got to #2 in the UK Charts, surely one of the most annoying tunes ever.

YARBROUGH AND PEOPLES - DON'T STOP THE MUSIC

Contemporary duo from Dallas, Texas, their only hit, Don't Stop the Music, reached #19 in the Billboard Hot 100. It also crossed the Atlantic, reaching #7 in the UK and #4 in Belgium.

It has been covered many times, Simon Harris being the best known version.

OH SO CLOSE... BUT NO CIGAR...

COAST TO COAST – THE HUCKLEBUCK

Coast to Coast, from Wellingborough, Northamptonshire, are best known for their version of the Hucklebuck (#5 in UK) and many think of them as one hit wonders. However, their follow-up, Let's Jump the Broomstick, actually charted at #28. Sorry guys.

Weird OHW Fact... the singer on the first hit was fired before the single charted, so the new guy got to mine to his predecessor's voice.

LANDSCAPE - EINSTEIN A GO-GO

A one hit wonder with Einstein A Go-Go? (#5 UK) Nope... their follow-up, Norman Bates, got to #40. Shame... such a good entry they would have made.

1982...

As the Commodore 64 Home Computer is launched for general use, the year begins...
Mark Thatcher disappears in the Sahara, the Falklands war begins, The Weather Channel airs for the first time, Aston Villa win the European Cup, E.T.: The Extra-Terrestrial is released, Vic Morrow dies in a helicopter accident, and Michael Jackson's Thriller is released.

ADRIAN GURVITZ - CLASSIC
Probably better known from his years with the Baker Gurvitz Army, and a one hit wonder with band, The Gun, in 1967, British singer-songwriter Adrian Gurvitz had a hit from the album of the same name. It reached #8 in the UK Charts.

ALDO NOVA - FANTASY
Canadian rock musician Aldo Nova achieved one-hit-wonder-ness on his first attempt; the first single from his debut album reached #23 in the Billboard Hot 100, and #14 in his native Canada. He never charted Top 40 again, sticking to songwriting and producing.

ALTON EDWARDS - I JUST WANNA SPEND SOME TIME WITH YOU
Perhaps the only Zimbabwean entry to our list, I Just Wanna Spend Some Time With You got to #20 in the UK Charts.

BARDO - ONE STEP FURTHER
Written by Simon Jefferis, and sung by duo Sally Ann Triplett and Stephen Fischer, it was the 1982 UK entry for the Eurovision Song Contest in Harrogate. It got to seventh place in the contest, and hit #2 in the UK Singles Chart.

BERTIE HIGGINS - KEY LARGO
Written by Bertie Higgins and Sonny Limbo, it was released from the album, Just Another Day in Paradise. It reached #8 in the Billboard Hot 100 chart, and spent 17 weeks in the Top 40. Elsewhere it got to #2 in

Australia, #3 in Canada, and #8 in New Zealand. It reached a disappointing #60 on the UK Singles Chart.

Billboard rated the song as #17 of 1982.

BLUE ZOO - CRY BOY CRY

British new wave band Blue Zoo, had three 'hit' singles in the UK. I'm Your Man got to #55, Cry Boy Cry" reached #13, staying in the chart for 8 weeks. The follow-up, (I Just Can't) Forgive And Forget, reached just #60.

BOYSTOWN GANG - CAN'T TAKE MY EYES OFF YOU

Reached #1 in the Netherlands, Belgium, and Spain.

San Francisco based disco band took Frankie Valli's hit and gave it a disco beat. The version reached number one in the Netherlands, Belgium, Spain and #4 in the UK Chart.

THE BRAT - CHALK DUST: THE UMPIRE STRIKES BACK

The Brat, aka Roger Kitter, was an English actor. He took this novelty song (mimicking John McEnroe's tennis tantrums) and went to #19 in the UK, staying in the chart for 8 weeks. It also got Top 10 in the Netherlands, Belgium and South Africa.

Weird OHW Fact... Kitter played Captain Alberto Bertorelli in series 7 of the TV sitcom 'Allo 'Allo!

BROWN SAUCE - I WANNA BE A WINNER

Comprising presenters from the BBC TV show, Multi-Coloured Swap Shop, Brown sauce were Keith Chegwin, Maggie Philbin and Noel Edmonds. Their only hit, written by Scot B.A. Robertson, reached #15 in the UK Charts, and stayed in the charts for 12 weeks.

BUCKNER & GARCIA - PAC-MAN FEVER

Sold over 2 million copies.

Buckner & Garcia were a parody/novelty song duo who first recorded in the early 70's. On momentum from the video game craze, they wrote and released their Pac man song, reaching #9 in the Billboard Hot 100. The follow-up did not chart, topping out at #103.

CHARLENE - I'VE NEVER BEEN TO ME

Reached #1 in Ireland, Canada, Australia, and the UK.

Written by Ron Miller and Kenneth Hirsch, this song is best known by American singer Charlene's recording. which is best known via a recording by American pop singer. As well as topping the charts above, it went top 40 in most charts, #5 in New Zealand and Norway, and #7 in Belgium and the Netherlands. (#7). It's one of the biggest one hit wonders.

CHÉRI - MURPHY'S LAW

Written by Geraldine Hunt and Freddie James, (They were the mother and brother of Chéri singer Rosalind Hunt), it was recorded by the Canadian/American duo. It reached #5 in the US Soul Chart, and a creditable #13 in the UK. It just sneaked into the Billboard Hot 100 at #39.

CLASSIX NOUVEAU - IS IT A DREAM

Reached #1 in Poland, Portugal, Yugoslavia, Israel, and Iceland.

Classix Nouveaux were a classic case for the one hit wonder bin; you'll never see a more likely list of countries to score a #1 hit in. Their song reached #11 in their native UK, their follow-up single, Because You're Young, only got to #43.

Weird OHW Fact... Their lead singer, Sal Solo, had a one hit wonder in his own right in 1984.

DAVID LASLEY - IF I HAD MY WISH TONIGHT

American singer/songwriter David Eldon Lasley is best known for his songs sung by other people. Lasley's only solo hit was, If I Had My Wish Tonight. It got to #36 in the Billboard Chart, and stayed in the chart for 10 weeks.

DAZZ BAND – LET IT WHIP

Out of Cleveland, Ohio, The Dazz Band is an American R&B, funk band. They peppered the US indie charts (R&B and Dance) in the 1980's but only had one charting US Single. Let it Whip got to a creditable #5 in the Billboard Hot 100, and cemented their credentials for the decade.

Weird OHW Fact... They are also a one hit wonder in the UK in 1984, with the single, Let It All Blow, (#12).

DEXYS MIDNIGHT RUNNERS & THE EMERALD EXPRESS – COME ON EILEEN

Reached #1 in Australia, Belgium, Canada, Ireland, New Zealand, South Africa, Switzerland, UK, and USA.

Sold over 2 million copies.

Written by the band, this single made Dexys Midnight Runners a household name all over the world. Topping world charts, it also reached top 40 in most others. They were one hit wonders in USA and Australia.

Billboard voted it the #13 song of 1983.

Weird OHW Fact... Front man, Kevin Rowland, fired the drummer during the video shoot; he's only seen in the first half of the official video.

DONALD FAGEN - I.G.Y. (WHAT A BEAUTIFUL WORLD)

Written by American musician Donald Fagen, he is best known as the iconic voice of jazz/rock legends, Steely Dan. From his debut solo album, The Nightfly, the track, I.G.Y. (What a Beautiful World) was the only hit. It reached #26 in the Billboard Hot 100.

EDDIE SCHWARTZ - ALL OUR TOMORROWS

Edward Sydney Schwartz is a Toronto native, who released three albums in the early 80's. The second album, No Refuge, gave him his only hit, charting in the Billboard Hot 100 at #28. The follow-up, Over the Line, topped out at #91.

EYE TO EYE - NICE GIRLS

A duo comprising American Deborah Berg and British keyboardist Julian Marshall (from Marshall Hain), had a hit from their first album. Nice Girls reached #37 in the U.S. Billboard Hot 100. The second album did not do so well, the wrongly titled follow up single, Lucky, just reached #88.

FAT LARRY'S BAND - ZOOM

American R&B outfit had more success in the UK than their native land. Their fourth single was their only hit, reaching #2 in the UK Charts.

FRANK ZAPPA FEATURING MOON UNIT ZAPPA - VALLEY GIRL
Perhaps the weirdest entry in the book; Moon Unit Zappa appeared on her father's recording, speaking 'valleyspeak'; slang terms used with her teenage girlfriends. The single got to #32 in the Billboard Hot 100, their highest entry.

GOOMBAY DANCE BAND - SEVEN TEARS
Reached #1 in the UK and Ireland.
The German group, somewhat in the style of Boney M, released the song from their third album, Holiday in Paradise. It was a hit all over Europe, #1 in UK and Ireland, #4 in the Netherlands, #6 in Belgium, #15 in Austria, #25 in Australia, and #28 in New Zealand.
Weird OHW Fact... it was only the second time a German artist had topped the UK charts. Kraftwerk with, The Model, had beaten them by just six weeks.

GREG GUIDRY - GOIN' DOWN
Written by Greg Guidry and David Martin, and taken from his album, Over the Line, reached #17 on the Billboard Hot 100. It did well in the Adult Contemporary Chart, #11.
Billboard ranked the song #97 of 1982.

HAIRCUT ONE HUNDRED - LOVE PLUS ONE
Written by front man, Nick Heyward, British new wave band Haircut One Hundred released this track from their debut album, Pelican West. It reached #3 in the UK Charts, and stayed in the chart for 12 weeks. Elsewhere it reached #22 in New Zealand. Heyward went solo immediately afterwards.

JENNIFER HOLLIDAY - AND I AM TELLING YOU I'M NOT GOING
Written by Tom Eyen and Henry Krieger from the Broadway musical Dreamgirls, Jennifer Holliday (who played the original role on Broadway) took the single to #22 in the Billboard Hot 100, and #32 in the UK Chart.

Holliday won a Tony Award and a Grammy for Best R&B Performance.

JOAN JETT AND THE BLACKHEARTS - I LOVE ROCK 'N' ROLL

Reached #1 in Australia, Canada, Netherlands, New Zealand, South Africa, Sweden, and USA.

Sold over 2 million copies.

Yup, amazingly Joan Jett is a one hit wonder in the UK.

Covering the 1975 Arrows hit, she made hers the definitive version. While it hit the top of many charts, (seven weeks at the top in the USA) it just reached #4 in the UK.

Billboard ranked it at the #3 song of 1982.

JUNIOR - MAMA USED TO SAY

Born in Wandsworth, London, Norman Washington Giscombe was a backing vocalist with the band Lynx. Turning solo, he had an immediate hit with Mama Used to Say. It hit #7 in the UK, and #30 in the Billboard Hot 100. He continued to have hits in the UK, but that was his only success stateside.

Weird OHW Fact... Junior Giscombe wrote some songs with Thin Lizzy's Phil Lynott just before Phil's death, but never released. Some of the rough demo's are still available on Youtube.

KARLA BONOFF - PERSONALLY

Written by Paul Kelly, and recorded by him in 1973, Bonoff's version from her album, Wild Heart of the Young, reached #19 in the US Billboard Hot 100.

Billboard ranked it at the #60 song of 1982.

LARRY ELGART AND HIS MANHATTAN SWING ORCHESTRA - HOOKED ON SWING

A band leader from the early 40's, Elgart's biggest break came with the swing part of the 'Hooked on Classics' series. Hooked on Swing got into the Billboard Chart, topping at #31. The follow-up album, imaginatively titled, Hooked on Swing 2, did not have a charting single.

LE ROUX - NOBODY SAID IT WAS EASY (LOOKIN' FOR THE LIGHTS)

From Baton Rouge, Louisiana, they were called Louisiana' LeRoux for their first four unsuccessful years. They dropped the state name, and had an instant hit. Their fourth album, last Safe Place spawned their only success; Addicted got to #8 in the Mainstream Rock chart, Nobody Said It Was Easy (Lookin' For the Lights) got to #18 in the Billboard Hot 100, their only charting hit. The follow-up, Last Safe Place on Earth, got to #77.

Weird OHW Fact... Okay, this is on a personal note; LeRoux's track, Take a Ride on a Riverboat is one of my most favorite songs.

LESLIE PEARL - IF THE LOVE FITS WEAR IT

Born in Pennsylvania, Leslie Pearl is an American singer-songwriter. She wrote hits for many mainstream artists; Crystal Gayle, Karen Carpenter, and Kenny Rogers. From her only solo album, she scored one hit, reaching #28 in the Billboard Hot 100.

Weird OHW Fact... Pearl wrote jingles for Pepsi, Folgers Coffee, Ford, Gillette and many others.

(MALCOLM MCLAREN AND) WORLD'S FAMOUS SUPREME TEAM - BUFFALO GALS

Malcolm McLaren formed the ensemble, and their hit took them by surprise. Buffalo Girls reached #3 in New Zealand, #9 in the UK and Switzerland, #13 in Sweden, #19 in Germany. The follow-up, Duck Rock, did not chart.

MARSHALL CRENSHAW - SOMEDAY, SOMEWAY

Born in Detroit, Michigan, Marshall Howard Crenshaw is a singer/songwriter, probably best known for his only hit. From his first album, Someday, Someway, reminds me of Buddy Holly, and it reached #36 in the Billboard Hot 100.

Weird OHW Fact... Crenshaw played Buddy Holly in the movie, La Bamba.

MOBILES - DROWNING IN BERLIN

Based in Eastbourne, England, the Mobiles were a synth pop group, whose only hit was Drowning in Berlin. It got to #9 in the UK, the follow-up, Amour, Amour, reached #45.

MONSOON - EVER SO LONELY

Written by Steve Coe, this single featured 16 year-old Sheila Chandra on vocals. The single reached #12 in the UK Chart, and stayed in the chart for 9 weeks.

MUSICAL YOUTH – PASS THE DUTCHIE

Reached #1 in the UK, Belgium, Canada, Ireland, Netherlands, New Zealand and Switzerland.

Sold over 5 million copies.

British Jamaican reggae 'kiddy' band Musical Youth, hit it big from the start; their first single from their debut album, The Youth of Today. They hit #2 in Austria and Germany, but perhaps more important, #10 in the Billboard Chart.

Weird OHW Fact... It was in fact a copy of two other songs; one, Pass The Kouchie, referred to drugs, so all such references were taken out.

NATASHA - IKO IKO

This much-covered New Orleans song about gang war was recorded by Scottish singer, Natasha England (born Dorothy Natasha Sherratt), taking the song to its highest UK chart position, #10. It also charted in Ireland and New Zealand.

NICOLE - A LITTLE PEACE

Nicole Hohloch, or Seibert, won the Eurovision Song Contest for West Germany in 1982. Written by Ralph Siegel, Bernd Meinunger and Paul Greedus. She reached #1 in the UK with an English version. **Weird OHW Fact...** After she won, she performed the song in English, French, Dutch and German.

PATRICE RUSHEN - FORGET ME NOTS

Written by Patrice Rushen, Freddie Washington, and Terri McFaddin, it was recorded for her album, Straight from the Heart. It charted well, reaching #23 in the Billboard Hot 100, #8 in the UK and New Zealand, #19 in Ireland, #24 in the Netherlands, and #29 in Australia.

Rushen received a Grammy nomination for Best Female R&B Vocal Performance.

PHD - I WON'T LET YOU DOWN
Reached #1 in Belgium and the Netherlands.
British band Ph.D consisted Scottish leader, Jim Diamond, and ex-Jeff Beck bandmates, Tony Hymas and Simon Phillips. Their only hit was a smash. Topping the Low Countries Charts, it reached #2 in Ireland, #3 in the UK and Italy, #4 in France, and #14 in Germany. Jim Diamond went solo.

PIGBAG - PAPA'S GOT A BRAND NEW PIGBAG
Written by Pigbag, the tune is a dance instrumental performed by the Cheltenham late-punk brass orientated band. It got to #2 in the UK Chart after a lot of club airplay and a re-release.

PINKEES - DANGER GAMES
From Basildon, Essex, with a sound immediately reminiscent of Squeeze, (Their lead singer sounds like Glenn Tilbrook) their second single became a hit in the UK. Danger Games reached #8 in the UK Chart. They didn't chart again.

PRISM - DON'T LET HIM KNOW
Written by Jim Vallance and Bryan Adams, it was recorded by Canadian rock band Prism on the band's sixth studio album, Small Change. It was Prism's biggest US hit, peaking at #1 on the Rock chart, and #39 the Billboard Hot 100. It only reached #49 in the Canadian Chart.

RAINBOW - STONE COLD
Unbelievably, despite all of their albums charting in the USA, Ritchie Blackmore's Rainbow are a one hit wonder in America.
With Joe Lynn Turner now on vocals, the ballad, Stone Cold, came from their sixth studio album, and although it reached #1 in the Hard Rock Chart, it just squeaked into the Billboard Hot 100 at #40. With no higher chart hit, Rainbow is a USA One hit wonder.

RAW SILK - DO IT TO THE MUSIC
New York dance band, Raw Silk will be best remembered for their song, Do It to the Music. However, they won't be remembered much in their

native USA, as they had more luck in the UK. The song reached #5 on the US Dance charts, but didn't break into the Billboard Hot 100. It reached #18 in the UK, their follow-up, Just in Time, hit the UK at #49.

RENEE AND RENATO - SAVE YOUR LOVE
Reached #1 in the UK, Ireland, Belgium, and Norway.
Written by Johnny Edward and his wife, Renée and Renato's version was a worldwide smash. It topped the UK charts for 4 weeks, until we were saved by Phil Collins, Can't Hurry Love.
Weird OHW Fact... The writer was the voice of Metal Mickey.
Weird OHW Fact... Renée (Hilary Lester) did not appear on the video; they used a beautiful model.

Rick Moranis and Dave Thomas (actors/comedians) as Bob and Doug MacKenzie, "Take Off" (No. 16, March 1982[22])

ROCKERS REVENGE FEATURING DONNIE CALVIN - WALKING ON SUNSHINE
Written by Eddy Grant with vocals added by Donnie Calvin, it was first recorded by Eddy Grant in 1979. Rockers Revenge, a studio band, covered the song, taking it to #4 in the UK Chart.

ROYAL PHILHARMONIC ORCHESTRA - HOOKED ON CLASSICS
Louis Clark and the Royal Philharmonic Orchestra, took the first track of their album to the charts in 1982. Titled simply Hooked on Classics Part 1 & 2, it reached #2 in the UK chart, #6 in New Zealand, #9 in Australis, then later, #10 in the Billboard Hot 100, and #21 in Canada.
Billboard ranked it at the #56 song for 1982.

SKYY - CALL ME
Brooklyn-based funk band Skyy have a weird distinction; they might be the only band in the book that are one-hit wonders in only the USA and Netherlands. Their song reached #26 in the Billboard Hot 100, and #34 in the Netherlands.

SNEAKER - MORE THAN JUST THE TWO OF US

This West Coast funk rock band, is best known for its only Billboard Hot 40 single. More Than Just the Two of Us reached #34 in the USA. Their follow-up, Don't Let Me In, only got to #63.

Weird OHW Fact... The group's name 'Sneaker' was taken from the Steely Dan song 'Bad Sneakers'.

SYLVIA - NOBODY

Born in Kokomo, Indiana, Sylvia Jane Kirby usually went by just her forename. In the song, Nobody, she had a hit, a country crossover, reaching #1 in the Country Chart, and #15 in the Billboard Hot 100. She was awarded Female Vocalist of the Year by the Academy of Country Music in the same year. In 1983 the BMI awarded the song; BMI Song of the Year For Most Air-Play.

TANÉ CAIN - HOLDIN' ON

Born in Los Angeles, California, she released her debut album on RCA Records in 1982. The first single, Danger Zone, did not chart, but the follow-up, Holdin' On, reached #37 on the Billboard Hot 100.

Weird OHW Fact... She contributed three songs to the soundtrack of Arnold Swartzenegger's movie, Terminator.

Weird OHW Fact... Tané Cain's maiden name is McClure; yup, she's the eldest child of actor, Doug McClure (Trampas from the Virginian)

TONI BASIL - MICKEY

Reached #1 in Australia, USA, and Canada.

Sold over 3 million copies.

Yup, this is one of the 'biggies'. Written by Mike Chapman and Nicky Chinn as "Kitty", and recorded by UK pop band, Racey, it was a smash hit for Toni Basil... but it did not chart quickly. With the title changed to 'Mickey', it was first released in the UK in May, 1981, but it did not chart. On its re-release in January 1982, it reached #2 in the UK, #3 in Ireland. In April it got to #1 in Australia, #2 in New Zealand, #3 in South Africa. Only then did North America catch onto the Toni basil coat-tails, the hit reaching #1 in USA and Canada.

Showing how late it charted in USA, Billboard ranked it at the #36 song for 1983.

TOTO COELO - I EAT CANNIBALS

Toto Coelo (renamed Total Coelo for the US release) was a British new wave group, put together by producer Barry Blue. Their only UK hit reached #8 in the UK Chart, and went to #4 in Australia, #3 in South Africa, #2 in Sweden, #11 in Ireland, and #38 in New Zealand.

The follow-up, Dracula's Tango (Sucker For Your Love), reached Top 40 in Australia, Ireland and Sweden, but only #54 in the UK.

TRIO - DA DA DA

Reached #1 in Austria, New Zealand, South Africa, and Switzerland.
Sold over 13 million copies.

German band Trio consisted of Stephan Remmler, Gert 'Kralle' Krawinkel, and Peter Behrens. This annoying song from their debut album was a complete hit in over 30 countries. It can't be counted as a #1 hit, but more as a Top 10, because it made the top 10 in most countries in the world. It ended up being the 18th biggest single ever sold, selling over 13 million copies.

It has been dubbed, copied, translated, lampooned and parodied. The writers don't care; they made millions.

THE WEATHER GIRLS - IT'S RAINING MEN

Sold more than 6 million copies.

Written by Paul Jabara and Paul Shaffer in 1979, this song was offered around for a couple of years... Diana Ross, Donna Simmer, and Cher all turned it down. The Weather Girls, Martha Wash and Izora Armstead, blew the competition away. It reached #2 in the UK, #5 in Ireland, #8 in Norway, #13 in New Zealand, and #16 in Australia. Despite their lack of mainstream success, it got to just #46 in the Billboard Hot 100, it still sold more than 6 million copies worldwide.

OH SO CLOSE... BUT NO CIGAR...

A FLOCK OF SEAGULLS – I RAN (SO FAR AWAY)

Reached number 1 in Australia.

This English new wave band will always be 'remembered' for their one hit wonder-ness, but in actual fact they only hold that accolade in

Australia and the Netherlands. They had 3 hits in the USA, I Ran (So Far Away) (#9), Space Age Love Song (#30), and Wishing (If I Had a Photograph of You) (#26) and in most other countries.

Weird OHW Fact... Amazingly, I Ran (So Far Away) was not a hit in their native UK (#43).

MADNESS – OUR HOUSE

I know, you fellow Britons, madness can't be a one hit wonder, can they?

No. Even in the hallowed halls of the Billboard Charts, the American chart cyphers miss one thing...

Yes, Our House (#5 UK, top ten everywhere) did reach #7 in the Billboard Chart... AND, they never reached that height again...

BUT... they had already hit #33 with IT Must Be Love, the year before... thus no bad name-calling here.

1983...

As Jim Henson's Fraggle Rock is shown in Canada and the United States, the year begins...
Bob Hawke is elected Prime Minister of Australia, the Space Shuttle Challenger is launched for the first time, Return of the Jedi opens in cinemas, GPS becomes available for civilian use, US troops invade Grenada, and Thor, sorry, actor Chris Hemsworth is born.

OHW SPECIAL FEATURE... THE 1983 ABBA WAR...
In 1982, with ABBA on an official break, and Benny and Björn working on their musical, Chess, it left the girls alone to work on their solo projects... the war had begun.
Unknown to most of the world's population, who thought of the ABBA boys as the main powerhouse, and considered the girls as simply eye candy, the girls were successful solo singers both before, during and after ABBA.
So... back to the war...
Part 1.
AGNETHA FÄLTSKOG (THE BLONDE ONE) - CAN'T SHAKE LOOSE
From her first solo English album, Wrap Your Arms Around Me, (She had already two European hits off the album which hadn't charted in the USA) this album track was a surprise hit in the US. It reached #23 in Canada, and #29 in the Billboard Hot 100. Despite great success in Europe, it would be her only US hit.
Weird OHW Fact... Agnetha has recorded 12 studio albums and released 43 solo singles.
Weird OHW Fact... Agnetha's solo albums have reached #1 in over 10 countries.
Part 2.
ANNI-FRID SYNNI LYNGSTAD, 'FRIDA' (THE BRUNETTE ONE) - I KNOW THERE'S SOMETHING GOING ON
Reached #1 in France, Belgium, Switzerland, and Costa Rica.

This song was the first single taken from her solo album, Something's Going On. The song was a worldwide hit; #5 in Australia, #3 in Sweden, #6 in South Africa. In America, it reached #11 in Canada, and #13 in the Billboard Hot 100.

Weird OHW Fact... Frida is a real princess; she married a German prince, and when he died, she now lives with a British Viscount.

Weird OHW Fact... The album was produced by Phil Collins, who also played drums.

Weird OHW Fact... Anni-Frid has recorded 5 studio albums and released 32 solo singles.

AFTER THE FIRE - DER KOMMISSAR

This London band went through many changes in its lifetime. Beginning as a Rock band in 1978, they ended as a synth unit, having their only hit, a version of, Falco's Der Kommissar. It got to #5 in the Billboard Hot 100, #12 in Canada, #2 in South Africa, but didn't break the Top 40 in the UK (#47).

Billboard ranked the song as #30 for 1983.

ASSEMBLY - NEVER NEVER

Assembly was a Vince Clarke (from London, bands; Yazoo, Erasure) project, featuring Londonderry vocalist Feargal Sharkey (The Undertones). The song reached #4 in the UK Chart, #6 in Ireland and top 40 on many other charts. It was their only hit.

BIG COUNTRY – IN A BIG COUNTRY

From their debut album, The Crossing, Scottish rockers Big Country thought to take over the world. The song topped at #17 in the Billboard Hot 100, and an impressive #3 in Canada; their only North American hit. The band would chart many singles; Fields of Fire, Look Away, and Wonderland.

Weird OHW Fact... The trademark bag-pipe wailing on their singles was done by electric guitar effects.

BILLY GRIFFIN - HOLD ME TIGHTER IN THE RAIN

From Baltimore, Maryland, Griffin released his first solo album, having a UK hit. It got to #17 in the UK Charts. The follow-up, Serious, just reached #64.

Weird OHW fact... Griffin is probably best known for placing Smokey Robinson as the lead singer of The Miracles in 1972.

BOOKER NEWBERRY III – LOVE TOWN

Booker Newberry III, from Youngstown, Ohio, is best remembered for his solo hit, Love Town. It reached #4 in the UK Chart. The follow-up, Teddy Bear, got close, but peaked at #44.

CHARLIE - IT'S INEVITABLE

This British rock band, formed by Terry Thomas, had all of their success in the USA. Their only charting hit, It's Inevitable, reached #38 in the Billboard Chart. The band broke up soon after.

F. R. DAVID – WORDS (DON'T COME EASY)

Reached #1 in Australia, Austria, Belgium, Denmark, Ireland, Italy, Norway, South Africa, Sweden and Switzerland.

Released in France and Monaco in 1981, this Tunisian French singer's sole hit took time to conquer the world. A wider release in 1983 gave him his hit. As well as topping charts, the song got to #2 in the UK, the Netherlands and France, #7 in New Zealand, and #19 in Australia

FLASH AND THE PAN - WAITING FOR A TRAIN

Written by band members Harry Vanda and George Young, who were both former members of the Australian band, The Easybeats (Friday on My Mind, 1966). Waiting For a Train is their only song that charted in the UK (#7) giving them one hit wonder status. The single also reached #26 in the Netherlands, and a poor #98 in their native country.

FRANKIE GOES TO HOLLYWOOD – RELAX

Reached #1 in Finland, France, Germany, Greece, Israel, Italy, Spain, Switzerland, Thailand, and the UK.

Sold over 5 million copies.

A debut single is never again going to be so controversial; banned by the BBC in their native UK, this was #1 in 14 countries (including UK) it also reached #10 in the Billboard Charts and New Zealand, #5 in Australia, and top ten most everywhere else.

Their follow-ups were just as impressive; Two Tribes, The Power of Love, and Welcome to the Pleasuredome... but these hits just topped at #43 and #48 in the USA charts, making Frankie Goes To Hollywood a one hit wonder in America.

FRANK STALLONE - FAR FROM OVER
Written by Frank Stallone and Vince DiCola, this song was on the soundtrack to the movie, Staying Alive. and was also featured in the film's soundtrack. The song reached #10 in the Billboard Hot 100, #15 in Canada. Elsewhere it reached #2 in Belgium, #5 in Switzerland, #6 in Netherlands, #11 in Germany, #16 in France, and #22 in Italy.

INCANTATION - CACHARPAYA (ANDES PUMPSA DAESI)
Incantation is a British/Chilean musical ensemble that was formed to play South American music. From their stage show they were given a record deal, and the one hit was Cacharpaya (Music of the Pan Pipes) reaching #12 in the UK Charts.

Weird OHW Fact... The British musicians had not played traditional American music, and had to learn the instruments from scratch.

INDEEP - LAST NIGHT A DJ SAVED MY LIFE
Written by Michael Cleveland for the band, it was released in February, hitting #13 in the UK Charts. It also reached #2 in the Dutch Charts, and in Belgium. Their subsequent singles did not chart.

JIM CAPALDI – THAT'S LOVE
Written by British singer/songwriter Jim Capaldi for his album, Fierce Heart, it was released, and became a hit in the USA, reaching #28 in the Billboard Charts. The song tells of two conflicting ways to look at love.

Weird OHW Fact... Both Steve Winwood and his wife, Nicole sang backing; they were having marriage problems at the time.

JIMMY THE HOOVER - TANTALISE (WO WO EE YEH YEH)

Managed by Malcolm McLaren, and supporting Bow Wow Wow on tour, they had only one hit, reaching #18 in the UK Charts. Later singles did not chart.

JOBOXERS – JUST GOT LUCKY

This British new wave group had already had a top ten hit in the UK (Boxerbeat #3), but it was their follow-up which became an international hit. Just Got Lucky reached #36 in the Billboard Hot 100.

KAJAGOOGOO – TOO SHY

Reached #1 in Belgium, Germany, Ireland, Japan and the UK.

Written by the band, it was the first single from their debut album, White Feathers. It shot straight to #1 in the UK, followed by topping other charts. It was a worldwide top 10 hit, reaching #5 in the USA, #6 in Australia, #8 in Canada, #2 in New Zealand, and #11 in South Africa.

Despite their other hits, Kajagoogoo are one hit wonders in USA, Austria, and Sweden.

Weird OHW Fact... Lead singer Limahl (a one hit wonder in 1984) sang the theme song to the movie, The NeverEnding Story.

KEITH HARRIS AND ORVILLE - ORVILLE'S SONG

Orville the Duck has bright green feathers, and wears a nappy (diaper) with a large safety pin. Keith Harris, the ventriloquist released Orvilles song... my daughter loved it... which got to #4 in the UK Charts.

Weird OHW Fact... Orville was named after one of the Wright Brothers, the pioneers of flight.

KISSING THE PINK - LAST FILM

This London band's first single, Don't Hide in the Shadows, flopped. But after a manager change, The Last Film reached #19 in the UK Singles Chart.

LOTUS EATERS - FIRST PICTURE OF YOU

The newly formed Lotus Eaters from Liverpool did a session for BBC DJ John Peel, producing their first single. It got to #15 in the UK Charts, and started the band making an album. The second single, was a disappointing #53 (Netherlands #37). The album charted at #96.

LYDIA MURDOCK - SUPERSTAR

American pop singer, Lydia Murdoch, gave an answer for Michael Jackson's Billie Jean. Th song reached #14 in the UK, and also charted in Canada.

THE MAISONETTES - HEARTACHE AVENUE

This English pop band (Lol Mason and Mark Tibenham) recorded two albums, their hit coming from the first. Heartache Avenue reached #7 in the UK Singles Chart, #12 in Canada.

Weird OHW Fact... The song was discovered in a pile of demo tapes, and released.

Weird OHW Fact... Mason's brother, Jeremy, played Richard Lord in UK soap Crossroads.

MARTIN BRILEY - THE SALT IN MY TEARS

Briley released three solo albums under Mercury Records, and scored one chart hit. The Salt in My Tears reached #36 in the Billboard Hot 100. The follow-up, Put Your Hands on the Screen, did not chart highly.

MARY JANE GIRLS - ALL NIGHT LONG

Mary jane Girls only released two albums, one spawned a one hit wonder in UK and Ireland, the other gave them the same moniker in the USA. All Night Long, written by Rick James, reached #13 in the UK, and #18 in Ireland. It did not break into the Billboard Hot 100.

MEN WITHOUT HATS - THE SAFETY DANCE

Reached #1 in South Africa.

The Canadian band is well remembered for this smash worldwide hit; the carnival video is ingrained in my mind, but the hit was a slow mover. It reached #11 in Canada in April before hitting #3 in the USA a few months later. In Europe it reached top ten in most countries, #6 in the UK, making then a one hit wonder there. It reached #2 in New Zealand, but not until early 1984.

Billboard ranked the song as #35 for 1983.

Weird OHW fact... Their 1987 hit, Pop Goes The World, was a hit in most countries, clearing them of one hit wonder-ness. The single did not chart in the UK.

MEZZOFORTE - GARDEN PARTY

Icelandic instrumental band, Mezzoforte, wove a web of jazz-funk into their music. Their biggest hit, Garden Party, came from their fourth album, Surprise, Surprise, and reached #17 in the UK Charts.

Weird OHW Fact... Herb Alpert covered the tune, but at a different speed. It is conjectured that he heard it played wrongly, and assumed it was correct.

MICHAEL SEMBELLO – MANIAC

Reached #1 in Canada and USA.

Written by Dennis Matkosky and Michael Sembello, this song from the movie, Flashdance, was a smash hit. It reached #1 in USA and Canada, #2 in Australia, Spain and Switzerland, and top 10 in many others (UK, #43).

Billboard ranked it as the #9 song for 1983.

MOVING PICTURES - WHAT ABOUT ME

Reached #1 in Australia.

Written by Garry Frost and Frances Swan, Australian rock band Moving Pictures recorded it on their album, Days of Innocence. After topping the Aussie charts, it made its way to USA, where it peaked at #29 in the Billboard Hot 100.

Billboard ranked it as the #88 song for 1983.

ORANGE JUICE - RIP IT UP

Scottish post-punks from Bearsden, Glasgow, Orange Juice was founded in 1979. Their only hit was Rip It Up, reaching #8 in the UK Singles Chart. It would be their only chart hit.

OXO - WHIRLY GIRL

Written by band singer/guitarist Ish "Angel" Ledesma, this song was recorded on their debut album. It reached #28 in the Billboard Hot 100. Their other singles did not chart.

Weird OHW Fact... The Whirly Girl in the title, is actually Ledesma's wife, Lori.

PATRICK SIMMONS - SO WRONG

Best known as a member of the rock band, The Doobie Brothers, (and the writer of their hit single, Black water) he released a solo album in 1983. So Wrong reached #30 in the Billboard Hot 100, but no follow-up reached so high.

PATTI AUSTIN AND JAMES INGRAM - BABY COME TO ME

The duet was the first of two, and is included on Austin's album, Every Home Should Have One. It only charted in the UK (#11), but after being used as a love tune on General Hospital, it got to #1 on the billboard Charts. #3 in Canada, and #9 in New Zealand. Their second duet, How Do You Keep the Music Playing, did not chart in the UK, making them one hit wonders there.

PETER SCHILLING – MAJOR TOM (COMING HOME)

Written by Peter Schilling and David Harland Lodge, this tribute to David Bowie's hero was an instant international hit. Originally recorded in German, it reached #1 in West Germany, Austria and Switzerland, #2 in the Netherlands, France,. The English version reached #1 in Canada, #14 in the U.S. Billboard Hot 100, #4 in South Africa, and #22 in Ireland. **Weird OHW Fact...** In 2011, William Shatner did a cover version on his album, Seeking Major Tom.

PIA ZADORA - THE CLAPPING SONG

Zadora covered the Shirley Ellis hit for the film score of the movie, The Lonely Lady. The surprise hit reached #36 in the Billboard Hot 100. She would not chart as a solo artist again.

RE-FLEX - THE POLITICS OF DANCING

Written by band member Paul Fishman and recorded on their debut album of the same name, the song was a success. It reached #24 in the Billboard Hot 100, #28 in the UK, #9 in Canada, #12 in both Australia and New Zealand.

ROBERT ELLIS ORRALL AND CARLENE CARTER - I COULDN'T SAY NO

Having already written hit songs for Shenandoah and Clay Walker, Orrall had a song-writing pedigree. His only solo hit came with a duet with Carlene Carter; I Couldn't Say No. It reached #32 in the mainstream Billboard Hot 100. Not quite the crossover he expected.

ROCKSTEADY CREW - (HEY YOU) THE ROCKSTEADY CREW

Reached #1 in the Netherlands.
The American breakdancing/hip hop group hit the ground running with their first single. It topped the Dutch charts, and #2 in Sweden, #4 in Switzerland, #5 in New Zealand and Ireland, #6 in the UK and Norway, and #33 in Australia. They would never chart so high again.

RYAN PARIS - DOLCE VITA

Reached #1 in Belgium, the Netherlands and Spain.
Born Fabio Roscioli, Italian Ryan Paris hit it worldwide with his single Dolce Vita, written by Pierluigi Giombini and Paul Mazzolini. Apart from topping charts, it reached #2 in Austria, Ireland, Norway and Sweden, #3 in Germany, South Africa and Switzerland, It reached #5 in the UK Charts, spending 10 weeks in the charts.

RYUICHI SAKAMOTO (WITH DAVID SYLVIAN) – FORBIDDEN COLOURS

This multi-talented Japanese star acted alongside David Bowie in the movie, Merry Christmas Mr. Lawrence. Sakamoto composed the film score, having a hit with the single, Forbidden Colours. It reached #16 in the UK Charts.

SAGA - ON THE LOOSE

From Oakville, Ontario, this Canadian band reached stardom with their fourth album, Worlds Apart. Wind Him Up got to #22 in Canada, and #7 in Germany. On the Loose reached #26 in the USA and Germany. Their subsequent hits underperformed, making them a USA one hit wonder.

TACO - PUTTIN' ON THE RITZ

Reached #1 in New Zealand and Sweden.

Sold over 1 million copies.

Indonesian born, Dutch singer, based in Germany, Taco Ockerse, released a version of the Irving Berlin song, Puttin' On the Ritz. The single was a worldwide smash reaching #4 in the Billboard Hot 100, #3 in Canada, and top ten in most countries in the world.

Weird OHW Fact... Irving Berlin, who was aged 95, became the oldest living person to have one of his songs hit the top 10.

THOMAS DOLBY - SHE BLINDED ME WITH SCIENCE

The English musician Thomas Dolby, released the song in late 1982, charting in the USA a few months later. It reached #5 in the Billboard Hot 100 and #1 in Canada's RPM Magazine. Elsewhere the song didn't live up to its US positions, #7 in New Zealand, #19 in Australia, #26 in South Africa, and a paltry #49 in his native UK. It would be his only mainstream USA chart entry.

Billboard ranked it as the #23 song for 1983.

VANDENBERG - BURNING HEART

Named after bandleader, Adrian Vandenburg, this Dutch rock band hit the big time with a whimper. Their first single from their first album, Burning Heart, reached #39 in the U.S. Billboard Hot 100 charts. Vandenberg opened for Ozzy Osbourne and KISS in the USA, but they never gained a following.

WILL POWERS - KISSING WITH CONFIDENCE

Written by Goldsmith, Jacob Brackman, Nile Rodgers, Todd Rundgren, and Steve Winwood.

Will Powers is the stage name of American artist Lynn Goldsmith. The single, taken from her album Dancing for Mental Health, reached #17 in the UK Chart.

Weird OHW Fact... Goldsmith used effects to sound like a man, and Carly Simon was the female voice.

OH SO CLOSE... BUT NO CIGAR...

ICEHOUSE - HEY LITTLE GIRL

This Australian rock band had hits galore in Australia and New Zealand. Hey Little Girl got worldwide airplay, and are considered UK one hit wonders... but not so. Hey Little Girl got to #17 in the UK. A later single, Crazy, got to #38. However, if you really want them to be one hit wonders, they are... Hey Little Girl, was their only hit in Switzerland and Austria.

ROMAN HOLLIDAY - DON'T TRY TO STOP IT
By the slimmest of margins, British band Roman Holliday came so close to being one hit wonders... Don't Try To Stop It got to #14 in the UK Charts... the follow-up, Motormania, reached #40.

TWISTED SISTER - I AM (I'M ME)
Dee Snider and the American rockers were knocking on the door of one hit wonder-ship in the UK with their single I Am (I'm Me). It reached #18 in the UK Charts; so far so good. But their follow-up, The Kids Are Back, got to #32. Ah well.

1984...

As George Orwell's 1984 arrives, and Apple put the MAC computer on sale, the year begins...
The Winter Olympics are held in Sarajevo, a year-long miners' strike begins in the UK, Marvin Gaye is shot by his father, Bruce Springsteen's Born in the USA is released, Indira Gandhi is assassinated, and Band Aid raises millions for Ethiopia with 'Do They Know It's Christmas'.

ALEXEI SAYLE - ULLO JOHN! GOTTA NEW MOTOR?
Written by the comedian Alexei Sayle, who had a recurring role on TV's irreverent sit-com, The Young Ones, it was released in 1982 to no avail. Re-released in 1984, it reached #15 in the UK Charts.

ALPHAVILLE - BIG IN JAPAN
Reached #1 in Germany, Switzerland, Sweden, and Brazil.
German band Alphaville had considerable success in the mid 80's all over Europe. However, they only broke the UK Top 40 once. From their album, Forever Young, they got to #8 in the UK, #2 in Italy, Spain, #4 in Austria and Ireland. Their follow up did not chart in the UK.

ART COMPANY - SUSANNA
Reached #1 in the Netherlands.
Written by Caroline Bogman and Ferdi Lancee, this Dutch band reached #12 with the English version of their original Dutch hit. They topped the charts in their native Netherlands.

BAND AID - DO THEY KNOW IT'S CHRISTMAS?
Reached #1 in the UK, Australia, Austria, Belgium, Denmark, Germany, Ireland, Italy, Netherlands, New Zealand, Norway, Sweden, Switzerland, and many more.
Sold more than 12 million copies.
Almost worth a chapter on its own, this charity ensemble changed history. Written by Bob Geldof (Boomtown Rats) and Midge Ure

(Ultravox), and sung/recorded in a single day by a plethora of British stars shot straight to #1 for Christmas, staying there for 5 weeks. With the record producers working for free, it sold a million copies in the first week, eventually over 12 million were sold, raising £8 million for Ethiopia.

It reached #13 in the Billboard Hot 100.

Weird OHW Fact... Band Aid II in 1989 also had a UK #1 with the song (see 1989 entry) with a new cast of singers and performers.

Weird OHW Fact... In 2004, Band Aid 20 did a 29 year anniversary version, (most of the singers were very young when it was first released). This also got to #1 in the UK, Denmark, Italy, Norway and New Zealand.

BELLE AND THE DEVOTIONS - LOVE GAMES

Written by Paul Curtis and Graham Sacher, this song was the UK's entry at the Eurovision Song Contest in 1984. It reached #11 in the UK Chart.

Weird OHW Fact... The song got some 'boos' at the contest, a push back against English football fans rioting in Luxemburg, the host venue of the show.

DAZZ BAND - LET IT ALL BLOW

Already US one hit wonder's in 1982, (Let It Whip, #5), The Dazz Band from Cleveland, Ohio, had their only foreign success with their 1984 release, Let it all Blow. Despite a poor rating in the Billboard Charts, (#84), this song got to #12 in the UK Charts.

DEBORAH ALLEN - BABY I LIED

Written by Deborah Allen, Rafe VanHoy and Rory Michael Bourke, it was the first single from the album, Cheat the Night. Crossing over from her country roots, it reached #4 on the Billboard Hot 100, and #31 in Australia.

DENNIS DEYOUNG - DESERT MOON

Written by Dennis DeYoung, the major song-writer in the band, Styx, this song was released from his first solo album. The song reached a very creditable #10 in the US Billboard Hot 100.

Billboard ranked it at the #97 song for 1984.

FACE TO FACE - 10-9-8

Face to Face, a new wave band from Boston, Massachusetts, had their only hit from their first album. 10-9-8 reached #38 in the Billboard Hot 100.

FICTION FACTORY – (FEELS LIKE) HEAVEN

Scottish group Fiction Factory released this song as a single from their debut album Throw the Warped Wheel Out. It was a European hit, reaching #2 in Switzerland, #6 in their native UK, #14 in Sweden and #20 in Austria. Their follow-ups did not chart.

ICICLE WORKS - BIRDS FLY (WHISPER TO A SCREAM)/LOVE IS A WONDERFUL COLOUR

This alternative rock band from Liverpool is kinda infamous in this book. They had two hit singles in two separate countries with no further chart entries, and therefore are one hit wonders twice over. Birds Fly (Whisper to a Scream) reached #37 in the Billboard Hot 100, but only #90 in their native UK. Love Is a Wonderful Colour reached #15 in the UK, but did not chart anywhere else.

So, Icicle Works, are one hit wonders twice over, with different songs.

Weird OHW Fact... The band was named after Frederick Pohl's science fiction short story 'The Day the Icicle Works Closed'.

JOE FAGAN - BREAKIN' AWAY/THAT'S LIVIN' ALRIGHT

Written by English singer Joe Fagin, Ian La Frenais, and Ken Ashby, the songs were used for the opening and closing credits on the ITV show Auf Wiedersehen, Pet. The double A side reached #3 in the UK Singles Chart.

Weird OHW Fact... Joe Fagan released a parody of the song, That's England Alright, for England's 2006 World Cup run... it didn't help the players performance.

JOHN WAITE - MISSING YOU

Reached #1 in Canada and USA.

English musician John Waite broke the mold when he co-wrote this song with David Thoener and Gary Gersh. Released as the first single from his second album, No Brakes, it Topped the Billboard Hot 100 for a week, and went to #1 in Canada too. A top 20 hit all over the world, it reached #9 in the UK, #5 in Australia, #6 in Ireland, #14 in South Africa, and #18 in New Zealand.

It was nominated for the 1985 Best Pop Vocal Performance Male Grammy Award.

Weird OHW Fact... The song is a one hit wonder in the UK, but not USA and Canada. Waite's later single, Every Step Of The Way, charted at #25 in the USA, and #39 in Canada.

JOYCE KENNEDY - THE LAST TIME I MADE LOVE

From Anguilla, Mississippi, Joyce Kennedy sang for the band, Mother's Finest. When the band broke up, she had her only hit single, reaching just #40 in the Billboard Chart; the thinnest margin of one-hit-wondership.

JULIA NIXON - BREAKIN' DOWN (SUGAR SAMBA)

Nixon was the leader of an ensemble called Julia & Company. The band released two singles, the first, Breakin' Down (Sugar Samba) charted in the UK at #15. The follow-up, I'm So Happy, only reached #56.

JUMP 'N THE SADDLE BAND - THE CURLY SHUFFLE

Written by singer Peter Quinn, this novelty song is a mash-up of the catchphrases of the Three Stooges. The song reached #15 on the US Billboard Hot 100.

Weird OHW Fact... The song was released by The Knuckleheads in Canada, charting far higher (#29) than the Jump 'N The Saddle version, which was available at the same time.

KENNY LOGGINS - FOOTLOOSE

Reached #1 in Australia, Canada, New Zealand, and the USA.

Written by Kenny Loggins and Dean Pitchford, it was released as a single from the movie of the same name. As well as topping four charts, it reached #6 in the UK and #4 in Switzerland, Germany and Ireland. Loggins' later single, Danger Zone, charted almost everywhere but the UK, where it reached just #45, making him a one hit wonder in the UK. Billboard ranked it at the #4 song for 1984.

LAID BACK - WHITE HORSE

Written by band members Tim Stahl and John Guldberg, the song was released as the B-side of the Danish band's single, Sunshine Reggae. The song became a minor hit in Europe, but it was the B-side that got played in the USA. When released as a single, it reached #26 in the Billboard Hot 100.

LIMAHL - THE NEVERENDING STORY

Reached #1 in Norway, Sweden, Spain, and Japan.
Written by Giorgio Moroder and Keith Forsey, it is the title song from the movie The NeverEnding Story. Limahl, lead singer with Kajagoogoo (also a one hit wonder 1983), topped the scandanavian charts, and reached #2 in Austria, Germany and Italy, #4 in the UK and ireland, #6 in Australia and #17 in the Billboard Hot 100.
Weird OHW Fact... the singer's stage name, Limahl, is an anagram of his name, Hamill.

MATTHEW WILDER - BREAK MY STRIDE

Reached #1 in Norway.
Written by Matthew Wilder and Greg Prestopino, this track from Wilder's debut album destined him for the one hit wonder bin. Break My Stride topped the Norwegian charts, reached #5 in the Billboard Hot 100 and #5 in Canada. Elsewhere it was top 10 all over the world, including #3 in Belgium, Ireland and New Zealand, #4 in the UK and South Africa.
Weird OHW Fact... In the USA, a later hit, This Kid's American, got to #33 in the USA, making him a one hit wonder everywhere else but his native USA.

MEL BROOKS - TO BE OR NOT TO BE (THE HITLER RAP)

This self-penned rap came loosely from the movie, The Producers. It reached #3 in the Australian Charts and #12 in the UK Charts.

MIKE RENO/ANN WILSON - ALMOST PARADISE (LOVE THEME FROM FOOTLOOSE)

With Mike Reno (Loverboy) and Ann Wilson (Heart) this duet was a guaranteed hit. It reached #7 in the Billboard Hot 100, staying in the chart for 13 weeks, the third song to chart from the movie, Footloose. It also reached #3 in Canada.

Billboard ranked it at the #4 song for 1984.

MURRAY HEAD - ONE NIGHT IN BANGKOK

Reached #1 in Belgium, Netherlands, Spain, South Africa, West Germany, Switzerland and Australia.

Written by ABBA's Benny Andersson, Björn Ulvaeus and Tim Rice, this song from the musical, Chess, was a worldwide hit. Apart from chart toppers, it also reached #3 in the USA and Canada, and #12 in the UK.

Weird OHW Fact… Murray Head is NOT a one hit wonder every country; his 1969 song, Superstar, (from the musical Jesus Christ Superstar) charted in USA (#14), Canada (#6), Germany (#9) and Australia (#5).

Weird OHW Fact… Murray Head's younger brother, Anthony Head, starred in the TV series Buffy the Vampire Slayer.

NEIL – HOLE IN MY SHOE

Nigel Planer, who played Neil in the BBC sitcom, The Young Ones, took this 1967 Traffic hit to #2 in the UK Charts. The song is sung in character.

Weird OHW Fact… Neil's version got to #2, exactly the same position as Traffic's original.

NENA – 99 LUFTBALLONS

Reached #1 in (German version) Australia, Austria, Belgium, Germany, Japan, Netherlands, New Zealand, Sweden, and Switzerland, and (English version) Canada, Ireland, and the UK..

Born Gabriele Susanne Kerner, or to use her stage name, Nena, is best remembered for her lone hit, 99 Luftballons/99 Red Balloons. The Original German and translated English versions vied around the globe for supremacy, but either way, it was money in the bank for Nena. Apart from chart topping, it reached #2 in the Billboard Hot 100.

Billboard ranked it as the #28 song for 1984.

Weird OHW Fact... In the official video, the band thought the explosions (provided by the Dutch Army) were getting out of hand, and so took cover; it was unscripted.

OLLIE & JERRY - BREAKIN... THERE'S NO STOPPING US
Written by the American duo from Los Angeles, California, Ollie Brown and Jerry Knight, the song was included on the soundtrack of the movie, Breakin'. The single got to #9 in the Billboard Hot 100, #5 in the UK, #7 in New Zealand, #27 in Belgium and the Netherlands, and #25 in Australia. Their follow-up, Electric Boogaloo, just stayed outside the charts, (#57 in UK).
Weird OHW Fact... Jean-Claude Van Damme, an extra in the movie, is seen dancing in the background at one point.

REBBIE JACKSON - CENTIPEDE
Sold more than 1 million copies.
Born in Gary, Indiana, Rebbie is the oldest child of the Jackson family. Written and produced by Michael Jackson, it is her only single to chart in the Billboard Hot 100, reaching #24.
Weird OHW Fact... Michael Jackson and the Weather Girls sing backing vocals on the single.

ROCKWELL - SOMEBODY'S WATCHING ME
Reached #1 in Belgium, France and Spain.
Born Kennedy William Gordy, he is better known as Rockwell. This self-penned song from the debut album took the world by storm. As well as topping the charts in three countries, he hit Top Ten in most others. It reached #2 in the Billboard Hot 100 and in Canada, #6 in the UK and Ireland, #5 in New Zealand and South Africa, and #12 in Australia. Billboard ranked it as the #26 song for 1984.
Weird OHW Fact... If you think it sounds very 'Jacksony', you're right; the song features Michael Jackson and Jermaine Jackson providing backing vocals.

ROMEO VOID - A GIRL IN TROUBLE (IS A TEMPORARY THING)
This American new wave band from San Francisco, California, had their only hit from their third, and final, album, Instincts. It reached #35 in

the Billboard Hot 100. Their earlier song, Never Say never, although it was popular on MTV, never charted.

SAL SOLO - SAN DAMIANO (HEART AND SOUL)

Reached #1 in Poland.

Already a one hit wonder as the lead singer with a previous band, Classix Nouveaux, (See 1982 entry) Sal reached the OHW bin by himself in 1984. Embracing the Catholic religion, Sal reached #15 in the UK Chart with San Damiano (Heart And Soul). He soon dropped out of the music industry.

SAM HARRIS - SUGAR DON'T BITE

As the winner of Star Search in its premiere season, Harris landed a contract with Motown Records. Sugar Don't Bite, was his only hit, reaching #36 in the Billboard Hot 100.

He has since sold millions of his nine studio albums.

Weird OHW Fact... Sam Harris co-created the hit TV series, Down To Earth.

SCANDAL - THE WARRIOR

Written by Nick Gilder and Holly Knight, this song was recorded on Scandal's debut and only album. The song reached #7 in the Billboard Hot 100, #6 in Australia, and #11 in New Zealand.

Weird OHW Fact... Two of the band's follow up singles got to #41 in the Billboard Chart; so close to breaking the one-hit-wonder moniker.

SHANNON - LET THE MUSIC PLAY

Written by Chris Barbosa and Ed Chisolm, it was Shannon's first single. It crossed over from 'dance' to mainstream charts all over the world. Hitting #8 in the Billboard Hot 100, it also reached #14 in the UK, #2 in New Zealand, #5 in Germany, #12 in Canada, and Top 40 in Europe. Billboard ranked it as the #49 song for 1984.

SMILEY CULTURE - POLICE OFFICER

Born David Victor Emmanuel, this London rapper was better known as Smiley Culture. He only had one charting single in the UK; Police Officer reached #12 in the UK Charts. The follow ups were, Cockney Translation, UK #71, and Schooltime Chronicle, UK #59.

Weird OHW Fact... He died in 2011 of a stab wound when police were searching his house for drugs.

SNOWY WHITE - BIRD OF PARADISE

Englishman Terence Charles White is probably best known for his years as a Thin Lizzy Guitarist, or for touring as a member of Pink Floyd. His one solo single, Bird of paradise, reached #6 in the UK Charts.

Weird OHW Fact... Playing live with Pink Floyd (1979-82), and Thin Lizzy(1980-82), and Roger Waters' The Wall Live(1980-81), made him a busy bee.

STRAWBERRY SWITCHBLADE - SINCE YESTERDAY

Written and recorded by Scottish female duo Jill Bryson and Rose McDowall, AKA Strawberry Switchblade, it was their second single from their debut album. It charted slowly, finally reaching #5 in the UK, #6 in Ireland, and #24 in the Netherlands.

Weird OHW Facts... The brass fanfare in the song's first few seconds, come from the third movement of Sibelius's Symphony No. 5.

THE STYLE COUNCIL - MY EVER CHANGING MOODS

Written by band leader, Paul Weller (Ex The Jam), despite having a decent hit portfolio in the UK, New Zealand and Australia, this was their only US hit. It reached #29 in the Billboard Hot 100, #5 in the UK, and #32 in New Zealand.

Weird OHW Fact... The Jam never charted in the USA, their highest position being #135 with, The Bitterest Pill.

SWANS WAY - SOUL TRAIN

A three-piece band formed in Birmingham, they had their only hit from their debut album, The Fugitive Kind. Soul Train got to #20 in the UK Charts. The follow up, The Anchor, only reached #57.

TALK TALK - IT'S MY LIFE

Written by Mark Hollis and Tim Friese-Greene, and released by English new wave band from their second album, it was a worldwide hit. It reached #31 in the Billboard Chart, #7 in Italy, #30 in Canada, #33 in New Zealand, and Top 40 in most European Charts. Although a subsequent single, Life's What You Make It, tracked higher in some countries, it did not chart in the USA.

TOMMY SHAW - GIRLS WITH GUNS
Written by Tommy Roland Shaw, this singer is best known for his time fronting rock band, Styx. In his first solo album, Girls With Guns, had its signature track reach #33 in the Billboard Hot 100. A follow-up single, Lonely School, charted at a weak #60.

THE TOY DOLLS - NELLIE THE ELEPHANT
This irreverent English punk outfit made a habit of recording parodies, usually speeded up. First released for Christmas 1982, the re-release got to #4 in the UK Charts, staying in the chart for 14 weeks.

TRACEY ULLMAN - THEY DON'T KNOW
Written by Kirsty MacColl in 1979, Comedian and Actress Tracey Ullman chose it as her second single. It reached #8 in the Billboard Hot 100, and #2 in the UK. MacColl sung backing vocals for Ullman, who charted many times in the UK, but never again in the USA.
Weird OHW Fact... The video shows a cameo of Paul McCartney; Ullman was in his movie, Give My Regards to Broad Street.

VAN STEPHENSON - MODERN DAY DELILAH
Before he joined BlackHawk, this Hamilton, Ohio native Stephenson had a short solo career. This, his second single, reached #22 in the Billboard Hot 100. The follow-up, What the Big Girls Do, only got to #45.

WANG CHUNG – DANCE HALL DAYS
English band Wang Chung, released this song as a single, quickly becoming a worldwide hit. It got to #16 in the Billboard Hot 100, where it was followed by a few other hits. It also reached #2 in Italy, #3 in Belgium, #5 in Germany, Switzerland, #21 in the UK, #12 in Ireland, and Top 40 in most of Europe. However, it was the band's only single to make charts in the UK and Europe, making them one hit wonders in UK and most of Europe.

Weird OHW Fact... Wang Chung is a re-working of Huang Chung, (their original name) the Chinese phrase for 'yellow bell'.

OH SO CLOSE... BUT NO CIGAR...

DEAD OR ALIVE - YOU SPIN ME ROUND (LIKE A RECORD)
The very first #1 by producers Stock, Aitken & Waterman; this single is commonly known as a one hit wonder in the USA... Yup, you know the drill... it's simply not the case.
Reaching #11 in the USA, it was soon pressed close by a follow-up single, Brand New Lover, which got to #15.
Close... not even... blah.

1985...

As the internet domain name idea begins, and USA For Africa raise millions, the year begins...
British Telecom announces the red telephone boxes are to be scrapped, both Neighbours and Eastenders are aired for the first time, Back to the Future opens in America, the wreck of the Titanic is located, the first Nintendo home video game is released, and Live Aid rocks the entire world.

ALED JONES - WALKING IN THE AIR
Written by Howard Blake for the Channel 4 animated film, The Snowman, and originally recorded for the movie by Peter Auty in 1982, it was recorded by boy soprano Aled Jones after the film became popular. The single reached #5 in the UK charts.
Weird OHW Fact... Although his voice broke at just 16, he had already sold over 6 million records.

ALISON MOYET - INVISIBLE
Despite being a regular performer in most of the world's charts, Alison Moyet only broke the US Top 40 once. Invisible reached #31 in the Billboard Hot 100, #4 in Netherlands, #6 in Ireland, and top 40 most other places.

ANIMOTION - OBSESSION
Written and recorded by Holly Knight and Michael Des Barres in 1983, Animotion, (Los Angeles-based synth/pop band), covered it a year later. Instant one-hit-wonder-ism, the song reached #6 in the Billboard Hot 100, #5 in the UK, #7 in Canada, and top 40 in most other major charts. They never even got close again.

ARCADIA - ELECTION DAY
Reached #1 in Italy.
Written by Nick Rhodes and Simon Le Bon, the song was recorded by the Duran Duran spinoff, Arcadia (Duran Duran were on a short break).

It reached #6 in the USA, #7 in the UK, #5 in Ireland. The song almost doesn't qualify, as subsequent singles did chart in the USA, UK, and Ireland. But... they are one hit wonders in Australia, New Zealand, Norway and Switzerland.

Weird OHW Fact... It topped the Italian charts for seven weeks.

Weird OHW Fact... Grace Jones is featured on vocals and a speaking part.

ARTISTS UNITED AGAINST APARTHEID - SUN CITY

Written by Steven Van Zandt as a protest against apartheid policies in South Africa, the song was a minor worldwide hit. Only reaching #38 in the Billboard Hot 100, it reached #21 in the UK, #4 in Australia, and #10 in Canada.

ASHFORD & SIMPSON - SOLID

Reached #1 in New Zealand.

Written by the husband-and-wife duo, Nickolas Ashford, and Valerie Simpson, it was released from the album of the same name. It reached #2 in Germany, #3 in the Netherlands, Switzerland and the UK.

Weird OHW Fact... In 2009, Ashford & Simpson rewrote the song for President Barack Obama, renaming it, Solid As Barack

AUTOGRAPH - TURN UP THE RADIO

This American glam/metal band from Pasadena, California, hit all the right one hit wonder buttons, charting with their first single from their debut album, Sign In Please. Turn Up The Radio reached #29 in the Billboard Hot 100, their only hit.

BALTIMORA - TARZAN BOY

Reached #1 in Belgium, Finland, France, Netherlands and Spain.

Written by Maurizio Bassi and Naimy Hackett, Tarzan Boy was the debut single by Italian-based Baltimora (featuring Northern Ireland's Jimmy McShane on synth and vocals). The song was a worldwide smash. Apart from chart-topping, it reached #2 in Austria, Ireland and Sweden, #3 in the UK, Germany and South Africa, as well as #13 in the Billboard Hot 100.

CHRISSIE HYNDE (WITH UB40) - I GOT YOU BABE

Reached #1 in Australia, Ireland, New Zealand, and UK.

Christine Ellen Hynde, from Akron, Ohio, is better known as lead singer in the band, The Pretenders. In 1985, she teamed up with British band, UB40, and released Cher's old song. It reached #1 in the UK Charts, #28 in the Billboard Hot 100, and to 10 in most European charts.

COCK ROBIN - WHEN YOUR HEART IS WEAK/THE PROMISE YOU MADE

Jamming two songs into one entry here. American band, Cock Robin, had more success in mainland Europe than anywhere else, but they did score two major one hit wonders from their debut album. In USA, When Your Heart Is Weak, reached #35. In the UK, The Promise You Made reached #28 in the UK Charts.

THE COLOURFIELD - THINKING OF YOU

The Colourfield was a musical venture by Terry Hall (lead singer of The Specials, and Fun Boy Three). Their only hit was Thinking Of You, reaching #12 in the UK, and #11 in Ireland.

COLONEL ABRAMS - TRAPPED

Written by Colonel Abrams and Marston Freeman, the song is Abrams only major hit. Although it reached #3 in the UK, and topped two Billboard Dance charts, it never charted mainstream.

Weird OHW Fact... Mike Stock (Stock Aitken Waterman) claimed the song influenced Rick Astley's Never Gonna Give You Up.

THE COMMENTATORS - N-N-NINETEEN (NOT OUT)

Edinburgh comedian, Rory Bremner, polished this song in night clubs, before releasing it as 'The Commentators'. A cricket parody of Paul Hardcastle's 19, it got to # 13 in the UK Charts, the only country it could possibly chart.

THE CROWD - YOU'LL NEVER WALK ALONE

Gerry Marsden, on hearing of an appeal for the Bradford City stadium fire, quickly organized a 'Band-Aid' type charity song. The list of stars attending was astounding, and the single got to #1 in the UK and Ireland.

Weird OHW Fact... Gerry Marsden made chart history as the first person to hit #1 with two versions of the same song. (A year later, the same feat would be equaled by Cliff Richard and Living Doll.)

Weird OHW Fact... Once Gerry had raised the money, he was told the appeal fund had been closed. He donated it to the Bradford Burns Research Unit instead.

Weird OHW Fact... Unlike the original Band-Aid, the record companies refused to let their share go... where's Bob Geldof when you need him?

CURTIS HAIRSTON - I WANT YOUR LOVIN'

Curtis Kinnard Hairston was an American soul/funk vocalist. Before signing with the B. B. & Q. Band, he scored his only solo hit, reaching #13 in the UK Chart. His other releases charted, but never broke into the Top 40.

DAVID FOSTER - LOVE THEME FROM ST. ELMO'S FIRE

This Canadian record producer and composer has so many credits to his name, I wouldn't know where to begin. However, he wrote and recorded the 'love' theme from the movie, St. Elmo's Fire. It reached #15 in the Billboard Hot 100.

DEE C. LEE - SEE THE DAY

Dee C. Lee sang backing vocals for Wham and The Style Council where she married Paul Weller. Her solo career was basically this one song. It reached #3 in the UK, #5 in Australia, and #36 in Germany and the Netherlands.

Weird OHW Fact... A 2005 cover, by Girls Aloud, reached #9 in the UK Singles Chart.

DEBARGE - RHYTHM OF THE NIGHT

Written by Diane Warren, the single was released by DeBarge (a mainly family group) from their fourth Motown album, Rhythm of the Night. Although they had hit the Billboard Chart before, this was their first UK hit, topping out at #4. It also reached #3 in the US, Canada and New

Zealand, #4 in the Netherlands, and #5 in Australia. The follow-up didn't break the top 40 in the UK, Australia or New Zealand.

DENISE LASALLE - MY TOOT TOOT

Recording a version of Rockin' Sidney's, My Toot Toot, LaSalle, born Ora Denise Allen, got her only hit in the UK. My Toot Toot reached #6 in the UK charts, a surprise for her. She had a previous US hit, Trapped by a Thing Called Love, in 1971.

DON HENLEY - THE BOYS OF SUMMER

Written by Don Henley and Mike Campbell, it was recorded on Henley's solo album, Building the Perfect Beast. Better known as the vocalist and drummer of the band, The Eagles, Henley had a successful solo career. In the UK, however, he only had one hit. The Boys of Summer reached #12 in the UK Charts. Two years before, Dirty laundry had just reached #59.

DOUBLE - THE CAPTAIN OF HER HEART

Written by the Swiss duo Kurt Maloo, Felix Haug, the single was from their album, Blue. It was a worldwide success; #3 in Italy, #6 in Ireland, #8 in the UK, #9 in Norway and France, as well as a creditable #16 in the Billboard Hot 100.
Weird OHW Fact... With this single, Double were the first Swiss act to break into the Billboard Top 40.

THE DREAM ACADEMY - LIFE IN A NORTHERN TOWN

From London, The Dream Academy peaked far too soon; the first single from their debut album reached #7 in the US Billboard Hot 100. It also reached #15 in their native UK and #9 in Ireland. **Weird OHW Fact...** They are one hit wonders in the UK and Ireland... but amazingly not America. Their follow-up, The Love Parade, hit the Billboard Chart at #36.

EDDY & THE SOUL BAND - THEME FROM SHAFT

Not much known about this one. Eddy & The Soul Band (whoever they were?) took their version to #13 hit in the UK Singles Chart. Their version featured in the final episode (Going To America) of sitcom, Father Ted.

FAR CORPORATION – STAIRWAY TO HEAVEN
Frank Farian (who created Bonery M and Milli Vanilli) put together a group for an album of cover songs. The band name was abbreviated from "Frank Farian Corporation", and included members of Barclay James Harvest, Toto, Boney M and Force Majeure.
Far Corporation's primary claim to fame is their cover of "Stairway to Heaven", never before released as a single by Led Zeppelin. It charted the Billboard Hot 100 at #89 and reached #8 on the UK Singles Chart. Explicit

THE FIRM - RADIOACTIVE
Written by Paul Rodgers (Free) and produced by Rodgers and Jimmy Page, this English supergroup comprised Rodgers (Free), Jimmy Page (Led Zeppelin), Chris Slade (Manfred Mann's Earth Band), and Tony Franklin. They had one hit, reaching #28 in the Billboard Hot 100. The single reached #75 and #76 in UK and Canada.

GARY MOORE/PHIL LYNOTT - OUT IN THE FIELDS
Written by former Thin Lizzy guitarist Gary Moore, it was an instant hit. With sounds of the old 'heavier' Thin Lizzy, it reached #3 in the Irish Charts and #5 in the UK Singles Chart.
It was one of the last recordings of Phil Lynott.

GIUFFRIA - CALL TO THE HEART
When Gregg Giuffria left the Washington D.C. glam rock band, Angel, he formed Giuffria. The debut album gave them their one hit wonder badge. Call to the Heart reached #15 in the Billboard Hot 100, but the follow-up just climbed to #57. They supported Deep Purple and Foreigner on tour.

GODLEY AND CREME – CRY
Kevin Godley and Lol Crème are probably best known for their time in the UK band, 10CC. Before turning their hand to video work, they had a brief solo career. Well known in the UK Charts, this was their only US

hit. It reached #16 in the Billboard Hot 100, #19 in the UK, #8 in Germany, #13 in the Netherlands, and #27 in Ireland.

Weird OHW Fact... The song is perhaps best remembered for the multitude of faces, blended into each other.

GRAHAM PARKER AND THE SHOT - WAKE UP (NEXT TO YOU)

Londoner Graham Parker had been in the music business since 1974, best known for his work with Graham Parker and the Rumor. His only US hit came from his album, Steady Nerves. Wake Up (next To You) reached #39 in the Billboard Hot 100.

HAROLD FALTERMEYER - AXEL F

Reached #1 in Ireland, Canada, and the Netherlands.

Written and performed by German composer Harold Faltermeyer, Axel F is the theme from the Eddie Murphy movie, Beverly Hills Cop. As well as chart-topping, the single reached #2 in Belgium, Germany, Switzerland and the UK, #3 in the Billboard Hot 100.

Weird OHW Fact... The title comes from both Murphy's character's name, Axel Foley, and the fact that the tune is also in the key of F.

Weird OHW Fact... Born Hans Hugo Harold Faltermeier, he was named after a US General, living/stationed in Germany.

JACK WAGNER - ALL I NEED

Written by Glen Ballard, David Pack and Clif Magness, it was recorded by American actor, Jack Wagner. Before the hit, he was probably best known for his character, Frisco Jones, on the TV show General Hospital. Since his single's success, he has starred in The Bold and the Beautiful and Melrose Place. The song hit #2 in the Billboard Hot 100, and #3 in Canada. His highest follow-up, Too Young, charted at #52.

JAN HAMMER - MIAMI VICE THEME

Reached #1 in USA.

Czech-born Jan Hammer is perhaps better known for his movie themes. Writing for Miami Vice, the theme hit the charts, reaching #1 in USA, #2 in Ireland, #3 in UK and Canada, and top 40 in most other charts. The follow up 'Crockett's Theme' also charted in most countries, but not in the USA or New Zealand, making it a one hit wonder in those countries.

Billboard rated the song as #27 of 1985.

Weird OHW Fact... As far as I can work out, this was the last instrumental to hit #1 in the Billboard Hot 100.

JENNIFER RUSH - THE POWER OF LOVE

Reached number 1 in Australia, Austria, Canada, Ireland, New Zealand, Spain and the UK.

Sold over 2 million copies.

Born Heidi Stern, Jennifer Rush co-wrote the song which launched her career. Rush's original version reached #1 in the UK Chart (5 weeks at #1), becoming the biggest-selling single of the year. Despite being a Canadian #1, it only reached #57 in the USA.

Weird OHW Fact... In 1993, Celine Dion's version reached #1 in USA.

JOHN HUNTER - TRAGEDY

American singer and musician John Hunter is best known for his only hit. From his first solo album, Famous At Night, the single reached #39 in the Billboard Hot 100. The follow-up did not chart.

JOHN PARR - ST. ELMO'S FIRE (MAN IN MOTION)

Reached #1 in Canada and U.S.A.

English musician John Parr has sold millions of records, but only one hit in the UK. St Elmo's Fire, from the movie, reached #6 in the UK Chart, and top 10 in most of the world's charts.

The follow-up, Rock'N'Roll Mercenaries, (UK #31) was a duet with Meatloaf, so doesn't count to his solo work. A previous 1984 single, Naughty, Naughty, reached #23 in the USA.

Weird OHW Fact... John Parr and David Foster originally wrote the song for Canadian athlete Rick Hansen, travelling around the world on a wheelchair for spinal charities. His ordeal was called the 'Man in Motion Tour.'

KATE BUSH - RUNNING UP THAT HILL

It's a shame that an artist of such stature gets labelled with a one hit wonder sticker, but in truth, America never quite 'got' Kate Bush. From her album, Hounds of Love, it reached #3 in the UK and Germany, #6 in Austria, Netherlands and Belgium, and #7 in France. Over the Atlantic, it reached #16 in Canada, but a poor #30 in the Billboard Hot 100. Her follow-up, Don't Give Up, a duet with Peter Gabriel got to #40 in Canada, but just #72 in the USA, where she remains a one hit wonder.

KATRINA AND THE WAVES - WALKING ON SUNSHINE

Written by band member Kimberley Rew for their first album, she has shared royalties equally with the band for 30 years. The song was an indie success; it reached #2 in Ireland, #3 in Canada, #4 in Australia, #9 in the United States, and #8 in the UK.

Billboard rated the song as #75 of 1985.

Weird OHW Fact... Rew conceived the song as a ballad, but lead singer Katrina Leskanich let it all go.

Weird OHW Fact... The band (having been paid a million pounds in royalties per year for 30 years) finally sold the rights for a one-off for £10 million pound deal.

Weird OHW Fact... This song is only a one hit wonder in the USA. Katrina and the Waves won the Eurovision contest in 1997, with, Love Shine A Light, charting almost everywhere.

THE LIMIT - SAY YEAH

A concept of Dutch record producers Bernard Oattes and Rob van Schaik, their first album held their only hit, Say Yeah. It did get to #7 in the US Dance Chart, but reached #17 in the UK Singles Chart, their only hit.

MARIA VIDAL - BODY ROCK

Born Maria Elena Fernandez-Vidal, this American singer-songwriter only had one solo hit. The theme from the movie of the same name reached #11 in the UK, and #5 in South Africa. It never broke into the Billboard Top 40, sticking at #48.

MARY JANE GIRLS - IN MY HOUSE

American R&B group released this as their first single from their second album, Four For You. It reached #7 in the Billboard Hot 100, #6 in Canada, Netherlands and New Zealand.

MIDNIGHT STAR - OPERATOR

Despite a variety of single success, Midnight Star only achieved one top 40 hit in the USA. Operator reached #18 in the Billboard Hot 100, (#66 in UK). They had 2 Top 20 hits in the UK in 1986, so just one hit wonders in USA.

OPUS - LIVE IS LIFE
Reached #1 in Austria, Canada, France, Germany, Spain and Sweden.
Sold over 5 million copies.
From Graz, Austria, this was their second single release. It charted everywhere, hitting many #1's and top 10's in most other countries. It reached #6 in the UK, and a poor #32 in the Billboard Hot 100. It is a musical standard at European sports venues.

PAT METHENY GROUP - THIS IS NOT AMERICA
Written by David Bowie, Pat Metheny and Lyle Mays, this jazz fusion song was Pat Metheny's only chart hit. From the soundtrack of the movie, The Falcon and the Snowman, and with vocals by David Bowie, the song reached #32 in the Billboard Hot 100, and #14 in the UK.

PAUL HARDCASTLE – 19
Reached #1 in Austria, Belgium, Germany, Ireland, Italy Netherlands Norway, New Zealand, Sweden Switzerland, and UK.
Sold over 8 million copies.
Written by Paul Hardcastle, William Coutourie, and Jonas McCord, '19' was recorded on Hardcastle's third album. Helped by versions in French, Spanish, German and Japanese, it was a number one all over the world; topping 13 charts.
In the USA, despite the Viet Nam subject matter, and despite reaching #2 in Canada, the song topped out at just #15 in the Billboard Charts.
Weird OHW Fact… Due to other hits, Paul Hardcastle is NOT a one hit wonder in UK, Ireland, New Zealand, Netherlands and Germany.
Weird OHW Fact… Manchester United used the track to celebrate their 19th Premier League title; the song dipped back into the UK Top 40.

PHILIP BAILEY (& PHIL COLLINS) - EASY LOVER
Reached #1 in UK, Canada, Netherlands, Ireland, and Japan.

Written by Philip Bailey, (of Earth, Wind & Fire), and Phil Collins (of Genesis), the song was recorded for Bailey's solo album, Chinese Wall. As well as chart topping 5 charts, it reached #2 in the Billboard Hot 100 and New Zealand, #5 in Finland and Germany, and top 20 in most other charts (Only #74 in Australia)

Billboard rated the song as #12 of 1985.

Weird OHW Fact... The whimsical video was staged as a music video showing the making of a music video.

PHYLLIS NELSON - MOVE CLOSER

Reached #1 in the UK.

Written and performed by American singer-songwriter Phyllis Nelson, although it had no entry in the Billboard Chart, it topped the UK Charts, reached #15 in Australia, #23 in New Zealand, and was a minor hit in Belgium and the Netherlands.

Weird OHW Fact... This was the first single to top the UK charts written and performed by the same black woman.

Weird OHW Fact... On UK re-release in 1994, it reached #34, making her a double one hit wonder.

SCRITTI POLITTI - PERFECT WAY

Written by band members Green Gartside and David Gamson, this british band from Leeds had a run of decent hits in the UK, but only one scratched the US. From their album, Cupid & Psyche, Perfect Way was only a #48 hit in the UK, but its dance beat sent it to #6 in the US Dance chart, and #11 in the Billboard Hot 100.

SHEILA E - THE BELLE OF ST MARK

Born in Oakland, California, Sheila Cecelia Escovedo is best known as Sheila E., or 'The Queen of Percussion'. Although she had hits in the USA, this was her only chart success in the UK, Ireland and New Zealand. The song reached #34 in the Billboard Hot 100, #18 in the UK and Ireland, #5 in New Zealand, #8 in the Netherlands, and #16 in Australia.

SOPHIA GEORGE - GIRLIE GIRLIE

Written by Sangie Davis, and on George's debut album, Fresh, it was the Jamaican born singer's only chart success. It reached #1 in her native Jamaica, and #7 in the UK Charts.

Weird OHW Fact... George was teaching deaf children when the single was released.

STARPOINT - OBJECT OF MY DESIRE

A R&B sextet from Maryland, Starpoint cracked the Billboard chart only once. Object of My Desire reached #25 in the Hot 100, while charting high in both Dance and Black charts.

Weird OHW Fact... In 2005, DJ Dana Rayne's eurotrance cover reached #7 in the UK.

STEVE ARRINGTON - FEEL SO REAL

Stephen Ralph Arrington, from Dayton, Ohio, had his best success with a solo album, Dancin' in the Key of Life. The title track hit both the R&B and Dance Charts, but his only real chart success came from, Feel So Real, which reached #5 in the UK Singles Chart.

TOTAL CONTRAST - TAKES A LITTLE TIME

An English techno soul duo from England, this band is probably the least one-hit-wondery of any of the entries, ever. Takes a Little Time reached #17 in the UK Chart and did well in the US dance charts, however their first hit single reached #41, and the follow-ups reached #44 and #63. Man they tried hard to beat the one hit wonder bin... but they're firmly in it.

TRANS-X - LIVING ON VIDEO

Reached #1 in Spain.

Written by band member Pascal Languirand, the Canadian synth group from Montreal took their only hit worldwide. Making it big on its re-release, it only reached #61 in the Billboard Hot 100, but got to #9 in the UK and Austria, #1 in Spain, #2 in Switzerland, #4 in Germany, and #17 in Ireland.

USA FOR AFRICA - WE ARE THE WORLD

Reached #1 in USA, UK, Australia, Ireland, Canada, New Zealand, and more than 20 other countries.

Sold over 10 million copies.

Written by Michael Jackson and Lionel Richie after an original idea by Harry Belafonte, the USA's charity record for Africa was released just seven weeks after Band Aid's super-hit, Do They Know It's Christmas? The US single topped the charts in too many countries to count, and charted everywhere, raising millions for Ethiopia.

It also starred 'everybody'.

However, despite the huge world sales, Billboard rated the song as only #20 of 1985.

Weird OHW Fact... To show unity with the British effort, Phil Collins played drums, and Bob Geldof sang on the chorus.

Weird OHW Fact... Again, Like Band Aid's 'aftershocks', We Are The World 25 For Haiti raised millions for the island after the earthquake of 2010.

OH SO CLOSE... BUT NO CIGAR...

A-HA – TAKE ON ME

Oh, the video, oh those chiseled good-looks, oh the synth strings, oh the perfect one-hit wondered-ness of it all...

Nope. A-Ha made many hits after this #1 world-breaker. The follow-up hit the charts well, The Sun Always Shines on TV, topped the UK charts and reached #20 in the Billboard Hot 100. Throw in a James Bond movie theme, The Living Daylights, and these guys were made for life, and NEVER one hit wonders.

EUROPE – FINAL COUNTDOWN

It's perhaps not surprising that this Swedish rock band is considered a one-hit-wonder, but they're not even close. The Final Countdown reached #1 in most countries around the world, but the follow-up, Rock The Night (UK #12) also charted well. Carrie (US #3) and Superstitious (Sweden and Norway #1) were also creditable hits, meaning this band should never be considered even close to being included in this book.

THE POWER STATION - SOME LIKE IT HOT

This supergroup, Robert Palmer, Chic drummer Tony Thompson, and the Taylor brothers from Duran Duran are sometimes considered a one hit wonder. Their premier hit, Some Like it Hot, was a hit in most charts. However, their follow-up, Get It On (Bang A Gong) also charted in UK, USA, Germany, and Australia. One hit wonders you may be in Austria, Belgium, etc, you don't get the in the select few.

Weird OHW Fact... The band was named after The Power Station recording studio where the album was conceived and recorded.

1986...

As the space shuttle Challenger disintegrates just 73 seconds after launch, the year begins...
Voyager 2 reaches Uranus, the Soviet Union launches the Mir space station, the Chernobyl nuclear power plant blows during a safety test, killing 4000+, the FIFA World Cup is held in Mexico, the Iran-Contra Affair begins, and Matt Groening creates Homer, Bart and The Simpsons.

ANITA BAKER - SWEET LOVE
Written by Anita Baker, Louis A. Johnson and Gary Bias, it was recorded by the American R&B singer on her second studio album, Rapture. It reached #8 in the Billboard Hot 100 and #13 in the UK.
Billboard ranked the song as #90 of 1986.

ANITA DOBSON - ANYONE CAN FALL IN LOVE
Written by Simon May, Leslie Osborne and Don Black, the song was recorded by Anita Dobson, famous for her role as Angie watts in BBC's soap, EastEnders. The single reached #4 in the UK Charts.

AURRA - YOU AND ME TONIGHT
This American soul group ran through a gamut of personel changes and nomenclature. At the time of their only hit, #12 in the UK Charts, they were Curt Jones and Starleana Young, and had the name Aurra.

BERLIN - TAKE MY BREATH AWAY
Reached #1 in Belgium, Canada, Ireland, Netherlands, UK, and USA.
Sold over 3 million copies.
American new wave band from Orange County had some limited chart success, but when they hit it big with, Take My Breath Away, from the movie Top Gun, they went worldwide. The song was written by Italian Giorgio Moroder and Tom Whitlock and went top 5 in most charts.
Billboard ranked the song as #27 of 1986.
Weird OHW Fact... It won the Academy Award AND Golden Globe for Best Original Song in 1986.

THE BLOW MONKEYS - DIGGING YOUR SCENE

Written by multi-instrumentalist Dr. Robert (Bruce Robert Howard) from Haddington, Scotland, it was recorded on their second album, Animal Magic. The song reached #14 in the Billboard Hot 100, #12 in the UK Chart, #24 in Italy, #25 in Germany, and #37 in the Netherlands and Italy. Their follow ups had sporadic success in the UK and in Europe, but they never charted in the USA again.

BOYS DON'T CRY - I WANNA BE A COWBOY

Boys Don't Cry only released two albums, but in pure one-hit-wondership, hit it big with their first single. I Wanna Be a Cowboy was a novelty song, reaching #12 in the Billboard Hot 100, and top 10 in Australia and South Africa.

Weird OHW Fact... The official video features a cameo appearance by Ian (Lemmy) Kilmister of rock band Motörhead.

BRUCE HORNSBY AND THE RANGE - THE WAY IT IS

Reached #1 in USA, Canada, and the Netherlands.

Written by Bruce Hornsby from the album of the same name, the single's success launched their career. The song topped three and reached #3 in Belgium, #8 in Ireland, #13 in South Africa, #15 in the UK and Switzerland, and #16 in Germany. The follow-ups were huge, Mandolin Rain, The Valley Road... but neither charted in the UK or Germany, making Bruce a one hit wonder in those countries.

CHRIS DE BURGH - LADY IN RED

Reached #1 in Belgium, Ireland, Norway, Poland, South Africa and the UK.

Written by Chris De Burgh (pronounced de burg), it topped six charts, and went top ten in most others, including #3 in the Billboard Hot 100. It quickly becoming de Burgh's best-selling single and his signature song. Due to other hits, he's basically a one hit wonder everywhere, except Ireland.

Billboard ranked the song as #21 of 1987.

Weird OHW Fact... In a 2001 poll, the song was voted the fourth most hated UK number-one single.

CLAIRE AND FRIENDS - IT'S 'ORRIBLE BEING IN LOVE (WHEN YOU'RE 8½)

Written by Mick Coleman and produced by Kevin Parrott, the novelty song was recorded by Stockport schoolgirl, Claire Usher and her friends. It reached #13 in the UK Charts.

Weird OHW Fact... Mick Coleman and Kevin Parrott are better known as Brian and Michael, who wrote and performed the 1978 #1 one hit wonder, Matchstalk Men and Matchstalk Cats and Dogs.

CLARENCE CLEMONS - YOU'RE A FRIEND OF MINE

Written by Narada Michael Walden and Jeffrey Cohen, the recording features a duet with Clarence Clemons and Jackson Browne (although Clemons gets top billing). It reached #18 in the Billboard Hot 100, and #9 in Australia.

Weird OHW Fact... Clarence Clemons is probably better known as Bruce Springsteen's E Street Band saxophone player.

Weird OHW Fact... Daryl Hannah, Clemons girlfriend, provided backing vocals.

CUTTING CREW - (I JUST) DIED IN YOUR ARMS

Reached #1 in USA, Canada, Norway and Finland.

Written by Nick Van Eede, the front-man of the London rock band, it was recorded on their debut album, Broadcast. Released first in the UK, it reached #4, and it quickly spread. Topping four charts, it hit #2 in Sweden and Ireland, #4 in Switzerland and Germany, #8 in Australia, and #9 in Austria and Netherlands.

Billboard ranked the song as #32 of 1987.

Weird OHW Fact... The title of the song came to Van Eede after making love; *le petit mort*, the little death being the term for orgasm in French.

DAVE DOBBYN - SLICE OF HEAVEN

Reached #1 in new Zealand and Australia.

With three #1's under his belt, you'd hardly consider New Zealander Dobbyn to be a one hit wonder, but he is. Slice of Heaven was his only song to break out of Australia and New Zealand, reaching #24 in the

Billboard Hot 100. It was #1 in new Zealand for eight weeks, topping the Australian chart for four weeks.

DAVID + DAVID - WELCOME TO THE BOOMTOWN
Written by Los Angeles studio musicians David Baerwald and David Ricketts, it was recorded on their debut album, Boomtown. The single reached #37 in the Billboard Hot 100. The follow-up, aptly titled, Ain't So Easy, reached #51.

DEVICE - HANGING ON A HEART ATTACK
This American pop-rock trio, comprising Holly Knight, Paul Engemann and Gene Black, only produced one album, 22B3. The hit single went to #35 in the Billboard Hot 100. The follow-up, Who Says, just reached #79.
Weird OHW Fact... Holly Knight wrote Love is a Battlefield, a hit for Pat Benatar.

DON JOHNSON – HEARTBEAT
Written by Eric Kaz, and Wendy Waldmanis, this track was recorded on Johnson's bebut album, heartbeat. The album reached #17, and the title track got to #5 in the Billboard Hot 100. Subsequent singles did not chart.

THE FABULOUS THUNDERBIRDS - TUFF ENUFF
Written by Jerry McCain in 1960, this modern cover version reached #10 in the Billboard Hot 100. There is also some news of top 20's placings in other charts, but I can't find details. Their follow-up, Wrap it up, reached #50.

FARLEY 'JACKMASTER' FUNK - LOVE CAN'T TURN AROUND
From Isaac Hayes' 1975 song, I Can't Turn Around, Steve "Silk" Hurley made a house version; it charted in the US Dance Chart, but did not crossover. Farley (who lived with Hurley) made his own version, changing the title slightly. Farley's version reached #10 in the UK Singles Chart.

FORCE MDS - TENDER LOVE

Written by Jimmy Jam and Terry Lewis, Staten Island New Yorkers, Force MD's recorded it for their second album, Chillin'. It reached #10 in the Billboard Hot 100, (#2 in the Adult Contemporary Chart), and #23 in the UK Singles Chart.

GAVIN CHRISTOPHER - ONE STEP CLOSER TO YOU
Written by Evan Rogers, Carl Sturken, Jeff Pescetto, and David Grant, this song was recorded by Chicago singer, becoming his biggest hit. It broke the top 25 on Dance, Pop and R&B, and reached #22 in the mainstream Billboard Hot 100.

GEORGIA SATELLITES - KEEP YOUR HANDS TO YOURSELF
Written by the group's lead singer, Dan Baird, this American southern rock group from Atlanta, Georgia had a hit on their hands. The song reached #2 in the Billboard Hot 100 and a poor #69 in the UK charts. The follow-up, Battleship Chains, I remember just as clearly, but it disappointed, just topping out at #86 in the USA, #44 in the UK.

GLORIA LORING AND CARL ANDERSON - FRIENDS AND LOVERS
Written by Jay Gruska and Paul Gordon, it was recorded as a duet by Glori Loring who had a major part in the daytime soap, Days of Our Lives. The song reached #2 in the Billboard Hot 100, and was performed on the show.

GRANGE HILL CAST - JUST SAY NO
The cast of BBC show, Grange Hill, entered the music business with their song, Just Say No, coinciding with a world campaign against children taking drugs. The song reached #5 in the UK Charts.

GTR - WHEN THE HEART RULES THE MIND
Written by the guitarists Steve Hackett and Steve Howe, this track was the first single released from 'Supergroup' GTR's debut album. It reached #14 in the Billboard Hot 100. The follow-up, The Hunter, just reached #85.
Weird OHW Fact... GTR is an abbreviation for the 'guitar' label used on mixing consoles.

GWEN GUTHRIE - AIN'T NOTHING GOIN' ON BUT THE RENT

Reached #1 in New Zealand.

Written and recorded by American singer Gwen Guthrie, it would be the biggest hit of her career. It only reached #42 in the Billboard Hot 100, but did hit #1 on the Dance Charts, #5 in the UK, and top 20 in many European charts.

Weird OHW Fact... The hook 'Ain't nothing goin' on now, but the rent-uh' is taken from the 1972 James Brown song 'Get on the Good Foot'.

HAYWOODE - ROSES

Sidney Haywoode, a London singer, peppered the outer regions of the UK Charts with a series of singles. Only one stuck. She will always be remembered for her #11 hit, from the album, Arrival.

Weird OHW Fact... Before the album was released in Japan, it was being sold on Amazon for $800.

HIPSWAY - THE HONEYTHIEF

Written by band members Grahame Skinner, Harry Travers, Johnny McElhone and Ally McLeod, this Scottish band hit high heights with their only hit. It reached #17 in the UK charts, and a creditable #19 in the Billboard Hot 100.

HOLLYWOOD BEYOND - WHAT'S THE COLOUR OF MONEY?

This Birmingham pop group only had one hit, but it was close... Their first single reached #7 in the UK Singles Charts, #21 in Germany and #14 in Switzerland. However, relegating them to the one hit wonder bin, the follow-up single, No More Tears, only reached #47 in the UK.

HONEYMOON SUITE - FEEL IT AGAIN

Written by band keyboardist, Ray Coburn, it was the first and only hit for this hard rock band from Niagara Falls, Canada. From their second album, The Big Prize, the single reached #34 in the Billboard Hot 100.

Weird OHW Fact... The band's name is a testament to Niagara Falls being the premier American honeymoon destination.

IT BITES – CALLING ALL THE HEROES

Written by front man Francis Dunnery, it was recorded on their debut album, The Big Lad in the Windmill. It reached #6 in the UK Charts, but brought them little attention elsewhere. The follow-up, Kiss Like Judas, did not chart.

IT'S IMMATERIAL - DRIVING AWAY FROM HOME (JIM'S TUNE)

British indie band, It's Immaterial, recorded the song after four 'John Peel Sessions'. It was their only hit, reaching #18 in the UK Charts. The follow-up, Ed's Funky Diner (Friday Night, Saturday Morning), charted at #65.

JOHN FARNHAM – YOU'RE THE VOICE

Reached #1 in Australia, Germany and Sweden.

Written by Andy Qunta, Keith Reid, Maggie Ryder and Chris Thompson, it was recorded by. Australian John Farnham for his album, Whispering Jack. It topped 3 charts, and reached #3 in Ireland and Switzerland, #6 in the UK and Austria, #12 in Canada, #13 in the Netherlands.

Weird OHW Fact... It only got to #82 in the USA. Heart covered it in 1991, reaching #20 in the Rock Chart.

JOHN TAYLOR - I DO WHAT I DO (THEME FOR 9½ WEEKS)

Written by Jonathan Elias, John Taylor, and Michael Des Barres, this song was used on the soundtrack of the movie, 9½ Weeks. It reached #23 in the Billboard Hot 100, and just #42 in the UK Charts.

Weird OHW Fact... John Taylor was the bassist for Duran Duran.

LATIN QUARTER - RADIO AFRICA

This British band were popular as a live act in Northern Europe, incorporating pop, rock, reggae and folk into their repertoire. Their only charting success only hit the UK Charts on its second issue, reaching #19.

LETITIA DEAN AND PAUL MEDFORD - SOMETHING OUTA NOTHING

Written by Simon May, Stewart James and Bradley James, for incorporation into the plot of BBC soap opera EastEnders. Actors Letitia Dean and Paul J. Medford recorded the song, which rose to #12 in the UK Singles Chart.

LOVEBUG STARSKI - AMITYVILLE (IT'S THE HOUSE ON THE HILL)
Bronx born Kevin Smith is a musician and producer. He began a solo career in 1981, but will be best remembered for his only chart single, Amityville (The House on the Hill). It reached #12 hit in the UK Singles Chart.

MAX HEADROOM - PARANOIMIA
English synthpop group Art of Noise recorded a version of this song on their album, In Visible Silence. For the single, they included Max Headroom on vocals. It was a hit, reaching #34 in the Billboard Hot 100, #12 in the UK, #6 in New Zealand, #7 in the Netherlands, #17 in Belgium, and #33 in Germany.

MODELS - OUT OF MIND, OUT OF SIGHT
Written by band member James Freud, it was recorded for the Australian new wave band's album of the same name. It topped the Australian Chart in 1985, and slipped to #37 in the Billboard Hot 100 in the following year.

MODERN TALKING - BROTHER LOUIE
Reached #1 in Germany, South Africa, Spain and Sweden.
Written by Dieter Bohlen, one half of the German Modern Talking duo, this pair had three #1's in their native land behind them before breaking the UK market. The song was a European success, finding the top of 4 charts, #2 in Austria, Ireland and Switzerland, #4 in the UK, and top 10 everywhere else. But despite much more mainland European success, the duo would never chart in the UK again.
Weird OHW Fact... This band has sold more than 120 million records, making them the biggest German music act ever.

NANCY MARTINEZ - FOR TONIGHT
French-Canadian singer from Montreal, Martinez peppered the Dance Charts, but only one song crossed over to the Billboard Hot 100. For Tonight reached #32.

NU SHOOZ - I CAN'T WAIT

Reached #1 in Canada.

Written by front man John Smith for the Portland band, and recorded on the album, Poolside, the song was originally released in 1984, to no success. Remixed and re-released, it reached #2 in the Billboard Hot 100, #2 in Germany and the UK, #3 in New Zealand, #4 in Switzerland, and #9 in Holland and Italy.

Billboard ranked the song as #99 of 1986.

ORAN "JUICE" JONES - THE RAIN

Written by Vincent Bell, Houston Texas born Oran Jones took the song for his debut album, Juice. It reached #9 in the Billboard Hot 100, #3 in Germany, #4 in the UK, #6 in Belgium and Ireland, #10 in the Netherlands, #12 in Switzerland, #16 in Austria, and #22 in New Zealand.

OWEN PAUL - MY FAVOURITE WASTE OF TIME

Written by Marshall Crenshaw in 1979, it was released by Glasgow singer, Owen Paul. It reached #3 in the UK, but his follow-ups failed to chart.

PATTI LABELLE (AND MICHAEL MACDONALD) - ON MY OWN

Reached #1 in USA, Canada and Netherlands.

Written by Burt Bacharach and Carole Bayer Sager, this song was the biggest single by either party. It reached #1 in the USA, where it stayed for three weeks. It also topped the Canadian and Dutch charts, hitting #2 in the UK, #4 in New Zealand, #12 in Australia, #15 in Sweden and #20 in Austria.

Billboard ranked the song as #4 of 1986.

Weird OHW Fact... The video was shot on two different coasts of the USA, the two singers did not meet.

PETER CETERA - GLORY OF LOVE

Reached #1 in USA and Sweden.

Written by Peter Cetera, David Foster and Diane Nini, it was recorded on his solo album, Solitude/Solitaire. It reached #1 in the Billboard Hot 100, #2 in Norway, #3 in the UK, and top 30 in all other major charts. Despite having a good solo career, follow-ups did not chart in UK,

Germany and Australia, making Cetera a one hit wonder in those countries.

Billboard ranked the song as #26 of 1986.

Weird OHW Fact... Peter Cetera is probably best known as an original member of Chicago (1967-1985).

PSEUDO ECHO - FUNKY TOWN

Reached #1 in Australia, Canada and New Zealand.

Making a heavier, rockier version of Lipps Inc's 1979 smash hit, Australian band Pseudo Echo rode this all the way to the bank. It topped the Australian, Canadian and New Zealand charts, then went #2 in South Africa, #6 in the Billboard Hot 100, #8 in the UK, and #12 in Ireland.

Billboard ranked the song as #99 of 1987.

Weird OHW Fact... In Australia, Pseudo Echo's version spent 7 weeks at #1 in Australia... Lipps Inc only got 2 weeks at #1.

REAL ROXANNE / HITMAN HOWIE TEE - BANG ZOOM LET'S GO

Before turning his hand to production, Howard Thompson (British born but raised in Brooklyn, NY) had a short solo career. His only charting hit reached #11 in the UK Charts. The first single, Romeo Part 1, just reached #64.

REGINA - BABY LOVE

Written by Stephen Bray, Regina Richards, and Mary Kessler, Baby Love was originally intended for Madonna, who turned it down. Brooklyn-born singer Regina, crossed over from Dance charts to #10 in the Billboard Hot 100.

Weird OHW Fact... Danni Minogue had a bigger hit with the song in 1991.

Weird OHW Fact... Regina's version was produced by writer Stephen Bray, who had produced for Madonna. The finished song sounded Madonna-esque.

RIC OCASEK - EMOTION IN MOTION

Written by Ric Ocasek, it was recorded on his second solo album, This Side of Paradise. Better known as the lead singer for The Cars, it was his only solo hit, reaching #15 in the Billboard Hot 100, #8 in Australia, and #35 in New Zealand.

ROBERT TEPPER - NO EASY WAY OUT

This American songwriter from New Jersey, is probably best known for his single hit, featured on the movie Rocky IV soundtrack. Stallone liked the song, and when released, it climbed to #22 in Billboard's Hot 100.

Weird OHW Fact... Another Tepper song, Angel of the City, was used as the main song in Stallone's movie, Cobra.

SLY FOX - LET'S GO ALL THE WAY

Written by band member Gary 'Mudbone' Cooper, it was recorded on American duo's only album of the same name. It charted in the UK first, reaching #3, then sales spread, #7 in the Billboard Hot 100, #5 in the Netherlands, #14 in Belgium, and #27 in New Zealand. Follow-ups bombed.

SPITTING IMAGE - THE CHICKEN SONG

Reached #1 in UK and Ireland.

This parody/novelty song from the Channel 4 TV series, Spitting Image, shot to #1 in Ireland and the UK. It makes fun of the ludicrous 'holiday' songs that we sing every time we Britons hit the sun and sangria.

Weird OHW Fact... The lyrics mention, 'those two wet gits with their girly curly hair'; an obvious reference to holiday band Black Lace.

STAN RIDGWAY - CAMOUFLAGE

Written by Stan Ridgway, Camouflage is from the album The Big Heat. The single did not chart at all in the USA, but was a considerable European success. It reached #2 in Ireland and Poland, #4 in the UK, #7 in Belgium, #8 in Germany, #11 in the Netherlands and Switzerland, #17 in Austria.

SU POLLARD - STARTING TOGETHER

Nottingham native Susan Georgina Pollard is probably best known for her role as chalet maid on the sitcom, Hi-de-Hi!. Her first single bombed, but her next single (the theme of BBC series, The Marriage) reached #2 in the UK Charts.

TA MARA AND THE SEEN - EVERYBODY DANCE

From Minneapolis, this Minnesota group took the quintessential one hit wonder route. Their first single from their debut album was their only hit. Everybody Dance reached #3 on the Dance Charts, crossing over to #24 in the mainstream Billboard Hot 100.

TIMBUK3 - THE FUTURE'S SO BRIGHT, I GOTTA WEAR SHADES

Written by band member Pat MacDonald, this Madison Wisconsin band only had one bite at the fame cherry. The Future's So Bright, I Gotta Wear Shades was issued from their debut album, Greetings from Timbuk3. It reached #19 in the Billboard Hot 100, #15 in Canada, #11 in Ireland, #21 in the UK, #18 in Australia, and #29 in New Zealand.

TIMEX SOCIAL CLUB - RUMOURS

Reached #1 in Canada.
San Francisco Bay music group recorded this song for their debut and only album, Vicious Rumors. It was a belter. It was a #1 in three lesser Billboard Charts, and reached #8 in the mainstream Billboard Hot 100, #2 in New Zealand, #3 in the Netherlands, #13 in the UK, and top 20 in most major music charts.

VESTA WILLIAMS - ONCE BITTEN TWICE SHY

From Ohio, Mary Vesta Williams was an American singer–songwriter. She had many lesser hits on the US R&B Charts, but only one broke the top 40 barrier. Once Bitten Twice Shy reached #14 in the UK Charts, #20 in the Netherlands, #21 in Ireland.
Weird OHW Fact... Williams had a 4 octave vocal range, very rare.

OH SO CLOSE... BUT NO CIGAR...

DOCTOR AND THE MEDICS - SPIRIT IN THE SKY

Taking a neat cover of Norman Greenbaum's 1969 hit to #1 in the UK Charts, London glam rockers, Doctor and the Medics are usually thought of as a one hit wonder band... but their follow-up, Burn, reached #29. So they dodge the one hit wonder bullet...

IGGY POP - REAL WILD CHILD (WILD ONE)

Reached #1 in New Zealand.

Written by Australians Johnny Greenan, Johnny O'Keefe, Dave Owens and Tony Withers in 1958, Iggy Pop covered it for his album, Blah-Blah-Blah. It charted in the UK at #10, and reached #11 in Australia, #16 in Ireland. His other 'hit', Candy, also hit most of the major charts, but not the UK, so, does that drop Iggy into the one hit wonder bin? No.

Singles in late 90's reached #22 and #26, so he's not a one hit wonder.

Weird OHW Facts... Iggy Pop's real name is James Newell Osterberg, Jr.

1987...

As Aretha Franklin is the first woman inducted into the Rock and Roll Hall of Fame, the year begins...
U2 release their album, The Joshua Tree, the first Rugby World Cup kicks off in New Zealand, Ronald Reagan challenges Mikhail Gorbachev to 'tear down' the Berlin Wall, Nazi Rudolf Hess is found dead in Spandau Prison, and 12 are killed by an IRA bomb at Enniskillen.

ABIGAIL MEAD & NIGEL GOULDING - FULL METAL JACKET (I WANNA BE YOUR DRILL INSTRUCTOR)
The musical score for the movie, Full Metal jacket, was written by director Stanley Kubrick's daughter, Vivian. Under the stage name, Abigail Mead, a single was released featuring many snippets from R. Lee Ermey's drill instructions. The single reached #2 in the UK Chart.

THE BARBUSTERS - LIGHT OF DAY
Written by Bruce Springsteen, it was released by the 'band' of Springsteen, Joan Jett and Michael J. Fox. It reached #33 in the Billboard Hot 100, and has been performed by both Springsteen and Joan Jett at their individual concerts.

BENJAMIN ORR - STAY THE NIGHT
Written by Benjamin Orr and Diane Grey Page, this song was Orr's only solo hit. Stay the Night reached #24 in the Billboard Hot 100 chart, and top 5 in both the Adult Contemporary and Album Rock track Charts.
Weird OHW Fact... Orr was the singer and bassist for the band, The Cars.

BILL MEDLEY/JENNIFER WARNES – (I'VE HAD) THE TIME OF MY LIFE
Reached #1 in USA, Australia, Netherlands, Belgium and Canada.
Written by Franke Previte, John DeNicola, and Donald Markowitz, it was chosen as the theme to the movie, Dirty Dancing. A worldwide hit, it topped many charts, and reached #3 in Austria, #5 in Germany, Spain, Switzerland and Ireland, #6 in the UK, and #12 in Sweden.

It won both Academy Award and Golden Globe for Best Original Song.
Weird OHW Fact... The song was originally written for Donna Summer and Joe Esposito, but they turned it down. It would have been Summer's biggest hit. Ah well.

BLACK - WONDERFUL LIFE
Reached #1 in Austria and Poland.
Written by Liverpool's Colin Vearncombe, (Black), he is best known for his solo single which was a worldwide hit. It topped the Austrian and Polish charts, reaching #2 in Switzerland, France, and Germany, #5 in Belgium, #7 in Spain, Australia, Ireland, and Netherlands, #8 in the UK, and #9 in Italy.

BOOGIE BOX HIGH – JIVE TALKIN'
Headed by Andros Georgiou, this ensemble consisted of Georgiou's cousin George Michael, Nick Heyward of Haircut One Hundred, Mick Talbot of The Style Council, and others. Their only hit release was originally just meant as a demo, but when released, it reached #7 in the UK.
Weird OHW Fact... Due to his contract with to Epic Records, George Michael was never credited in any way... this might have had a huge impact on the song's success.

BOURGEOIS TAGG - I DON'T MIND AT ALL
The project of American guitarist Lyle Workman, this band's first single hit it big-ish, then disappeared. The song, from the album, Yoyo, reached #38 in the Billboard Hot 100.

BREAKFAST CLUB - RIGHT ON TRACK
Written by band members Dan Gilroy and Stephen Bray, this New York band charted high, reaching #7 in the Billboard Hot 100, #4 in Australia, and a poor #54 in the UK. A follow-up, Kiss and Tell, reached #48 in the USA... so one hit wonders.

BROKEN ENGLISH - COMIN' ON STRONG
Written by Steve Elson who was performing in a British Rolling Stones tribute band. Inspired by the song, a band was put together for the

project. Having a distinct Rolling Stones 'feel and sound', the first single got to #18 in the UK Chart, but follow-up material was not up to the quality of the first offering.

BRUCE WILLIS - RESPECT YOURSELF
Bruce Willis skirted with a solo pop career before delving deep into the movies. His first single with the Pointer Sisters, reached #5 in the Billboard Hot 100, #7 in the UK. His follow-up, the Drifters, Under The Boardwalk, reached #2 in the UK, but didn't chart in the US.

CHICO DEBARGE - TALK TO ME
Jonathan Arthur DeBarge had a long career, hitting the fringes of the Billboard and R&B Charts. In true One Hit Wonder fashion, his only hit came from his debut album. Talk To Me rose to #21 in the Billboard Hot 100, and #7 on the R&B Chart. He did chart several times, but never again broke the Top 40.

CLUB NOUVEAU - LEAN ON ME
Reached #1 in Canada, New Zealand, and USA.
Written by legend Bill Withers in 1972, Club Nouveau's version reached higher than the original. It topped the charts in the USA, Canada and New Zealand, while reaching #3 in the UK, #4 in Netherlands, #5 in Ireland and Australia, and Top 20 in many other major charts.
Weird OHW Fact... It is one of only nine songs to have reached Billboard #1with two different artists.

THE COMMUNARDS - DON'T LEAVE ME THIS WAY
Reached #1 in Belgium, Ireland, Netherlands, and UK.
Written by Kenneth Gamble, Leon Huff and Cary Gilbert. And already having been a huge hit for Harold Melvin & the Blue Notes (1975) and Thelma Houston (1977), you might have thought the British pop duo had little original to offer... wrong. Their version was upbeat, synth strong and a worldwide dance hit. It reached #1 in many charts, and #2 in Switzerland, New Zealand and Australia, #5 in Germany and Italy, #6 in Spain and France. It is, however The Communards only US chart entry, at #40, a very squeaky one hit wonder.

COMPANY B - FASCINATED
Written by Cuban band member, Ish Ledesma, Fascinated was the girl band's only hit. It reached #1 in the US Dance Charts, and a creditable #21 in the Billboard Hot 100, where it spent 8 weeks in the chart.

DANNY WILSON - MARY'S PRAYER
Written by band member Gary Clark, this pop band from Dundee, Scotland, took their first hit single to dizzy heights. Through a couple of releases, the band hit #3 in the UK, #5 in Ireland, #10 in South Africa, #23 in the Billboard Hot 100, and #35 in Germany.
Weird OHW Fact... The band performed the song at the opening gala of the Ryder Cup in 2014.

DONNA ALLEN – SERIOUS
This Floridian courted a few bands before turning to a solo career, and may be best known for singing on tour for Gloria Estefan for nine years. She had three top 40 hits in the UK, and a few on the R&B Charts, but this first single was her only chart entry in the US, #21 in the Billboard Chart, #8 in the UK.
Weird OHW Fact... She was a cheerleader for the Tampa Bay Buccaneers.

FERRY AID - LET IT BE
Reached #1 in Norway, Switzerland and the UK.
This charity ensemble were organized by Gary Bushell to raise money after the Zeebrugge ferry disaster (It capsized, killing 193). Headed by McCartney, the song rose to #1 in the UK, Norway and Switzerland, #2 in Ireland, #3 in Holland, #4 in Austria, #8 in France, and #9 in Sweden.

FREDDIE MCGREGOR - JUST DON'T WANT TO BE LONELY
Written by Bobby Eli, John Freeman and Vinnie Barrett in 1973, Jamaican Freddie McGregor covered the song, but did it in a reggae beat. It reached #9 in the UK chart. His follow-up, That Girl (Groovy Situation), only reached #47.

GLENN AND CHRIS - DIAMOND LIGHTS

Written by Bob Puzey, Diamond Lights is the unlikely only hit for ex Tottenham Hotspur and England footballers Glenn Hoddle and Chris Waddle. It reached #12 in the UK Chart and was lampooned for their 'live' performances.

GRATEFUL DEAD - TOUCH OF GREY
Written by Jerry Garcia, and Robert Hunter, for the album, In the Dark, Touch of Grey is the Grateful Dead's only hit single. It reached #9 in the Billboard Hot 100, and #1 in the Mainstream Rock Tracks chart.

GREGORY ABBOTT - SHAKE YOU DOWN
Reached #1 in Spain and USA.
Written by Gregory Abbot, it would be his biggest hit, charting worldwide. It topped the Spanish and Billboard Hot 100, and reached #2 in Canada, #3 in Netherlands and New Zealand, #5 in Ireland, #6 in the UK, #7 in Belgium, and top 20 in most other major music charts. Billboard ranked the song as #3 for 1987.
Weird OHW Fact... He has taught English at Berkeley University.

JEFF LORBER - FACTS OF LOVE
From Pennsylvania, Lorber recorded the track for the album, Private Passion. Featuring Karyn White, the song was his biggest hit, reaching #27 in the Billboard Hot 100.

JENNIFER RUSH - THE FLAMES OF PARADISE
Born Heidi Stern, despite this New yorker's 1985 worldwide smash hit, The Power of Love (US #57), this duet with Elton John was her only other Billboard Hot 100 entry, reaching #36.

THE JETS - CRUSH ON YOU
Written by Jerry Knight and Aaron Zigman, it was the second single from their debut album. It reached #3 in the Billboard Hot 100, and #5 in the UK Charts. They had many more hits in the USA, but none in the UK.

JONATHAN BUTLER - LIES

Jonathan Kenneth Butler, a native of Cape Town, South Africa, is a R&B Gospel singer. His hit, Lies, reached #25 in the Billboard Hot 100, and #18 in the UK, spending 12 weeks in the UK Chart.

KANE GANG - MOTORTOWN

This band from North East England may be one hit wonders twice over, (in 1984, respect Yourself got to #19 in Australia), but Motortown, the hit single from their album, Miracle, reached #36 in the Billboard Hot 100, their only US hit.

KAREL FIALKA - HEY MATTHEW

Written by British musician Karel Fialka, it was recorded for his album, Human Animal. It reached #9 in the UK, and was his only hit.

LEVERT - CASANOVA

Written by Reggie Calloway, it was a hit for the Cleveland, Ohio R&B group. It reached #5 in the Billboard Hot 100, #9 in the UK, #16 in Canada, #17 in Ireland, #26 in New Zealand, and #27 in the Netherlands.
Billboard ranked it as #71 song of 1987.

LIVING IN A BOX - LIVING IN A BOX

Written by Marcus Vere and Steve Piggot, the Sheffield band would not have a bigger success than their first single. It reached #5 in the UK Charts, and #17 in the Billboard Hot 100. It was a worldwide hit, reaching #2 in Switzerland, #4 in Germany and Sweden, #6 in Ireland, and Top 20 in most major music charts. This song makes them one hit wonders in USA, Canada, France, and New Zealand.

MARRS - PUMP UP THE VOLUME / ANITINA (THE FIRST TIME I SEE SHE DANCE)

Reached #1 in Canada, Italy, Netherlands, New Zealand and the UK.
Written by band members Martyn Young and Steve Young, it was the only single by this ensemble. It topped five charts, and reached Top Ten in most major charts of the world, hitting #13 in the Billboard Hot 100.

MEL SMITH (WITH KIM WILDE) - ROCKIN' AROUND THE CHRISTMAS TREE

Written by Johnny Marks and first recorded by Brenda Lee in 1958, this song has been covered by hundreds of artists. Kim Wilde, and comedian Mel Smith did their own comedy version for Comic Relief. It reached #3 in the UK Chart, and #9 in Norway, not surprisingly, a one hit wonder.

MENTAL AS ANYTHING - LIVE IT UP

Written by band member Greedy Smith (Andrew McArthur Smith), these Australian rockers were no strangers to the Australian charts before hitting it huge with Live it Up. The track was included on the soundtrack of Crocodile Dundee, and it sold all over the world. The song reached #3 in the Billboard Hot 100 and the UK, #2 in Australia and Ireland, #4 in Norway, #6 in Germany and New Zealand, #15 in Austria and #20 in Sweden.

MICHAEL CRAWFORD - THE MUSIC OF THE NIGHT

Michael Patrick Smith, CBE, is possibly better known in Britain for his comedy role as the hapless Frank Spencer in Some Mother's Do 'Ave 'Em. In 1986, he assumed the lead role in The Phantom of the Opera, taking this single to #7 in the UK Chart.

Weird OHW Fact... He played the role over 1300 times, in London, Broadway and Los Angeles.

MIDNIGHT OIL - BEDS ARE BURNING

Reached #1 in Canada, New Zealand, South Africa.

Written by band members Rob Hirst, Jim Moginie and Peter Garrett, this was the song that gave the Australian band world attention. It reached #1 in New Zealand, South Africa and Canada, but surprisingly just #6 in their native land. It also reached #3 in the Netherlands, #5 in France, #6 in the United Kingdom, #11 in Ireland and #17 in the United States and Sweden.

Subsequent singles were hits in most countries (including Truganini, #29 UK) but they never reached inside the Billboard top 40 again (Blue Sky Mine reached #47).

THE NYLONS - KISS HIM GOODBYE

This a cappella group from Toronto, Ontario, Canada, have covered many popular songs. The only charting single got to #12 in the Billboard Hot 100, and #21 in Canada.

THE OTHER ONES - HOLIDAY
Formed in Berlin, this mixed Australian/German band hit it worldwide with their first single. Holiday reached #29 in the Billboard Hot 100, #4 in Germany, #10 in New Zealand, #13 in Austria, and #22 in Switzerland. They disbanded in 1990.

THE PARTLAND BROTHERS - SOUL CITY
G.P. Partland and Chris Partland, a Canadian rock duo from Toronto, Ontario, are probably best remembered for their only charting hit. Soul City reached #27 in the Billboard Hot 100, and #27 in Canada.
Weird OHW Fact... G.P. Partland was a policeman before hitting the music business.

THE PSYCHEDELIC FURS - HEARTBREAK BEAT
Written by band members Richard Butler, John Ashton, and Tim Butler, and probably best known for their song, pretty in Pink, this was the London band's only US hit. From the album, Midnight to Midnight, it reached #26 in the Billboard Hot 100.

RAINMAKERS - LET MY PEOPLE GO GO
This Kansas City, Missouri rock band is famous for not having a single in their own country. Let My People Go–Go was a hit in the UK, reaching #18 in the UK Charts.
Weird OHW Fact... The band went on to be more famous in Norway than any other country. Oh the fickle ways of the music business.

ROBERT CRAY BAND - SMOKING GUN
Written by Robert Cray, Bruce Bromberg and Richard Cousins, this song reached #2 on the Billboard Album Rock Tracks chart, and got to #22 in the mainstream Billboard Hot 100.
For this song, Cray was nominated for the 1987 MTV Video Music Awards for Best New Artist.

SHIRLEY MURDOCK - AS WE LAY

Written by Larry Troutman and Billy Beck, it was recorded on her debut album. A regular visitor to the R&B Charts, this song was the American singer/songwriter's only mainstream hit. It reached #23 in the Billboard Hot 100.

SPAGNA - CALL ME

Written by Giorgio Spagna, Alfredo Larry Pignagnoli and Ivana Spagna, this was the Italian singer's biggest hit. It reached #2 in Italy and the UK, #3 in Ireland, #4 in the Netherlands, France and Norway, #7 in Switzerland, and #8 in Sweden.

Although it never charted in the Billboard Hot 100, Billboard ranked it as the #43 song of 1987.

STEVE "SILK" HURLEY - JACK YOUR BODY

Reached #1 in Ireland and the UK.

Written by Steve Hurley, it was recorded on his only album, Hold on to Your Dream. It topped both the UK and Irish Charts,

Weird OHW Fact... It was the first UK #1 single to get most of its sales in 12" format.

Weird OHW Fact... Busy working hard on the album, Hurley had to be told that his single had reached #1.

Weird OHW Fact... It was the only UK #1 not to be played on radio 1 before it reached the top of the chart.

STEVE WALSH - I FOUND LOVIN'

This British disc jockey jumped to the other side of the studio to record his only hit. His version of the Fatback Band's, I Found Lovin, reached #9 in the UK Charts.

Weird OHW Fact... Walsh died after a car crash in Ibiza, Spain, the following year.

Weird OHW Fact... Ironically, his last chart entry (#44 UK) was Ain't No Stopping Us Now.

THE SYSTEM - DON'T DISTURB THIS GROOVE

Written by synth/pop duo David Frank and Mic Murphy, this was recorded on the album of the same name. It topped the R&B Chart and reached #4 in the Billboard Hot 100.

TAFFY - I LOVE MY RADIO
Written by Claudio Cecchetto, Graziano Pegoraro and Pier Michele Bozzetti, it was recorded by American disco singer Taffy, (Katherine Quaye). It reached #5 in Italy in 1985, then #6 in the UK in late 1986. It also reached #6 in the US Dance Chart, #26 in Austria, and #35 in Germany.

TIMOTHY B. SCHMIT - BOYS NIGHT OUT
From his second solo album, Schmit is probably better known as the bass player for The Eagles. His only solo chart hit reached #25 in the Billboard Hot 100.
Weird OHW Fact... Schmit played on... Crosby, Stills and Nash's, Southern Cross, and Don Henley's, Dirty Laundry.

T'PAU - HEART AND SOUL
Reached #1 in Canada.
Written by band members Carol Ann Decker and Ronald Rogers, this English band's first single hit the worldwide charts with gusto. Partly because of its use in a jeans commercial, Heart and Soul topped the Canadian chart, and reached #4 in the Billboard Hot 100, the UK, and Ireland, and top 20 in most major world charts. Although their 'follow-up' single topped many charts, for some reason it did nothing in the USA, making them a one hit wonder with this song.
Weird OHW Fact... The band is named after the Star Trek character.

WA WA NEE - SUGAR FREE
Written by band singer Paul Gray, this Australian band, although they charted many times in their home land, only had one US hit. Sugar Free reached #35 in the Billboard Hot 100, and #10 in Australia.

WAX - BRIDGE TO YOUR HEART
Written by the duo; American singer-songwriter Andrew Gold and 10cc bass player Graham Gouldman, this was a great start to their

partnership. It reached #12 in the UK Charts, #8 in Spain, #9 in Sweden, and just missed breaking America, #43 in the Billboard Hot 100. They never charted again.

WHEN IN ROME – THE PROMISE
Written by band members Clive Farrington, Michael Floreale and Andrew Mann, in true one hit wonder style, this British band scored with their first single from their debut album... then vanished without trace. The single reached #11 in the Billboard Hot 100. The follow-up, Heaven Knows, only got to #95.

WORLD PARTY - SHIP OF FOOLS (SAVE ME FROM TOMORROW)
Written by Karl Wallinger, who was the one man band known as World Party. Formerly of the band, Waterboys, the song was released from his debut album, Private Revolution. It reached #27 in the Billboard Hot 100, #4 in Australia, and just missed the UK chart (#42).

ZODIAC MINDWARP & THE LOVE REACTION - PRIME MOVER
This British heavy rock band had a surprise hit with Prime Mover. It reached #18 in the UK Charts, but their heavy style was not mainstream.
Weird OHW Fact... Supposedly the song was inspired by Hawkwind's, Quark, Strangeness and Charm... basically, I don't see the connection,

OH SO CLOSE... BUT NO CIGAR...

SPEAR OF DESTINY - NEVER TAKE ME ALIVE
This British conglomeration have had many member changes, but they're not one hit wonders. Yes, the single, Never Take me Alive, got to #14 in the UK Charts, but a later single, So In Love With You, reached #36.

WESTWORLD - SONIC BOOM BOY
This British electronic rock band are usually known as one hit wonders; their biggest hit reached #11 in the UK Charts. However, as their position in this book indicates, this is not the case. The follow-up single,

Ba-Na-Na-Bam-Boo, got to #37 just a few months later. Sorry guys, you just blew it!

Weird OHW Fact... the band are named after the sci-fi movie, Westworld, starring Yul Brunner.

1988...

As The Phantom of the Opera, the longest running Broadway play, opens, the year begins...

The Winter Olympics are held in Calgary, a new British political party is formed, the Liberal Democrats, Sonny Bono is elected mayor of Palm Springs, Piper Alpha is destroyed in the North Sea, the Summer Olympics are held in Seoul, Pan Am 103 is blown up over Lockerbie, Scotland.

ADVENTURES - BROKEN LAND

Written by band guitarist Pat Gribben, this was the band's biggest hit, making them one hit wonders everywhere but Ireland. Broken Land reached #20 in the UK, #8 in Ireland, and #25 in Italy. The follow-up, Drowning in the Sea of Love, reached #15 in Ireland.

Weird OHW Fact... Despite its mediocre chart showing, the song was the most-played song on BBC Radio 1 in 1988.

ANGRY ANDERSON - SUDDENLY (WEDDING THEME FROM 'NEIGHBOURS')

From the Australian Rock band, Rose Tattoo, Gary Stephen "Angry" Anderson found himself with a hit on his hands when a track from his second solo album, Beats From a Distant Drum, was used as the wedding theme on Aussie TV soap, Neighbours. Kylie and Jason's wedding took Suddenly to #3 in the UK, #2 in Australia, #3 in Ireland, #11 in New Zealand, and a surprise #35 in the Billboard Hot 100.

Weird OHW Fact... the song was stopped being #1 in Australia by Kylie Minogue's debut single, Locomotion.

BARDEUX - WHEN WE KISS

This American dance duo tried hard not to be a one hit wonder. Their first single, Three Time Lover, hit #10 on Hot Dance Singles, and the second single, Magic Carpet Ride shot to #5 in the same chart, hitting #81 in the Billboard Hot 100. When We Kiss got to #36 in the Billboard Hot 100, but the success had gone.

BOBBY MCFERRIN - DON'T WORRY BE HAPPY

Reached #1 in Australia, Austria, Germany, U.S.A. and Canada.

Written by Bobby McFerrin, it became the first a cappella song to reach #1 in the Billboard Hot 100; the recording contained no musical instruments, just mouth noises. It topped charts all over the world, and became McFerrin's best seller by far. It also reached #2 in the UK, Belgium, Netherlands, New Zealand, Sweden, and Switzerland, and #3 in Ireland.

Weird OHW Fact... Used by George Bush on his campaign, McFerrin supposedly dropped the song from his repertoire.

Weird OHW Fact... The title is taken from a famous quotation by Indian mystic and sage, Meher Baba.

BOY MEETS GIRL - WAITING FOR A STAR TO FALL

Reached #1 in Canada.

Written by the duo, Shannon Rubicam and George Merrill, it was offered to both Whitney Houston and Belinda Carlisle, but when they refused, the duo recorded it on their second album, Reel Life. It reached #1 in the Billboard Adult Contemporary Chart, and #5 in the Billboard Hot 100, #5 in Ireland, #22 in Germany, #25 in New Zealand, and #35 in Australia.

BREATHE - HANDS TO HEAVEN

School friends from Hampshire, England, this band had considerable success in the Billboard Hot 100, with five Top 40 entries. In their native UK, however, just one song charted. Hands To Heaven reached #2 in the Billboard Hot 100, #4 in the UK, #10 in New Zealand, #14 in Sweden, and #29 in Germany. Amazingly the only country listed above where they are NOT a one hit wonder, is USA.

BRYAN FERRY - KISS AND TELL

Written by Bryan Ferry, the vocalist for Roxy Music, it would be the second single from his album Bête Noire. The song reached #31 in the Billboard Hot 100, but only a disappointing #41 in his native UK.

BVSMP - I NEED YOU

This American hip hop group had three hit singles, the most remembered being their debut, I Need You. The song reached #3 in the UK and Germany, #7 in Ireland and Netherlands, #13 in Belgium, #14 in Sweden. Their follow-ups did not chart as high.

Weird OHW Fact... B.V.S.M.P. is short for Baby Virgo Shocking Mister P. (Don't ask me why.)

CHERYL PEPSII RILEY - THANKS FOR MY CHILD

Born in Brooklyn, New York, Cheryl Ann Riley worked as a nurse for handicapped children before her singing career. Thanks for My Child was the first single, and the only one to break into the Billboard Hot 100 (#38). The song did reach #1 on the Hot Black Singles chart.

CLIMIE FISHER - LOVE CHANGES (EVERYTHING)

Written by the duo, Simon Climie and Rob Fisher and Dennis Morganno, this song was not a rapid riser. Originally meant for Rod Stewart (who refused it), the duo recorded it themselves. It did not fare well, reaching just #67 in the UK and #30 in The Netherlands. On re-release, however, it went worldwide. It reached #2 in the UK and South Africa, #7 in Germany, #8 in Switzerland, #15 in Austria, and #23 in Australia. In USA, however, where the band would have no further success, it reached #23 in the Billboard hot 100.

Weird OHW Fact... Fisher co-wrote Rick Astley's, Cry for Help, UK #7.

THE CHURCH – UNDER THE MILKY WAY

Written by band member Steve Kilbey and Karin Jansson, this song was included on the album, Starfish. From Sydney, Australia, the band took the song to #24 in the Billboard Hot 100, #22 in Australia, and #25 in New Zealand.

Weird OHW Fact... There are some weird bagpipes in the song somewhere, but they're like someone stepped on the bag by mistake.

Weird OHW Fact... In 1990, they hit the US Alt Chart with, Metropolis, but never hit mainstream again.

DAN REED NETWORK - RITUAL

From Portland, Oregon, this funk/rock band had one minor hit in the USA, and later peppered the UK charts. Their one stateside hit was

Ritual, reaching #38 in the Billboard Chart. In 1990, they one-hit-wondered (it's a verb, trust me) the UK with the song, Stardate 1990.

THE DEELE - TWO OCCASIONS
Written by Kenneth 'Babyface' Edmonds, Darnell Bristol and Sid Johnson, it was released by the Cincinnati, Ohio group for the band's third album, Eyes of a Stranger. As well as top 10 in other US Charts, including R&B, it rose to #10 in the Billboard Hot 100.

DENISE LOPEZ - SAYIN' SORRY (DON'T MAKE IT RIGHT)
From Queens, New York, Lopez achieved modest success, bubbling under the Billboard Charts for years. Winning an album deal with A&M Records, Truth in Disguise was released, giving her only hit. The song reached #31 in the Billboard Hot 100. She continued to make music, but never charted again.

DESIRELESS - VOYAGE VOYAGE (REMIX)
Reached #1 in Germany, Norway and Spain.
Sold more than 2 million copies.
Written by Dominique Albert Dubois and Jean-Michel Rivat, it was recorded by French singer Desireless. Sung entirely in French, it was a European hit, eventually hitting the top of three charts and peaking in the UK at #5, #4 in Ireland, and Top 10 in the rest of the major European charts.

EDIE BRICKELL & NEW BOHEMIANS - WHAT I AM
Reached #1 in Canada.
Written by band members Edie Brickell and Kenny Withrow, the song was recorded for the debut album of this Dallas band, Shooting Rubberbands at the Stars. It reached #7 in the Billboard Hot 100, #11 in New Zealand, #18 in Australia, #23 in Ireland, and #31 in the UK, becoming a one hit wonder almost everywhere.
Billboard ranked the song as #84 of 1989.
Weird OHW Fact... in 1990, Edie left the band and married Paul Simon.

E.U. - DA BUTT

Written by Marcus Miller, this song was recorded by D.C.-based go-go band E.U. (Experience Unlimited). The song was their only major hit, reaching #35 in the Billboard Hot 100. Spike Lee directed the official video.

FREIHEIT - KEEPING THE DREAM ALIVE
Freiheit, or to give them their full name, Münchener Freiheit, are named after a square in Munich, Germany. Taken from their fifth studio album, the single, Keeping the Dream Alive, reached #14 in the UK Charts.
Weird OHW Fact... In German, the song is called; So lang' man Träume noch leben kann.

FUNKY WORM - HUSTLE! TO THE MUSIC
This British project was assembled by record producer, Mark Brydon, taking its name from the song, Funky Worm, by the Ohio Players. Their only hit was the track, Hustle! To the Music, which reached #1 in the US Dance chart before reaching #13 in the UK Singles Chart.

GIANT STEPS - ANOTHER LOVER
Written by band members Colin Campsie, and George McFarlane and producer Gardner Cole, it was recorded for the debut album of the English duo. It reached #13 in the Billboard Hot 100, and featured Top 10 in the US Dance, Club Play, and Cash Box charts. Their follow-up single, Into You, did not chart so high; #58 in 1989.

HARRY ENFIELD - LOADSAMONEY (DOIN' UP THE HOUSE)
Born in Sussex, English Comedian Henry Richard Enfield charted early in his career. Loadsamoney (Doin' Up the House) reached #4 in the UK Charts. In the song, his character is an obnoxious Cockney plasterer boasting about how much money he earned.

HITHOUSE - JACK TO THE SOUND OF THE UNDERGROUND
Dutch DJ Peter Slaghuis worked under the stage-name Hithouse. He helped bring House Music to Europe, and eventually had a hit. The song reached #14 in the UK Chart. His follow-ups did not chart.
Weird OHW Fact... Hithouse is a literal translation of his surname, Slaghuis.

Weird OHW Fact... His career was brought to an abrupt halt in 1991, when his car crashed into an oncoming truck at 136mph.

HUMANOID - STAKKER HUMANOID

Humanoid is a project by video artists Mark McClean and Colin Scott, and music man Brian Dougans. The song reached #17 in the UK Singles Chart, but the partnership soon dissolved.
Weird OHW Fact... Supposedly the name Stakker was 'added' to the song's title to avoid contractual problems.

IVAN NEVILLE - NOT JUST ANOTHER GIRL

From the first of four solo albums, If My Ancestors Could See Me Now, Neville's debut single reached #26 in the Billboard Hot 100. It was featured on the movie, My Stepmother Is an Alien.
Weird OHW Fact... Ivan is the son of Aaron Neville.

JACK'N'CHILL - THE JACK THAT HOUSE BUILT

Written by band member Vlad Naslas, this British house duo consisted of Naslas and Edward Stratton. The song reached #6 in the UK Singles Chart, and stayed in the charts for 18 weeks.

JANE WIEDLIN - RUSH HOUR

Written by Jane Wiedlin, (Jane Marie Genevieve Wiedlin) and Peter Rafelson, it was included in this Wisconsin's second album. It reached #9 in the Billboard Hot 100, #8 in Ireland, #12 in the UK Chart, and #31 in New Zealand.
Weird OHW Fact... Wiedlin was the guitarist in the band, The Go Go's.

J. J. FAD - SUPERSONIC

From Rialto, California, this band originally chose their name by their first initials; Juana, Juanita, Fatima, Anna, and Dania. The song, written by the band reached #10 in the Dance/Club Play Songs and #22 on the Hot R&B/Hip-Hop Charts. More importantly, it also reached #30 in the Billboard Hot 100.

KRUSH - HOUSE ARREST

Krush, a UK dance/music group, had a series of minor hits, but their big break came with House Arrest. The sampled song reached #3 in the UK Charts, but the band did not chart again.

MORRIS DAY - FISHNET

A Prince protégé, and former lead singer of The Time, Morris Day's only solo contribution to the US Charts was his one single, Fishnet. It reached #23 in the Billboard Hot 100, and #12 on the Dance Charts.

MORRIS MINOR AND THE MAJORS - STUTTER RAP (NO SLEEP 'TIL BEDTIME)

Written by Tony Hawks (Antony Gordon Hawksworth), and performed with Paul Boross and Phil Judge, the parody novelty song mimics the Beastie Boys 'No Sleep 'Til Brooklyn. The song reached #4 in the UK, #2 in Australia, and #14 in Canada.

Weird OHW Fact... In the video, John Deacon (Queen Bassist) makes a cameo appearance; he's wearing a blue wig and playing the guitar solo.

Weird OHW Fact... In Australia, they actually had a second charting single. This Is the Chorus, which parodied Stock/Aitken/Waterman, reached #22.

Weird OHW Fact... On the strength of the song's success, they got a TV series, Morris Minor's Marvellous Motors. It only ran for one season.

OFRA HAZA - IM NIN ALU

Reached #1 in Germany, Norway, Spain and Switzerland.
Sold over 3 million copies worldwide.
This traditional 17th century Hebrew poem was set to music by Ofra Haza as early as 1978. Topping many charts, it did well worldwide, reaching #2 in Sweden and Austria, #6 in France, and #15 in the UK. It also reached top 20 in both Billboard's Hot Dance Club Play chart and the Hot Modern Rock Tracks.

PATRICK SWAYZE FEATURING WENDY FRASER - SHE'S LIKE THE WIND

Written by Patrick Swayze and Stacy Widelitz, this power ballad has main vocals by Swayze himself. It reached #3 in the Billboard Hot 100,

#4 in Ireland, #6 in Australia, #7 in Norway, #8 in Sweden, #17 in the UK, and top 20 in most other major music charts.

Weird OHW Fact... Written in 1984, it was meant to be on the soundtrack of the movie, Grandview, U.S.A., and about Jamie Lee Curtis' character.

PEBBLES - GIRLFRIEND

Written by Kenneth Edmonds and Antonio Reid, the song was originally intended for Vanessa Williams, but pebbles (born Perri Arlette McKissack) offered the writers more money and two cars. Girlfriend reached #5 in the Billboard Hot 100, #8 in the UK, #9 in Ireland#17 in Canada, and #23 in New Zealand.

Pebbles has had a formidable career since, but this was the only single to chart in the UK and Ireland.

Weird OHW Fact... Unsurprisingly, Vanessa Williams never spoke to those writers again.

THE PRIMITIVES - CRASH

Written by band members Paul Court, Steve Dullaghan, and Tracy Spencer, it was recorded for the Coventry band's debut album, Lovely. It reached #5 in the UK Chart, and #15 in South Africa. It also reached #3 in the U.S. Modern Rock Tracks Chart.

It has since charted by cover versions by Chloë, and Matt Willis.

THE PROCLAIMERS - I'M GONNA BE (500 MILES)

Reached #1 in Australia, Iceland and New Zealand.

Sold more than 2 million copies.

Written and performed by Scottish twins Charlie and Craig Reid, it was released as the duo's first single from their album, Sunshine on Leith. It reached #11 in the UK Chart, and #14 in Ireland, but hit down under with a bang, topping both charts. In 1993, after its inclusion in the soundtrack of the movie, Benny & Joon, a re-release reached #3 in the Billboard Chart, #4 in Canada, and #5 in Austria.

Weird OHW Fact... Their favorite Football team, Edinburgh's Hibernian F.C., play Sunshine on Leith at every game, and it has become the team's anthem.

ROB BASE AND DJ E-Z ROCK - IT TAKES TWO

These New York rappers Rob Base and DJ E-Z Rock mixed a song that would inspire many cover versions. The 'original' reached #36 in the Billboard Hot 100, and #24 in the UK Charts.

ROBBIE ROBERTSON - SOMEWHERE DOWN THE CRAZY RIVER

Written by Robbie Robertson, who was born Jaime Royal Robertson, on the Six Nations Reserve near Toronto, Ontario. This lazy track was produced by Daniel Lanois and Peter Gabriel, and it rose to #15 in the UK Charts, and #24 in the Mainstream Rock Tracks Chart.

ROBIN BECK - THE FIRST TIME

Reached #1 in the UK, Australia, Netherlands, Germany, Ireland, Norway, and Switzerland.

Written by Gavin Spencer, Tom Anthony, and Terry Boyle, this song was originally destined to be a Coca Cola commercial. After the commercial ran for the first time, they released it as a single; in USA it bombed. In the UK, it took off. Bam, topped charts, and rocketed Robin Beck to stardom. As well as chart-topping, it reached #2 in Sweden and Spain, #4 in France.

Weird OHW Fact... In 2006, Swedish band, Sunblock, covered the song with Robin Beck, taking it to #9 in the UK Singles Chart.

SABRINA - BOYS (SUMMERTIME LOVE)

Reached #1 in France and Switzerland.

Sabrina, born Norma Sabrina Salerno, was every schoolboy's dream and this Italian model had two hit European singles. The first, Boys (Summertime Love), reached #1 in France and Switzerland, #2 in Belgium, Germany and Finland, #3 in the UK, Ireland, Italy, Norway and Spain. The second single, Hot Girl, did well in Europe, but not in the UK, making her a one hit wonder there.

Weird OHW Fact... The video shows Sabrina dancing in a pool as her bikini slips down, revealing her nipples. It is MUCH downloaded on the internet. Yup, for research purposes, I had to check it out. (I am devoted to my work)

SCARLETT AND BLACK - YOU DON'T KNOW

Written by the duo Robin Hild and Sue West (Scarlett and Black), the trach was included on their debut album. The song reached #20 in the Billboard Hot 100, whilst also achieving some success with Billboard's Dance and Hot Dance charts. Their follow-ups did not chart.

STAR TURN ON 45 (PINTS) - PUMP UP THE BITTER (BRUTAL MIX)

This English novelty musical ensemble only had one hit, modelled loosely on MARRS Pump Up The Volume. It had a spot on Top of the Pops, and reached #12 in the UK Charts.

STRYPER - HONESTLY

Written by band leader Michael Sweet, this Christian rock band from Orange County, California strode into the Top 40. The power ballad reached #23 in the Billboard Hot 100, and became their best known song.

SUAVE - MY GIRL

From Los Angeles, California, Suave (born Waymond Anderson) reached the charts when he covered the Temptations song, My Girl. His version reached, #20 in the Billboard Hot 100. His follow-ups had some success in the ZR&B Charts, but he did not chart mainstream again.

TAJA SEVELLE - LOVE IS CONTAGIOUS

Born Nancy Richardson, this singer and musician from Minneapolis, Minnesota, got her big break on her first single. Love Is Contagious reached #7 in the UK Charts, and #20 in Netherlands. It only reached #62 in the Billboard Hot 100. Her follow-up, Wouldn't You Love to Love Me?, did badly, leaving her a one hit wonder.

TIMELORDS - DOCTORIN' THE TARDIS

Reached #1 in the UK and New Zealand.
Bill Drummond (alias King Boy D) and Jimmy Cauty (alias Rockman Rock) are visible in various guises in the UK Charts; The KLF, The Justified Ancients of Mu Mu, The JAMs and The Timelords, being just some. This single went straight to the UK and NZ #1 slot, #2 in Australia, #4 in Ireland, #7 in Belgium, #10 in Norway. It did reach Top

20 in the US Dance and Hot Modern Charts, but just #66 in the Billboard Hot 100.

Weird OHW Fact... The song features samples of The Sweet's Blockbuster, and Gary Glitter's Rock and Roll Parts 1 and 2.

Weird OHW Fact... With an American police car driving round Britain, and daleks in the video, who can forget this?

TIMES TWO - STRANGE BUT TRUE

Written by duo Shanti Jones and Johnny Dollar, (from Point Reyes, California) this band was hired to support Debbie Gibson's tour. The single from their album, X2, reached #21 in the Billboard Hot 100. It would be their only US hit.

Weird OHW Fact... Cecelia, a cover of the Simon and Garfunkel song, reached #1 in New Zealand, making them a one hit wonder there too.

TRACY CHAPMAN - FAST CAR

Reached #1 in Belgium, Canada, Ireland, and the Netherlands

Yes, perhaps I'm embarrassed to admit it, but American singer-songwriter Tracy Chapman is a one hit wonder in the UK. Her debut single from her debut album, made more famous for an appearance on the Nelson Mandela 70th Birthday Tribute, shot her to worldwide stardom. Fast Car reached #1 in Belgium, Canada, Ireland, and the Netherlands, #4 in the UK, and #6 in the Billboard Hot 100.

Her subsequent hit singles, Give Me One Reason, Talkin' 'bout a Revolution, and Crossroads, did not chart in the UK.

TWO MEN A DRUM MACHINE AND A TRUMPET - (I'M) TIRED OF GETTING PUSHED AROUND

This song was written by Fine Young Cannibals band members Andy Cox and David Steele between their first two FYC albums. With a new sound and name, they reached #18 in the UK Charts, and Top 20 in the US Dance Charts.

WEE PAPA GIRL RAPPERS - WEE RULE

Twin sisters Sandra and Samantha Lawrence made up the Female rap duo Wee Papa Girl Rappers. Their biggest hit was Wee Rule, which reached #1 in Belgium, #2 in the Netherlands, #4 in Ireland and

Switzerland, #6 in the UK Chart, #10 in Germany, #12 in Austria, #13 in Sweden and #17 in New Zealand. Their earlier hit reached #21 in the UK, #15 in the Netherlands, and #28 in Belgium. Subtract one list from the other and you have the list of countries they are one hit wonders in.

Weird OHW Fact... Before finding solo fame, the twins were backing singers for Feargal Sharkey.

ZIGGY MARLEY AND THE MELODY MAKERS - TOMORROW PEOPLE

The children of Bob and Rita Marley, were formed into a band, and signed by Virgin Records. Their only US Chart single was Tomorrow People, which reached #39 in the Billboard Hot 100. The follow-up, Tumblin' Down, reached #1 on the Hot Dance Music chart, but it never breached the mainstream chart.

OH SO CLOSE... BUT NO CIGAR...

GLEN GOLDSMITH - DREAMING

From Buckinghamshire in England, Goldsmith is often thought of as a one hit wonder. However, he's not even close. In 1987, I Won't Cry, reached #34 in the UK Charts, and the follow-up, What You See Is What You Get, got one place higher. Now his big hit, Dreaming, did reach the dizzy heights of #12 in the UK, but he's hardly a one hit wonder.

THE MAC BAND, FEATURING THE MCCAMPBELL BROTHERS - ROSES ARE RED

Written and produced by LA Reid and Kenneth 'Babyface' Edmonds, peppering the US R&B Charts, these four brothers from Flint, Michigan, are probably best remembered for their only real hit. Roses are Red reached #8 in the UK Chart.

However... the follow-up, Stalemate, reached #40, breaking the criteria for a one hit wonder. Sorry lads.

1989...

As George H. W. Bush is sworn in as the 41st President of the USA, the year begins...

Thomas & Friends airs in the U.S., the last Soviet Union forces leave Afghanistan, Thatcher's Poll tax is levied in Scotland, riots in Tiananmen Square, Beijing, force China to declare martial law, Hurricane Hugo devastates the Caribbean, Bette Davis dies at 81, and Taylor Swift is born.

A GUY CALLED GERALD - VOODOO RAY

Written by Aniff Akinola, and Gerald Simpson (A Guy Called Gerald), Voodoo Ray is an acid house single sampling British comedians Peter Cook and Dudley Moore. From Manchester, England, Simpson reached #12 in the UK Chart.

ALANNAH MYLES - BLACK VELVET

Reached number 1 in USA, Sweden, Switzerland, and Norway.
1 million sold, and 4 million airplays.
Written by Christopher Ward (Alannah's Boyfriend) and producer David Tyson, it topped half a dozen charts and reached #2 in UK, Austria, Belgium, Germany and New Zealand, #3 in Australia and Netherlands, #4 in Ireland, a disappointing #10 in her native Canada, and Top Ten in most major music charts.
Billboard ranked it as the #18 song of 1989.

BAND AID II - DO THEY KNOW IT'S CHRISTMAS?

Driven by Bob Geldof's phone call to the Stock, Aitken and Waterman team, the young stars flocked, the song got re-recorded, and money was raised for the ongoing plight in Ethiopia. The re-do reached #1 in Ireland and the UK, #8 in New Zealand, and #30 in Australia. Not quite the same impact as the original, but a good effort.
Weird OHW Fact... The only persons to perform on the original song and re-do were Bananarama.

THE BELLE STARS - IKO IKO

This British girl group from London had a hit with their version of the Dixie Cups 1965 song. It was included in the soundtrack for the movie, Rain Man, and reached #14 in the Billboard Hot 100, and #35 in their native UK.

Weird OHW Fact... Their soundtrack inclusion is in the first few minutes of the movie.

BIZ MARKIE – JUST A FRIEND

Written by American hip hop artist Biz Markie, he released it as the first single from the album, The Biz Never Sleeps. It became his biggest hit, reaching #9 in the Billboard Hot 100, #3 in the US Rap Chart.

Billboard ranked it as the #94 song of 1989.

BOYS CLUB - I REMEMBER HOLDING YOU

From Minneapolis, Minnesota, Boys Club was pop duo Gene Hunt and Joe Pasquale. Their one hit was, I Remember Holding You, which reached #9 in the U.S. Billboard Hot 100.

DEON ESTUS - HEAVEN HELP ME

Born Jeffery Deon Estus, this Michigan musician is probably best known as the bass player in pop group Wham! His solo album, Spell, spawned three singles, the most noticeable was Heaven Help Me, with the help of George Michael's vocals, which reached #5 in the Billboard Hot 100.

EDELWEISS - BRING ME EDELWEISS

Reached #1 in Austria, Sweden and Switzerland.

Sold more than 5 million copies.

This Austrian electronic dance band is best known for their multi-mixed smash hit, Bring Me Edelweiss. Borrowing heavily from ABBA's SOS, the song topped three European charts, and reached #2 in Germany and the Netherlands, #5 in the UK, #7 in US Dance Chart, and #24 in US Rock Chart.

GRAYSON HUGH - TALK IT OVER

American singer songwriter Hugh signed to RCA Records in 1987; it would be his one road to fifteen-minute fame. His second album spawned three singles, only one of which charted Top 40. Talk It Over reached #19 in the Billboard Hot 100, #9 in US Adult Contemporary, and #4 in Australia.

HALO JAMES - COULD HAVE TOLD YOU SO
This short-lived London Pop band only released one album, Witness. The only hit from the album reached #6 in the UK Charts, and #3 in Ireland. The single spent 11 weeks in the UK Chart, but their other singles were not so successful, Wanted, topping out at #45, and Baby at #43.

THE JEFF HEALEY BAND - ANGEL EYES
Written by band members John Hiatt, and Fred Koller, the song would be recorded on their first album, See the Light. Perennial chart hitters in Healey's native Canada, this would be the only US hit for the Toronto band. It reached #5 in the Billboard Hot 100, and #16 in Canada, promising a great US Career. The success was never repeated.
Billboard ranked the song as #70 of 1989.

JIMMY HARNEN WITH SYNCH - WHERE ARE YOU NOW?
Written by Jimmy Harnen, and Rich Congdon, this power ballad was recorded by the Pennsylvania-based band, and released in 1986. It only reached #77, and the band was dropped by Colombia Records. In 1989, the song was featured on the Disney Channel sitcom, Liv and Maddie. The subsequent re-release under the new name, Jimmy Harnen with Synch, took it to #10 in the Billboard Hot 100.

KAOMA – LAMBADA
Reached #1 in Austria, Belgium, Finland, France, Germany, Italy, Netherlands Norway, Spain, Sweden, and Switzerland.
Sold over 15 million copies.
French pop group Kaoma, with guest vocals by Brazilian, Loalwa Braz, hit it big right out of the blocks. First single from their debut album blew their world apart. It reached #1 in eleven countries and #4 in the UK, and Ireland, #5 in Australia, #10 in New Zealand, #12 in Japan, and a lowly #46 in the Billboard Hot 100.

Weird OHW Fact... Kaoma's version was unauthorized by the original writers, Bolivian pop group Los Kjarkas, and they successfully sued for damages in 1990.

KIX - DON'T CLOSE YOUR EYES

Written by Bob Halligan Jr, John Palumbo, and Donnie Purnell, Maryland rockers Kix recorded this power ballad on their fourth studio album, Blow My Fuse. It reached #11 in the Billboard Hot 100, a height they never reached again.

Weird OHW Fact... The lyrics are a plea for the listener not to commit suicide.

KON KAN - I BEG YOUR PARDON

Written by Barry Harris, Joe South, this song by Canadian synth/pop band features many factions of other songs. Released as their debut single, it reached #3 in the Netherlands, #5 in the UK, #7 in New Zealand, #8 in Germany, and #19 in Canada.

L.A. GUNS - THE BALLAD OF JAYNE

Not surprisingly formed in Los Angeles, California, and named after their guitarist, Tracii Guns, this rock group scored in the late 80's, then faded. From their album, Locked and Loaded, this song got to #25 in the Rock Chart, and #33 in the Billboard Hot 100. Their next singles did not fly quite so high; It's Over Now, peaked at #62.

LIZA MINELLI - LOSING MY MIND

Written by Stephen Sondheim in 1971 for the musical, Follies, this 'Pet Shop Boys' re-vamped version with the legendary Liza at the helm, sailed to a new worldwide audience. It reached #2 in Ireland, #6 in the UK, #7 in Spain, #15 in Belgium, #17 in Germany, #19 in Austria, and #23 in New Zealand.

Weird OHW Fact... Although it hit #11 of the US Maxi Chart, and #26 on the US Dance Chart, it did not enter the Billboard Hot 100.

LOVE AND ROCKETS – SO ALIVE

Reached #1 in Canada.

Written by band guitarist Daniel Ash, it was recorded on the British band's fourth studio album. It was a minor world hit, topping the Canadian charts, #1 on the Billboard Modern tracks chart, #3 in the Billboard Hot 100, #16 in New Zealand, #24 in Australia, and a disappointing #79 in their native UK.

LYNNE HAMILTON - ON THE INSIDE/THEME FROM PRISONER: CELL BLOCK H

Written by Allan Caswell, an Australian songwriter with more than 1200 published songs to his credit. On the Inside, is the theme song for the Australian soap opera Prisoner (or 'Prisoner: Cell Block H'). A #1 hit in Australia and New Zealand when the show first premiered in 1979, it became a #3 hit in the UK Charts when the series was broadcast in a late-night slot in the UK.

ONE 2 MANY - DOWNTOWN

Reached #1 in Norway.

Flash in the pan Norwegian band, One 2 Many, only made one album, but it spawned a hit single, Downtown, hitting the top of the Norwegian charts for 5 weeks, #29 in Netherlands, #37 in the Billboard Hot 100, and #38 in Belgium.

Weird OHW Fact... By the time the record company was issuing follow-up releases, the band had already split up.

REAL LIFE – SEND ME AN ANGEL

Reached #1 in Germany and New Zealand.

Written by David Sterry and Richard Zatorski for Australian new-wave band, Real Life, it charted quite well in 1983, topping the NZ and German charts, #2 in Switzerland, #6 in Australia and #29 in the Billboard Hot 100. However, a re-vamped edition charted SIX YEARS later... #26 in the Billboard Hot 100, and #22 in New Zealand.

REYNOLDS GIRLS - I'D RATHER JACK

This British vocal duo, comprising sisters Linda and Aisling Reynolds, will always be best known for their hit single, I'd Rather Jack, an irreverent hit at the few awards given to 'current artists... "I'd rather

jack, than Fleetwood Mac". The song, picked up by PWL Records, reached #6 in Ireland, #7 in Belgium, and #8 in the UK.
Weird OHW Fact... After just one hit, The Reynolds Girls were dropped by their PWL label

ROACHFORD - CUDDLY TOY (FEEL FOR ME)
Written by front man Andrew Roachford, it was the first hit by the London band, the second single from their debut album. It reached #4 in the UK, and #25 in the Billboard Hot 100. Regular charters in the UK, it was their only US hit.

ROBIN ZANDER - SURRENDER TO ME
Written by Richard Marx and Ross Vanelli, this power ballad was recorded by Heart's singer Ann Wilson and Cheap Trick's singer, Robin Zander. Spurred by being featured on the soundtrack of the Mel Gibson movie, it reached #6 in the Billboard Hot 100.

ROB N RAZ FEATURING LAILA K - GOT TO GET
Written by Rob n Raz, MC ll Fresh, and Laila K, Got to Get was a huge hit in Europe, reaching Top Ten in most major music charts. It got to #8 in the UK Charts, and reached #49 in the Billboard Hot 100. It also reached #57 in the Australian Chart, staying in the chart for 20 weeks.

SA-FIRE - THINKING OF YOU
Written by Wilma Cosmé (aka Sa-Fire), and Russ DeSalvo, this Puerto Rican singer released it as her third single. It reached #12 in the Billboard Hot 100, and #4 in the Adult Contemporary Chart.

SAM BROWN - STOP
Reached number 1 in Belgium.
Written by Sam Brown, Gregg Sutton, and Bruce Brody, this song charted on its second release, reaching #2 in France and Netherlands, #3 in Austria, #4 in the UK, Ireland and Australia, Top 10 in most other major charts, and notably #9 in Canada, #16 in New Zealand.
Weird OHW Fact... The song featured on the soundtrack of the movie, Bitter Moon.

SHARON BRYANT - LET GO
Sharon Bryant is probably best known as the lead singer for Atlantic Starr. Following a solo career, she eventually had her sole solo hit, Let Go. The song reached #34 in the Billboard Hot 100. The follow-up, Foolish Heart, did not chart.

SHERIFF - WHEN I'M WITH YOU
Reached #1 in USA.

Written by band member Arnold Lanni, this power ballad was released in 1982, reaching #8 in the band's native Canada, a disappointing #61 in the USA. The band, subsequently disillusioned, split up. However, their story didn't end there; a DJ in WKTI in Milwaukee put the song on his playlist, and three months later it was #1 in the US Billboard Hot 100.

Weird OHW Fact... Two of Sheriff's members did not want to re-form to milk the single, but lead singer Freddy Curci and guitarist Steve DeMarchi, formed the band, Alias, and had a #2 single in 1990 with, More Than Words Can Say.

SILVER BULLET - 20 SECONDS TO COMPLY
Silver Bullet, aka Richard David Brown, is a British rapper from London. His first single, Bring Forth the Guillotine, did not chart, but he hit #11 in the UK Charts with his second release.

STARLIGHT - NUMERO UNO
Black Box members Daniele Davoli, Valerio Semplici, and Mirko Limoni created music under many different musical aliases. One such, Starlight, had a single hit with Numero Uno. It reached #9 in the UK Charts.

STEFAN DENNIS - DON'T IT MAKE YOU FEEL GOOD
Australian actor Stefan Dennis is probably best known for his portrayal of Paul Robinson in the soap opera Neighbours. On a hiatus from the show, he tried singing; his only solo hit reached #16 in both the UK and Irish charts.

SYBIL - DON'T MAKE ME OVER
Reached #1 in New Zealand.

Written by Burt Bacharach and Hal David, and previously a hit for Dionne Warwick, American singer/songwriter Sybil Anita Lynch took it back into the charts. It charted high in the Dance and R&B charts, and reached #19 in the UK, and #20 in the Billboard Hot 100. Her follow up, Walk On By, another Bacharach/David composition, did not chart in the USA.

Weird OHW Fact... Her version of, Walk On By, reached #6 in the UK, the highest charting position for this song.

TEN CITY - THAT'S THE WAY LOVE IS

Chicago-based dance trio, Ten City, had a hit on their hands from their debut album, Foundation. The song reached #1 in the US Dance chart, #12 in the R&B Chart, and #8 in the UK Charts.

VAN MORRISON (WITH CLIFF RICHARD) - WHENEVER GOD SHINES HIS LIGHT

Written by Northern Irish Van Morrison, it was recorded as a duet with Cliff Richard for Morrison's album, Avalon Sunset. The song was released in November for the Christmas market, and reached #6 in Ireland, and #20 in the UK Charts.

WATERFRONT - CRY

Written by band member Chris Duffy, this Welsh duo from Cardiff had a hit on both sides of the Atlantic. It reached #17 in the UK Charts, and #10 in the Billboard Hot 100, and #1 in the Adult Contemporary Chart. Their follow-up, Nature Of Love, just reached #70 in the Billboard Hot 100.

OH SO CLOSE... BUT NO CIGAR...

STEVIE NICKS - ROOMS ON FIRE

Written by Stevie Nicks and Rick Nowels, this song almost put Stevie Nicks firmly in the one hit wonder bin. It reached #9 in Canada and #16 in both USA and UK. However, a later single, Sometimes It's a Bitch, got to #40 in the UK, tipping her away from one hit wonder ignominy.

WILL TO POWER   BABY I LOVE YOUR WAY – FREEBIRD/I'M NOT IN LOVE

Reached #1 in Canada, Norway and USA.

This medley by the South Florida band Will to Power is often considered a one hit wonder... but then again, most people are often wrong. Yes, it topped the charts in Canada, Norway and the US Billboard Hot 100, #3 in Ireland, #6 in the UK and New Zealand, #18 in Germany, and #20 in Australia. BUT. Most people forget that in 1990, they also had a minor hit with 10cc's, I'm Not In Love, reaching #7 in the USA, #8 in Norway, #15 in New Zealand, #29 in the UK, and #38 in Australia. No one hit wonder-ship for them.

DID I MISS ONE OUT?

Did I miss a one hit wonder; oh, I know I did a lot of research, but I know I've probably missed more than a few.

Send them to me at kansasscot@aol.com and I'll check them out. If they fit the criteria, I'll include them in future editions.

INDEX: THE ALPHABETIC LIST OF SONGS

Writing an index is always a tricky thing, do I count all the 'the's' in the T section, or do people remember 'The House of the Rising Sun' with the 'The' at the start?

So I made a decision... The 'A's...?

I've left them all in.

And the the's? I've left them all out. If you're looking for The House of the Rising Sun, you'll find it under 'H'.

Okay?

So with the semantics done, here's the alphabetical list of song titles...

THE NUMBERS...

5.7.0.5. (1978) CITY BOY - 5.7.0.5.

5-10-15-20 (25-30 YEARS OF LOVE) (1970) THE PRESIDENTS

7 AND 7 (1966) IS LOVE

7 TEEN (1980) REGENTS

10-9-8 (1984) FACE TO FACE

11TH HOUR MELODY (1956) LOU BUSCH AND HIS ORCHESTRA

19 (1985) PAUL HARDCASTLE

20 SECONDS TO COMPLY (1989) SILVER BULLET

96 TEARS (1966) ? & THE MYSTERIANS

99 LUFTBALLONS (1984) NENA

867-5309/JENNY (1981) TOMMY TUTONE

1900 YESTERDAY (1970) LIZ DAMON'S ORIENT EXPRESS

A...

ABRAHAM, MARTIN AND JOHN (1969) MOMS MABLEY

A CASUAL LOOK (1956) THE SIX TEENS

A FALLEN STAR (1957) JIMMY C NEWMAN

A FIFTH OF BEETHOVEN (1976) WALTER MURPHY AND THE BIG APPLE BAND

AFTERNOON DELIGHT (1976) STARLAND VOCAL BAND

AFTER SCHOOL (1957) RANDY STARR

AFTER THE GOLD RUSH (1974) PRELUDE

A GIRL IN TROUBLE (IS A TEMPORARY THING) (1984) ROMEO VOID

AH! LEAH! (1980) DONNIE IRIS

AIN'T NO STOPPIN' US NOW (1979) MCFADDEN & WHITEHEAD

AIN'T NOTHING GOIN' ON BUT THE RENT (1986) GWEN GUTHRIE

AIN'T UNDERSTANDING MELLOW (1972) BRENDA LEE EAGER

AIRPORT (1978) MOTORS

AIRPORT LOVE THEME (1970) VINCENT BELL

ALABAMA JUBILEE (1955) FERKO STRING BAND

AL DI LÀ (1962) EMILIO PERICOLI

A LITTLE BIT OF SOAP (1961) THE JARMELS

A LITTLE PEACE (1982) NICOLE

ALL ALONG THE WATCHTOWER (1968) THE JIMI HENDRIX EXPERIENCE

ALLEY CAT (1962) BENT FABRIC AND HIS PIANO

ALLEY OOP (1960) DANTE & THE EVERGREENS

ALLEY OOP (1960) THE HOLLYWOOD ARGYLES

ALL I NEED (1985) JACK WAGNER

ALL NIGHT LONG (1983) MARY JANE GIRLS

ALL OUR TOMORROWS (1982) EDDIE SCHWARTZ

ALL OUT OF LOVE (1980) AIR SUPPLY

ALL THE YOUNG DUDES (1972) MOTT THE HOOPLE

ALMOST PARADISE (1957) LOU STEIN

ALMOST PARADISE (LOVE THEME FROM FOOTLOOSE) (1984) MIKE RENO/ANN WILSON

ALMOST PERSUADED (1966) DAVID HOUSTON

ALMOST SUMMER (1978) CELEBRATION FEATURING MIKE LOVE

ALONE (WHY MUST I BE ALONE) (1957) SHEPHERD SISTERS

A LOVER'S HOLIDAY (1980) CHANGE

ALRIGHT NOW (1970) FREE

ALSO SPRACH ZARATHUSTRA (2001) (1973) EUMIR DEODATO

AMAZING GRACE (1972) ROYAL SCOTS DRAGOON GUARDS

AMERICAN CITY SUITE (1972) CASHMAN AND WEST

AMERICANS (A CANADIAN'S OPINION) (1974) BYRON MACGREGOR/GORDON SINCLAIR

AMIE (1975) PURE PRAIRIE LEAGUE

AN AMERICAN TRILOGY (1972) MICKEY NEWBURY

AMIGO (1980) BLACK SLATE

A MILLION TO ONE (1960) JIMMY CHARLES

AMITYVILLE (IT'S THE HOUSE ON THE HILL) (1986) LOVEBUG STARSKI

AND I AM TELLING YOU I'M NOT GOING (1982) JENNIFER HOLLIDAY

ANGELA JONES (1960) JOHNNY FERGUSON

ANGELA JONES (1960) MICHAEL COX

ANGEL BABY (1960) ROSIE AND THE ORIGINALS

ANGEL IN YOUR ARMS (1977) HOT

ANGEL EYES (1989) THE JEFF HEALEY BAND

ANGEL OF THE MORNING (1968) MERRILEE RUSH AND THE TURNABOUTS

ANGEL ON MY SHOULDERS (1961) SHELBY FLINT

ANNIE'S SONG (1978) JAMES GALWAY

AN OPEN LETTER TO MY TEENAGE SON (1967) VICTOR LUNDBERG

ANOTHER LOVER (1988) GIANT STEPS

ANYONE CAN FALL IN LOVE (1986) ANITA DOBSON

ANYTHING YOU WANT (1976) JOHN VALENTI

APACHE (1961) JØRGEN INGMANN AND HIS GUITAR

APRIL IN PARIS (1956) COUNT BASIE

A QUESTION OF TEMPERATURE (1968) THE BALLOON FARM

ARE FRIENDS ELECTRIC? (1979) TUBEWAY ARMY

ARE YOU READY? (1970) PACIFIC GAS AND ELECTRIC

ARIEL (1977) DEAN FRIEDMAN

ARMED AND EXTREMELY DANGEROUS (1973) FIRST CHOICE

ARMS OF MARY (1976) SUTHERLAND BROTHERS & QUIVER

(MAIN THEME) AROUND THE WORLD (1957) VICTOR YOUNG AND HIS SINGING STRINGS

ASHES BY NOW (1980) RODNEY CROWELL

ASIA (1961) MINOR KOKOMO

A SONG OF JOY (HIMNO A LA ALEGRIA) (1970) MIGUEL RÍOS

AS THE YEARS GO BY (1970) MASHMAKHAN

THE ASTRONAUT (PART 1 AND 2) (1961) JOSE JIMENEZ (BILL DANA)

AS WE LAY (1987) SHIRLEY MURDOCK

AT MY FRONT DOOR (CRAZY LITTLE MAMA) (1955) EL DORADOS

AT THE HOP (1958) NICK TODD

AUTOBAHN (1975) KRAFTWERK

AUTOMATIC LOVER (1978) DEE D. JACKSON

AUTUMN LEAVES (1955) STEVE ALLEN

A WALK IN THE BLACK FOREST (1965) HORST JANKOWSKI

A WALK IN THE PARK (1980) NICK STRAKER BAND

A WAY OF LIFE (1969) THE FAMILY DOGG

A WONDERFUL DREAM (1962) THE MAJORS

AXEL F (1985) HAROLD FALTERMEYER

B...

BABE (1980) STYX

BABY, COME BACK (1968) THE EQUALS

BABY COME TO ME (1983) PATTI AUSTIN AND JAMES INGRAM

BABY FACE (1976) WING AND A PRAYER FIFE AND DRUM CORPS

BABY I LIED (1984) DEBORAH ALLEN

BABY I LOVE YOUR WAY/FREEBIRD/I'M NOT IN LOVE (1989) WILL TO POWER

BABY IT'S YOU (1969) SMITH

BABY LOVE (1986) REGINA

BABY, OH BABY (1961) THE SHELLS

BABY THE RAIN MUST FALL (1965) GLENN YARBROUGH

BABY SITTIN' BOOGIE (1960) BUZZ CLIFFORD

BACK HOME (1970) 1970 ENGLAND WORLD CUP SQUAD

BACK ON THE STREET AGAIN (1967) THE SUNSHINE COMPANY

BACK TO SCHOOL AGAIN (1958) TIMMIE 'OH YEAH' ROGERS

BACK WHEN MY HAIR WAS SHORT (1973) GUNHILL ROAD

BAD BOY (1957) THE JIVE BOMBERS

BAKER STREET (1978) GERRY RAFFERTY

THE BALLAD OF DAVY CROCKETT (1955) THE VOICES OF WALTER SCHUMANN

THE BALLAD OF IRVING (1966) FRANK GALLOP

THE BALLAD OF JAYNE (1989) L.A. GUNS

BAND OF GOLD (1956) KIT CARSON

BANG A GONG (GET IT ON) (1972) T. REX

BANG ZOOM LET'S GO (1986) REAL ROXANNE / HITMAN HOWIE TEE

BARBADOS (1975) TYPICALLY TROPICAL

BARBARA (1960) THE TEMPTATIONS

BAREFOOTIN'(1966) ROBERT PARKER

BATMAN THEME (1966) NEAL HEFTI

BATTLE HYMN OF LT. CALLEY (1971) C. COMPANY FEATURING TERRY NELSON

BATTLE HYMN OF THE REPUBLIC (1959) MORMON TABERNACLE CHOIR

BAUBLES, BANGLES AND BEADS (1958) KIRBY STONE FOUR

BEACH BABY (1974) THE FIRST CLASS

BEAUTIFUL SUNDAY (1972) DANIEL BOONE

BEAUTIFUL PEOPLE (1967) KENNY O'DELL

BECAUSE THE NIGHT (1978) PATTI SMITH GROUP

BEDS ARE BURNING (1987) MIDNIGHT OIL

BEEN SO LONG (1958) THE PASTELS

THE BELLE OF ST MARK (1985) SHEILA E

BE THANKFUL FOR WHAT YOU GOT (1974) WILLIAM DEVAUGHN

BETTER TELL HIM NO (1961) THE STARLETS

BETTY DAVIS EYES (1981) KIM CARNES

BIG BAD JOHN (1961) JIMMY DEAN

BIG IN JAPAN (1984) ALPHAVILLE

BIG YELLOW TAXI (1970) THE NEIGHBORHOOD

THE BIRDIE SONG (BIRDIE DANCE) (1981) THE TWEETS

BIRD OF PARADISE (1984) SNOWY WHITE

THE BIRDS AND THE BEES (1965) JEWEL AKENS

BIRDS FLY (WHISPER TO A SCREAM)/LOVE IS A WONDERFUL COLOUR (1984) ICICLE WORKS

BIRTHDAY (1969) UNDERGROUND SUNSHINE

BIRTHDAY PARTY (1963) THE PIXIES THREE

BLACK PEARL (1969) THE CHECKMATES, LTD.

BLACK IS BLACK (1977) BELLE EPOQUE

BLACK IS BLACK (1966) LOS BRAVOS

BLACK SLACKS (1957) JOE BENNETT & THE SPARKLETONES

BLACK VELVET (1989) ALANNAH MYLES

THE BLOB (1958) THE FIVE BLOBS

BLUE GIRL (1963) THE BRUISERS

BLUE STAR (1955) FELICIA SANDERS

BLUE'S THEME (1967) DAVIE ALLAN AND THE ARROWS

BLUE SUEDE SHOES (1956) CARL PERKINS

BOBBY'S GIRL (1962) MARCIE BLANE

BOBBY'S GIRL (1962) SUSAN MAUGHAN

BODY ROCK (1985) MARIA VIDAL

BONGO ROCK (1959) PRESTON EPPS

BONGO STOMP (1962) LITTLE JOEY AND THE FLIPS

BORN FREE (1968) THE HESITATIONS

BORN TO BE ALIVE (1979) PATRICK HERNANDEZ

BORN TO BE WILD (1968) STEPPENWOLF

BORN TOO LATE (1958) THE PONI-TAILS

THE BOY FROM NEW YORK CITY (1964) THE AD LIBS

THE BOY NEXT DOOR (1963) THE SECRETS

THE BOYS ARE BACK IN TOWN (1976) THIN LIZZY

BOYS NIGHT OUT (1987) TIMOTHY B. SCHMIT

THE BOYS OF SUMMER (1985) DON HENLEY

BOYS (SUMMERTIME LOVE) (1988) SABRINA

BREAKING AWAY (1981) BALANCE

BREAKIN' AWAY/THAT'S LIVIN' ALRIGHT (1984) JOE FAGAN

BREAKIN' DOWN (SUGAR SAMBA) (1984) JULIA NIXON

BREAKING... THERE'S NO STOPPING US (1984) OLLIE & JERRY

BREAK MY STRIDE (1984) MATTHEW WILDER

THE BREEZE AND I (ANDALUCIA) (1955) CATERINA VALENTE

BRIDGE TO YOUR HEART (1987) WAX

BRING ME EDELWEISS (1989) EDELWEISS

BROKEN LAND (1988) ADVENTURES

BROTHER LOUIE (1986) MODERN TALKING

BROTHER LOUIE (1973) STORIES

BUFFALO GALS (1982) (MALCOLM MCLAREN AND) WORLD'S FAMOUS SUPREME TEAM

BURNING HEART (1983) VANDENBERG

BUSTIN' LOOSE, PART 1 (1979) CHUCK BROWN AND THE SOUL SEARCHERS

BUST OUT (1963) THE BUSTERS

BUT IT'S ALRIGHT (1966) J. J. JACKSON

BUZZ BUZZ BUZZ (1957) THE HOLLYWOOD FLAMES

C...

CACHARPAYA (ANDES PUMPSA DAESI) (1983) INCANTATION

CALIFORNIA SUN (1964) THE RIVIERAS

CALLING ALL THE HEROES (1986) IT BITES

CALL ME (1987) SPAGNA

CALL ME (1982) SKYY

CALL TO THE HEART (1985) GIUFFRIA

CAMOUFLAGE (1986) STAN RIDGWAY

CAN'T GET ENOUGH (1974) BAD COMPANY

CAN THIS BE REAL (1974) NATURAL FOUR

CAN'T SHAKE LOOSE (1983) AGNETHA FÄLTSKOG (THE BLONDE ONE)

CAN'T TAKE MY EYES OFF YOU (1982) BOYSTOWN GANG

CAN'T YOU HEAR MY HEARTBEAT (1965) GOLDIE & THE GINGERBREADS

ÇA PLANE POUR MOI (1978) PLASTIC BERTRAND

CAPTAIN BEAKY (1980) CAPTAIN BEAKY & HIS BAND

THE CAPTAIN OF HER HEART (1985) DOUBLE

CAR 67 (1979) DRIVER 67

CARS (1980) GARY NUMAN

CAROLINE, NO (1966) BRIAN WILSON

CASANOVA (1987) LEVERT

CAST YOUR FATE TO THE WIND (1965) SOUNDS ORCHESTRAL

CAST YOUR FATE TO THE WIND (1963) VINCE GUARALDI TRIO

CAT SCRATCH FEVER (1977) TED NUGENT

CENTIPEDE (1984) REBBIE JACKSON

CHA-HUA-HUA (1958) THE PETS

CHAIN GANG (1956) BOBBY SCOTT

CHALK DUST: THE UMPIRE STRIKES BACK (1982) THE BRAT

(THE) CHASE (1979) GIORGIO MORODER

CHANSON D'AMOUR (SONG OF LOVE) (1958) ART AND DOTTY TODD

CHATTANOOGA CHOO CHOO (1978) TUXEDO JUNCTION

THE CHEATER (1966) BOB KUBAN AND THE IN-MEN

CHERRY BABY (1977) STARZ

CHEVY VAN (1975) SAMMY JOHNS

CHICK-A-BOOM (DON'T YA JES' LOVE IT) (1971) DADDY DEWDROP

THE CHICKEN SONG (1986) SPITTING IMAGE

CINCO ROBLES (FIVE OAKS) (1957) RUSSELL ARMS

CINDERELLA (1962) JACK ROSS

CINDERELLA ROCKEFELLA (1968) ESTHER AND ABI OFARIM

CINDY, OH CINDY (1956) VINCE MARTIN AND THE TARRIERS

CINNAMON CINDER (IT'S A VERY NICE DANCE) (1963) THE PASTEL SIX

CITY OF ANGELS (1956) THE HIGHLIGHTS

CITY OF NEW ORLEANS (1972) ARLO GUTHRIE

THE CLAPPING SONG (1983) PIA ZADORA

CLASSIC (1982) ADRIAN GURVITZ

CLASSICAL GAS (1968) MASON WILLIAMS

CLOSE TO CATHY (1962) MIKE CLIFFORD

COLOR HIM FATHER (1969) THE WINSTONS

COME ON DOWN TO MY BOAT (1967) EVERY MOTHER'S SON

COME ON EILEEN (1982) DEXYS MIDNIGHT RUNNERS & THE EMERALD EXPRESS

COME SOFTLY TO ME (1959) THE FLEETWOODS

COME TO ME (1979) FRANCE JOLI

COME WHAT MAY (1972) VICKY LEANDROS

COMIN' ON STRONG (1987) BROKEN ENGLISH

COMMUNICATION (1966) DAVID MCCALLUM

CONCRETE AND CLAY (1965) EDDIE RAMBEAU

CONCRETE AND CLAY (1965) UNIT 4 + 2

CONFIDENTIAL (1956) SONNY KNIGHT

CONVENTION '72 (1972) THE DELEGATES

CONVOY (1976) CW MCCALL

COOL AID (1971) PAUL HUMPHREY AND THE COOL AID CHEMISTS

COOL JERK (1966) THE CAPITOLS

COULD THIS BE MAGIC (1957) THE DUBS

COUNT EVERY STAR (1961) DONNIE AND THE DREAMERS

COULD HAVE TOLD YOU SO (1989) HALO JAMES

CRASH (1988) THE PRIMITIVES

CRAZY MAMA (1972) J. J. CALE

CRUEL TO BE KIND (1979) NICK LOWE

CRUSH ON YOU (1987) THE JETS

CRY (1985) GODLEY AND CRÈME

CRY (1989) WATERFRONT

CRY BABY (1956) BONNIE SISTERS

CRY BOY CRY (1982) BLUE ZOO

CRY ME A RIVER (1955) JULIE LONDON

CRY TO ME (1963) BETTY HARRIS

CUDDLY TOY (FEEL FOR ME) (1989) ROACHFORD

THE CURLY SHUFFLE (1984) JUMP 'N THE SADDLE BAND

D...

D.O.A. (1971) BLOODROCK

DADDY-O (1955) BONNIE LOU

DA BUTT (1988) E.U.

DA DA DA (1982) TRIO

DADDY'S HOME (1961) SHEP AND THE LIMELITES

DAISY A DAY (1973) JUD STRUNK AND THE MIKE CURB CONGREGATION -

DAISY A DAY (1973) LOUDON WAINWRIGHT III

DANCE ACROSS THE FLOOR (1978) JIMMY "BO" HORNE

DANCE HALL DAYS (1984) WANG CHUNG

DANCING IN THE CITY (1978) MARSHALL HAIN

DANCING IN THE MOONLIGHT (1972) KING HARVEST

DANCIN' MAN (1977) Q

DANGER GAMES (1982) PINKEES

DARK MOON (1957) BONNIE GUITAR

DARLIN'(1978) FRANKIE MILLER

THE DAWN OF CORRECTION (1965) THE SPOKESMEN

DAY BY DAY (1972) GODSPELL CAST

DAY FOR DECISION (1966) JOHNNY SEA

DEAR ONE (1962) LARRY FINNEGAN

DECK OF CARDS (1959) WINK MARTINDALE

DELICIOUS (1958) JIM BACKUS AND FRIEND

DENISE (1963) RANDY & THE RAINBOWS

DER KOMMISSAR (1983) AFTER THE FIRE

DESERT MOON (1984) DENNIS DEYOUNG

DESIDERATA (1971) LES CRANE

DEVIL'S GUN (1977) C.J. AND CO.

DIAMOND LIGHTS (1987) GLENN AND CHRIS

DIAMONDS AND PEARLS (1960) THE PARADONS

DID YOU BOOGIE (WITH YOUR BABY) (1976) FLASH CADILLAC & THE CONTINENTAL KIDS

DID YOU SEE HER EYES (1969) THE ILLUSION

DIGGING YOUR SCENE (1986) THE BLOW MONKEYS

DING-DONG! THE WITCH IS DEAD (1967) THE FIFTH ESTATE

DINNER WITH DRAC–PART 1 (1958) JOHN ZACHERLEY

DIRTY WATER (1966) THE STANDELLS

DISCO DUCK (1976) RICK DEES AND HIS CAST OF IDIOTS

DISCO LUCY (I LOVE LUCY THEME) (1977) WILTON PLACE STREET BAND

DOCTORIN' THE TARDIS (1988) TIMELORDS

DOCTOR'S ORDERS (1975) CAROL DOUGLAS

DOES YOUR MAMA KNOW ABOUT ME (1968) BOBBY TAYLOR & THE VANCOUVERS

DOING IT TO DEATH (1973) FRED WESLEY AND THE J.B.'S

DO IT AGAIN A LITTLE BIT SLOWER (1967) JON AND ROBIN AND THE IN-CROWD

DO IT, DO IT AGAIN (1978) RAFFAEL CARRÀ

DO IT TO THE MUSIC (1982) RAW SILK

DOLCE VITA (1983) RYAN PARIS

DOMINIQUE (1963) THE SINGING NUN

DON'T BE ANGRY (1955) NAPPY BROWN

DON'T BRING ME DOWN (1964) PRETTY THINGS

DON'T CLOSE YOUR EYES (1989) KIX

DON'T CRY FOR ME ARGENTINA (1977) JULIE COVINGTON

DON'T DISTURB THIS GROOVE (1987) THE SYSTEM

DON'T EVER WANNA LOSE YA (1979) NEW ENGLAND

DON'T GIVE IT UP (1981) ROBBIE PATTON

DON'T GIVE UP ON US (1977) DAVID SOUL

DON'T GO BREAKING MY HEART (1976) ELTON JOHN/KIKI DEE

DON'T GO NEAR THE INDIANS (1962) REX ALLEN

DON'T GO TO STRANGERS (1960) ETTA JONES

DON'T HANG UP (1962) THE ORLONS

DON'T HOLD BACK (1979) CHANSON

DON'T IT MAKE YOU FEEL GOOD (1989) STEFAN DENNIS

DON'T LEAVE ME THIS WAY (1987) THE COMMUNARDS

DON'T LEAVE ME THIS WAY (1976) THELMA HOUSTON

DON'T LET HIM KNOW (1982) PRISM

DON'T LET ME BE MISUNDERSTOOD (1978) SANTA ESMERALDA

DON'T MAKE ME OVER (1989) SYBIL

DON'T MESS UP A GOOD THING (1965) BOBBY MCCLURE

DON'T THINK TWICE (1965) THE WONDER WHO?

DON'T PUSH IT DON'T FORCE IT (1980) LEON HAYWOOD

DON'T STOP THE MUSIC (1981) YARBROUGH AND PEOPLES

DON'T TRY TO STOP IT (1983) ROMAN HOLLIDAY

DON'T WORRY BE HAPPY (1988) BOBBY MCFERRIN

DON'T YOU JUST KNOW IT (1958) HUEY "PIANO" SMITH AND THE CLOWNS

DON'T YOU WRITE HER OFF (1979) MCGUINN, CLARK AND HILLMAN

DO THEY KNOW IT'S CHRISTMAS? (1984) BAND AID

DO THEY KNOW IT'S CHRISTMAS? (1989) BAND AID II

DOUBLE BARREL (1971) DAVE AND ANSELL COLLINS

DOUBLE DUTCH BUS (1981) FRANKIE SMITH

DOUBLESHOT (OF MY BABY'S LOVE) (1966) THE SWINGIN' MEDALLIONS

DO WHAT YOU WANNA DO (1970) FIVE FLIGHTS UP

DOWN THE AISLE OF LOVE (1958) THE QUIN-TONES

DOWNTOWN (1989) ONE 2 MAN

DO YOU LOVE ME (1962) THE CONTOURS

DO YOU WANNA MAKE LOVE (1977) PETER MCCANN

DREAMING (1988) GLEN GOLDSMITH

DRIVING AWAY FROM HOME (JIM'S TUNE) (1986) IT'S IMMATERIAL

DRIVER'S SEAT (1979) SNIFF 'N' THE TEARS

DROWNING IN BERLIN (1982) MOBILES

THE DUCK (1966) JACKIE LEE

DUELING BANJOS (1973) ERIC WEISSBERG AND STEVE MANDELL

DYNOMITE (1975) BAZUKA

E...

EARLY IN THE MORNING (1958) THE RINKY DINKS

EARTH ANGEL (WILL YOU BE MINE) (1955) THE PENGUINS

EASY LIVIN' (1972) URIAH HEEP

EASY LOVER (1985) PHILIP BAILEY (& PHIL COLLINS)

EASY LOVIN' (1971) FREDDIE HART

ECHO PARK (1969) KEITH BARBOUR

ECHO BEACH (1980) MARTHA AND THE MUFFINS

EDDIE MY LOVE (1956) THE TEEN QUEENS

EIGHTEEN WITH A BULLET (1975) PETE WINGFIELD

EINSTEIN A GO-GO (1981) LANDSCAPE

ELECTION DAY (1985) ARCADIA

THE ELEPHANT SONG (1975) KAMAHL

ELOISE (1956) KAY THOMPSON

EL WATUSI (1963) RAY BARRETTO

EMOTION (1977) SAMANTHA SANG

EMOTION IN MOTION (1986) RIC OCASEK

THE ENCHANTED SEA (1959) THE ISLANDERS

THE END (1958) EARL GRANT

ENDLESS SLEEP (1958) JODY REYNOLDS

THE ENTERTAINER (1974) MARVIN HAMLISCH

THE ENTERTAINER (1965) TONY CLARKE

ELUSIVE BUTTERFLY (1966) BOB LIND

ERES TU (TOUCH THE WIND) (1974) MOCEDADES

ERNIE (THE FASTEST MILKMAN IN THE WEST) (1971) BENNY HILL

EVE OF DESTRUCTION (1965) BARRY MCGUIRE

EVERLASTING LOVE (1981) RACHEL SWEET

EVERLASTING LOVE (1967) ROBERT KNIGHT

EVER SO LONELY (1982) MONSOON

EVERYBODY DANCE (1986) TA MARA AND THE SEEN

EVERYBODY'S GOT TO LEARN SOMETIME (1980) THE KORGIS

EVERYONE'S GONE TO THE MOON (1965) JONATHAN KING

EVIL WOMAN (DON'T PLAY YOUR GAMES WITH ME) (1970) CROW

EXODUS (1961) EDDIE HARRIS

EYE LEVEL (1973) SIMON PARK ORCHESTRA

F...
FACTS OF LOVE (1987) JEFF LORBER

FALLING (1977) LEBLANC & CARR

FALLIN' IN LOVE (1974) THE SOUTHER, HILLMAN, FURAY BAND

FANNIE MAE (1960) BUSTER BROWN

FANTASY (1982) ALDO NOVA

FAR FROM OVER (1983) FRANK STALLONE

FARMER JOHN (1964) THE PREMIERS

FASCINATED (1987) COMPANY B

FAST CAR (1988) TRACY CHAPMAN

FEELINGS (1975) MORRIS ALBERT

FEEL IT AGAIN (1986) HONEYMOON SUITE

(FEELS LIKE) HEAVEN (1984) FICTION FACTORY

FEELS LIKE I'M IN LOVE (1980) KELLY MARIE

FEEL SO REAL (1985) STEVE ARRINGTON

FINAL COUNTDOWN (1985) EUROPE

FIRE (1968) THE CRAZY WORLD OF ARTHUR BROWN

FIRST PICTURE OF YOU (1983) LOTUS EATERS

THE FIRST TIME (1988) ROBIN BECK

FISHNET (1988) MORRIS DAY

THE FLAMES OF PARADISE (1987) JENNIFER RUSH

FLOAT ON (1977) THE FLOATERS

THE FLORAL DANCE (1977) BRIGHOUSE AND RASTRICK BRASS BAND

THE FLORAL DANCE (1978) TERRY WOGAN AND THE HANWELL BRASS BAND

FLOWERS ON THE WALL (1966) THE STATLER BROTHERS

FLY ME TO THE MOON–BOSSA NOVA (1963) JOE HARNELL AND HIS ORCHESTRA

THE FOOL (1956) SANFORD CLARK

FOOLED AROUND AND FELL IN LOVE (1976) ELVIN BISHOP

FOOL (IF YOU THINK IT'S OVER) (1978) CHRIS REA

FOOTLOOSE (1984) KENNY LOGGINS

FOOTSIE (1975) WIGAN'S CHOSEN FEW

FOOT STOMPIN'-PART 1 (1961) THE FLARES

FORBIDDEN COLOURS (1983) RYUICHI SAKAMOTO (WITH DAVID SYLVIAN)

FOREVER (1960) THE LITTLE DIPPERS

FOREVER (1964) PETER DRAKE AND HIS TALKING STEEL GUITAR

FOREVER AUTUMN (1978) JUSTIN HAYWARD

FORGET ME NOTS (1982) PATRICE RUSHEN

FOR THE GOOD TIMES (1971) RAY PRICE

FOR TONIGHT (1986) NANCY MARTINEZ

FOR WHAT IT'S WORTH (STOP, HEY WHAT'S THAT SOUND) (1967) BUFFALO SPRINGFIELD

FOR YOUR LOVE (1958) ED TOWNSEND

FOR YOUR PRECIOUS LOVE (1967) OSCAR TONEY, JR.

FREIGHT TRAIN (1957) CHARLES MCDEVITT SKIFFLE GROUP

FRIDAY ON MY MIND (1967) THE EASYBEATS

FRIENDS AND LOVERS (1986) GLORIA LORING AND CARL ANDERSON

FROM A JACK TO A KING (1963) NED MILLER

FULL METAL JACKET (I WANNA BE YOUR DRILL INSTRUCTOR) (1987) ABIGAIL MEAD & NIGEL GOULDING

FUNKIN' FOR JAMAICA (N.Y.) (1980) TOM BROWNE

THE FUNKY JUDGE (1968) BULL & THE MATADORS

FUNKY MOPED (1975) JASPER CARROT

FUNKY NASSAU (1971) THE BEGINNING OF THE END

FUNKYTOWN (1980) LIPPS INC.

FUNKY TOWN (1986) PSEUDO ECHO

FUNNY HOW TIME SLIPS AWAY (1962) JIMMY ELLEDGE

FUNNY (HOW TIME SLIPS AWAY) (1964) JOE HINTON

THE FUTURE'S SO BRIGHT, I GOTTA WEAR SHADES (1986) TIMBUK3

G...

GALLANT MEN (1967) SENATOR EVERETT MCKINLEY DIRKSE

GAMES (1971) REDEYE

GAMES PEOPLE PLAY (1969) JOE SOUTH

GARDEN OF EDEN (1956) JOE VALINO

GARDEN PARTY (1983) MEZZOFORTE

GEE WHIZ (1980) BERNADETTE PETERS

GENERAL HOSPI-TALE (1981) THE AFTERNOON DELIGHTS

GENIUS OF LOVE (1981) TOM TOM CLUB

GET A JOB (1958) THE SILHOUETTES

GET IT ON (1971) CHASE

GET READY (1970) RARE EARTH

GET TOGETHER (1969) THE YOUNGBLOODS

GET USED TO IT (1979) ROGER VOUDOURIS

(GHOST) RIDERS IN THE SKY (1961) THE RAMRODS

GIMME DAT DING (1970) THE PIPKINS

GIMME GIMME GOOD LOVIN' (1969) CRAZY ELEPHANT

GINNIE BELL (1961) PAUL DINO

GIRLFRIEND (1988) PEBBLES

GIRLIE GIRLIE (1985) SOPHIA GEORGE

THE GIRL FROM IPANEMA (1964) ASTRUD GILBERTO

GIRL OF MY DREAMS (1979) BRAM TCHAIKOVSKY

GIRLS (1975) MOMENTS & WHATNAUTS

GIRLS WITH GUNS (1984) TOMMY SHAW

GIRL WATCHER (1968) THE O'KAYSIONS

GIVING IT UP FOR YOUR LOVE (1981) DELBERT MCCLINTON

GLORY OF LOVE (1986) PETER CETERA

GO BACK (1970) CRABBY APPLETON

GOD, LOVE AND ROCK AND ROLL (1970) TEEGARDEN AND VAN WINKLE

GOLDFINGER (1965) SHIRLEY BASSEY

GOIN' DOWN (1982) GREG GUIDRY

GONE (1972) JOEY HEATHERTON

GONNA FIND ME A BLUEBIRD (1957) MARVIN RAINWATER

GONNA FLY NOW (1977) BILL CONTI

GONNA FLY NOW (1977) MAYNARD FERGUSON

GOOD MORNING STARSHINE (1969) OLIVER

GOOD OLD ROCK AND ROLL CAT (1969) MOTHER & THE ALL NIGHT NEWS BOYS

THE GOOD, THE BAD AND THE UGLY (1968) HUGO MONTENEGRO

GOOD TIME CHARLIE'S GOT THE BLUES (1972) DANNY O'KEEFE

GOTTA TRAVEL ON (1959) BILLY GRAMMER

GOT TO BE REAL (1978) CHERYL LYNN

GOT TO GET (1989) ROB N RAZ FEATURING LAILA K

GRADUATION DAY (1956) THE ROVER BOYS

THE GRADUATION SONG... (1961) POMP AND CIRCUMSTANCE ADRIAN KIMBERLY

GRANDAD (1971) CLIVE DUNN

GRAZING IN THE GRASS (1968) HUGH MASEKELA

GREEN TAMBOURINE (1968) THE LEMON PIPERS

THE GROOVE (1980) RODNEY FRANKLIN

GROOVY GRUBWORM (1969) HARLOW WILCOX AND THE OAKIES

GUESS WHO (1959) JESSE BELVIN

GUITAR BOOGIE (1959) SHUFFLE THE VIRTUES

H...

HALLELUJAH (1971) SWEATHOG

HANDS TO HEAVEN (1988) BREATHE

HANGING ON A HEART ATTACK (1986) DEVICE

HANG ON IN THERE BABY (1974) JOHNNY BRISTOL

HANG ON SLOOPY (1965) THE MCCOYS

HAPPY DAYS (1976) PRATT & MCCLAIN

HAPPY, HAPPY BIRTHDAY BABY (1957) THE TUNE WEAVERS

THE HAPPY REINDEER (1959) DANCER, PRANCER AND NERVOUS

THE HAPPY WHISTLER (1956) DON ROBERTSON

HARLEM NOCTURNE (1966) THE VISCOUNTS

HARLEM SHUFFLE BOB & EARL

HARPER VALLEY P.T.A. (1968) JEANNIE C. RILEY

HAUNTED HOUSE (1964) JUMPIN' GENE SIMMONS

HAVE I THE RIGHT (1977) THE DEAD END KIDS

HAVE I THE RIGHT? (1964) THE HONEYCOMBS

HAVEN'T STOPPED DANCING YET (1979) GONZALEZ

HAWAII TATTOO (1965) THE WAIKIKIS

HEARTACHE AVENUE (1983) THE MAISONETTES

HEART AND SOUL (1961) THE CLEFTONES

HEART AND SOUL (1987) T'PAU

HEARTBEAT (1986) DON JOHNSON

HEARTBREAK BEAT (1987) THE PSYCHEDELIC FURS

HEAVEN HELP ME (1989) DEON ESTUS

HEAVEN KNOWS (1979) BROOKLYN DREAMS

HEAVEN ON THE 7TH FLOOR (1977) PAUL NICHOLAS

HE'LL HAVE TO STAY (1960) JEANNE BLACK

HELLO HELLO (1967) SOPWITH CAMEL

HELLO MUDDAH, HELLO FADDUH (1963) ALLAN SHERMAN

HELLO WALLS (1961) FARON YOUNG

HELP ME MAKE IT THROUGH THE NIGHT (1971) SAMMI SMITH

HERE COMES SUMMER (1959) JERRY KELLER

HERE COMES THE SUN (1971) RICHIE HAVENS

HERE COMES THE JUDGE (1968) PIGMEAT MARKHAM

HERE COMES THE JUDGE (1968) SHORTY LONG

HE'S GOT THE WHOLE WORLD IN HIS HANDS (1958) LAURIE LONDON

HEY! BABY (1961) BRUCE CHANNEL

HEY JOE (1966) THE LEAVES

HEY LITTLE GIRL (1983) ICEHOUSE

HEY LITTLE GIRL (1957) THE TECHNIQUES

HEY MATTHEW (1987) KAREL FIALKA

HEY! MR. BANJO (1955) THE SUNNYSIDERS

HEY THERE LONELY GIRL (1974) EDDIE HOLMAN

(HEY YOU) THE ROCKSTEADY CREW (1983) ROCKSTEADY CREW

HIDE AND GO SEEK–PART 1 (1962) BUNKER HILL

HIDEAWAY (1961) FREDDY KING

HIGH-HEEL SNEAKERS (1964) TOMMY TUCKER

HIGH SCHOOL U.S.A. (1959) TOMMY FACENDA

HI HO SILVER LINING (1967) JEFF BECK

HIPPY HIPPY SHAKE (1959) CHAN ROMERO

HIPPY HIPPY SHAKE (1964) THE SWINGING BLUE JEANS

HISTORY REPEATS ITSELF (1966) BUDDY STARCHER

HOCUS POCUS (1973) FOCUS

HOKEY COKEY (1981) SNOWMEN

HOLDIN' ON (1982) TANÉ CAIN

HOLD ME TIGHTER IN THE RAIN (1983) BILLY GRIFFIN

HOLD ON (1979) IAN GOMM

HOLD YOUR HEAD UP (1972) ARGENT

HOLE IN MY SHOE (1984) NEIL

HOLIDAY (1987) THE OTHER ONES

HONESTLY (1988) STRYPER

THE HONEYTHIEF (1986) HIPSWAY

HOOKED ON CLASSICS (1982) ROYAL PHILHARMONIC ORCHESTRA

HOOKED ON SWING (1982) LARRY ELGART AND HIS MANHATTAN SWING ORCHESTRA

HOOTENANNY (1963) THE GLENCOVES

HOOTS MON (1958) LORD ROCKINGHAM'S XI

THE HORSE (1968) CLIFF NOBLES AND CO.

HOT CHILD IN THE CITY (1978) NICK GILDER

HOT PASTRAMI (1963) THE DARTELLS

HOT ROD LINCOLN (1972) COMMANDER CODY AND HIS LOST PLANET AIRMEN

HOT ROD LINCOLN (1960) CHARLIE RYAN AND THE TIMBERLANE RIDERS

HOT ROD LINCOLN (1960) JOHNNY BOND

HOT SMOKE & SASAFRASS (1969) BUBBLE PUPPY

HOUSE ARREST (1988) KRUSH

THE HOUSE OF BLUE LIGHTS (1955) CHUCK MILLER

THE HOUSE OF THE RISING SUN (1970) RIJID PINK

HOW 'BOUT US (1981) CHAMPAIGN

HOW DO I SURVIVE (1980) AMY HOLLAND

HOW DO YOU DO (1972) MOUTH & MACNEAL

HOW LONG? (1975) ACE

HOWZAT (1976) SHERBET

THE HUCKLEBUCK (1981) COAST TO COAST

HUNGRY FOR LOVE (1965) SAN REMO GOLDEN STRINGS

HUSHABYE (1959) THE MYSTICS

THE HUSTLE (1975) VAN MCCOY

HUSTLE! TO THE MUSIC (1988) FUNKY WORM

HYPNOTIZED (1967) LINDA JONES

I...

I AINT GOT TIME ANYMORE (1971) THE GLASS BOTTLE

I AM (I'M ME) (1983) TWISTED SISTER

I AM THE BEAT (1981) LOOK

I BEG YOUR PARDON (1989) KON KAN

I BELIEVE IN YOU (1980) DON WILLIAMS

I CAN HELP (1974) BILLY SWAN

I CAN SING A RAINBOW/LOVE IS BLUE (1969) THE DELLS

I CAN'T GROW PEACHES ON A CHERRY TREE (1966) JUST US

I CAN'T STAND THE RAIN (1973) ANN PEEBLES

I CAN'T STAND THE RAIN (1978) ERUPTION

I CAN'T WAIT (1986) NU SHOOZ

I COULD BE SO GOOD FOR YOU (1980) DENNIS WATERMAN BAND

I COULDN'T SAY NO (1983) ROBERT ELLIS ORRALL AND CARLENE CARTER

I'D LIKE TO TEACH THE WORLD TO SING (IN PERFECT HARMONY) (1972) THE HILLSIDE SINGERS

I'D LOVE TO CHANGE THE WORLD (1971) TEN YEARS AFTER

I DO (1965) THE MARVELOWS

I DON'T MIND AT ALL (1987) BOURGEOIS TAGG

I DO WHAT I DO (THEME FOR 9½ WEEKS) (1986) JOHN TAYLOR

I'D RATHER JACK (1989) REYNOLDS GIRLS

I'D REALLY LOVE TO SEE YOU TONIGHT (1976) ENGLAND DAN AND JOHN FORD COLEY

I EAT CANNIBALS (1982) TOTO COELO

IF (1975) TELLY SAVALAS

IF I HAD A GIRL (1960) ROD LAUREN

IF I HAD MY WISH TONIGHT (1982) DAVID LASLEY

IF I HAD WORDS (1978) SCOTT FITZGERALD & YVONNE KEELY

(IF LOVING YOU IS WRONG) I DON'T WANT TO BE RIGHT (1979) BARBARA MANDRELL

I FOUND LOVIN' (1987) STEVE WALSH

IF THE LOVE FITS WEAR IT (1982) LESLIE PEARL

IF WE MAKE IT THROUGH DECEMBER (1974) MERLE HAGGARD

IF YOU WANT IT (1979) NITEFLYTE

IF YOU GOT TO MAKE A FOOL OF SOMEBODY (1962) JAMES RAY

IF YOU SHOULD SAIL (1980) NIELSEN/PEARSON

I GOT A LINE ON YOU (1969) SPIRIT

I GOT A WIFE (1959) THE MARK IV

I GOT A WOMAN, PART 1 (1962) JIMMY MCGRIFF

I GOT MY MIND MADE UP (YOU CAN GET IT GIRL) (1979) INSTANT FUNK

I GOT YOU (1980) SPLIT ENZ

I GOT YOU BABE (1985) CHRISSIE HYNDE (WITH UB40)

I.G.Y. (WHAT A BEAUTIFUL WORLD) (1982) DONALD FAGEN

(I JUST) DIED IN YOUR ARMS (1986) CUTTING CREW

I JUST DON'T UNDERSTAND (1961) ANN-MARGRET

I JUST WANNA SPEND SOME TIME WITH YOU (1982) ALTON EDWARDS

I KNOW THERE'S SOMETHING GOING ON (1983) ANNI-FRID SYNNI LYNGSTAD, 'FRIDA' (THE BRUNETTE ONE)

I KNOW (YOU DON'T LOVE ME NO MORE) (1962) BARBARA GEORGE

IKO IKO (1989) THE BELLE STARS

IKO IKO (1982) NATASHA

I LIKE IT LIKE THAT, PART 1 (1961) CHRIS KENNER

I'LL BE THE OTHER WOMAN (1974) THE SOUL CHILDREN

I'LL TAKE YOU HOME AGAIN, KATHLEEN (1974) LIEUTENANT PIGEON

I LOST MY HEART TO A STARSHIP TROOPER (1978) SARAH BRIGHTMAN & HOT GOSSIP

I LOVE (1974) TOM T. HALL

I LOVED 'EM EVERY ONE (1981) T.G. SHEPPARD

I LOVE MY RADIO (1987) TAFFY

I LOVE ROCK 'N' ROLL (1982) JOAN JETT AND THE BLACKHEARTS

I LOVE THE NIGHTLIFE (DISCO 'ROUND) (1978) ALICIA BRIDGES

I LOVE YOU (1968) PEOPLE!

I LOVE YOU (1962) THE VOLUMES

I LOVE YOU FOR ALL SEASONS (1971) THE FUZZ

I LOVES YOU, PORGY (1959) NINA SIMONE

IMAGE OF A GIRL (1960) THE SAFARIS

I'M A FOOL TO CARE (1961) JOE BARRY

I'M AVAILABLE (1957) MARGIE RAYBURN

I'M DOIN' FINE NOW (1973) NEW YORK CITY

I'M EASY (1976) KEITH CARRADINE

(I'M GETTIN') NUTTIN' FOR CHRISTMAS (1955) RICKY ZAHND AND THE BLUE JEANERS

I'M GONNA BE (500 MILES) (1988) THE PROCLAIMERS

I'M GONNA MAKE YOU LOVE ME (1968) MADELINE BELL

I'M GONNA TAKE CARE OF EVERYTHING (1978) RUBICON

I'M HAPPY THAT LOVE HAS FOUND YOU (1980) JIMMY HALL

IMMIGRATION MAN (1972) CROSBY & NASH

IM NIN ALU (1988) OFRA HAZA

I'M NOT LISA (1975) JESSI COLTER

I'M INTO SOMETHIN' GOOD (1964) EARL-JEAN

I'M STICKIN' WITH YOU (1957) JIMMY BOWEN WITH THE RHYTHM ORCHIDS

(I'M THE GIRL ON) WOLVERTON MOUNTAIN (1962) JO ANN CAMPBELL

(I'M) TIRED OF GETTING PUSHED AROUND (1988) TWO MEN A DRUM MACHINE AND A TRUMPET

IN A BIG COUNTRY (1983) BIG COUNTRY

I NEED YOU (1988) BVSMP

IN MY HOUSE (1985) MARY JANE GIRLS

INTO THE NIGHT (1980) BENNY MARDONES

INVISIBLE (1985) ALISON MOYET

IN A BROKEN DREAM (1972) PYTHON LEE JACKSON

IN-A-GADDA-DA-VIDA (1968) IRON BUTTERFLY

IN A MOMENT (1969) THE INTRIGUES

INDIANA WANTS ME (1970) R. DEAN TAYLOR

INDIAN RESERVATION (1968) DON FARDON

I NEED YOUR LOVING (1962) DON GARDNER AND DEE DEE FORD

IN THE MIDNIGHT HOUR (1973) CROSS COUNTRY

IN THE MOOD (1977) HENHOUSE FIVE PLUS TOO

IN THE MOOD (1959) ERNIE FIELDS

IN THE SUMMERTIME (1970) MUNGO JERRY

IN THE YEAR 2525 (EXORDIUM AND TERMINUS) (1969) ZAGER AND EVANS

I ONLY WANNA BE WITH YOU (1979) THE TOURISTS

I RAN (SO FAR AWAY) (1982) A FLOCK OF SEAGULLS

I REALLY LOVE YOU (1961) THE STEREOS

I REMEMBER HOLDING YOU (1989) BOYS CLUB

I REMEMBER YOU (1962) FRANK IFIELD

IS IT A DREAM (1982) CLASSIX NOUVEAU

IS IT YOU? (1981) LEE RITENOUR

ISN'T SHE LOVELY (1977) DAVID PARTON

I SOLD MY HEART TO THE JUNKMAN (1962) THE BLUE-BELLES

ISRAELITES (1969) DESMOND DEKKER AND THE ACES

ITCHY TWITCHY FEELING (1958) BOBBY HENDRICKS

IT MUST BE LOVE (1979) ALTON MCCLAIN AND DESTINY

IT'S A CRAZY WORLD (1977) MAC MCANALLY

IT'S ALMOST TOMORROW (1955) THE DREAM WEAVERS

IT'S ALRIGHT (1965) ADAM FAITH WITH THE ROULETTES

IT'S GOOD NEWS WEEK (1965) HEDGEHOPPERS ANONYMOUS

IT'S 'ORRIBLE BEING IN LOVE (WHEN YOU'RE 8½) (1986) CLAIRE AND FRIENDS

IT SHOULD HAVE BEEN ME (1976) YVONNE FAIR

IT'S INEVITABLE (1983) CHARLIE

IT'S MY LIFE (1984) TALK TALK

IT'S MY PARTY (1981) BARABARA GASKIN (WITH DAVE STEWART)

IT'S NOW OR NEVER (1981) JOHN SCHNEIDER

IT'S RAINING MEN (1982) THE WEATHER GIRLS

IT TAKES TWO (1988) ROB BASE AND DJ E-Z ROCK

IT TAKES TWO (1967) KIM WESTON & MARVIN GAYE

I'VE BEEN LONELY FOR SO LONG (1972) FREDERICK KNIGHT

I'VE FOUND SOMEONE OF MY OWN (1971) THE FREE MOVEMENT

I'VE GOT A TIGER BY THE TAIL (1965) BUCK OWENS AND THE BUCKAROOS

I'VE GOT THE MUSIC IN ME (1974) THE KIKI DEE BAND

I'VE HAD IT (1959) THE BELL NOTES

(I'VE HAD) THE TIME OF MY LIFE (1987) BILL MEDLEY/JENNIFER WARNES

I'VE NEVER BEEN TO ME (1982) CHARLENE

IVORY TOWER (1956) CATHY CARR

I WANNA BE A COWBOY (1986) BOYS DON'T CRY

I WANNA BE A WINNER (1982) BROWN SAUCE

I WANNA LOVE HIM SO BAD (1964) THE JELLY BEANS

(I WANNA) TESTIFY (1967) THE PARLIAMENTS

I WANT'A DO SOMETHING FREAKY TO YOU (1975) LEON HAYWOOD

I WANT YOU, I NEED YOU (1981) CHRIS CHRISTIAN

I WANT YOUR LOVIN' (1985) CURTIS HAIRSTON

I WANT YOU TO BE MY BABY (1955) LILLIAN BRIGGS

I WAS KAISER BILL'S BATMAN (1967) WHISTLING JACK SMITH

I WILL STILL LOVE YOU (1978) STONEBOLT

I WISH THAT WE WERE MARRIED (1962) RONNIE & THE HI-LITES

I WISH YOU LOVE (1964) GLORIA LYNNE

I WONDER WHAT SHE'S DOING TONIGHT (1963) BARRY & THE TAMERLANES

I WON'T LET YOU DOWN (1982) PHD

J...

THE JACK THAT HOUSE BUILT (1988) JACK'N'CHILL

JACK TO THE SOUND OF THE UNDERGROUND (1988) HITHOUSE

JACK YOUR BODY (1987) STEVE "SILK" HURLEY

THE JAM–PART 1 (1962) BOBBY GREGG AND HIS FRIENDS

JAMIE (1962) EDDIE HOLLAND

JAPANESE BOY (1981) ANEKA (MARY SANDEMAN)

JAZZ CARNIVAL (1980) AZYMUTH

JEALOUS KIND OF FELLA (1969) GARLAND GREEN

JEANS ON (1977) DAVID DUNDAS

JENNIE LEE (1958) JAN AND ARNIE

JENNIFER TOMKINS (1970) THE STREET PEOPLE

THE JERK (1965) THE LARKS

JESUS IS A SOUL MAN (1969) LAWRENCE REYNOLDS

JE T'AIME... MOI NON PLUS (1969) JANE BIRKIN & SERGE GAINSBOURG

JILTED JOHN (1978) JILTED JOHN

JIM DANDY (1974) BLACK OAK ARKANSAS

JIVE TALKIN' (1987) BOOGIE BOX HIGH

JOANNE (1970) MICHAEL NESMITH AND THE FIRST NATIONAL BAND

JOHNNY GET ANGRY (1962) JOANIE SOMMERS

JOHNNY REGGAE (1971) THE PIGLETS

THE JOKER (THAT'S WHAT THEY CALL ME) (1957) BILLY MYLES

JOURNEY TO THE CENTER OF THE MIND (1968) AMBOY DUKES

JOY (1972) APOLLO 100 FEATURING TOM PARKER

JUDY (1958) FRANKIE VAUGHAN

JUDY IN DISGUISE (WITH GLASSES) (1968) JOHN FRED AND HIS PLAYBOY BAND

JUDY MAE (1975) BOOMER CASTLEMAN

JUMP TO THE BEAT (1980) STACY LATTISAW

JUNGLE FEVER (1972) THE CHAKACHAS

JUNK FOOD JUNKIE (1976) LARRY GROCE

JUST A FRIEND (1989) BIZ MARKIE

JUST COME HOME (1960) HUGO & LUIGI

JUST DON'T WANT TO BE LONELY (1987) FREDDIE MCGREGOR

JUST GOT LUCKY (1983) JOBOXERS

(JUST LIKE) ROMEO AND JULIET (1964) THE REFLECTIONS

JUST ONE LOOK (1963) DORIS TROY

JUST SAY NO (1986) GRANGE HILL CAST

JUST SO LONELY (1981) GET WET

JUST THE TWO OF US (1981) GROVER WASHINGTON JR.

JUST WHEN I NEEDED YOU MOST 1979 (1979) RANDY VANWARMER

K...

K-JEE (1971) THE NITE-LITERS

KEEM-O-SABE (1969) THE ELECTRIC INDIA

KEEPING THE DREAM ALIVE (1988) FREIHEIT

KEEP ON DANCING (1965) THE GENTRYS

KEEP YOUR HANDS TO YOURSELF (1986) GEORGIA SATELLITES

KEY LARGO (1982) BERTIE HIGGINS

KILLER JOE (1963) THE ROCKY FELLERS

KILLIN' TIME (1981) SUSAN ANTON

THE KIND OF BOY YOU CAN'T FORGET (1963) THE RAINDROPS

THE KING IS GONE (1977) RONNIE MCDOWELL

KING OF THE COPS (1976) BILLY HOWARD

KING TUT (1978) STEVE MARTIN

KISS AN ANGEL GOOD MORNING (1972) CHARLEY PRIDE

KISS AND TELL (1988) BRYAN FERRY

KISS HIM GOODBYE (1987) THE NYLONS

KISSING WITH CONFIDENCE (1983) WILL POWERS

KISS IN THE DARK (1979) PINK LADY

KNOCK ON WOOD (1979) AMII STEWART

KOOKIE, KOOKIE (LEND ME YOUR COMB) (1959) EDWARD BYRNES

KUNG FU FIGHTING (1974) CARL DOUGLAS

L...

LADY IN RED (1986) CHRIS DE BURGH

LAMBADA (1989) KAOMA

L'AMOUR EST BLEU (LOVE IS BLUE) (1968) VICKY LEANDROS

LAND OF A THOUSAND DANCES (1965) CANNIBAL & THE HEADHUNTERS

LANGUAGE OF LOVE (1960) JOHN D. LOUDERMILK

THE LAST FAREWELL (1975) ROGER WHITTAKER

LAST FILM (1983) KISSING THE PINK

LAST KISS (1964) J. FRANK WILSON AND THE CAVELIERS

LAST KISS (1974) WEDNESDAY

LAST NIGHT (1961) THE MAR-KEYS

LAST NIGHT A DJ SAVED MY LIFE (1983) INDEEP

THE LAST TIME I MADE LOVE (1984) JOYCE KENNEDY

LAY A LITTLE LOVIN' ON ME (1970) ROBIN MCNAMARA

LAYLA (1972) DEREK AND THE DOMINOS

LEADER OF THE LAUNDROMAT (1965) THE DETERGENTS

LEAN ON ME (1987) CLUB NOUVEAU

LEAVING ME (1973) THE INDEPENDENTS

LET GO (1989) SHARON BRYANT

LET IT ALL BLOW (1984) DAZZ BAND

LET IT BE (1987) FERRY AID

LET IT OUT (LET IT ALL HANG OUT) (1967) THE HOMBRES

LET IT WHIP (1982) DAZZ BAND

LET ME GO, LOVER! - JOAN WEBER

LET ME IN (1962) THE SENSATIONS

LET MY PEOPLE GO GO (1987) RAINMAKERS

LET'S ALL CHANT (1978) MICHAEL ZAGER BAND

LET'S GO (PONY) (1962) THE ROUTERS

LET'S GO ALL THE WAY (1986) SLY FOX

LET'S GO TO SAN FRANCISCO (1967) THE FLOWER POT MEN

LET'S LIVE TOGETHER (1976) THE ROAD APPLES

LET'S THINK ABOUT LIVING (1960) BOB LUMAN

THE LETTER (1969) THE ARBORS

LETTER FROM SHERRY (1964) DALE WARD

LET THE GOOD TIMES ROLL/FEELS SO GOOD (1967) BUNNY SIGLER

LET THE FOUR WINDS BLOW (1957) ROY BROWN

LET THE LITTLE GIRL DANCE (1960) BILLY BLAND

LET THE MUSIC PLAY (1984) SHANNON

LIAR, LIAR (1965) THE CASTAWAYS

LIECHTENSTEINER POLKA (1957) WILL GLAHÉ AND HIS ORCHESTRA

LIES (1987) JONATHAN BUTLER

LIES (1966) THE KNICKERBOCKERS

LIFE IN A NORTHERN TOWN (1985) THE DREAM ACADEMY

LIFE IS A ROCK (BUT THE RADIO ROLLED ME) (1974) REUNION

LIGHT OF DAY (1987) THE BARBUSTERS

(LIGHT OF EXPERIENCE) DOINA DE JALE (1976) GHEORGHE ZAMFIR

LIZZIE AND THE RAINMAN (1975) TANYA TUCKER

LITTLE ARROWS (1968) LEAPY LEE

LITTLE BAND OF GOLD (1963) JAMES GILREATH

LITTLE BIT O' SOUL (1967) THE MUSIC EXPLOSION

LITTLE BITTY PRETTY ONE (1957) THURSTON HARRIS

LITTLE DIPPER (1959) MICKEY MOZART QUINTET

THE LITTLE DRUMMER BOY (1959) HARRY SIMEONE CHORALE

LITTLE GIRL (1966) SYNDICATE OF SOUND

LITTLE HONDA (1964) THE HONDELLS

LITTLE OLE MAN (UPTIGHT–EVERYTHING'S ALRIGHT) (1967) BILL
COSBY

THE LITTLE SPACE GIRL (1959) JESSE LEE TURNER

LITTLE STAR (1958) THE ELEGANTS

LITTLE THINGS MEAN A LOT (1955) KITTY KALLEN

LIVE IS LIFE (1985) OPUS

LIVE IT UP (1987) MENTAL AS ANYTHING

LIVING IN A BOX (1987) LIVING IN A BOX

LIVING NEXT DOOR TO ALICE (1977) SMOKIE

LIVING ON VIDEO (1985) TRANS-X

LIVIN' IT UP (FRIDAY NIGHT) (1979) BELL AND JAMES

LOADSAMONEY (DOIN' UP THE HOUSE) (1988) HARRY ENFIELD

LOLLIPOP (1958) RONALD & RUBY

LO MUCHO QUE TE QUIERO (THE MORE I LOVE YOU) (1969) RENÉ
Y RENÉ

LONELY FOR YOU (1959) GARY STITES

THE LONELY SURFER (1963) JACK NITZSCHE

THE LONE RANGER (1979) QUANTUM JUMP

LONG HAIRED LOVER FROM LIVERPOOL (1972) LITTLE JIMMY OSMOND

LONG LONESOME HIGHWAY (1970) MICHAEL PARKS

LOOK FOR A STAR (1960) DEANE HAWLEY

LOOK FOR A STAR (1960) GARRY MILES

LOOK FOR A STAR (1960) GARRY MILLS

LOOKIN' FOR LOVE (1980) JOHNNY LEE

LOOP DE LOOP (1963) JOHNNY THUNDER

LOOP DI LOVE (1972) SHAG

THE LORD'S PRAYER (1974) SISTER JANET MEAD

LOSING MY MIND (1989) LIZA MINELLI

LOST LOVE (1961) H.B. BARNUM

LOVE (CAN MAKE YOU HAPPY) MERCY

LOVE CAN'T TURN AROUND (1986) FARLEY 'JACKMASTER' FUNK

LOVE CHANGES (EVERYTHING) (1988) CLIMIE FISHER

LOVE GAMES (1984) BELLE AND THE DEVOTIONS

LOVE GROWS (WHERE MY ROSEMARY GOES) (1970) EDISON LIGHTHOUSE

LOVE HURTS (1975) NAZARETH

LOVE IN C MINOR (1977) CERRONE

LOVE IS BLUE (1968) PAUL MAURIAT

LOVE IS CONTAGIOUS (1988) TAJA SEVELLE

LOVE IS IN THE AIR (1978) JOHN PAUL YOUNG

LOVE IS STRANGE (1957) MICKEY & SYLVIA

LOVE IS THE DRUG (1976) ROXY MUSIC

LOVE JONES (1972) BRIGHTER SIDE OF DARKNESS

LOVE LETTERS (1962) KETTY LESTER

LOVE LIKE A MAN (1970) TEN YEARS AFTER

LOVELY ONE (1956) THE FOUR VOICES

LOVE MAKES A WOMAN (1968) BARBARA ACKLIN

LOVE MAKES THE WORLD GO ROUND (1966) DEON JACKSON

LOVE MEANS (YOU NEVER HAVE TO SAY YOU'RE SORRY) (1971) SOUNDS OF SUNSHINE

LOVE ME FOREVER (1958) MARION RYAN

THE LOVE OF MY MAN (1963) THEOLA KILGORE

LOVE OF THE COMMON PEOPLE (1970) NICKY THOMAS

LOVE PLUS ONE (1982) HAIRCUT ONE HUNDRED

LOVE POWER (1968) THE SANDPEBBLES

LOVERS ISLAND (1961) THE BLUE JAYS

LOVE THEME FROM ST. ELMO'S FIRE (1985) DAVID FOSTER

LOVE TOWN (1983) BOOKER NEWBERRY III

LOVE WON'T LET ME WAIT (1975) MAJOR HARRIS

LOVE YOU LIKE I NEVER LOVED BEFORE (1981) JOHN O'BANION

LOVE YOU SO (1960) RON HOLDEN

LOVIN' YOU (1975) MINNIE RIPERTON

LULLABY OF BIRDLAND (1956) THE BLUE STARS

M...
MA BELLE AMIE (1970) TEE SET

MACARTHUR PARK (1968) RICHARD HARRIS

THE MADISON (1960) AL BROWN'S TUNETOPPERS FEATURING COOKIE BROWN

THE MADISON TIME-PART 1 (1960) RAY BRYANT TRIO

MAGIC (1974) PILOT

MAGIC FLY (1977) SPACE

MAGNET AND STEEL (1978) WALTER EGAN

MAJOR TOM (COMING HOME) (1983) PETER SCHILLING

MAKE BELIEVE (1969) WIND

MAKE YOURSELF (1955) COMFORTABLE PEGGY KING

MAKIN' LOVE (1959) FLOYD ROBINSON

MAKING OUR DREAMS COME TRUE (1976) CYNDI GRECCO

MAKIN' IT (1979) DAVID NAUGHTON

MAMA DIDN'T LIE (1963) JAN BRADLEY

MAMA SING A SONG (1962) STAN KENTON

MAMA USED TO SAY (1982) JUNIOR

MANHATTAN SPIRITUAL (1959) REG OWEN

MANIAC (1983) MICHAEL SEMBELLO

THE MAN IN THE RAINCOAT (1955) MARION MARLOWE

THE MAN IN THE RAINCOAT (1955) PRISCILLA WRIGHT

MAIN THEME FROM THE MAN WITH THE GOLDEN ARM (1956) ELMER BERNSTEIN

(THEMES FROM) THE MAN WITH THE GOLDEN ARM (1956) RICHARD MALTBY AND HIS ORCHESTRA

MARIA ELENA (1963) LOS INDIOS TABAJARAS

MARIANNE (1957) TERRY GILKYSON AND THE EASY RIDERS

MARINA (1959) ROCCO GRANATA AND THE INTERNATIONAL QUINTET

MARTIAN HOP (1963) THE RAN-DELLS

MARY LOU (1959) RONNIE HAWKINS AND THE HAWKS

MARY'S PRAYER (1987) DANNY WILSON

MASTER JACK (1968) FOUR JACKS AND A JILL

MATCHSTALK MEN AND MATCHSTALK CATS AND DOGS (1978) BRIAN AND MICHAEL

MAY THE BIRD OF PARADISE FLY UP YOUR NOSE (1965) LITTLE JIMMY DICKENS

ME AND BOBBY MCGEE (1971) JANIS JOPLIN

ME AND MRS. JONES (1972) BILLY PAUL

MEDICINE MAN (1969) THE BUCHANAN BROTHERS

THE MEN IN MY LITTLE GIRL'S LIFE (1966) MIKE DOUGLAS

MERCY, MERCY, MERCY (1967) CANNONBALL ADDERLEY

MEXICO (1961) BOB MOORE AND HIS ORCHESTRA

MIAMI VICE THEME (1985) JAN HAMMER

MICHELLE (1966) DAVID AND JONATHAN

MICHELLE (1966) THE OVERLANDERS

MICKEY (1982) TONI BASIL

MIDNIGHT MARY (1964) JOEY POWERS

MIDNIGHT IN MOSCOW (1962) KENNY BALL AND HIS JAZZMEN

MIDNIGHT RIDER (1973) GREGG ALLMAN

MISDEMEANOR (1973) FOSTER SYLVERS

MIDNIGHT STROLL (1959) THE REVELS

MIRROR, MIRROR (1966) PINKERTON'S ASSORTED COLOURS

MISSING YOU (1984) JOHN WAITE

MISSISSIPPI (1970) JOHN PHILLIPS

MISSISSIPPI QUEEN (1970) MOUNTAIN

MISTER SANDMAN (1981) EMMYLOU HARRIS

MIXED-UP, SHOOK-UP GIRL (1964) PATTY & THE EMBLEMS

MOCKINGBIRD (1963) INEZ AND CHARLIE FOXX

MODERN DAY DELILAH (1984) VAN STEPHENSON

MONA LISA (1959) CARL MANN

MONEY (THAT'S WHAT I WANT) (1959) BARRETT STRONG

MONEY (THAT'S WHAT I WANT) (1977) THE FLYING LIZARDS

THE MONSTER MASH (1973) BOBBY 'BORIS' PICKETT AND THE CRYPT-KICKERS

MONTEGO BAY (1970) BOBBY BLOOM

MONY MONY (1968) TOMMY JAMES AND THE SHONDELLS

MOONFLIGHT (1969) VIK VENUS

MOONLIGHT SWIM (1957) TONY PERKINS

MOONGLOW AND THEME FROM PICNIC (1956) MORRIS STOLOFF AND THE COLUMBIA PICTURES ORCHESTRA

MORE (1963) KAI WINDING

MORE THAN IN LOVE (1981) KATE ROBBINS AND BEYOND

MORE THAN JUST THE TWO OF US (1982) SNEAKER

MORE TODAY THAN YESTERDAY (1969) SPIRAL STARECASE

MORGEN (1959) IVO ROBIC AND THE SONG-MASTERS

MORNING DANCE (1979) SPYRO GYRA

MORNING GIRL (1969) THE NEON PHILHARMONIC

MOTHER-IN-LAW (1961) ERNIE K-DOE

MOTHER OF MINE (1972) NEIL REID

MOTORCYCLE MAMA (1972) SAILCAT

MOTORTOWN (1987) KANE GANG

MOUNTAIN OF LOVE (1960) HAROLD DORMAN

MOVE CLOSER (1985) PHYLLIS NELSON

MOVIN' (1976) BRASS CONSTRUCTION

MR. BIG STUFF (1971) JEAN KNIGHT

MR. CUSTER (1960) LARRY VERNE

MR. LEE (1957) THE BOBBETTES

MR. WONDERFUL (1956) TEDDI KING

MULE SKINNER BLUES (1960) THE FENDERMEN

MURPHY'S LAW (1982) CHÉRI

MUSIC (1976) JOHN MILES

MUSIC BOX DANCER (1979) FRANK MILLS

THE MUSIC OF THE NIGHT (1987) MICHAEL CRAWFORD

MUSIC TO WATCH GIRLS BY (1967) BOB CREWE GENERATION

MY ANGEL BABY (1978) TOBY BEAU

(MY BABY DON'T LOVE ME) NO MORE (1955) DEJOHN SISTERS

MY BABY LOVES LOVIN' (1970) WHITE PLAINS

MY BOOMERANG WON'T COME BACK (1962) CHARLIE DRAKE

MY EVER CHANGING MOODS (1984) THE STYLE COUNCIL

MY FAVOURITE WASTE OF TIME (1986) OWEN PAUL

MY GIRL (1988) SUAVE

MY GIRL JOSEPHINE (1967) JERRY JAYE

MY LOVE, FORGIVE ME (AMORE, SCUSAMI) (1965) ROBERT GOULET

MY MARIA (1973) B. W. STEVENSON

MY PLEDGE OF LOVE (1969) JOE JEFFREY GROUP

MY RESISTANCE IS LOW (1976) ROBIN SARSTEDT

MY SHARONA (1979) THE KNACK

MY SWEET LADY (1974) CLIFF DEYOUNG

MY TOOT TOOT (1985) DENISE LASALLE

N...

NADIA'S THEME (THE YOUNG AND THE RESTLESS) (1976) BARRY DEVORZON AND PERRY BOTKIN, JR.

NAG (1961) THE HALOS

NA NA HEY HEY KISS HIM GOODBYE (1970) STEAM

NATIVE NEW YORKER (1978) ODYSSEY

NATURAL BORN BUGIE (1969) HUMBLE PIE

NATURALLY STONED (1968) THE AVANT-GARDE

NEANDERTHAL MAN (1970) HOTLEGS

THE NEED TO BE (1974) JIM WEATHERLY

NEL BLU DIPINTO DI BLU (VOLARE) (1958) DOMENICO MODUGNO

NELLIE THE ELEPHANT (1984) THE TOY DOLLS

THE NEVERENDING STORY (1984) LIMAHL

NEVER NEVER (1983) ASSEMBLY

NEVER ON SUNDAY (1960) LYN CORNELL

NEVER TAKE ME ALIVE (1987) SPEAR OF DESTINY

NEW ROMANCE (IT'S A MYSTERY) (1980) SPIDER

NEW YORK GROOVE (1978) ACE FREHLEY

NEXT PLANE TO LONDON (1967) THE ROSE GARDEN

NICE GIRLS (1982) EYE TO EYE

NICOLE (1981) POINT BLANK

THE NIGHT CHICAGO DIED (1974) PAPER LACE

NIGHT GAMES (1981) GRAHAM BONNET

THE NIGHT THE LIGHTS WENT OUT IN GEORGIA (1973) VICKI LAWRENCE

N-N-NINETEEN (NOT OUT) (1985) THE COMMENTATORS

NOBODY (1982) SYLVIA

NOBODY BUT ME (1968) THE HUMAN BEINZ

NOBODY BUT YOU BABE (1969) CLARENCE REID

NOBODY SAID IT WAS EASY (LOOKIN' FOR THE LIGHTS) (1982) LE ROUX

NOBODY'S CHILD (1969) KAREN YOUNG

NO CHARGE (1976) J.J. BARRIE

NO CHARGE (1974) MELBA MONTGOMERY

NO CHEMISE, PLEASE (1959) GERRY GRANAHAN

NO EASY WAY OUT (1986) ROBERT TEPPER

NO MATTER WHAT SHAPE (YOUR STOMACH'S IN) (1966) THE T-BONES

NOTHING BUT A HEARTACHE (1969) THE FLIRTATIONS

NOT JUST ANOTHER GIRL (1988) IVAN NEVILLE

NUMERO UNO (1989) STARLIGHT

THE NUT ROCKER (1962) B. BUMBLE AND THE STINGERS

O...

OBJECT OF MY DESIRE (1985) STARPOINT

OBSESSION (1985) ANIMOTION

OH, BABE, WHAT WOULD YOU SAY? (1973) HURRICANE SMITH

OH HOW HAPPY (1966) THE SHADES OF BLUE

OH JULIE (1958) THE CRESCENDOS

OH SUSANNAH (1955) THE SINGING DOGS

OH WELL (1979) THE ROCKETS

THE OLDEST SWINGER IN TOWN (1981) FRED WEDLOCK

OLD FASHIONED BOY (YOU'RE THE ONE) (1977) STALLION

THE OLD PHILOSOPHER (1956) EDDIE LAWRENCE

ONCE BITTEN TWICE SHY (1986) VESTA WILLIAMS

ONCE UPON A TIME (1961) ROCHELL AND THE CANDLES

ONCE YOU UNDERSTAND (1972) THINK

ONE DAY AT A TIME (1979) LENA MARTELL

ONE DAY AT A TIME (1974) MARILYN SELLARS

ONE HAS MY NAME (THE OTHER HAS MY HEART) (1966) BARRY YOUNG

ONE IN A MILLION YOU (1980) LARRY GRAHAM

ONE NATION UNDER A GROOVE (1978) FUNKADELIC

ONE NIGHT IN BANGKOK (1984) MURRAY HEAD

ONE STEP CLOSER TO YOU (1986) GAVIN CHRISTOPHER

ONE STEP FURTHER (1982) BARDO

ONE SUMMER NIGHT (1958) THE DANLEERS

ONE TIN SOLDIER (1970) THE ORIGINAL CASTE

ONE TIN SOLDIER (THE LEGEND OF BILLY JACK) (1971) COVEN

ONE TOKE OVER THE LINE (1971) BREWER & SHIPLEY

ONLY A LONELY HEART SEES (1980) FELIX CAVALIERE

ONLY YOU (1959) FRANCK POURCEL'S FRENCH FIDDLES

ON MY OWN (1986) PATTI LABELLE (AND MICHAEL MACDONALD)

ON THE INSIDE/THEME FROM PRISONER: CELL BLOCK H (1989) LYNNE HAMILTON

ON THE LOOSE (1983) SAGA

ON TOP OF SPAGHETTI (1963) TOM GLAZER AND THE DO-RE-MI CHILDREN'S CHORUS

O-O-H CHILD (1970) THE FIVE STAIRSTEPS

OOH POO PAH DOO–PART II (1960) JESSIE HILL

OO WEE BABY, I LOVE YOU (1965) FRED HUGHES

OPEN THE DOOR TO YOUR HEART (1966) DARRELL BANKS

OPERATOR (1985) MIDNIGHT STAR

ORVILLE'S SONG (1983) KEITH HARRIS AND ORVILLE

O SUPERMAN (1981) LAURIE ANDERSON

OUR HOUSE (1982) MADNESS

OUR WINTER LOVE (1963) BILL PURSELL

OUT IN THE FIELDS (1985) GARY MOORE/PHIL LYNOTT

OUT OF MIND, OUT OF SIGHT (1986) MODELS

OVER THE MOUNTAIN; ACROSS THE SEA (1957) JOHNNIE & JOE

OVER THE RAINBOW (1960) THE DEMENSIONS

OVERTURE FROM TOMMY (A ROCK OPERA) (1970) ASSEMBLED MULTITUDE

P...
PAC-MAN FEVER (1982) BUCKNER & GARCIA

PADRE (1958) TONI ARDEN

PAINTED LADIES (1974) IAN THOMAS

PAPA'S GOT A BRAND NEW PIGBAG (1982) PIGBAG

PAPER ROSES (1973) MARIE OSMOND

PARANOIMIA (1986) MAX HEADROOM

PART TIME LOVE (1963) LITTLE JOHNNY TAYLOR

PARTY DOLL (1957) BUDDY KNOX

PARTY LIGHTS (1962) CLAUDINE CLARK

PASS THE DUTCHIE (1982) MUSICAL YOUTH

PATA PATA (1967) MIRIAM MAKEBA

PEANUT BUTTER (1961) THE MARATHONS

PEANUTS (1956) LITTLE JOE AND THE THRILLERS

PENETRATION (1964) THE PYRAMIDS

PERCOLATOR (TWIST) (1962) BILLY JOE AND THE CHECKMATES

PERFECT WAY (1985) SCRITTI POLITTI

PERSONALLY (1982) KARLA BONOFF

PETITE FLEUR (LITTLE FLOWER) (1959) CHRIS BARBER'S JAZZ BAND

PICTURES OF MATCHSTICK MEN (1968) STATUS QUO

PIECE OF MY HEART (1968) BIG BROTHER AND THE HOLDING COMPANY

PILLOW TALK (1973) SYLVIA

PILOT OF THE AIRWAVES (1980) CHARLIE DORE

PINK SHOE LACES (1959) DODIE STEVENS

PIPELINE (1963) THE CHANTAYS

PLAYBOY (1968) GENE AND DEBBE

PLAYGROUND IN MY MIND (1973) CLINT HOLMES

PLAY THAT FUNKY MUSIC (1976) WILD CHERRY

PLEASE COME TO BOSTON (1974) DAVE LOGGINS

PLEASE DON'T LEAVE (1979) LAUREN WOOD

PLEASE DON'T TALK TO THE LIFEGUARD (1963) DIANE RAY

PLEASE HELP ME, I'M FALLING (1960) HANK LOCKLIN

PLEASE LOVE ME FOREVER (1961) CATHY JEAN AND THE ROOMMATES

PLEDGE OF LOVE (1957) KEN COPELAND

PLEDGING MY LOVE (1955) JOHNNY ACE

POLICE OFFICER (1984) SMILEY CULTURE

THE POLITICS OF DANCING (1983) RE-FLEX

POLK SALAD ANNIE (1969) TONY JOE WHITE

POPCORN (1972) HOT BUTTER

POP MUSIK (1979) M

POP POP POP-PIE (1962) THE SHERRYS

POPSICLES AND ICICLES (1964) THE MURMAIDS

PORTUGUESE WASHERWOMEN (1956) JOE 'FINGERS' CARR

THE POWER OF LOVE (1985) JENNIFER RUSH

PRECIOUS AND FEW (1972) CLIMAX

PRECIOUS, PRECIOUS (1971) JACKIE MOORE

PRECIOUS TO ME (1981) PHIL SEYMOUR

PRETTY GIRLS EVERYWHERE (1959) EUGENE CHURCH AND THE FELLOWS

PRETTY LITTLE ANGEL EYES (1961) CURTIS LEE

PRIME MOVER (1987) ZODIAC MINDWARP & THE LOVE REACTION

PRISCILLA (1956) EDDIE COOLEY

THE PROMISE (1987) WHEN IN ROME

PSYCHOTIC REACTION (1966) COUNT FIVE

PUMP UP THE BITTER (BRUTAL MIX) (1988) STAR TURN ON 45 (PINTS)

PUMP UP THE VOLUME / ANITINA (THE FIRST TIME I SEE SHE DANCE) (1987) MARRS

PURPLE PEOPLE EATER (1958) SHEB WOOLEY

THE PUSHBIKE SONG (1971) THE MIXTURES

PUSHIN' TOO HARD (1967) THE SEEDS

PUTTIN' ON THE RITZ (1983) TACO

PUT YOUR HAND IN THE HAND (1971) OCEAN

Q...
QUENTIN'S THEME (1969) CHARLES RANDOLPH GREAN SOUNDE

QUICK JOEY SMALL (RUN JOEY RUN) (1968) KASENETZ-KATZ SINGING ORCHESTRAL CIRCUS

R...
RACE WITH THE DEVIL (1968) THE GUN

RADAR LOVE (1973) GOLDEN EARRING

RADIOACTIVE (1985) THE FIRM

RADIO AFRICA (1986) LATIN QUARTER

THE RAIN (1986) ORAN "JUICE" JONES

RAINBOW (1957) RUSS HAMILTON

RAINBOW CONNECTION (1979) KERMIT THE FROG

RAMA LAMA DING DONG (1961) THE EDSELS

THE RAPPER (1970) THE JAGGERZ

RAPPER'S DELIGHT (1979) THE SUGARHILL GANG

RAUNCHY (1957) BILL JUSTIS

RAUNCHY (1957) ERNIE FREEMAN

REACH OUT OF THE DARKNESS (1968) FRIEND & LOVER

REAL WILD CHILD (WILD ONE) (1986) IGGY POP

RECONSIDER ME (1969) JOHNNY ADAMS

REFLECTIONS OF MY LIFE (1969) MARMALADE

RELAX (1983) FRANKIE GOES TO HOLLYWOOD

REMEMBER ME (1964) RITA PAVONE

REMEMBER THEN (1963) THE EARLS

RESPECT YOURSELF (1987) BRUCE WILLIS

RESURRECTION SHUFFLE (1971) ASHTON, GARDNER AND DYKE

RETURN OF DJANGO/DOLLAR IN THE TEETH (1969) THE UPSETTERS

RHYTHM OF THE NIGHT (1985) DEBARGE

RIDE CAPTAIN RIDE (1970) BLUES IMAGE

RIGHT ON TRACK (1987) BREAKFAST CLUB

RIGHT PLACE WRONG TIME (1973) DR. JOHN

RING MY BELL (1979) ANITA WARD

RINGO (1964) LORNE GREENE

RINGS (1971) CYMARRON

RIP IT UP (1983) ORANGE JUICE

RIP VAN WINKLE (1964) THE DEVOTIONS

RITUAL (1988) DAN REED NETWORK

RIVERS OF BABYLON (1978) BONEY M

ROBBIN THE CRADLE (1959) TONY BELLUS

ROCK-A-BYE YOUR BABY WITH A DIXIE MELODY (1956) JERRY LEWIS

ROCK AND ROLL DREAMS COME THROUGH (1981) JIM STEINMAN

ROCK AND ROLL, HOOCHIE KOO (1974) RICK DERRINGER

ROCKIN' AROUND THE CHRISTMAS TREE (1987) MEL SMITH (WITH KIM WILDE)

ROCKIN' CHAIR (1975) GWEN MCCRAE

ROCKIN ROBIN (1958) BOBBY DAY

ROCKIN' LITTLE ANGEL (1960) RAY SMITH

ROCK ME GENTLY (1974) ANDY KIM

ROCK ON (1974) DAVID ESSEX

ROCK THE BOAT (1974) THE HUES CORPORATION

RODRIGO'S GUITAR CONCERTO DE ARANJUEZ (1976) MANUEL & THE MUSIC OF THE MOUNTAINS

ROLENE (1979) MOON MARTIN

ROMEO'S TUNE (1980) STEVE FORBERT

ROOMS ON FIRE (1989) STEVIE NICKS

ROSE GARDEN (1970) LYNN ANDERSON

ROSES (1986) HAYWOODE

ROSES ARE RED (1988) THE MAC BAND, FEATURING THE MCCAMPBELL BROTHERS

ROSIE LEE (1957) THE MELLO-TONES

RUBBER DUCKIE (1970) ERNIE

RUBY DUBY DU (1960) TOBIN MATTHEWS AND CO.

RUMOURS (1986) TIMEX SOCIAL CLUB

RUNAROUND (1955) THE THREE CHUCKLES

RUN FOR HOME (1978) LINDISFARNE

RUNNING UP THAT HILL (1985) KATE BUSH

RUN RUN RUN (1972) JO JO GUNNE

RUSH HOUR (1988) JANE WIEDLIN

RHYTHM OF THE RAIN (1962) THE CASCADES

S...
SAD EYES (1979) ROBERT JOHN

SAD SWEET DREAMER (1974) SWEET SENSATION

THE SAFETY DANCE (1983) MEN WITHOUT HATS

SAILOR (YOUR HOME IS THE SEA) (1960) LOLITA

SALLY GO 'ROUND THE ROSES (1963) THE JAYNETTS

THE SALT IN MY TEARS (1983) MARTIN BRILEY

SAN DAMIANO (HEART AND SOUL) (1984) SAL SOLO

SANDY (1960) LARRY HALL

SAN FRANCISCO (BE SURE TO WEAR FLOWERS IN YOUR HAIR) (1967) SCOTT MCKENZIE

SATIN SHEETS (1973) JEANNE PRUETT

SATURDAY NIGHT (1979) HERMAN BROOD

SAUSALITO SUMMERNIGHT (1981) DIESEL

SAVANNAH NIGHTS (1980) TOM JOHNSTON

SAVE ALL YOUR KISSES FOR ME (1976) BROTHERHOOD OF MAN

SAVE YOUR LOVE (1982) RENEE AND RENATO

SAYIN' SORRY (DON'T MAKE IT RIGHT) (1988) DENISE LOPEZ

SAY MAN (1959) BO DIDDLEY

SAY WHAT (1981) JESSE WINCHESTER

SAY YEAH (1985) THE LIMIT

SEA CRUISE (1959) FRANKIE FORD

SEA OF LOVE (1959) PHIL PHILLIPS WITH THE TWILIGHTS

SEARCHING FOR MY LOVE (1966) BOBBY MOORE & THE RHYTHM ACES

SEASIDE SHUFFLE (1972) TERRY DACTYL AND THE DINOSAURS

SEASONS IN THE SUN (1974) TERRY JACKS

SEE THE DAY (1985) DEE C. LEE

SEE YOU IN SEPTEMBER (1959) THE TEMPOS

SELFISH ONE (1964) JACKIE ROSS

SEND ME AN ANGEL (1989) REAL LIFE

SERIOUS (1987) DONNA ALLEN

SET ME FREE (1980) UTOPIA

SEVEN TEARS (1982) GOOMBAY DANCE BAND

SEVEN YEAR ACHE (1981) ROSANNE CASH

SHADDAP YOU FACE (1981) JOE DOLCE MUSIC THEATRE

SHAGGY DOG (1964) MICKEY LEE LANE

SHAKE IT (1979) IAN MATTHEWS

SHAKE YOU DOWN (1987) GREGORY ABBOTT

SHAKIN' ALL OVER (1960) JOHNNY KIDD & THE PIRATES

SHAME, SHAME (1968) THE MAGIC LANTERNS

SHAME, SHAME, SHAME (1975) SHIRLEY & COMPANY

SHANGRI-LA (1964) ROBERT MAXWELL AND HIS HARP AND ORCHESTRA

SHANNON (1976) HENRY GROSS

SHAPE OF THINGS TO COME (1968) MAX FROST AND THE TROOPERS

SHAVING CREAM (1975) BENNY BELL

SHE BLINDED ME WITH SCIENCE (1983) THOMAS DOLBY

THE SHEFFIELD GRINDER / CAPSTICK COMES HOME (1981) TONY CAPSTICK

SHE'S ALL I GOT (1971) FREDDIE NORTH

SHE'S LIKE THE WIND (1988) PATRICK SWAYZE FEATURING WENDY FRASER

SHE'S NEAT (1958) DALE WRIGHT WITH THE ROCK-ITS

SHE'S THE ONE (1964) THE CHARTBUSTERS

SHIP OF FOOLS (SAVE ME FROM TOMORROW) (1987) WORLD PARTY

SHORT PEOPLE (1978) RANDY NEWMAN

SHOUT! SHOUT! (KNOCK YOURSELF OUT) (1962) ERNIE MARESCA

SHOULD'VE NEVER LET YOU GO (1980) DARA AND PAUL SEDAKA

(SHU-DOO-PA-POO-POOP) LOVE BEING YOUR FOOL (1975) TRAVIS WAMMACK

SILHOUETTES/DADDY COOL (1957) THE RAYS

SILVER THREADS AND GOLDEN NEEDLES (1962) THE SPRINGFIELDS

SIMON SAYS (1967) 1910 FRUITGUM COMPANY

SINCE I MET YOU BABY (1956) IVORY JOE HUNTER

SINCE YESTERDAY (1984) STRAWBERRY SWITCHBLADE

SIT DOWN, I THINK I LOVE YOU (1967) THE MOJO MEN

SITTIN' IN THE BALCONY (1957) JOHNNY DEE

SIX DAYS ON THE ROAD (1963) DAVE DUDLEY

SKIP A ROPE (1968) HENSON CARGILL

SLICE OF HEAVEN (1986) DAVE DOBBYN

SLIDE (1977) SLAVE

SLOW DOWN (1977) JOHN MILES

SLOW WALK (1956) SIL AUSTIN

SMALL BEGINNINGS (1972) FLASH

SMALL SAD SAM (1962) PHIL MCLEAN

SMILE A LITTLE SMILE FOR ME (1969) THE FLYING MACHINE

SMILING FACES SOMETIMES (1971) THE UNDISPUTED TRUTH

SMOKE FROM A DISTANT FIRE (1977) THE SANFORD-TOWNSEND BAND

SMOKE GETS IN YOUR EYES (1973) BLUE HAZE

SMOKING GUN (1987) ROBERT CRAY BAND

SMOKY PLACES (1962) THE CORSAIRS

THE SMURFING SONG (1978) FATHER ABRAHAM & THE SMURFS

SNAP YOUR FINGERS (1962) JOE HENDERSON

SNOOPY VS. THE RED BARON (1973) THE HOTSHOTS

SO ALIVE (1989) LOVE AND ROCKETS

SO FINE (1959) THE FIESTAS

SOFTLY WHISPERING I LOVE YOU (1972) THE ENGLISH CONGREGATION

SOLID (1985) ASHFORD & SIMPSON

SOMEBODY'S BEEN SLEEPING (1970) 100 PROOF (AGED IN SOUL)

SOMEBODY'S KNOCKIN' (1981) TERRI GIBBS

SOMEBODY'S WATCHING ME (1984) ROCKWELL

SOMEDAY, SOMEWAY (1982) MARSHALL CRENSHAW

SOMEDAY (YOU'LL WANT ME TO WANT YOU) (1958) JODIE SANDS

SOME LIKE IT HOT (1985) THE POWER STATION

SOMETHING IN THE AIR (1969) THUNDERCLAP NEWMAN

SOMETHING OUTA NOTHING (1986) LETITIA DEAN AND PAUL MEDFORD

SOMETHING'S BURNING (1970) KENNY ROGERS & THE FIRST EDITION

SOMETIMES (1977) FACTS OF LIFE

SOMETIMES WHEN WE TOUCH (1978) DAN HILL

SOMEWHERE, MY LOVE (1966) RAY CONNIFF

SOMEWHERE DOWN THE CRAZY RIVER (1988) ROBBIE ROBERTSON

SONIC BOOM BOY (1987) WESTWORLD

SORRY (I RAN ALL THE WAY HOME) (1959) THE IMPALAS

SOUL CITY (1987) THE PARTLAND BROTHERS

SOUL MAKOSSA (1973) MANU DIBANGO

SOUL SONG (1973) JOE STAMPLEY

SOUL TRAIN (1984) SWANS WAY

SO WRONG (1983) PATRICK SIMMONS

THE SPARROW (1979) THE RAMBLERS

SPIRIT IN THE SKY (1986) DOCTOR AND THE MEDICS

SPIRIT IN THE SKY (1970) NORMAN GREENBAUM

SPRING RAIN (1977) SILVETTI

STAND BY ME (1967) SPYDER TURNER

STANDING IN THE ROAD (1971) BLACKFOOT SUE

STAY (1960) MAURICE WILLIAMS AND THE ZODIACS

STAY AWHILE (1971) THE BELLS

STEAL AWAY (1964) JIMMY HUGHES

ST. ELMO'S FIRE (MAN IN MOTION) (1985) JOHN PARR

STAIRWAY TO HEAVEN (1985) FAR CORPORATION

STAND BY ME (1980) MICKEY GILLEY

STARTING TOGETHER (1986) SU POLLARD

STAY THE NIGHT (1987) BENJAMIN ORR

STICK SHIFT (1961) THE DUALS

STILL (1963) BILL ANDERSON

STONE COLD (1982) RAINBOW

STOP (1989) SAM BROWN

STAKKER HUMANOID (1988) HUMANOID

STRANGE BUT TRUE (1988) TIMES TWO

STRANDED IN THE JUNGLE (1956) THE CADETS

STRANDED IN THE JUNGLE (1956) THE GADABOUTS

STRANDED IN THE JUNGLE (1956) THE JAY HAWKS

STRANGER ON THE SHORE (1962) ACKER BILK

STREET LIFE (1979) THE CRUSADERS

STREET SINGIN' (1976) LADY FLASH

STREETS OF LONDON (1975) RALPH MCTELL

STRONGER THAN BEFORE (1981) CAROLE BAYER SAGER

STUCK IN THE MIDDLE WITH YOU (1973) STEALERS WHEEL

STUMBLIN' IN (1979) SUZI QUATRO

STUTTER RAP (NO SLEEP 'TIL BEDTIME) (1988) MORRIS MINOR AND THE MAJORS

ST. VALENTINE'S DAY MASSACRE (1981) MOTÖR HEADGIRL SCHOOL

SUAVECITO (1972) MALO

SUBSTITUTE (1978) CLOUT

SUCH A WOMAN (1979) TYCOON

SUDDENLY (WEDDING THEME FROM 'NEIGHBOURS') (1988) ANGRY ANDERSON

SUGAR BABY LOVE (1974) RUBETTES

SUGAR DON'T BITE (1984) SAM HARRIS

SUGAR FREE (1987) WA WA NEE

SWEET BABY (1981) STANLEY CLARKE AND GEORGE DUKE

SWEET LOVE (1986) ANITA BAKER

SUGAR ON SUNDAY (1969) CLIQUE

SUGAR SUGAR (1969) THE ARCHIES

SUKIYAKI (1963) KYU SAKAMOTO

SUMMER SAMBA (SO NICE) (1966) WALTER WANDERLEY

SUMMERTIME BLUES (1968) BLUE CHEER

SUMMERTIME CITY (1975) MIKE BATT WITH THE NEW EDITION

SUPERFLY MEETS SHAFT (1973) JOHN & ERNEST

SUMMERTIME, SUMMERTIME (1958) THE JAMIES

SUMMER SET (1960) MONTY KELLY

SUN CITY (1985) ARTISTS UNITED AGAINST APARTHEID

SUNSHINE (1971) JONATHAN EDWARDS

SUNSHINE GIRL (1967) PARADE

SUPERSONIC (1988) J. J. FAD

SUPERSTAR (1983) LYDIA MURDOCK

SURRENDER TO ME (1989) ROBIN ZANDER

SUSANNA (1984) ART COMPANY

SUSIE DARLIN'(1958) ROBIN LUKE

SWEET DREAMS (1966) TOMMY MCLAIN

THE SWEETEST THING THIS SIDE OF HEAVEN (1967) CHRIS BARTLEY

SWEET INSPIRATION (1968) THE SWEET INSPIRATIONS

SWEET LUI-LOUISE (1979) IRONHORSE

SWEET MARY (1971) WADSWORTH MANSION

SWINGIN' ON A STAR (1963) BIG DEE IRWIN (WITH LITTLE EVA)

THE SWINGIN' SHEPHERD BLUES (1957) MOE KOFFMAN QUARTETTE

SWING YOUR DADDY (1975) JIM GILSTRAP

T...

TAINTED LOVE (1981) SOFT CELL

TAKE A LITTLE RHYTHM (1980) ALI THOMSON

TAKE FIVE (1961) DAVE BRUBECK QUARTET

TAKES A LITTLE TIME (1985) TOTAL CONTRAST

TAKE ON ME (1985) A-HA

TAKE MY BREATH AWAY (1986) BERLIN

TALK IT OVER (1989) GRAYSON HUGH

TALK TO ME (1987) CHICO DEBARGE

TALK TO ME (1963) SUNNY & THE SUNGLOWS

TALK TALK (1967) THE MUSIC MACHINE

TALL COOL ONE (1959) THE WAILERS

TANTALISE (WO WO EE YEH YEH) (1983) JIMMY THE HOOVER

TAR AND CEMENT (1966) VERDELLE SMITH

TARZAN BOY (1985) BALTIMORA

TEACH ME TONIGHT (1962) GEORGE MAHARIS

TEA FOR TWO CHA CHA (1958) THE TOMMY DORSEY ORCHESTRA AND WARREN COVINGTON

TEDDY BEAR (1976) RED SOVINE

THE TEDDY BEAR SONG (1973) BARBARA FAIRCHILD

TEEN ANGEL (1960) MARK DINNING

TELEPHONE MAN (1977) MERI WILSON

TELL HIM (1962) THE EXCITERS

TELL HIM NO (1959) TRAVIS AND BOB

TELL LAURA I LOVE HER (1960) RICHIE VALENCE

TELL ME A LIE (1974) SAMI JO

TELSTAR (1962) THE TORNADOS

TENDER LOVE (1986) FORCE MDS

TENNESSEE BIRD WALK (1970) JACK BLANCHARD & MISTY MORGAN

TEQUILA (1958) THE CHAMPS

TEQUILA (1958) EDDIE PLATT

THANK GOD IT'S FRIDAY (1978) LOVE & KISSES

THANKS FOR MY CHILD (1988) CHERYL PEPSII RILEY

THAT'S HOW HEARTACHES ARE MADE (1963) BABY WASHINGTON

THAT'S LOVE (1983) JIM CAPALDI

THAT'S THE WAY LOVE IS (1989) TEN CITY

THAT STRANGER USED TO BE MY GIRL (1962) TRADE MARTIN

THEME FROM BEN (1962) CASEY VALJEAN

THEME FROM SHAFT (1985) EDDY & THE SOUL BAND

THEME FROM SUMMER OF '42 (1971) PETER NERO

THEME FROM THE GREATEST AMERICAN HERO (BELIEVE IT OR NOT) (1981) JOEY SCARBURY

THEME SONG FROM M*A*S*H (SUICIDE IS PAINLESS) (1980) MASH

THEME SONG FROM WHICH WAY IS UP (1978) STARGARD

THEN YOU CAN TELL ME GOODBYE (1967) THE CASINOS

THERE'LL NEVER BE (1978) SWITCH

THERE'S A MOON OUT TONIGHT (1961) THE CAPRIS

THERE'S NO ONE QUITE LIKE GRANDMA (1980) ST WINIFRED'S SCHOOL CHOIR

THERE'S SOMETHING ON YOUR MIND (1960) BOBBY MARCHAN

(THERE WAS A) TALL OAK TREE (1960) DORSEY BURNETTE

THEY DON'T KNOW (1984) TRACEY ULLMAN

THEY'RE COMING TO TAKE ME AWAY, HA-HAAA! (1966) NAPOLEON XIV

THINKING OF YOU (1985) THE COLOURFIELD

THINKING OF YOU (1989) SA-FIRE

THINK IT OVER (1978) CHERYL LADD

THIRD RATE ROMANCE (1975) AMAZING RHYTHM ACES

THIS HEART (1974) GENE REDDING

THIS IS NOT AMERICA (1985) PAT METHENY GROUP

THIS SHOULD GO ON FOREVER (1959) ROD BERNARD

THIS TIME (1961) TROY SHONDELL

(A THEME FROM) THE THREE PENNY OPERA (MORITAT) (1956) RICHARD HAYMAN AND JAN AUGUST

THREE STARS (1959) TOMMY DEE

THREE HEARTS IN A TANGLE (1961) ROY DRUSKY

THOSE OLDIES BUT GOODIES (REMIND ME OF YOU) (1961) LITTLE CAESAR & THE ROMANS

THUNDER AND LIGHTNING (1972) CHI COLTRANE

TIE ME KANGAROO DOWN, SPORT (1963) ROLF HARRIS

TIGHTER, TIGHTER (1970) ALIVE N KICKIN'

TILL DEATH DO US PART (1962) BOB BRAUN

TILL THEN (1963) THE CLASSICS

TIMOTHY (1971) THE BUOYS

TIP TOE THRU' THE TULIPS WITH ME (1968) TINY TIM

TIRED OF TOEIN' THE LINE (1980) ROCKY BURNETTE

TOAST (1978) STREETBAND

TOAST AND MARMALADE FOR TEA (1971) TIN TIN

TOBACCO ROAD (1964) THE NASHVILLE TEENS

TO BE OR NOT TO BE (THE HITLER RAP) (1984) MEL BROOKS

TO BE YOUNG, GIFTED AND BLACK (1970) BOB & MARCIA

TOCCATA (1980) SKY

TOGETHER (1981) TIERRA

TOGETHER WE ARE BEAUTIFUL (1980) FERN KINNEY

TO KNOW HIM IS TO LOVE HIM (1958) TEDDY BEARS

TOKYO MELODY (1964) HELMUT ZACHARIAS

TOMORROW PEOPLE (1988) ZIGGY MARLEY AND THE MELODY MAKERS

TONIGHT (COULD BE THE NIGHT) (1961) THE VELVETS

TONIGHT YOU BELONG TO ME (1956) THE LENNON SISTERS

TOO SHY (1983) KAJAGOOGOO

TORERO (1958) RENATO CAROSONE

TORN BETWEEN TWO LOVERS (1977) MARY MACGREGOR

TORTURE (1962) KRIS JENSEN

TOUCH OF GREY (1987) GRATEFUL DEAD

TRACY (1969) THE CUFF LINKS

TRACY'S THEME (1960) SPENCER ROSS

TRAGEDY (1985) JOHN HUNTER

TRAGEDY (1959) THOMAS WAYNE AND THE DELONS

THE TRAIL OF THE LONESOME PINE (1975) LAUREL & HARDY WITH THE AVALON BOYS FEATURING CHILL WILLS

TRAPPED (1985) COLONEL ABRAMS

TRAPPED BY A THING CALLED LOVE (1971) DENISE LASALLE

TRIANGLE (1961) JANIE GRANT

TRUE LOVE (1956) GRACE KELLY

TRUE LOVE (1956) JANE POWELL

TRYIN' TO LOVE TWO (1977) WILLIAM BELL

TSOP (THE SOUND OF PHILADELPHIA) (1974) MFSB

TUBULAR BELLS (1974) MIKE OLDFIELD

TUFF ENUFF (1986) THE FABULOUS THUNDERBIRDS

TURNING JAPANESE (1980) THE VAPORS

TURN THE BEAT AROUND (1976) VICKI SUE ROBINSON

TURN UP THE RADIO (1985) AUTOGRAPH

TWINE TIME (1965) ALVIN CASH AND THE CRAWLERS

TWO OCCASIONS (1988) THE DEELE

U...

UH! OH! PART 2 (1959) THE NUTTY SQUIRRELS

ULLO JOHN! GOTTA NEW MOTOR? (1984) ALEXEI SAYLE

UNCHAINED MELODY (1955) AL HIBLER

UNDERCOVER ANGEL (1977) ALAN O'DAY

UNDER THE MILKY WAY (1988) THE CHURCH

UNITED WE STAND (1970) THE BROTHERHOOD OF MAN

UNION MAN (1976) CATE BROS

UP IN A PUFF OF SMOKE (1975) POLLY BROWN

UPTOWN TOP RANKING (1978) ALTHEA & DONNA

V...

VALLEY GIRL (1982) FRANK ZAPPA FEATURING MOON UNIT ZAPPA

VEHICLE (1970) IDES OF MARCH

VENUS (1970) SHOCKING BLUE

VIDEO KILLED THE RADIO STAR (1979) THE BUGGLES

VILLAGE OF LOVE (1962) NATHANIEL MAYER AND THE FABULOUS TWILIGHTS

VOODOO RAY (1989) A GUY CALLED GERALD

VOYAGE VOYAGE (REMIX) (1988) DESIRELESS

W...

WAITING FOR A STAR TO FALL (1988) BOY MEETS GIRL

WAITING FOR A TRAIN (1983) FLASH AND THE PAN

WAKE UP (NEXT TO YOU) (1985)GRAHAM PARKER AND THE SHOT

THE WALK (1957) JIMMY MCCRACKLIN WITH HIS BAND

WALKING IN THE AIR (1985) ALED JONES

WALKING ON SUNSHINE (1985) KATRINA AND THE WAVES

WALKING ON SUNSHINE (1982) ROCKERS REVENGE FEATURING DONNIE CALVIN

WALKIN' MY CAT NAMED DOG (1966) NORMA TANEGA

WALK ON THE WILD SIDE-PART 2 (1962) JIMMY SMITH

WALK ON THE WILD SIDE (1973) LOU REED

WAND'RIN' STAR (1970) LEE MARVIN

THE WARRIOR (1984) SCANDAL

WASHINGTON SQUARE (1963) THE VILLAGE STOMPERS

WATER BOY (1961) DON SHIRLEY

WATERLOO (1959) STONEWALL JACKSON

THE WAY IT IS (1986) BRUCE HORNSBY AND THE RANGE

THE WAYWARD WIND (1956) GOGI GRANT

(WE AIN'T GOT) NOTHIN' YET (1967) BLUES MAGOOS

WE ARE THE WORLD (1985) USA FOR AFRICA

WE BELONG TOGETHER (1958) ROBERT & JOHNNY

WE CAN'T HIDE IT ANYMORE (1976) LARRY SANTOS

THE WEDDING (1965) JULIE ROGERS

THE WEDDING SONG (THERE IS LOVE) (1971) PAUL STOOKEY

WEE RULE (1988) WEE PAPA GIRL RAPPERS

WE GOTTA GET YOU A WOMAN (1970) TODD RUNDGREN

WE JUST DISAGREE (1977) DAVE MASON

WELCOME BACK (1976) JOHN SEBASTIAN

WELCOME TO THE BOOMTOWN (1986) DAVID + DAVID

WE'LL SING IN THE SUNSHINE (1964) GALE GARNETT

WE LOVE YOU BEATLES (1964) THE CAREFREES

WE'RE GONNA MAKE IT (1965) LITTLE MILTON

WEREWOLVES OF LONDON (1978) WARREN ZEVON

WET DREAM (1969) MAX ROMEO

WHAM BAM (1976) SILVER

WHAT ABOUT ME (1983) MOVING PICTURES

WHAT ARE WE DOIN' IN LOVE (1981) DOTTIE WEST

WHAT I AM (1988) EDIE BRICKELL & NEW BOHEMIANS

WHAT'S THE COLOUR OF MONEY? (1986) HOLLYWOOD BEYON

WHAT THE WORLD NEEDS NOW IS LOVE/ABRAHAM, MARTIN AND JOHN (1971) TOM CLAY

WHAT'S YOUR NAME? (1962) DON AND JUAN

WHAT YOU WON'T DO FOR LOVE (1978) BOBBY CALDWELL

WHEN (1958) THE KALIN TWINS

WHEN I DIE (1969) MOTHERLODE

WHENEVER GOD SHINES HIS LIGHT (1989) VAN MORRISON (WITH CLIFF RICHARD)

WHEN I'M DEAD AND GONE (1970) MCGUINESS FLINT

WHEN I'M WITH YOU (1989) SHERIFF

WHEN THE BOYS TALK ABOUT THE GIRLS (1958) VALERIE CARR

WHEN THE HEART RULES THE MIND (1986) GTR

(WHEN SHE NEEDS GOOD LOVIN') SHE COMES TO ME (1966) CHICAGO LOOP

WHEN THE WHITE LILACS BLOOM AGAIN (1956) HELMUT ZACHARIAS

WHEN WE GET MARRIED (1961) THE DREAMLOVERS

WHEN WE KISS (1988) BARDEUX

WHEN YOU DANCE (1956) THE TURBANS

WHEN YOUR HEART IS WEAK/THE PROMISE YOU MADE (1985) COCK ROBIN

WHEN YOU WERE SWEET SIXTEEN (1981) FUREYS WITH DAVEY ARTHUR

WHERE ARE YOU NOW? (1989) JIMMY HARNEN WITH SYNCH

WHERE DO YOU GO TO MY LOVELY (1969) PETER SARSTEDT

WHIP IT (1980) DEVO

WHIRLY GIRL (1983) OXO

WHISPERING/CHERCHEZ LA FEMME/SE SI BON (1977) DR. BUZZARD'S ORIGINAL SAVANNAH BAND

WHISPERING GRASS (DON'T TELL THE TREES) (1975) WINDSOR DAVIES AND DON ESTELLE

WHITE HORSE (1984) LAID BAC

THE WHITE KNIGHT (1976) CLEDUS MAGGARD & THE CITIZEN'S BAND

WHITE LIES, BLUE EYES (1972) BULLET

WHITE ON WHITE (1964) DANNY WILLIAMS

WHITE SILVER SANDS (1957) DAVE GARDNER

WHO DO YOU LOVE (1964) THE SAPPHIRES

WHO DO YOU THINK YOU ARE? (1974) CANDLEWICK GREEN

WHO PUT THE BOMP (IN THE BOMP, BOMP, BOMP) (1961) BARRY MANN

WHO WROTE THE BOOK OF LOVE? (1958) THE MONOTONES

WHY CAN'T WE LIVE TOGETHER (1973) TIMMY THOMAS

WIGGLE WOBBLE (1963) LES COOPER AND HIS SOUL ROCKERS

WILDFIRE (1975) MICHAEL MARTIN MURPHEY

WILDFLOWER (1973) SKYLARK

WILD THING (1967) SENATOR BOBBY

WILD WEEKEND (1963) THE REBELS

WILLIE AND THE HAND JIVE (1958) JOHNNY OTIS SHOW

WILL YOU BE STAYING AFTER SUNDAY (1969) THE PEPPERMINT RAINBOW

WINCHESTER CATHEDRAL (1966) THE NEW VAUDEVILLE BAND

THE WINDMILLS OF YOUR MIND (1969) NOEL HARRISON

WIPE OUT (1963) THE SURFARIS

WISH SOMEONE WOULD CARE (1964) IRMA THOMAS

THE WITCH (1970) THE RATTLES

WITCH DOCTOR (1958) DON LANG & HIS FRANTIC FIVE

THE WITCH QUEEN OF NEW ORLEANS (1971) REDBONE

WITH ALL MY HEART (1957) JODIE SANDS

WITHOUT YOUR LOVE (1980) ROGER DALTREY

WITH YOU I'M BORN AGAIN (1980) BILLY PRESTON & SYREETA

WOLVERTON MOUNTAIN (1962) CLAUDE KING

WOMAN TO WOMAN (1974) SHIRLEY BROWN

WOMEN'S LOVE RIGHTS (1971) LAURA LEE

WONDERFUL LIFE (1987) BLACK

WONDERING WHERE THE LIONS ARE (1980) BRUCE COCKBURN

WORDS (DON'T COME EASY) (1983) F. R. DAVID

WONDERFUL SUMMER (1963) ROBIN WARD

THE WONDER OF YOU (1959) RAY PETERSON

WOODSTOCK (1970) MATTHEWS SOUTHERN COMFORT

WOO HOO (1959) THE ROCK-A-TEENS

THE WORST THAT COULD HAPPEN (1969) BROOKLYN BRIDGE

Y...

YAKETY SAX (1963) BOOTS RANDOLPH

YELLOW BALLOON (1967) THE YELLOW BALLOON

YELLOW BIRD (1961) ARTHUR LYMAN

YELLOW RIVER (1970) CHRISTIE

YES I'M READY (1980) TERI DESARIO

YESTERDAY, WHEN I WAS YOUNG (1969) ROY CLARK

YOGI (1960) THE IVY THREE

YOU (1958) THE AQUATONES

YOU, I (1969) THE RUGBYS

YOU AIN'T SEEN NOTHING YET (1974) BACHMAN-TURNER OVERDRIVE

YOU AND ME TONIGHT (1986) AURRA

YOU ARE MY STARSHIP (1976) NORMAN CONNORS

YOU BETTER MOVE ON (1962) ARTHUR ALEXANDER

YOU CAN MAKE IT IF YOU TRY (1958) GENE ALLISON

YOU CAN'T SIT DOWN, PART 2 (1961) PHILIP UPCHURCH COMBO

YOU CAN'T TURN ME OFF (IN THE MIDDLE OF TURNING ME ON) (1977) HIGH INERGY

YOU CHEATED (1958) FRANKIE ERVIN

YOU COULD TAKE MY HEART AWAY (1981) SILVER CONDOR

YOU DON'T HAVE TO BE A BABY TO CRY (1963) THE CARAVELLES

YOU DON'T KNOW (1988) SCARLETT AND BLACK

YOU GONNA MAKE ME LOVE SOMEBODY ELSE (1979) JONES GIRLS

YOU LIGHT UP MY LIFE (1977) DEBBY BOONE

YOU'LL ALWAYS FIND ME IN THE KITCHEN AT PARTIES/STOP THE CAVALRY (1980)
JONA LEWIE

YOU'LL LOSE A GOOD THING (1962) BARBARA LYNN

YOU'LL NEVER WALK ALONE (1985) THE CROWD

YOUR BABY AIN'T YOUR BABY ANYMORE (1974) PAUL DA VINCI

YOU'RE A FRIEND OF MINE (1986) CLARENCE CLEMONS

YOU'RE MOVIN' OUT TODAY (1977) CAROLE BAYER SAGER

YOU'RE MY WORLD (1964) CILLA BLACK

YOU'RE SO FINE (1959) THE FALCONS

YOU'RE THE REASON (1961) BOBBY EDWARDS

YOU'RE THE VOICE (1986) JOHN FARNHAM

YOUR LOVE (1975) GRAHAM CENTRAL STATION

YOUR MA SAID YOU CRIED IN YOUR SLEEP LAST NIGHT (1961) KENNY DINO

YOUR WILD HEART (1957) JOY LAYNE

YOU SPIN ME ROUND (LIKE A RECORD) (1984) DEAD OR ALIVE

YOU TALK TOO MUCH (1960) JOE JONES

YOU TURN ME ON (TURN ON SONG) (1965) IAN WHITCOMB AND BLUESVILLE

YOU'VE GOT TO HIDE YOUR LOVE AWAY (1965) THE SILKIE

YOU'VE GOT YOUR TROUBLES (1965) THE FORTUNES

YOU WERE MINE (1959) THE FIREFLIES

Z...
ZOOM (1982) FAT LARRY'S BAND

DID I MISS ONE OUT?

Did I miss a one hit wonder; oh, I know I did a lot of research, but I know I've probably missed more than a few.

Send them to me at <u>kansasscot@aol.com</u> and I'll check them out. If they fit the criteria, I'll include them in future editions.

ABOUT THE AUTHOR

Ian Hall is an award-winning novelist and author of over 50 novels in many genres.

Born in Edinburgh, Scotland, he now lives in Kansas, USA.

He is a master story-teller, and hopes his love of history shines through in all his fiction works.

Learn more about Ian and his books at his website; ianhallauthor.com

At the website you can get a free book and sign up for his newsletter.

OTHER NON-FICTION BY IAN HALL

Ridiculously Comprehensive Dictionary of British Slang

Thousands of entries and definitions, rude words and all. The truly comprehensive guide to all British words and phrases; includes thousands of examples of Cockney Rhyming slang.

Churchill's Secret Armies; Ungentlemanly Warfare

A look at the various departments, secret units, and skullduggery that British Prime Minister Winston Churchill set in motion in the first years of the Second World War.

WORLD WAR 2 SPY SCHOOL; Counter Espionage

A complete transcript of the entire manual of the SOE, dated 1943, that proved the birth of modern counter espionage. Newly formatted, edited and provided with the author's introduction.

Other Novel Series by Ian Hall

The Jamie Leith Chronicles

Real life adventure; Scotland's attempt to colonize Panama in 1698

The Avenging Steel series.

Alternative Fiction; set in 1940's Edinburgh after the German invasion of Britain.

James Baird, a philosophy student at Edinburgh University becomes a reluctant member of the Scottish resistance movement against the occupying Nazis.

(6 books)

Caledonii; Birth of a Celtic Nation

Alternative/Speculative Historical Fiction; set in Scotland in 80AD as the Romans advance north.

With the aid of the druid movement, Calach, chief's son of clan Caledonii, must unite the bickering tribes against the new menace.

(5 books)

Star-Eater Chronicles

Ray-guns and rockets Science Fiction; set in the 25th century.

Seth Gingko is one of a thousand MacCollies Scouts sent out to map the galaxy. On reaching the furthermost star, and looks into the void beyond, he finds far more than he was bargaining for.

(8 books)

Space Academy Rebels

Teen/Young Adult Science Fiction; set in 2617.

The new intake of Space Academy would change the universe forever. As their paranormal abilities grow, they find their benefactors are not as squeaky-clean as they first thought.

(Trilogy)

Vampire High School.

Young Adult/Teen Horror; set in Arizona, USA.

When his best friend is murdered in front of his eyes, Lyman Bracks is mortified. When it happens in the middle of the school marching band, it's difficult to ignore.

(4 books, plus others)

A Connecticut Vampire.

Time-Travel Horror; set in Tudor England.

Vampire Francis is at the top of the food chain in modern USA. When he is transported back to 1500's England, he finds himself at the sharp end of a very different society.

(Trilogy)

One Last Thing

If you enjoyed this book, I'd be very grateful if you could post a short 5-star review on Amazon. Your support really does make a difference, and I read all the reviews so I can get your feedback and make this book even better.

Thanks again for your support.

Ian Hall

71966855R00278

Made in the USA
Middletown, DE
02 May 2018